ON PHOTO—GRAPHS

DAVID CAMPANY

THE MIT PRESS | CAMBRIDGE, MASSACHUSETTS

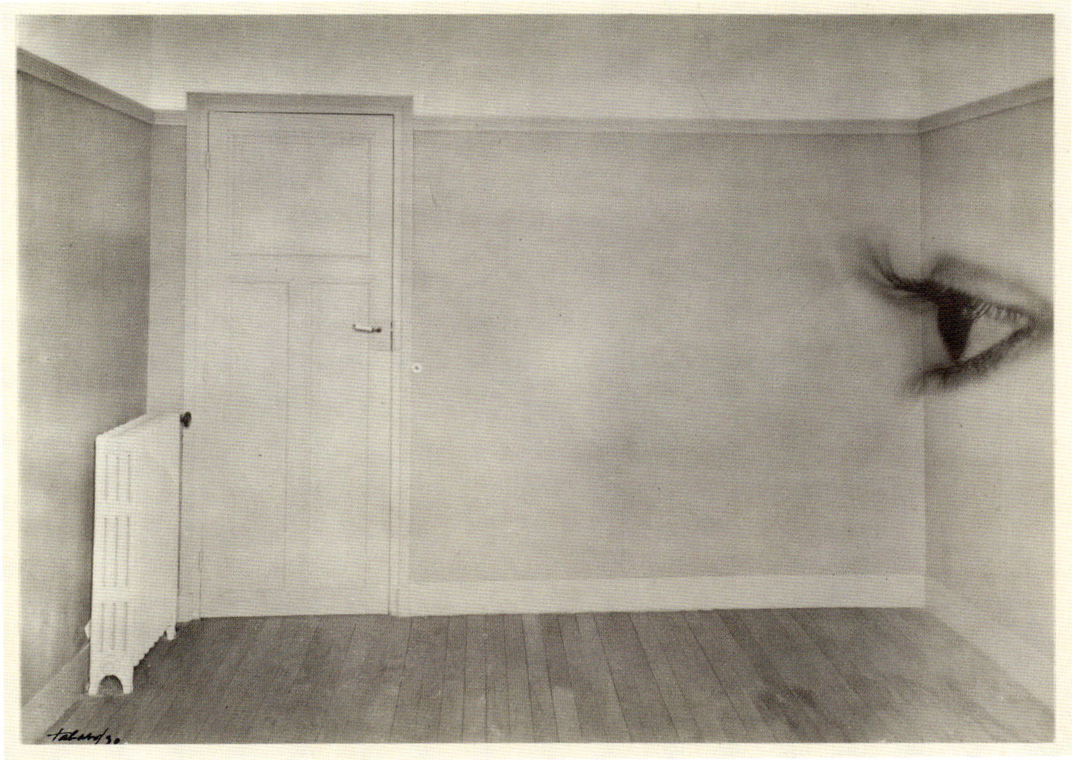

ON PHOTO— GRAPHS

FOR A.A.K.

David Campany is a writer, curator and educator. His books include *So Present, So Invisible: Conversations on Photography* (2018), *A Handful of Dust* (2015), *The Open Road: Photography and the American Road Trip* (2014), *Walker Evans: The Magazine Work* (2014), *Jeff Wall: Picture for Women* (2011), *Photography and Cinema* (2008) and *Art and Photography* (2003). He is Managing Director of Programs at the International Center of Photography, New York.

On the cover: Guy Bourdin, *Charles Jourdan, Spring 1978*, 1978 (see page 26)

Endpapers: Alexander Rodchenko, *Stars*, 1938

Page 3: Maurice Tabard, *Room with Eye*, 1930

Published by arrangement with Thames & Hudson Ltd, London by the MIT Press

ISBN 978-0-262-04424-0

Library of Congress Control Number 2019955427

Printed and bound in China by Toppan Leefung

The MIT Press
Massachusetts Institute of Technology
Cambridge, Massachusetts 02142
http://mitpress.mit.edu

CONTENTS

INTRODUCTION

PHOTOGRAPHS ARE OFTEN thought of as ways to hold things still, to calm the flux of a restless world. They allow us to gaze at fixed appearances, for pleasure or knowledge, or both. But very little else about them could be described as 'still'. From the beginning, photography's technologies have been in a state of constant change and development, and the tasks we have given the medium have continued to mutate and expand beyond measure. Moreover, photographs are highly mobile. They move over time, across cultures and between contexts. They lose meanings, and acquire meanings. Indeed, they could not be quite so mobile were they not quite so fixed. The mute stillness of photographs permits their promiscuity and proliferation. And so, paradoxically, photographs have helped to produce the flux they promise to calm. They confuse as much as fascinate, conceal as much as reveal, distract as much as compel. They are unpredictable communicators. They cannot carry meanings in any straightforward way. A single photograph is unable to account for the appearance it describes, or even account for itself. Like Herman Melville's Bartleby, a photograph is insistently there, yet enigmatic. In each one there is a kind of madness.

All of this leaves photography open to those wanting to take charge of it, to use it in one way or another. Broadly, there are two ways this happens. The first is to give photography pictorial conventions. Images that follow a formula are less likely to surprise, and will give the impression of meeting needs and expectations, of being 'functional'. Through convention, photography masks its madness. The second way is to accompany photographs with words. Writing, speech, discourse.

PHOTOGRAPHS CONFUSE AS MUCH AS FASCINATE, CONCEAL AS MUCH AS REVEAL, DISTRACT AS MUCH AS COMPEL. THEY ARE UNPREDICTABLE COMMUNICATORS.

Think of the complex legal system that secures the status of the police photo; or the connoisseur declaring this photograph better than that; the advertisement making claims in words for a product it depicts; the returning tourist narrating their holiday snapshots to friends; the caption for a news picture; or the photographic artist stating their intentions. The image cannot achieve any of this by itself. Words do many things for photographs, but in general they are used to oversee and direct them, the way parents supervise wayward children. Photographs can be bent to limitless wills, but never precisely so. They always have the potential to exceed the demands imposed upon them. And in that excess, photographs work upon us in ways we still barely comprehend.

If a photograph compels, if it holds our attention, it will be for more than one reason. The reasons may be unexpected, and even contradictory (mixed feelings are often the most compelling). When we are drawn to look at a photograph again and again, it is likely that our second or third response will not be quite the same as our first. Of course, most photographs do not stay in the mind for long at all, but this does not mean we can predict which ones will, or why, or whether a brief encounter with an image will leave some ineffable mark upon us. Photographs need less explanation than our responses to them.

The format of word and image sitting opposite each other on the pages of a book is perfectly familiar. Photography was presented this way almost from the start. In 1844 William Henry Fox Talbot published the first instalment of *The Pencil of Nature*, his remarkable account of the photographic process he had pioneered. He wrote short texts to accompany his pictures. At first glance the arrangement appeared straightforward, as if Talbot were telling readers about each image, but he had grasped that what photographs do and mean is complicated. With great foresight he understood the madness of his invention: the overwhelming detail, the world beyond intention, and the way photographs work upon our conscious and unconscious thought. At times, what he wrote bore little immediate relation to the image with which he had paired it. The reader/viewer was free to make her own connections.

Similarly, *On Photographs* cannot explain the various images it presents, although it is an account of how they can slip away from explanation and keep us interested. As such, it is a book concerned less with *what* we think about photographs than with *how* we think about them; and less with photographers' intentions than with what happens when we look. On the pages that follow, you will find more than one hundred photographs and writings. The images do not illustrate a written argument, and the writing is not a script for looking, but together they may bring you closer to the madness. Each double-page spread can be looked at and read on its own terms, or the whole book can be approached as one continuous essay. Or, the words can be ignored entirely to allow each image to be encountered for itself, and as part of an unbroken sequence built upon visual association and suggestion.

Asked who was the greatest photographer, the seasoned curator and writer John Szarkowski replied without hesitation: 'Anonymous.' His answer can be understood in different ways. First, extraordinary images can come from anyone, anytime, in any situation. Photography is ideally placed to take advantage of the gifts offered by the world before it. In addition, the craft of photography can be learned within a matter of weeks (although it may take a lifetime to master). This means that photographs can result almost

WHEN WE ARE DRAWN TO LOOK AT A PHOTOGRAPH AGAIN AND AGAIN, IT IS LIKELY THAT OUR SECOND OR THIRD RESPONSE WILL NOT BE QUITE THE SAME AS OUR FIRST.

SETS, SERIES, SEQUENCES, PHOTO-ESSAYS, TYPOLOGIES, PROJECTS, ALBUMS, ARCHIVES, FOLDERS, FEEDS – PHOTOGRAPHY IS ALMOST UNIMAGINABLE OUTSIDE OF ONE KIND OF GROUPING OR ANOTHER.

entirely from the photographer's disposition or attitude towards the world. The medium is perfectly welcoming to anyone who stumbles into it, just as a lens welcomes the light that passes through it.

Secondly, most photographs in daily life are consumed with little regard as to who actually made them. As well as having a deep respect for the 'accidental masterpieces' of amateurs and vernacular image-makers, Szarkowski admired the French photographer Eugène Atget, who worked in near obscurity in the late nineteenth and early twentieth centuries, making pictorially sophisticated documents of Paris, on commission and for his own pleasure. He became 'Atget', the great figure in the modern history of photography, only after he had died. Every photographer is anonymous until they are not, and every photograph is potentially a work of art, although it will never entirely cease being a document. This idea is both liberating and disturbing.

Authorship and intention may be the least compelling pieces of information appended to photographs. Without them, we are at much greater liberty to look for ourselves, although interpretation can be more intense when it is undirected. The composer John Cage called this 'response-ability'. When it is not made easy by instruction, responding to culture is difficult, but the rewards are all the richer.

While there may be something perfectly singular about any individual photograph, our visual culture is defined by numbers. Photographic images are reproducible, and often have no 'original'. They can exist in many places at the same time, be seen by many people, and they belong wherever they are placed, be it wall, page or screen. Just as importantly, photographs are rarely made to be encountered on their own. Sets, series, sequences, photo-essays, typologies, projects, albums, archives, folders, feeds – photography is almost unimaginable outside of one kind of grouping or another. The documentary photographer takes many shots to cover a subject that escapes the single picture. The fashion photographer makes images of the collection of garments, to flow across multiple pages. Artists produce projects, or bodies of work (very few make photographs to be seen with no relation to any other). As the German photographer August Sander put it, 'A successful photo is only a preliminary step toward the intelligent use of photography … Photography is like a mosaic that becomes a synthesis only when it is presented *en masse*.' Walker Evans said something similar: 'Photography is editing, editing after the taking. After knowing what to take you have to do the editing.' Meaning is made as much between images as within them.

There is almost always another photograph waiting just beyond our attention span, on the next page, further down the screen, along the gallery wall, or up the street. Looking at photographs is very often a matter of displacement, from one image to the next. And yet, none of this detracts from the discrete unity of each and every photographic image. Even when put together, they are not exactly like links in a chain, words in a sentence, or even shots in a movie. Each possesses and demands at least some measure of individuality. Looking at that individuality has its own merits. It can also tell us valuable things about the flux from which it came, and to which, inevitably, it will return.

Lastly, a word about the title of this book. When I was a student, I once spent an afternoon with Susan Sontag, the essayist, film-maker, novelist and author of the book *On Photography*, which remains the most widely read book on the subject. I admired Sontag's work very much, but about an hour into our conversation she asked curiously, 'What is it about my writings on photography that worries you?' I respected her enough to be honest. 'You don't have much to say about any particular images,' I replied. 'That's true,' she accepted. 'My book is more about photography as a *phenomenon*, social and artistic.' She paused, and smiled. 'Perhaps one day you will write a book titled *On Photographs*.'

THE PHOTO—GRAPHS

ROBERT CUMMING

1826; Niepce's Pewter Picture, 1980

THE OLDEST SURVIVING photograph made with a camera dates from 1826: *View from the Window at Le Gras*, created by the French inventor Joseph Nicéphore Niépce.

As early as 1822, Niépce had used heliography – a chemical-based process of his own devising – to make copies of printed engravings and drawings, without the use of a camera. First he would coat a plate of glass, copper or pewter in a type of light-sensitive bitumen, or asphalt. Then, a paper-based image would be laid on the sensitized plate and the two exposed to daylight for three to four hours. The sun's rays passing through the lighter areas of the paper print made the bitumen beneath soluble in lavender oil. Washing the plate gently revealed an impression, which could then be reproduced. Thus, the first photographic image was in fact an image of an image of an image, of an image. The earliest surviving example of this type of camera-less contact print, a copy of a seventeenth-century Flemish engraving on paper of a man leading a horse, was made by Niépce in 1825.

From 1824 the Frenchman had also experimented with placing a sensitized plate in a small lightproof box fitted with a lens that could focus an image of the world before it. *View from the Window at Le Gras* was made this way. It is distinct enough to show light hitting opposite sides of buildings, suggesting an exposure time of around eight hours, during which the sun would have moved considerably.

Niépce died in 1833, but not before partnering with Louis-Jacques-Mandé Daguerre, who advanced the process. In 1839 Daguerre gave to the French state the rights to the technique in exchange for lifetime pensions for himself and Niépce's son. Detailed instructions were published, and photography was 'free to the world'. The announcement reached others who had been working on similar processes, notably William Henry Fox Talbot (pages 198, 224) in England.

With photography, Niépce had introduced profound complications into the understanding of originality, artistry, science, authorship, time, realism, reproduction and proliferation. They haunt image-making to this day. And so here is Niépce's image incorporated into another. On to what looks like a windowpane, the American artist Robert Cumming has taped a flat diagram of a simple box camera. Lines indicate the passage of light through its lens, and in place of the received image we see *View from the Window at Le Gras*. Beneath the diagram, and slightly out of focus, is a modern camera on a tripod. If it is taking the image we are looking at, then it is not a glass window Cumming has used, but a mirror. The mirror and the window are the two most enduring metaphors for photography. Further out of focus, we see a chair and a trestle, and beyond this what looks like a tree, or perhaps a very large photograph of a tree. Cumming has specialized in this kind of complex visual puzzle, exploring perception, fascination and our easily duped faith in photography. Niépce and the other pioneers would have appreciated this playful homage.

Photography's past lives on in the minds of those to whom it means something, and in meaning something it remains contemporary.

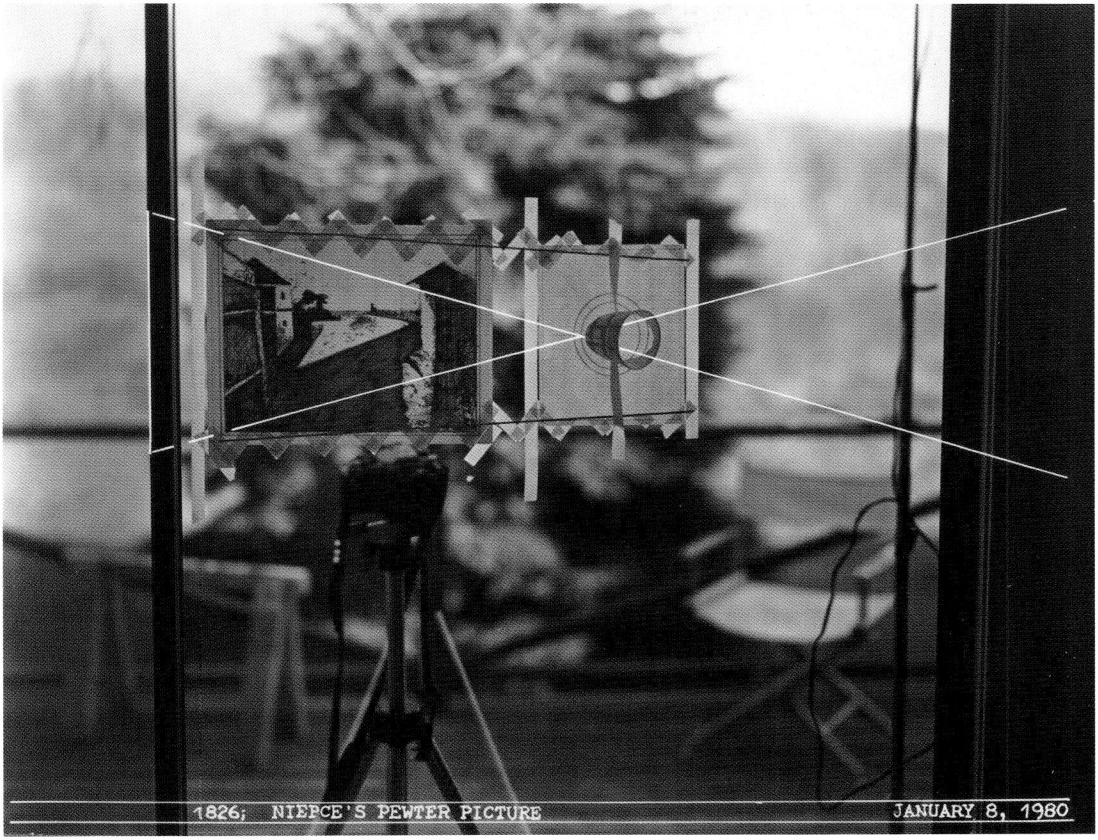
1826; NIEPCE'S PEWTER PICTURE
JANUARY 8, 1980

FREDERICK S. CHURCH

George Eastman aboard the SS *Gallia*, en route to England from America, 1890

THE NATURAL SHAPE OF THE IMAGE formed by a lens is circular. Eyeballs are spherical. Yet for the industrial age, the circle and the sphere were wastes of space. Circles do not tessellate, and spheres do not stack efficiently. Photography needed to be given straight edges and corners.

Nobody understood this better than George Eastman, founder of Eastman Kodak, the North American company responsible for making photography a popular amateur pursuit and a billion-dollar industry. Film, paper and cameras had to be standardized. Kodak's 'Box Brownie' camera, introduced in 1900, was to mass-market photography what Henry Ford's Model T would become to motoring just a few years later.

But here is Eastman pictured by his friend Frederick Church in a photograph without right angles. It was taken in 1890, a year after Eastman had launched the Kodak No. 1 camera. The image cast by its mass-produced lens was hazy in the corners, so only the sharp area in the middle was used (later models had an improved lens). The camera was sold pre-loaded with enough paper-based roll film to take 100 shots. Once the roll had been exposed, the whole camera would be returned to the factory, where the circular images, 6.4 centimetres (2½ in.) in diameter, would be printed on rectangular paper.

Intentionally or not, this image is a celebration of circles. Church photographed Eastman photographing him, their camera lenses eyeing each other on the deck of the SS *Gallia*, somewhere mid-Atlantic. They were heading to England, across an ocean that appears flat but is, in fact, curved. The circular image finds its echo in the circular lens at its centre and the round windows of the ship's open portholes. (Why are portholes circular? Corners cause cracks and corrosion.)

Perspective, which remains the basis of the Western pictorial tradition, based itself on the imagined view through the four corners of a 'picture window'. Optics and then photography reaffirmed the laws of perspective, but their roundness was rejected. Circular images remain rare and anomalous, and often confound our sense of composition. Frederick Church happened to compose a remarkable exception.

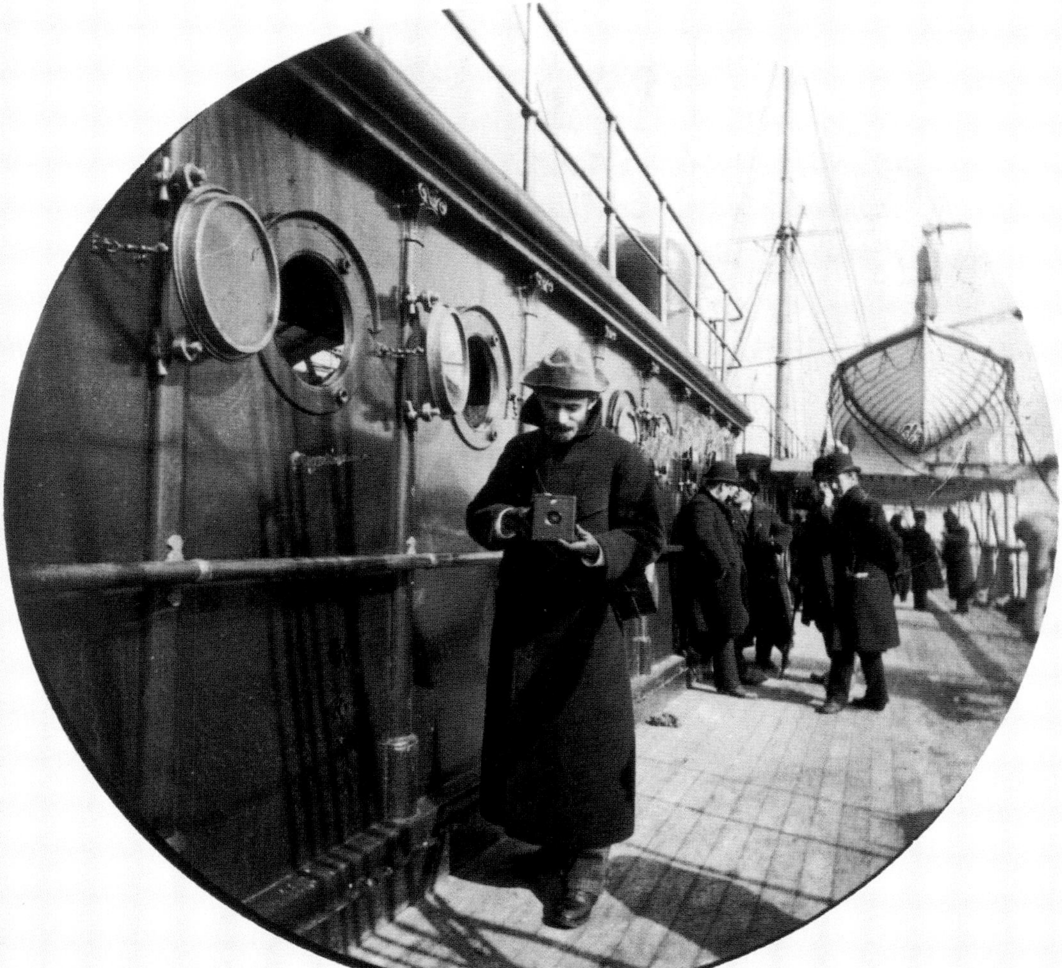

LEE FRIEDLANDER

Peter Exline, Spokane, Washington, 1970

WHEN A VIRTUOSO PHOTOGRAPHER enters a domestic situation, ordinary events may be lifted suddenly into another realm. Here is a photograph by Lee Friedlander. It was taken in 1970 and given the title *Peter Exline, Spokane, Washington*. On a basic level, then, it is a portrait of the man in the dark-rimmed spectacles and buttoned-down shirt. We do not know the names of the two people in the background, but we might assume all three, or four including the photographer, knew at least something of each other.

The picture is neither formal nor informal, on a line Friedlander has danced disarmingly for more than six decades. The artist R. B. Kitaj once described Friedlander and his art as a 'cross between the penny-plain and the complexly interesting'. Friedlander has a deep love and acute understanding of the amateur's happy accident. You or I could have taken this picture of friends in our backyard, but we did not. Or, if we did achieve something like it once, we have precious little chance of doing it again. Friedlander has made hundreds of images with this playful complexity.

Everything we expect of a domestic photo is present: the relaxed semi-performance of the people in a familiar setting, and a photographer belonging to the situation, yet separate enough from it to make a picture. But the dynamics are all askew. Each person seems to dramatize in a different way the act of photographic seeing. The figure on the left looks back through a camera. The boy on the right is caught behind a pillar by Friedlander's camera flash. A sliver of shadow bisects his chest as it passes over his right eye. And in the middle sits Mr Exline, comically low in the frame, in finely slatted sunshine. On the white shed behind him falls a triangle of light, its apex almost touching his eye. It is like a diagram from a book about optics.

So this is much more than a portrait. It is a meditation on domestic photography and its value, on backyard psychodrama, on picture-making, on light, sight, vision, geometry and the transformative nature of photography. Mr Exline sits there, wry and enigmatic. Is he in on this brief and layered amusement, or the butt of it?

FRIEDLANDER HAS A DEEP LOVE AND ACUTE UNDERSTANDING OF THE AMATEUR'S HAPPY ACCIDENT. YOU OR I COULD HAVE TAKEN THIS PICTURE OF FRIENDS IN OUR BACK-YARD, BUT WE DID NOT.

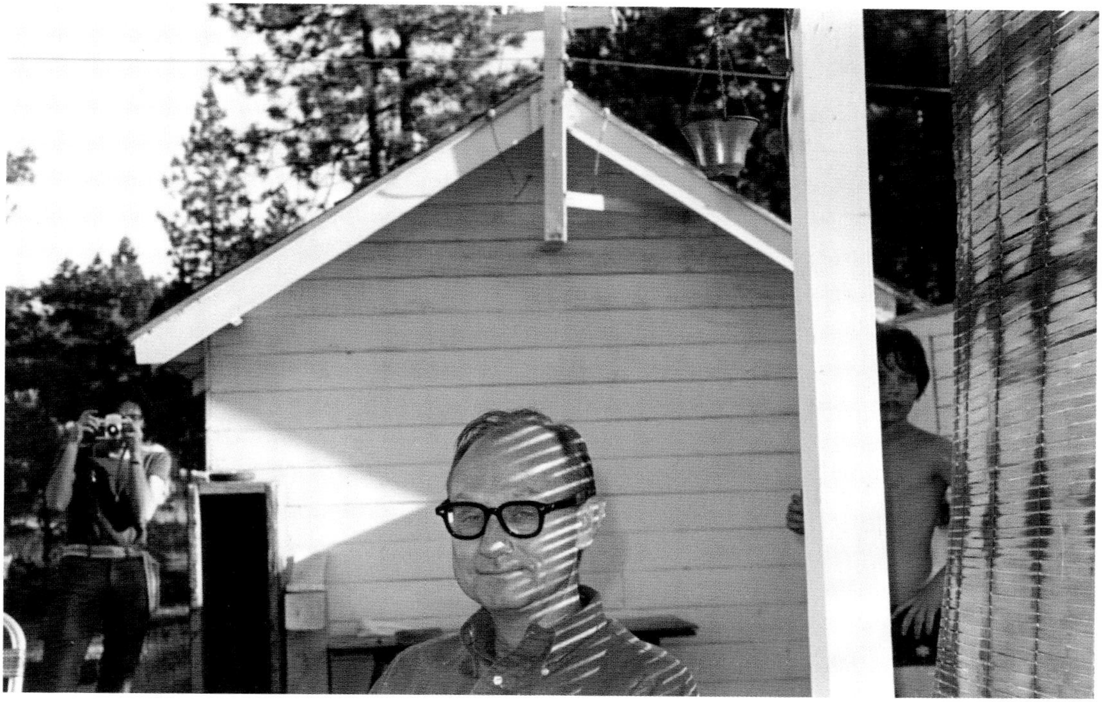

EUGÈNE ATGET

Fête du Trône, 1925

EUGÈNE ATGET (1857–1927) photographed an old Paris endangered by the forces of modernization. He made approximately 8,500 glass-plate negatives, each measuring 18 × 24 centimetres (7 × 9½ in.). He photographed speculatively, hoping to sell pictures to salon painters, cartoonists, sculptors, illustrators, avant-garde artists, sign painters, set designers, couturiers, industrial designers, architects, town planners, topographers, libraries and lovers of the city. He also took commissions, but many of his photographs seem to have been made for his pleasure alone. In his final years, they grew thick with the mystery and poetry of the everyday.

Atget was drawn to the well-worn delights of street fairs, and photographed them a number of times. He understood showmanship from the inside, having been a journeyman actor. He liked the ornate carousels and the stalls of the exotic fortune tellers. He made two images of this particular scene, the first taking in the front of the tent with its painted text and lurid illustrations. He then stepped towards the entrance, like a curious bystander.

As a rule, Atget would shoot early in the morning. Along the lower edge of the composition we see the makeshift barrier placed to prevent entry, but a strange assembly is visible. An outsized chair and enormous shoe sit on a dresser beside a miniature chair and a tiny shoe. Two photos of different dimensions both show two men, one little and one large. They are Armand the Giant and the smallest man in the world, Robert the Dwarf. Armand stood 2.28 metres (7½ ft) tall, Robert a mere 78 centimetres (30¾ in.).

Like photographs, humans come in all shapes and sizes, often with particularities you simply could not invent. Life's timid averages are what we misguidedly call 'normal'. The light bulb is a regular size, but it does nothing to illuminate the black backdrop, velvety as a magician's cape. Two paper signs bearing the price of admission add to the symmetry. They flap in the light breeze that blows through the long exposure.

Atget had a modest apartment in Montparnasse, on rue Campagne-Première. The young Man Ray (page 154) also resided on that street (years later, the artist Yves Klein did too). In 1926 Man Ray acquired four prints from Atget for reproduction in the journal *La Révolution surréaliste*. Word spread that this quiet but industrious man was making remarkable images. Upon his death in 1927, many vanguard journals published his work. The Paris-based *L'Art vivant* called him a 'precursor of modern photography'. In 1930 the first book of his work was published.

Atget left no clue as to how, or even if, he wished his work to be received. As that of a modernist? A surrealist? A lyric poet of the camera? A chronicler? Man Ray claimed that Atget wanted no credit and had a sign over his door: 'Documents pour artistes'. This clarifies nothing. The enigma of Atget and his photographs endures.

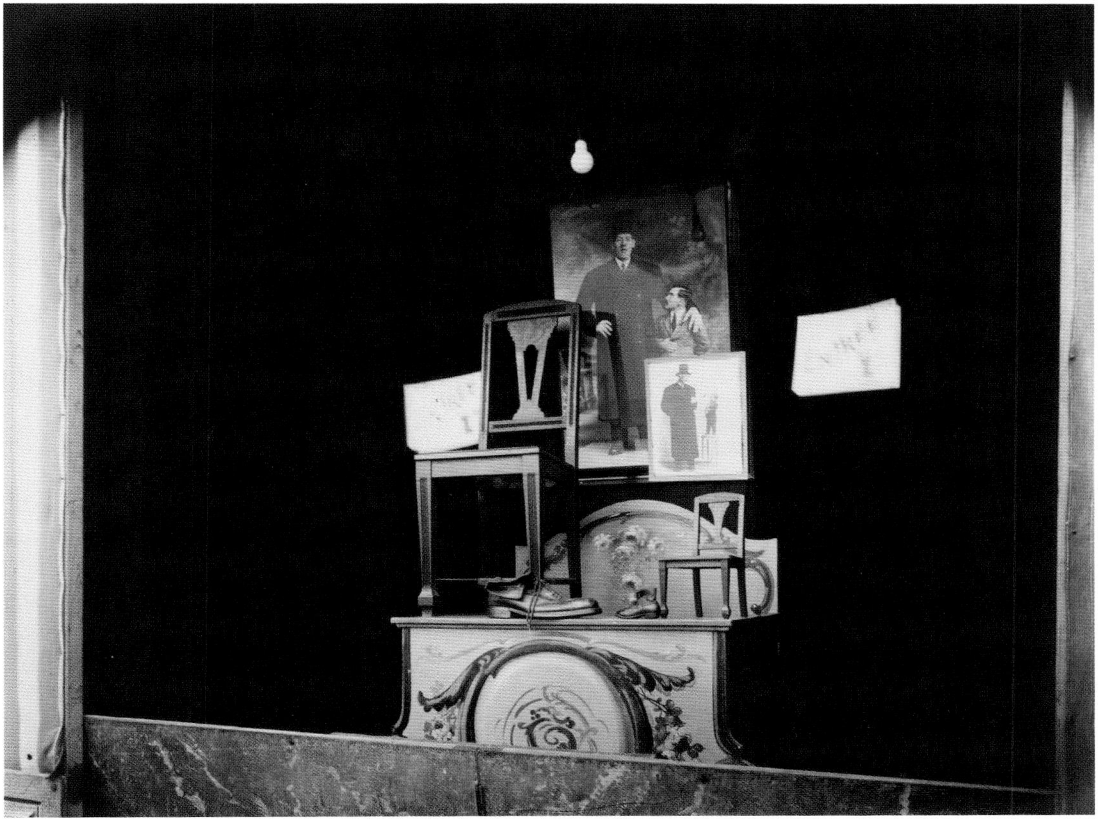

MANUEL ÁLVAREZ BRAVO

Parábola óptica, 1931

IN THE SPIRIT OF SURREALISM, THE FINAL FORM OF THE PHOTOGRAPH CAME ABOUT BY ACCIDENT.

MANUEL ÁLVAREZ BRAVO (1902–2002) enjoyed one of the longest careers of any photographer. For many decades he was a key figure in Mexican art and culture, and for almost as many he was celebrated worldwide. In 1938 Bravo met André Breton, the unofficial leader of French surrealism, and his images began to appear in its journals, such as *Minotaure*. With interests in the uncanny and the unsettling double, photographers associated with surrealism made frequent use of mirrors; but they made almost no use of the reversed image created by turning over the negative before printing. Bravo's *Parábola óptica* (Optical Parable) is a rich and strange exception.

We see an optometrist's window, photographed in Mexico City. It is all glass, reflections and doubling. There are seven eyes and a pair of spectacles. These are visual motifs we can read either way round. There is also writing that appears to be the wrong way round. Are we inside, looking out through the reflective glass? No, but we are not fully outside either. The shop is called Optica Moderna, or 'Modern Optics', which takes on wider resonance for a picture presented as a 'parable'. One photograph becomes a meditation on optics and photography in general.

In everyday speech, the phrase 'point of view' refers to values or opinions about things ('What is your point of view?'). In photography, it also refers to where the camera is placed in relation to the subject. It is often tempting to draw a parallel between a photographer's values or opinions about the world and the position from which they shoot it. There is always some kind of relation, but there can be no formula. Part of the unspoken fascination of photographs comes from how they confront us with this uncertainty. This is especially true of Bravo's image, since its point of view is imaginary.

In the spirit of surrealism, the final form of the photograph came about by accident. Bravo was checking over some printer's proofs in readiness for publication and saw it had been reversed by mistake. He found he preferred it this way. It was a moment of recognition in which his image appeared to have found some other intention, some other point of view beyond his own.

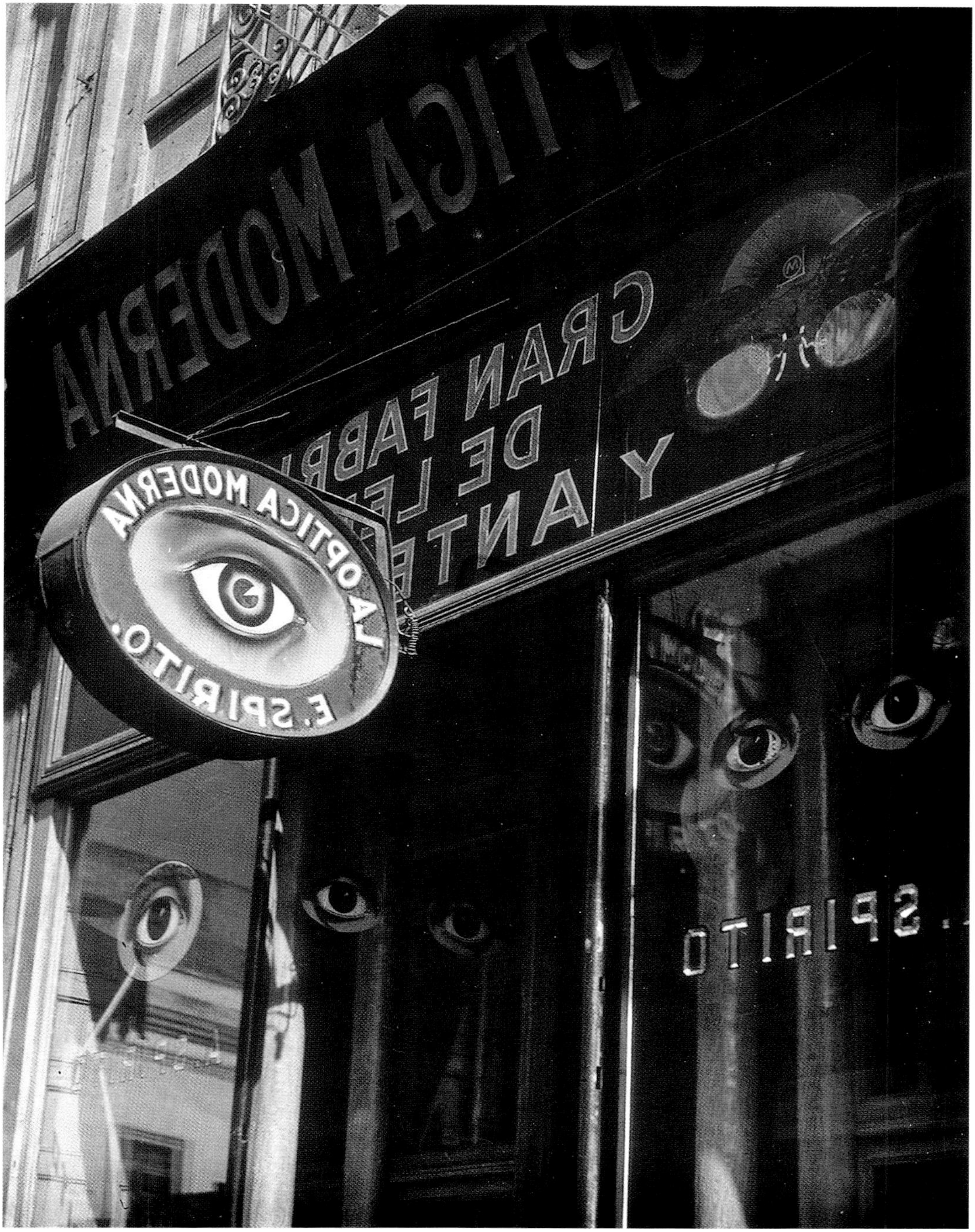
OPTICA MODERNA
GRAN FABRI
DE LE
Y ANTE
LA OPTICA MODERNA
E. SPIRITO.
SPIRITO

WILLIAM KLEIN

New York Fashion, 1959

ORIGINALLY, IT WAS TO BE a highly controlled *Vogue* magazine fashion shoot in a well-appointed Manhattan studio. But no image-maker has fed on the energy and chance of the urban scene with quite the same appetite as William Klein.

Three years before this photograph was taken, Klein had published *Life is Good & Good for You in New York: Trance, Witness, Revels*, a groundbreaking photographic book on the charms and horrors of the city. His gritty and anarchic street shots and wildly inventive page layouts broke every rule of good taste. In the uptight pages of 1950s *Vogue*, however, even a change of pose or a new locale could seem radical. Klein left the static formality of the studio (which belonged to another celebrated photographer, Richard Avedon; page 206) and took the models up to the rooftop.

In the centre of the photograph, facing the camera, is Isabella Albonico. On the left is Evelyn Tripp, and, on the right, Nena von Schlebrügge (the mother of the actress Uma Thurman). For the magazine page, the image was cropped at Albonico's feet and placed beside the following editorial:

'You don't replace black in fashion (or pearls, or furs, or cashmere sweaters), but you can, with astonishingly pretty results, give black that notable fashion tonic – a breather. Six pages of ways here, beginning with beige. Summer prerequisites for beige are a confirmed sun tan, or an intentional fairness; a stock of smallish velvet hats; brownish shoes. Later prop: a little black coat. Near right: Mirrored close-up of the kind of beige dress that proves that a good time to start wearing beige is anytime. Pale-beige silk crêpe like this is marvelously jewel-able in later hours, later months, is worn here with a darker beige velvet turban, off-white gloves. By Talmack, about $125. Saks Fifth Avenue; Halle Bros. Centre: Bell-sleeved apricot-beige that's like discovering a new fashion continent – or a particularly fortunate face powder. Velvet hat is black. Shoes are camel shade with no actual colour relation to apricot-beige, but everything in common. By Mollie Parnis, in rayon-and-acetate crêpe, about $110. Saks Fifth Avenue; Hutzler's. Far right: A profile of a bisque crêpe shirt reflected at a walk in the mirror – two views out of about a dozen we can think of, offhand, for a dress like this. Hat is black-grey, shoes are pitch brown. Dress by Herbert Sondheim, in rayon-and-acetate crêpe, about $70. Saks Fifth Avenue; Harzfeld's; Meier & Frank. All hats: Lilly Daché.'

Klein and the women then went out into the Manhattan traffic, still carrying their mirrors, improvising ironic poses, multiplying the spectacle as they mocked it. Klein knew the fashion business was a shallow game, but he also loved it – and played it well. In 1966 he made *Who Are You, Polly Maggoo?*, a feature film now regarded as the best account of fashion's seductive absurdity. Even *Vogue*'s text for this photograph now reads like a parody. Perhaps it always was.

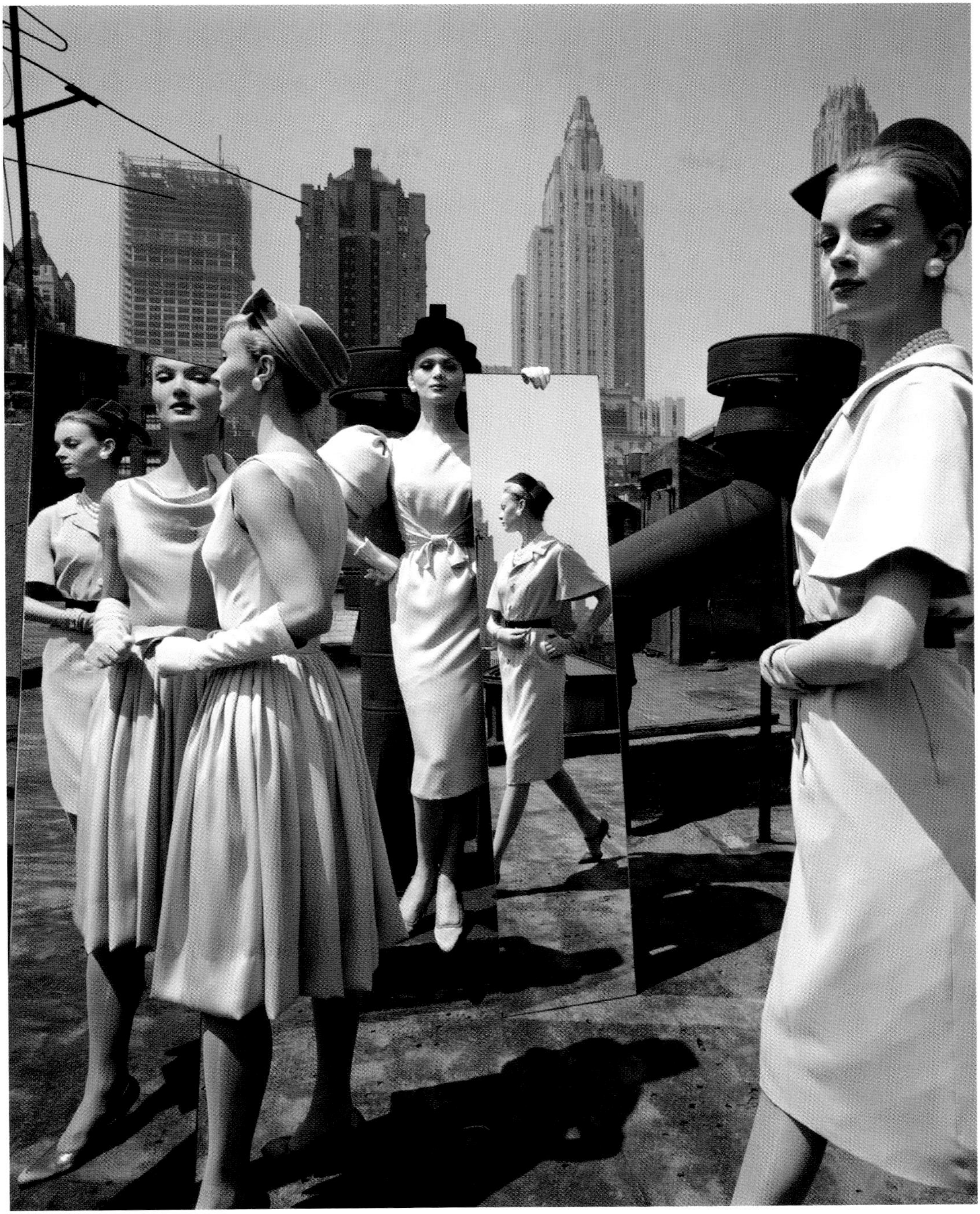

GUY BOURDIN

Charles Jourdan, Spring 1978, 1978

IN GENERAL, THE COMMERCIAL IMAGES that survive their principal function are the ones that are better than the principal function required, or deserved. The history of commercial photography is peppered with image-makers who had ambitions and standards that were entirely their own. Whether photojournalists, fashion photographers, industrial photographers or even advertising photographers, they used the parameters of the commission, and the financial support it offered, to further their own vision.

The French fashion photographer Guy Bourdin has become one of the most celebrated examples of such image-makers, but wider recognition of his work took a while. He rarely exhibited it, preferring to concentrate his attention on the printed pages of the magazines for which it had been conceived. In the years since his death in 1991, however, Bourdin's photographs have come to be recognized for their perfectionist blend of classical surrealism and hyper-vivid colour. Key to Bourdin's development was his friendship with Man Ray (page 154), who, in the 1920s and 1930s, had been not only a central figure in the avant-garde but also a highly sought-after portrait and fashion photographer.

Bourdin first worked for French *Vogue* in 1954, and in the next decade he began producing campaigns for the shoe company Charles Jourdan, which became his primary client. In both contexts, Bourdin was entrusted with unprecedented levels of creative freedom. This image was made during the shooting of a Charles Jourdan campaign.

In 1976 Bourdin was commissioned to photograph a women's lingerie catalogue for Bloomingdale's department store. The result was 'Sighs and Whispers', a luxurious, eighteen-page mail-order booklet given away as an insert in the *New York Times*. A highly stylized suite of staged narrative images, it was the only publication Bourdin produced in his own lifetime. Despite its purpose, it had the feel of a fully controlled and authored book. On a trip to New York, the British artist Victor Burgin (page 158) noticed it, and brought a copy back to London to give to the writer Rosetta Brooks. In 1981 Brooks published an essay on 'Sighs and Whispers' in the vanguard art and culture journal *ZG*. Drawing on psychoanalysis and semiotics, Brooks discussed the relations between product and image, desire and seduction, art and commissions, and photography and deathliness – concepts that Bourdin's self-reflexive images seemed to relish. Brooks's essay is credited with launching the serious critical study of fashion photography, a genre that until then had received little attention.

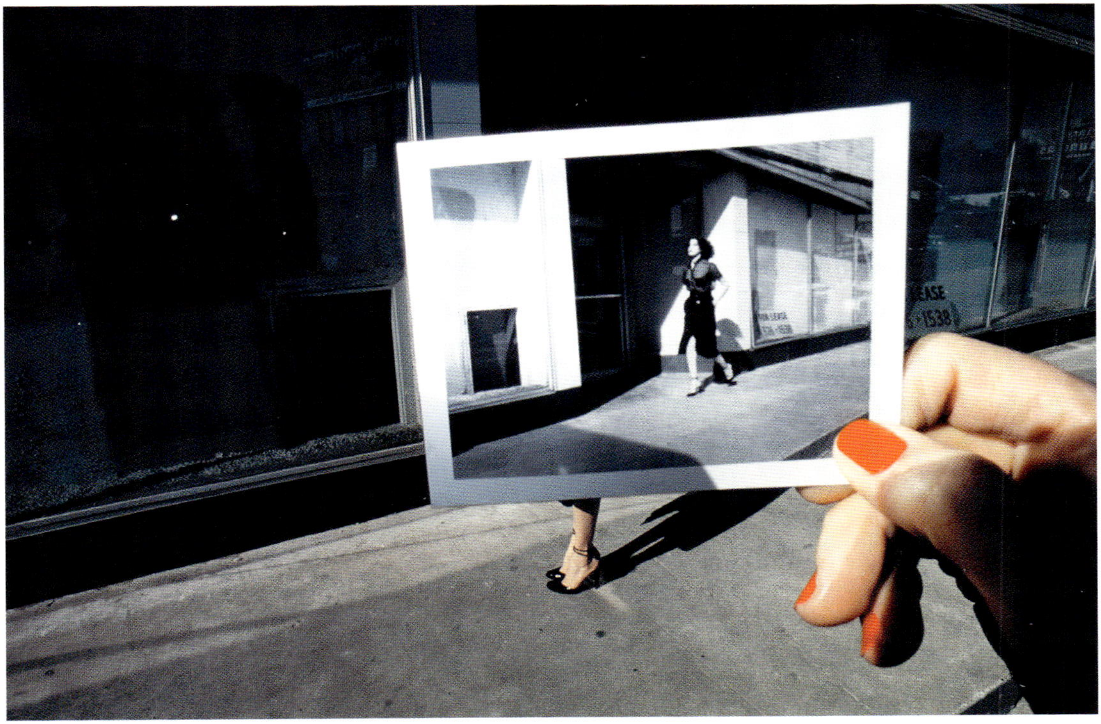

PHOTOGRAPHER UNKNOWN

Preparations for the British Exhibition of War Pictures, Grafton Galleries, London, c.1917

THE LARGE-SCALE PHOTOGRAPH has been familiar to audiences of contemporary art at least since the 1970s. It took photography away from the scale of the printed page, and towards a relationship with large paintings. Scale was one of the ways in which photography secured its link to the picture gallery, museum and art market.

However, a large scale does more than make a connection with the embodied experience historically associated with looking at paintings. One of its practical and social advantages is that many viewers are able to behold a large image at once. Response can be communal. This was the motivation for many of the earliest experiments with grand-scale photography. Before the artistic possibilities were fully realized, photographs were enlarged for exhibitions looking to marshal and choreograph a collective response.

Here we see uniformed soldiers carrying oak-framed prints into the Grafton Galleries, London. In the last two years of the First World War, a number of spectacular exhibitions set out to entertain and boost morale for the war effort. They were seen by people in their hundreds of thousands. Many of the images on display were hand-coloured composites assembled from pieces of various photographs, some of which were documentary in character and some staged enactments. The reasons for this were a mix of the aesthetic and the practical. At this point in photography's technical history, it was difficult to get shots of action; and when they were achieved, they rarely expressed the broader sense of the battle. So these tableaux were often constructed with more than one point of interest, like panoramas of small incidents.

The driving force behind the exhibitions was Ivor Castle, a photographer employed by the Canadian War Records Office. Working with the printer Raines & Co., Castle oversaw exhibitions often featuring military operations with a significant Canadian presence, notably the victory at Pilckem Ridge and the Somme offensive. Soon, Castle became involved in his own battle. His rival was the Australian photographer Frank Hurley, something of a hero since his return from Shackleton's near calamitous Antarctic expedition of 1914–17. Hurley was appointed to the Australian War Records Section in June 1917 and set about staging his own exhibition, also at the Grafton Galleries. Like Castle, he felt the only way to make convincing battle scenes was with composite prints. Moreover, Hurley set out to make the world's largest photographs. While more pictorially sophisticated, they did not exceed the size of Castle's efforts, the largest of which was around 6 metres (19½ ft) wide.

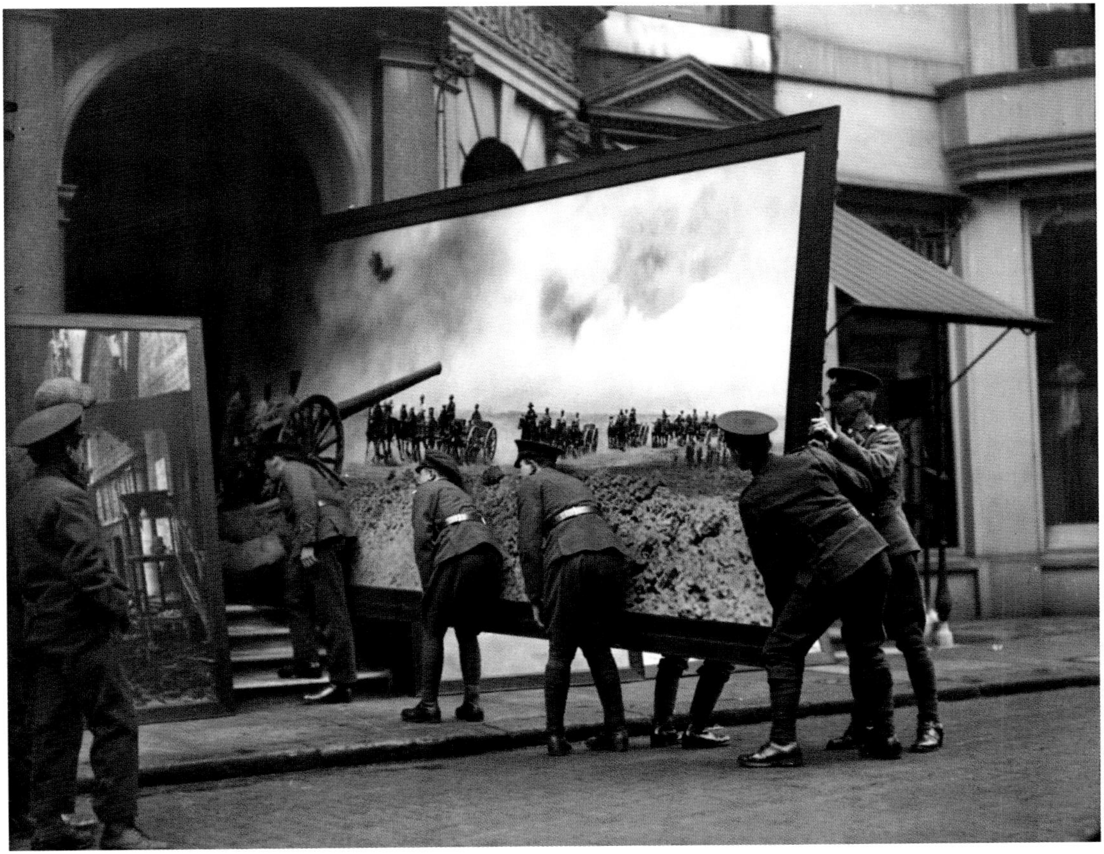

SUSAN MEISELAS

Monimbo, Nicaragua, July 2004, 2004

FROM THE SERIES 'RE-FRAMING HISTORY', 2005

IN THE WORLD OF PHOTOGRAPHY, an agency is an organization that distributes and sells photographers' images to publications and websites. Agencies grew alongside magazine photojournalism in the late 1920s and 1930s. To consider the word another way, however, 'agency' is what photographers might lose if they cannot control how their images are used.

The American photographer Susan Meiselas began her association with the Magnum Photos agency in 1976. Magnum is a cooperative owned by its photographer-members. It was set up in 1947, by Robert Capa, Henri Cartier-Bresson (page 82), George Rodger and David 'Chim' Seymour. Part of the motivation behind Magnum's founding was to try to protect its photographers' independence.

In 1978 Meiselas travelled to Nicaragua to cover the popular insurrection against the Somoza dictatorship. She stayed much longer than most other photojournalists, getting to know the people and the situation. She would send to the Magnum office in New York her exposed rolls of film along with written notes and captions. On her return to the office, after just over a year, she saw how various international magazines had used her photographs, sometimes in ways she was not expecting.

Meiselas made a book of her Nicaragua work, published in 1981. This gave her more control, and gave her project greater longevity, if a smaller audience. She also curated exhibitions that placed pages from the aforementioned magazines alongside spreads from her book, framed prints and outtakes. As she recalled: 'It was an attempt to de-mask for readers, and for me myself too, since I was a reader of my own images as they appeared in the media. Could I reveal to people what they don't usually get to see, rather than just showing a fine print of an image used on the cover of a magazine? Could I show the choices that determine why an image might be reproduced two-by-two inches or as a double spread? Could I show the different cultural resonances of the image choices around the world? Which images are used in Brazil or Germany?'

This restlessness over the way in which images are trafficked soon became central to each of Meiselas's projects. She has continued to visit Nicaragua, notably to make a documentary film about her experience, about the fate of the country since 1979, and about the fate of her photographs. Many of her images remain well known there. In 2004, twenty-five years after the overthrow of Somoza, she returned with nineteen of her photographs printed mural-size on fabric. These were installed close to the locations where the photographs had been taken. The effect was a haunting and provocative return of the country's recent history. Their placement was temporary, and, once removed, the giant images then travelled the world in exhibitions.

One of Meiselas's best-known Nicaragua images shows three people crouching in a forest with their faces hidden by traditional dance masks. They are making bombs in preparation for the revolution. The photograph made the cover of several publications, including the *New York Times Magazine*. Looking back, Meiselas feels she was being used to some extent by a group wanting to get its message out. Over time, however, the photograph developed a life of its own, with varied meanings. A photographer cannot always regulate the use of her images. In recognition of this fact, Meiselas makes projects that reflect on the limits of a photographer's agency, in both senses of the word.

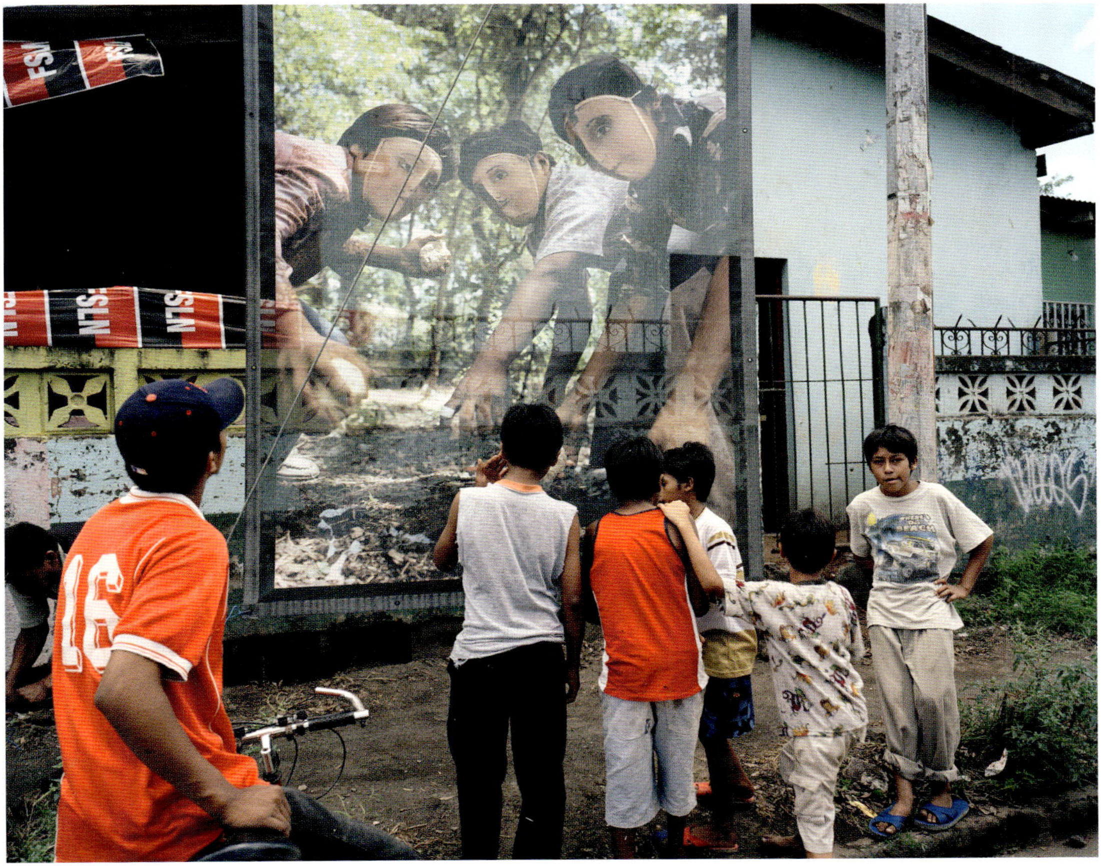

JOHN STEZAKER

Pair I, 2007

IT IS IN THE NATURE OF IMAGES, *all* images, to misbehave and exceed meaning in ways that are anarchic, elusive, enigmatic and ambiguous. This is why images are so often accompanied by words that tame and stabilize them. Essentially, however, they remain wild, and therefore have always been a source of great fascination, and great suspicion.

The anxiety that the world of images might disturb civil society is a familiar one. How often do we hear that we are 'bombarded' by or 'under siege' from images, as if somehow they were pursuing us? And amid such narcissism, we may delude ourselves that it is a new problem afflicting only us, and only now. The arrival of photography in the 1830s and its development into a mass medium certainly introduced new problems, new pleasures, new disturbances into the family of images. They might contain details that not even the photographer planned or intended.

Even the most conventional photographs contain other worlds. John Stezaker's source materials are almost banal: old postcards, vintage film stills and pictures from half-forgotten illustrated books. He combines them in disarmingly simple ways, often doing no more than placing one on top of another. Out of the familiarity something strange and startling can emerge, like unconscious wishes disrupting routine. Stezaker makes his collages in a state of reverie, like daydreaming, feeling as though he is being guided by an invisible hand. Time seems to stop, and the pictures begin to suggest their unspoken affinities. It is as if images have their own secret wishes. They wait in silence for their unpredictable energies to be released.

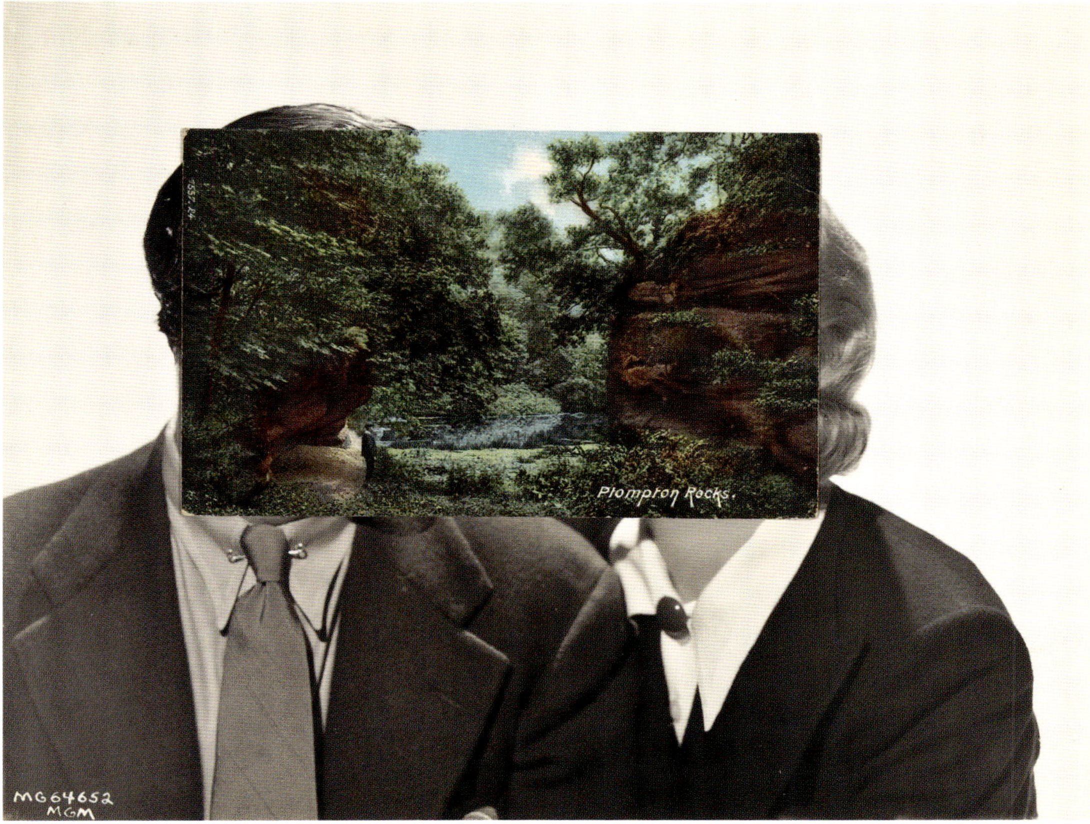
Plompton Rocks.
MG64652
MGM

HELENA ALMEIDA

Inhabited Painting, 1975

WHAT IS THE SURFACE OF A PHOTOGRAPH? Is it anything at all? The light-sensitive emulsions on the earliest photographic papers were hand-brushed, and the prints felt crafted. By the 1850s, papers had acquired an industrial smoothness that was unusual in the graphic arts. Manufacturers even double- and triple-coated their photographic papers to emphasize this. Before long, a high-gloss surface became standard and ceased to call attention to itself. On a screen, a photograph truly has no surface; but even when printed it tends to feel glassed-in and cut-off, its membrane difficult to see. The eye will slide.

In many ways photography gave up its own surface the better to explore the surfaces of the world around it. From the roughness of rock to the smoothness of steel and glass, the camera records it all in detail. Arguably, the medium became a modern art when it embraced its industrially smooth character rather than fighting it, or trying to overcome it. The modernity of a photograph could be expressed anywhere – as an exhibited print, on the pages of a book or magazine, projected on to a wall, or pasted as a billboard. Nevertheless, the elusive surface of photography has been a constant source of fascination.

The Portuguese artist Helena Almeida (1934–2018) moved freely between photography, painting, drawing, performance, film and sculpture. For her extended series 'Inhabited Paintings' (1974–77), she posed over and over again before her camera, often with a paintbrush in hand. The paint was added later, directly to the surface of the photograph itself. Sometimes Almeida appears to be emerging from behind the blue acrylic paint. Sometimes she seems to be in the process of obliterating herself, as if behind the painted surface and within the illusionistic space of the photograph. It was a deceptively simple formal game but also a feminist gesture. Abstract painting was associated with heroic male artists, notably Jackson Pollock (who, for publicity, had at one point been filmed from below while dripping his paint on to glass) and Yves Klein (page 46), famous for using a similar blue pigment, sometimes applied directly to the bodies of naked women. Almeida was a woman in control of her own body and image, literally and symbolically.

As you look, it is worth remembering that the image opposite is not the artist's work itself. It is an industrially standard photomechanical reproduction. Its surface is no different to any other page in this book. Close your eyes and run your finger across it. It will tell you nothing.

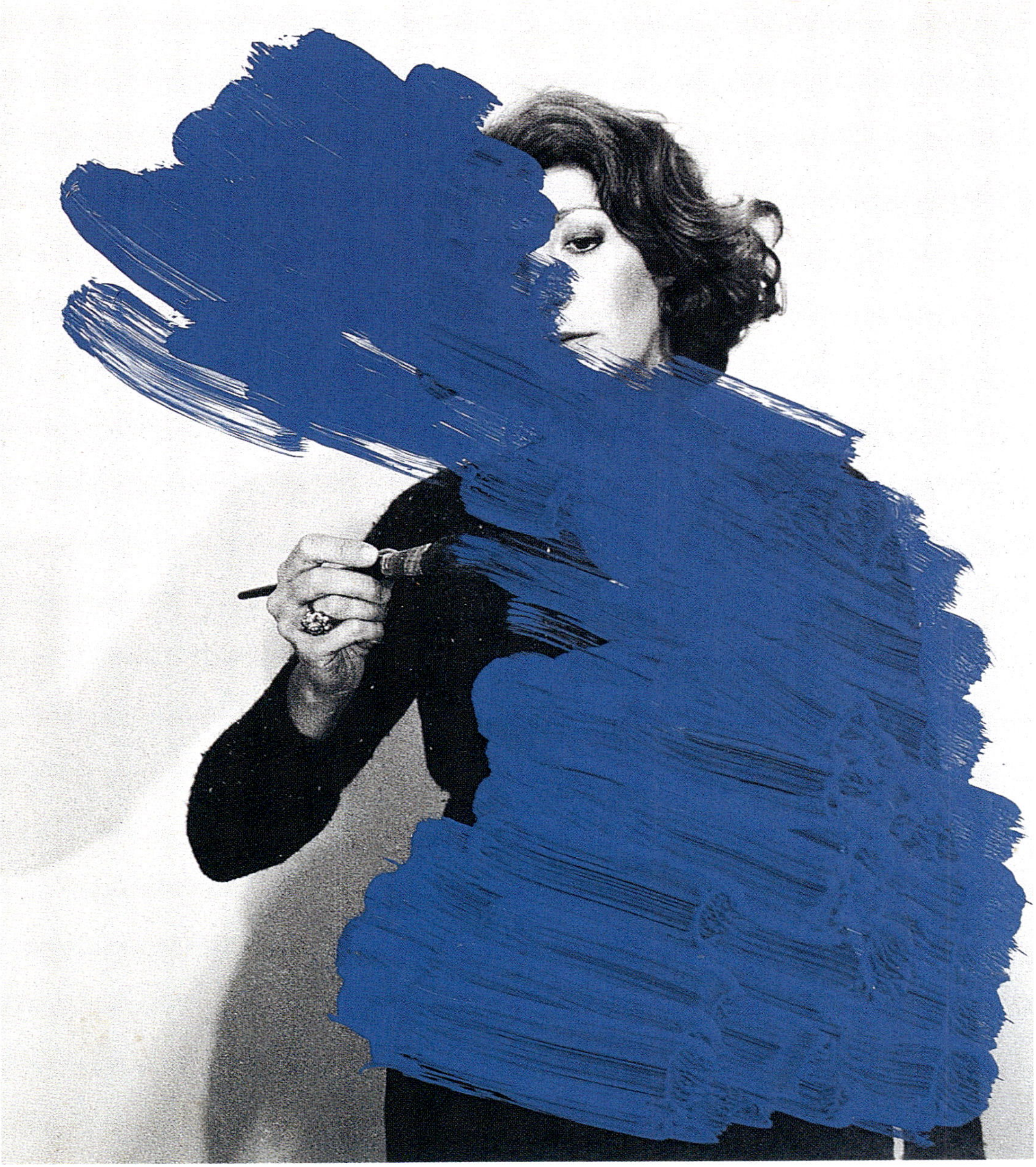

WILLIAM EGGLESTON

Untitled

FROM THE *LOS ALAMOS* PORTFOLIO, 1965–74

IN THE TWENTIETH CENTURY, difficulties slowed the artistic development of colour photography. First, it was for a long time notoriously tricky to print colour with any nuance. While negatives and transparencies captured colour with great subtlety, print technology was limited. It was almost impossible to control contrast and saturation, although many photographers adapted their art to the limitations and made fine work. Only the expensive dye-transfer print process offered prints that came close to the full richness. Cinema, however, being pure light, did not have to print, and for decades it raced far ahead in its aesthetic exploration of colour. Nothing in printed photography could rival the sumptuous colour of Powell and Pressburger's film *A Matter of Life and Death* (1946), for example.

Secondly, black-and-white photography preceded colour photography. The habits and criteria for art photography were formed in relation to black and white, and were entrenched by those who could not see beyond colour's association with commerce and entertainment. The photographer Paul Strand went so far as to claim that 'higher emotions cannot be communicated in colour', a sentiment that would have sounded ridiculous to such painters as Hilma af Klint or Georgia O'Keefe. The supposedly greater seriousness of black and white was also present in magazine photojournalism, which remained distinct from the pages of colour advertising well into the 1950s.

Thirdly, black and white and colour are not opposites. A colour image contains the black-and-white version of itself, but not the other way round. In the digital era, all the colour can be removed from an image at the touch of a button. Adding colour to a black-and-white original is painstaking, and akin to painting. When colour first became widespread in cinema, in magazines and then in domestic snapshots, it did indeed feel like an addition. The critic Roland Barthes felt that colour was 'a coating applied later on to the original truth of the black-and-white photograph [...] an artifice, a cosmetic (like the kind used to paint corpses)'.

Lastly, the meaning of colour is unstable and difficult to define. What does a red umbrella in a rainy grey street mean? Or the blue of a car? Or the green of a tree? The presence of each can transform a scene dramatically, without any particular meaning. Observational photographers, especially those working in the post-Second World War consumer societies, had to confront colour not as something extra, not as a layer on top of black and white, but as something fundamental. Colour is intrinsic to the world and to its photographic picturing.

The American William Eggleston was not the first to grasp this, but it is his work that has had the greatest influence on subsequent colour photographers, museum curators and critics. Of this particular image, he has said: 'It's of a place in Memphis that's long gone, and I was entranced by what [the woman] was wearing – her sweater and dress, light red and white – and how the color of her lips and fingernails went beautifully with those colors. The wall – those multicolors – is just incidental.'

In the flow of daily life, a reactive photographer cannot look at everything. Eggleston gazed through his viewfinder at the clothes, lips and nails, the overall composition, and quickly pressed his shutter. That glorious colour grid could well have been incidental. The fact that the woman's hair, right in the centre, would look almost the same in a black-and-white photo may have been incidental too. But neither is incidental to the resulting picture.

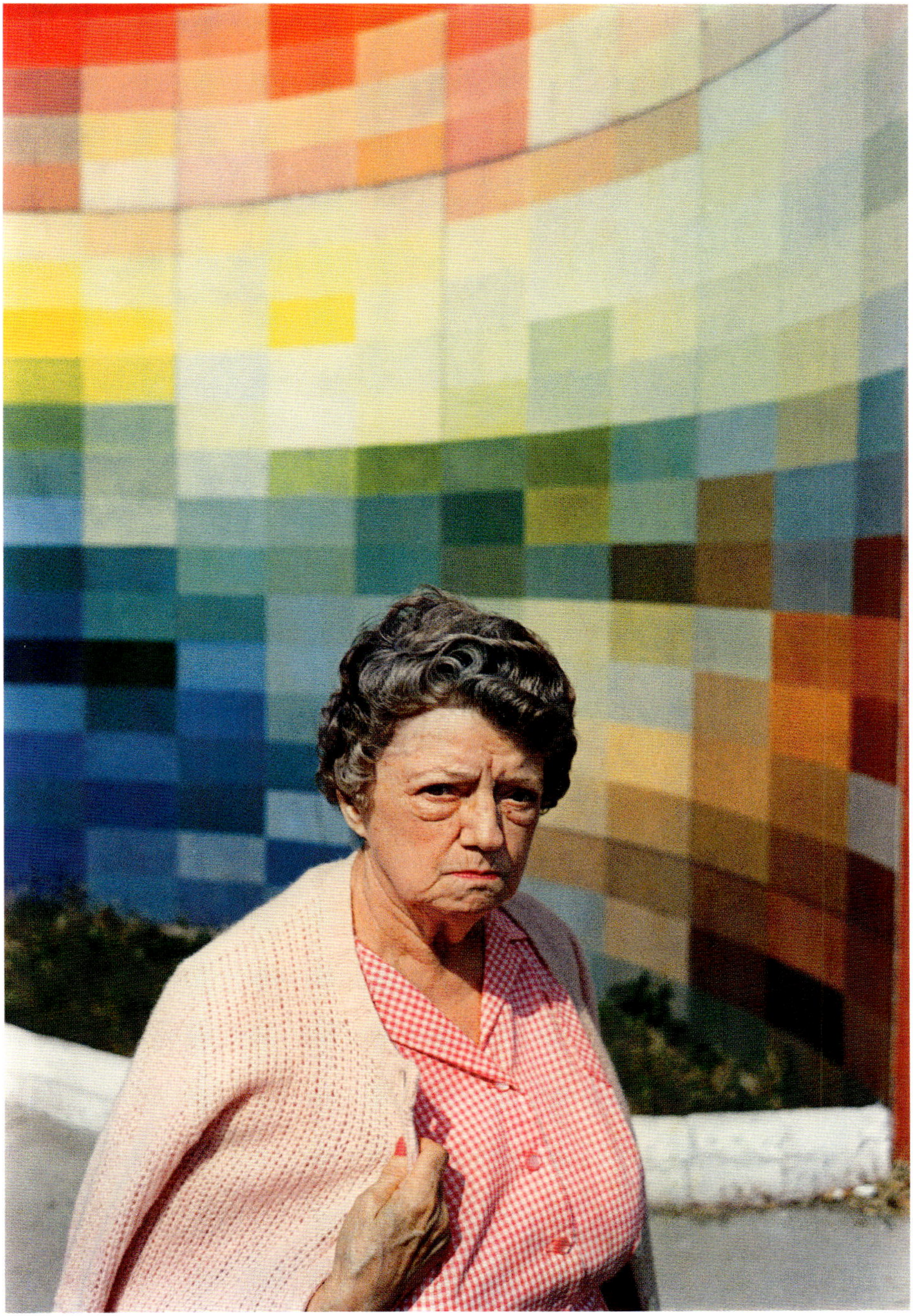

RUTH ORKIN

American Girl in Italy, 1951

AMERICAN GIRL IN ITALY was one of nine photographs by Ruth Orkin that appeared in the September 1952 issue of *Cosmopolitan*, in a feature titled 'When You Travel Alone'.

'Solo voyaging need hold no terrors for the feminine tourist,' begins the accompanying commentary. 'It's fun, it's easy, and it's the best way in the world to meet new people – men, for instance. Having no-one but yourself to depend on and being away from friends who expect you always to be yourself, you are likely to develop a brand-new self-reliance and charm. Besides, two girls or a group traveling together look like a closed corporation, and are less likely to be invited to join other people's fun.'

Orkin, aged twenty-nine, was not entirely alone, and neither was the woman in the picture,a twenty-three-year-old American calling herself Jinx Allen. Orkin was on her way back from an assignment in Israel; Allen was on a six-month tour of Europe. The two met in Florence, at the American Express office where ex-patriots collected their mail. They discussed life away from home, and the next morning they headed out for a free-spirited collaboration. Orkin photographed while Allen posed as if asking for directions, looked confused with foreign currency, and gazed at statues. Orkin made two attempts at this particular shot, asking Allen to repeat her walk, and asking the man on the motorcycle not to look at the camera. A minute later, Allen hopped on his passenger seat for another picture.

The issue of *Cosmopolitan* came and went, but this image has lasted. By accident or design its form is more classical, and its drama more theatrical, than Orkin's other shots from that day. There are compositions like this in the Renaissance paintings of Florence's Uffizi Gallery.

In the ensuing decades, the photograph became very well known. It was frequently reproduced in books and as a popular poster. The two women insisted there was no 'message' here about harassment or patriarchy, or feminism. Still, the mood of the photograph may not feel as light to a contemporary audience as the duo intended. Allen clutches her shawl to her chest, knuckles a little white. The bag and sketchbook are held close to her body. In that unpredictable fraction of a second, her eyelids drop, her mouth hangs open a little, and the angle of her head *could* suggest apprehension. The stride is forthright but her body seems to withdraw, as if moving through the scene as men's gazes meet the side of her face. This is not to say Allen or Orkin felt that way.

Once it is in the world, a photograph can acquire meaning well beyond intention. And if a photograph becomes 'iconic', as this one has, it is not because it carries some universal meaning; rather, it is open to different interpretations.

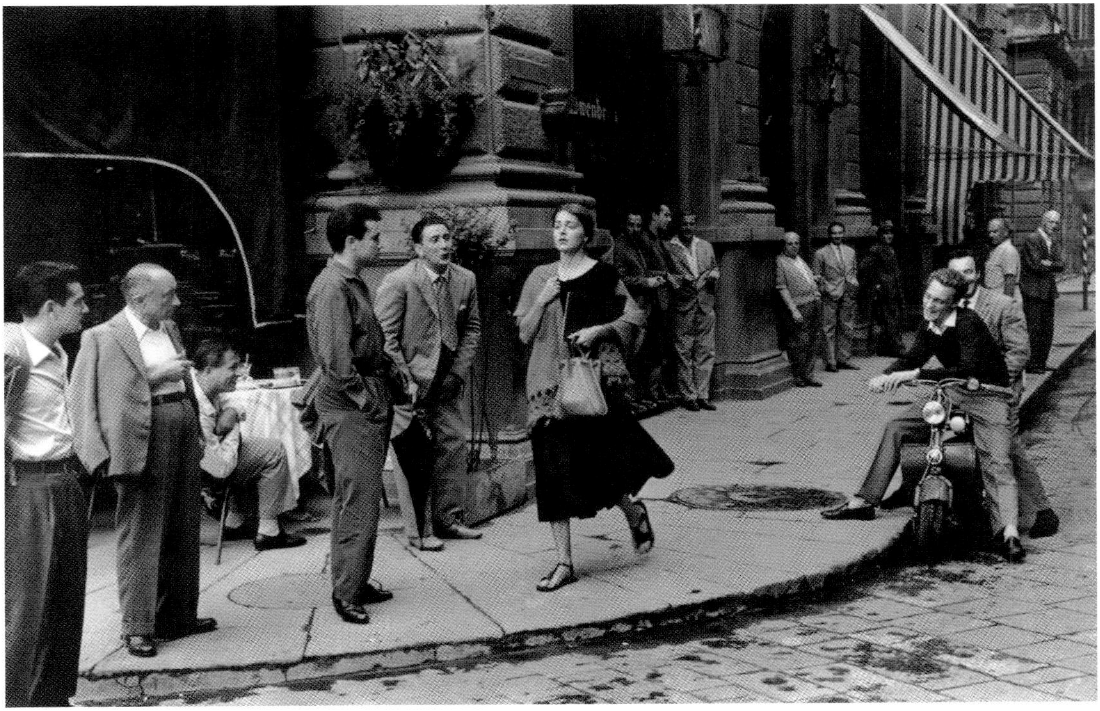

GÉRARD CASTELLO-LOPES

Lisboa, 1957

THE WORK OF GÉRARD CASTELLO-LOPES is not well known outside Portugal. Together with Sena da Silva and Carlos Afonso Dias, he was one of a loose group of photographers who made remarkable images in the 1950s. Castello-Lopes was also involved in cinema, as a critic and an actor, and for a while had his own film production and distribution company. He was a jazz-lover as well, and in 1948 co-founded Lisbon's legendary Hot Clube de Portugal.

Little of Castello-Lopes's photography was seen until the early 1980s, when it was shown at Lisbon's Ether Gallery. Portugal was in the process of discovering its own history of photography. The attention prompted Castello-Lopes to pick up his camera once more. He made new work and exhibited until a few years before his death in 2011. Throughout, his deepest inspiration had been the work of Henri Cartier-Bresson (page 82), whose book *The Decisive Moment* had been published to great acclaim in 1952. This photograph could easily be mistaken for one by the French master.

Castello-Lopes captures a moment of action in a photograph of formal geometry and great poise. But what is going on? Is the figure in the jacket pretending to be shot? No, there is a ball just visible behind his right hand. He is probably a goalkeeper in a street game among boys. Soccer shot. Gun shot. Camera shot.

The photograph came to wider attention when it was used on the cover of an English-language edition of *The Book of Disquiet*, by the celebrated Portuguese writer Fernando Pessoa. The image appears at first to have little to do with the book. There are, however, intriguing parallels. As with the delayed appreciation of the image, Pessoa's book was published posthumously (in 1982). Like a group of photographs, the book is an assemblage of vivid but enigmatic fragments that can be appreciated in almost any order. And Pessoa certainly had a deep affinity for the life and poetry of the street: 'There is no difference between me and these streets, save they being streets and I a soul, which perhaps is irrelevant when we consider the essence of things.'

More profoundly, Pessoa's *Book of Disquiet* explores the idea of the 'heteronym' – an invented persona to be adopted in order to bypass entrenched habits. Under a heteronym, you might be able to escape yourself and live differently, create differently. Perhaps Castello-Lopes made this photograph while trying to shoot like Cartier-Bresson. The idea is not as strange as it seems. Many photographers will admit to stepping into the shoes of those they admire, if only to get the admiration out of their system. But in the process, remarkable photographs do get made. If you produce a work of art while pretending to be someone else, who made it? Is authorship ever completely free of influence? The question runs throughout Pessoa's book. In art and literature, we expect authors and makers to be unique; in photography especially, this is rare.

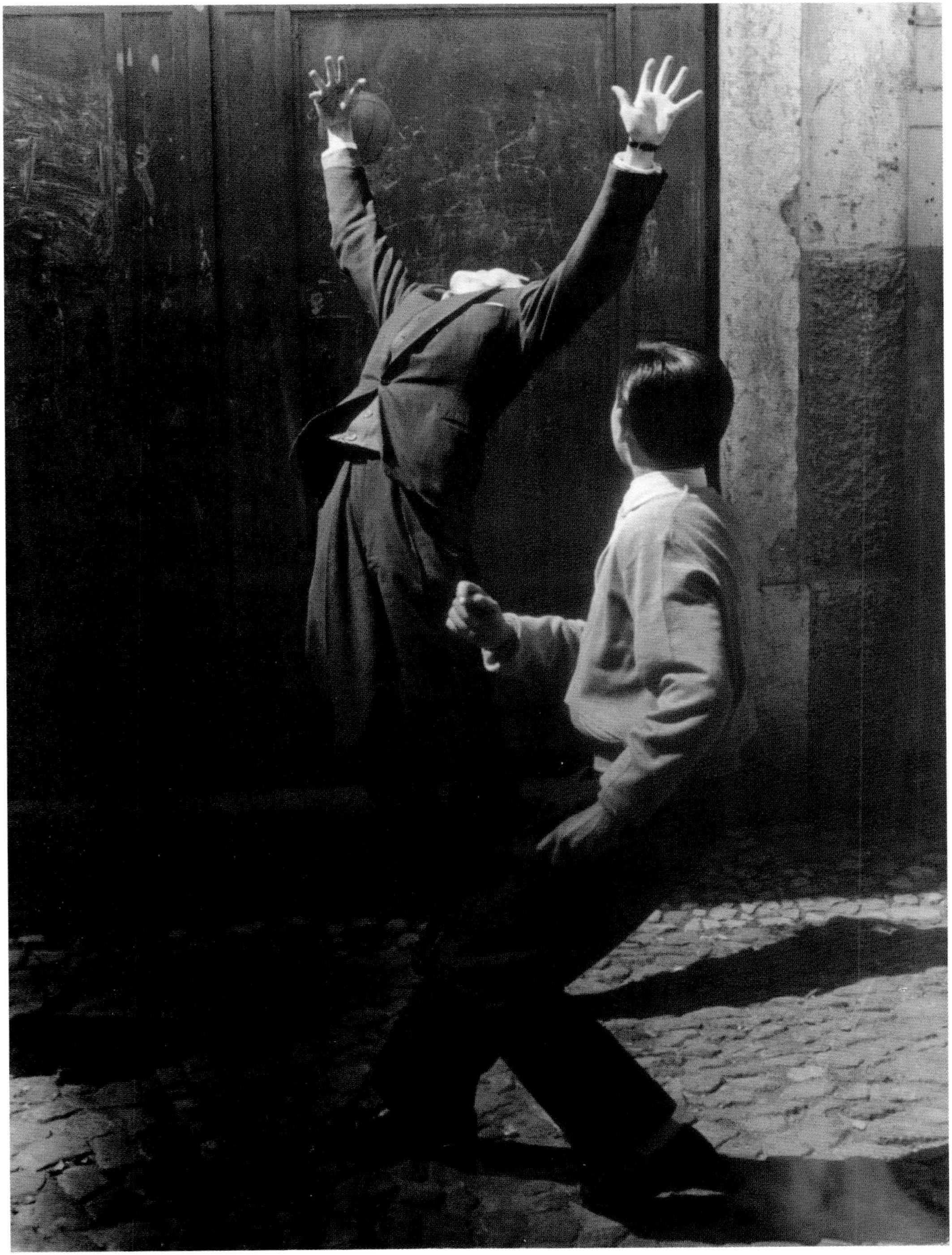

GARRY WINOGRAND

Albuquerque, New Mexico, 1957

THERE ARE NO WRONG OR RIGHT INTERPRETATIONS OF A PHOTOGRAPH, AND THIS MAKES IT IDEALLY SUITED TO THE PICTURING OF MIXED FEELINGS.

SINCE HIS DEATH IN 1984, aged just fifty-six, Garry Winogrand has come to symbolize the phenomenon of the compulsive photographer. He took hundreds of thousands of photographs, with enormous energy and prodigious intensity. He was at home in the chaos of dense city streets, but his subject was really the USA in total, and what it looked like photographed. In his final years, he was not even looking at the images he was making. He left behind 2,500 rolls of undeveloped film, 6,500 developed rolls, and 3,000 rolls developed and contact-printed. That's around 432,000 exposures. Others have gone through this work, choosing, publishing and exhibiting what they have thought to be the best of it.

Although he lived fast, Winogrand took a while to reach his extremes. This photograph, made in the sun of New Mexico, comes from early in his career. At this point, he was still working as a freelance photojournalist and advertising photographer, and those obligations were perhaps keeping his wilder impulses in check. Two of his images had been included in the world-touring exhibition 'The Family of Man' (1955), but he had not yet had a solo show. He was still finding his feet.

We see a toddler at the edge of the unknown, emerging from a home at the edge of the desert. The tiny figure is bright white against the blackness of the garage interior. In the deep shadow there is a second child. As they step into the sun, the pupils of their eyes are no doubt constricting, like camera apertures. Winogrand photographed and printed this image at the very limit of what the technology could then keep visible. So among other things, this picture could be about eyesight and exposure. It is also an image of possibility and foreboding, of excitement and dread. Commentators tend to swing one way or the other in their response to it, but if a photograph compels, it is usually for its ambiguity. There are no wrong or right interpretations of a photograph, and this makes it ideally suited to the picturing of mixed feelings.

It certainly turned out to be a prescient image. The conflicted experience of suburbia and our increasingly uneasy relationship with the natural landscape soon became central themes in North American photography and cinema. The house Winogrand photographed on the ouskirts of Albuquerque was soon subsumed by urban sprawl. And, as with so many cities in the US, the new townscape was being determined by the automobile. Almost nothing is in walking distance, and many streets even lack sidewalks. There is no car in Winogrand's image, although it has shaped so much of what we see here, and so much of what those children are about to experience.

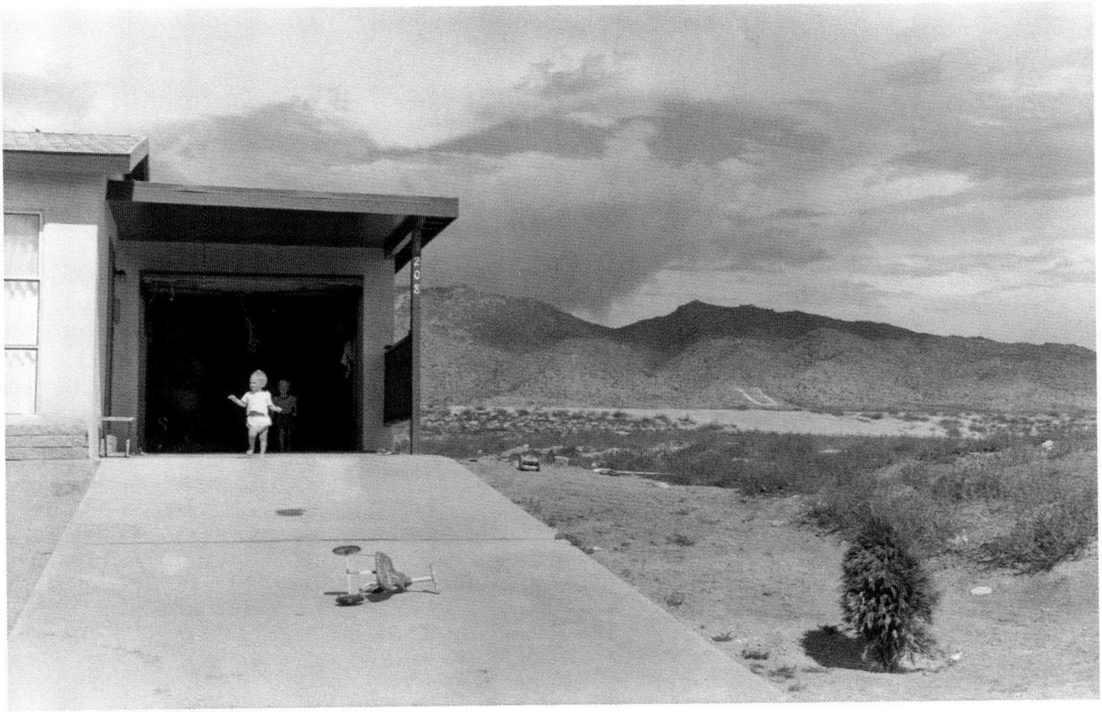
208

PHOTOGRAPHER UNKNOWN

Franz Reichelt, the 'Flying Tailor', demonstrates his parachute suit to the French press prior to his fateful leap from the Eiffel Tower, 1912

FRANZ REICHELT (1879–1912) was a French tailor of Austrian birth who invented a suit for aviators that was also a parachute. In the early days of manned flight, many pilots were killed through not being unable to jump safely from failing aircraft. Reichelt hoped his stylish invention would save lives. In late January 1912, he demonstrated his suit for a news photographer by jumping from low buildings. When the parachute did not open fully, Reichelt excitedly explained that his jumps were not high enough. Soon after, he announced that he would conduct a test from the Eiffel Tower, using a full-size human dummy.

On 12 February, photographers and newsreel cameramen gathered along with a large crowd at the foot of the tower. It soon became clear that Reichelt was intending to jump himself. Friends tried to dissuade him. As he climbed the steps to the first platform, his every move was being recorded. He got himself into position at the edge, paused, looked around, and leapt. The parachute failed to open and Reichelt plummeted to the icy ground. The next day's newspapers were covered in photos of the incident, and news footage played in cinemas. In the film, it is clear that Reichelt was terrified.

Reichelt's death is considered one of the first to be influenced by the presence of the media. If the cameras had not been there, he may not have felt the pressure to take such a risk. Let us remember the Flying Tailor as he made his test jump, brave and optimistic.

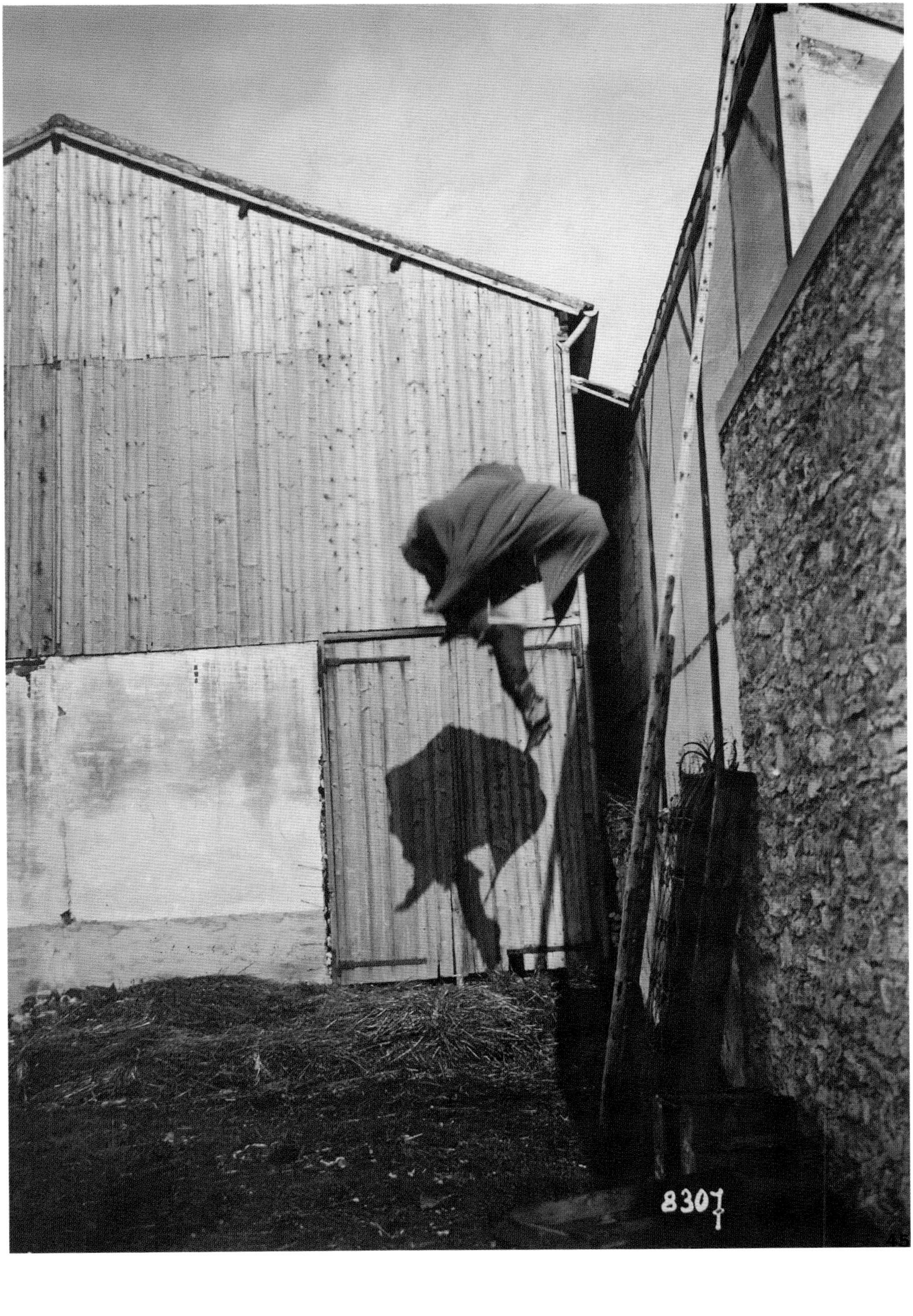
8307

HARRY SHUNK AND JÁNOS KENDER

Saut dans le vide

PHOTOMONTAGE OF A PERFORMANCE BY YVES KLEIN AT RUE GENTIL-BERNARD, FONTENAY-AUX-ROSES, FRANCE, 23 OCTOBER 1960

IN THE LATE 1950s, various kinds of art practice emerged that made use of photography. Artists within Pop, conceptual art, performance art, minimalism and land art would find they needed the help of a photographer to realize an idea or project, or to document a complex installation or performance. The situation gave rise to a new, hybrid kind of image that was often somewhere between a document and an artwork in its own right. It also gave rise to a new kind of photographer, one who could solve problems and create in collaboration.

The German photographer Harry Shunk and his Hungarian partner, János Kender, were the most prolific and well connected of this new breed. Between 1957 and 1973 they worked internationally, and with dozens of the best-known artists of the time. Their work was attributed to 'Shunk–Kender', but the credit usually took second place to the artists who had engaged them. Sometimes they were not credited at all.

In 1960 the French painter and provocateur Yves Klein engaged Shunk–Kender to help him produce *Saut dans le vide* (Leap into the Void), a performance made explicitly for the camera. Voids had been central to Klein's work for some time. He had been exploring their aesthetic and existential charge in his monochrome paintings, as well as in his exhibition 'The Specialization of Sensibility in the Raw Material State into Stabilized Pictorial Sensibility', presented at the Galerie Iris Clert, Paris, in 1958. Also known simply as 'The Void', the show consisted of nothing more than white walls and empty display cases.

The athletic Klein appears to make an ecstatic jump from a high wall on a quiet street. With no apparent care for his safety, he aims for the sky. In the background, a cyclist is unaware of what is going on, adding to the otherworldly atmosphere. In truth, Klein landed safely on a tarpaulin, stretched out by several friends. The image is a montage of two separate photographs. *Saut dans le vide* was then published on the front cover of Klein's single-edition newspaper, *Dimanche (Le Journal d'un seul jour)*. In many ways, the most remarkable feat here is not so much the leap but the perfectly realized image, created in the Shunk–Kender darkroom.

For decades, the name 'Shunk–Kender' was barely known to art audiences, and to a great extent this added to the effect of the art that the duo had helped to produce. If Yves Klein is perceived as the author of *Saut dans le vide*, our attention is on the leap itself (Klein even claimed he had made an earlier jump from a two-storey building). Once the emphasis shifts to the authorship of the photograph, then we are in the realm of contrivance, artifice and manipulation.

Much of the art of the last seventy years has emerged from the kind of ambivalent creative space in which Shunk–Kender operated so successfully. Photography can slip so easily between record and invention, casual document and carefully considered publicity. However, this slipperiness has come to be seen by curators, art writers and audiences as fascinating in itself, and key to our understanding of photography. In recent years, the work of Shunk–Kender has been the subject of a number of exhibitions, moving their inventiveness and authorship into the spotlight.

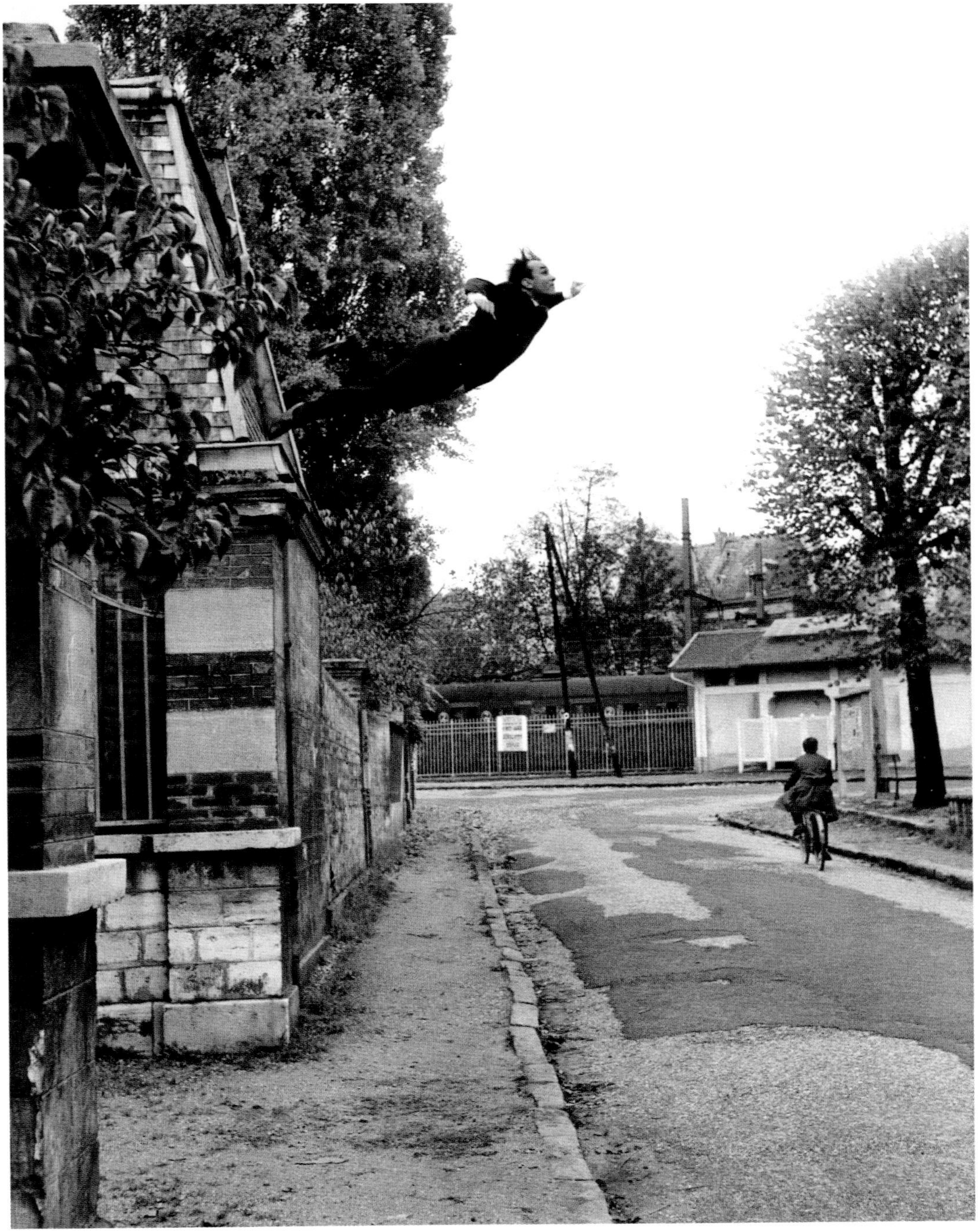

EADWEARD MUYBRIDGE

Chickens Scared by a Torpedo, 1884–87

FEW PHOTOGRAPHS HAVE HAD anything like the impact of Eadweard Muybridge's studies of human and animal locomotion, made in the 1870s and 1880s. They have come to symbolize a seismic and irreversible shift in the understanding of vision, living bodies, nature, science and art. The project was so singular, bold and uncompromising that historical time seems to split into 'before and after Muybridge'.

Muybridge's images are vivid, uncompromising and authoritative. They are also ambiguous, voyeuristic and obsessive. Why were they made? What were they for? How are we supposed to look at them? They fascinate in ways that exceed scientific purpose. Many nineteenth-century pioneers strike us as historical curiosities, but Muybridge captured secrets fundamental to modern experience. All subsequent generations have considered him theirs, if never in quite the same way.

The project began in 1872 with a commission to solve the question of whether or not all four hooves of a galloping horse are off the ground at the same time. Cameras were assembled in a row, each with a shutter to be set off by a trip wire. The horse would snag the wires as it passed and thus photograph itself in sequence. All its hooves *did* leave the ground. But the answer raised more questions, triggering an epic series of investigations that would last for years. Muybridge refined the technique, automating his cameras, but the essentials remained the same.

Tight systems and repetitions tend to have their pathologies. For some commentators, Muybridge's obsessive compulsion to control and repeat is located in his own damaged psyche: having discovered that his wife had given birth to a child by another man, he promptly tracked down the interloper and shot him. Muybridge was tried but acquitted. He departed for South America to clear his mind with other projects, but returned to the locomotion studies with inexhaustible vigour. Perhaps he really was replaying the traumatic instants when he found he'd been cuckolded and exacted his revenge. Perhaps not, but *something* motivated the relentless drive to freeze thousands of specimens in ecstatic stillness. Settling the horse question hardly justifies his extended parade of *Homo sapiens* and other beasts.

Nearly every book about the history of cinema offers Muybridge as one of its 'parents'. We have all grown up with movies, so it is difficult not to connect his instantaneous consecutive images with cinema. And while it is true that Muybridge himself devised a way of animating his photos (the Zoopraxiscope of 1879), the serious project was to stop and stare. Nevertheless, the fact that a movie camera is just a still camera that takes photos in an unusual way can never be quite overcome.

One of Muybridge's very last locomotion studies was *Chickens Scared by a Torpedo*. Science barely justifies its wild perversity. Soon after, Muybridge put his cameras aside and turned to gardening.

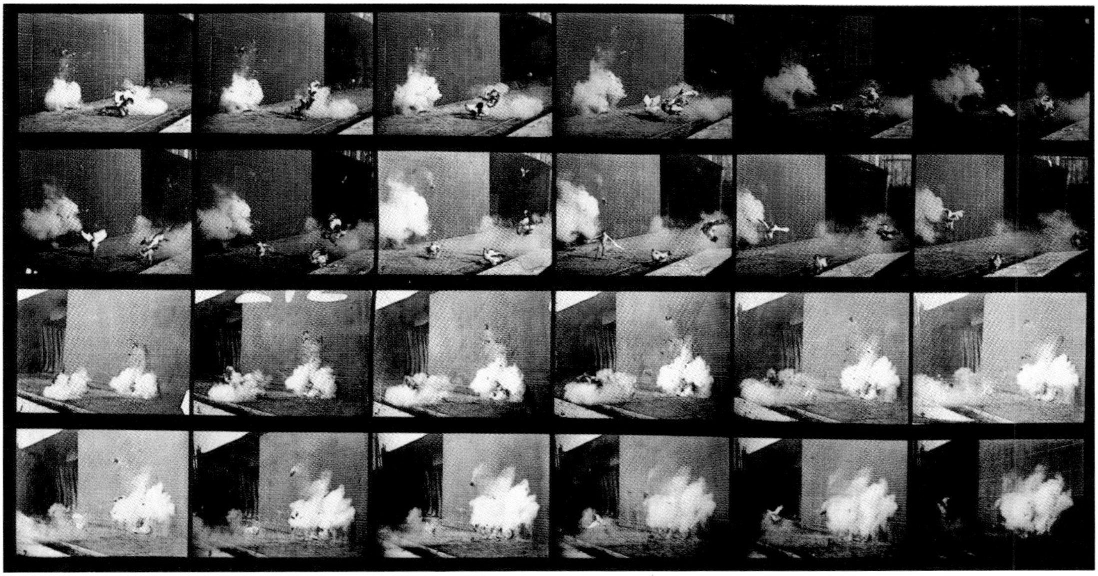

FRANK AND LILLIAN GILBRETH

Cyclegraphic image of a woman working at a gridded table, c. 1914

FOR CENTURIES, HUMANS had work songs. To keep both body and mind going through the hard and necessary labour of harvesting, washing, building and preparing food, people would sing. The rhythms and melodies helped maintain the pace so that the work got done. With the coming of the age of mechanization, this relationship was reversed. Now it was the rhythm of machines that set the pace, and the workers had to keep up with them. From mechanized looms to automobile production lines, standardized manufacture would standardize the worker. In theory, at least.

From the drive to greater efficiency, there emerged in the early twentieth century a whole new industry: 'time and motion study'. Time had long been studied in the workplace. Performance could be measured against a stopwatch, for example, and workers could simply be instructed to work faster. Studying motion meant looking at how the body of the worker performed the task. Combining the two could refine workers' movements so that time and energy were not wasted.

Lillian Gilbreth was a psychologist and one of the first women to earn a PhD in industrial engineering. Her husband, Frank Gilbreth, was an engineer and consultant. Key to their version of the time and motion study was the Cyclegraph, or Chronocyclegraph, an innovation of their own devising. A selected worker would sit or stand before a gridded background, with small light bulbs attached to the body parts that were doing the work (most often the hands, although the head was often wired too). While the worker performed a given task, a camera made a long exposure. On the photographic plate, the lights would register as white traces over blurred body movement. A smooth flow of light would indicate the task was being performed efficiently. If the light trace was erratic, there was room for improvement. The Gilbreths promoted their approach to efficiency as caring and humane, focused on working *better*, not simply harder.

Photographs like this one illustrated the Gilbreths' various published reports. The images certainly looked scientific and purposeful, but whether or not precise and practical conclusions could be drawn from the visual data has long been a point of contention. Regardless, the Gilbreths were skilled self-publicists. Their project met with wide acclaim, and the couple became popular symbols of the growing field of scientific management. And in the century since, the use of cameras to monitor work productivity has increased dramatically.

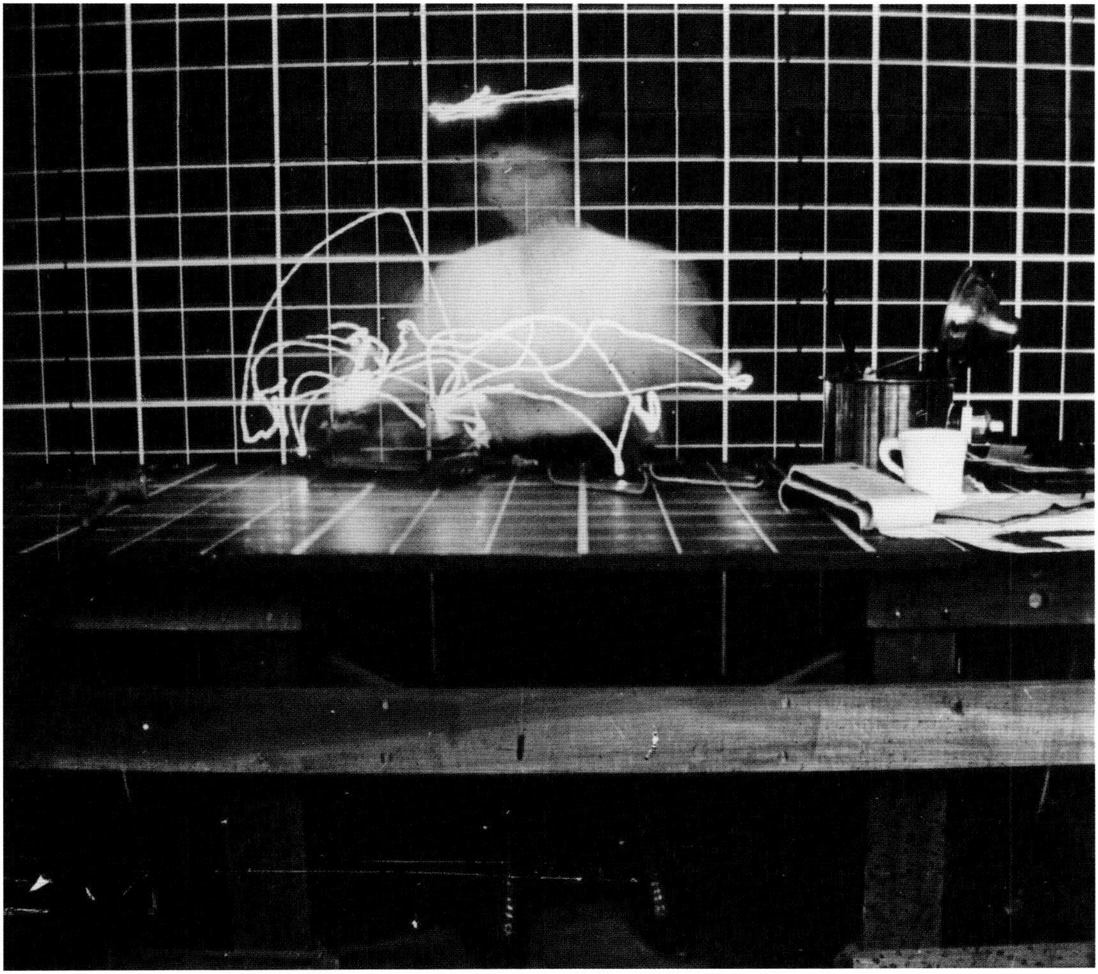

ÉTIENNE-JULES MAREY

Vertical Ball Drop, 1890

THERE ARE MANY WAYS in which still photography can register time and motion. The French scientist, physiologist and inventor Étienne-Jules Marey did it by making multiple high-speed exposures on a single photosensitive plate. This technique combined the freezing of movement with a technical impression of movement itself.

Matters of measurement – what to measure, how to measure, and how to interpret the results – were at the heart of all Marey's inventions. From an interest in human blood flow, respiration and muscle movement came his sphygmograph of 1863, the first wearable device for measuring pulse rates. His chronophotographic gun (1882) could take twelve consecutive photographs of animals and humans in movement, even flight. He also pioneered the study of aerodynamics by releasing smoke trails into a wind tunnel, and photographing the airflow around objects. His version of the movie camera could shoot sixty frames per second. What mattered was detail, demonstrated in precise photographs, and recounted in his many illustrated publications.

Late in life, Marey returned to the photographic analysis of movement. This image shows the result of an attempt to demonstrate how photography could be used to determine the rate of acceleration of a falling object. If the height of the drop is known, and the timing of the intervals between exposures is known, then a calculation can be made. A white ball is released, falling in front of a black backdrop that marks the height. In the centre of the frame is a circular mechanical device that indicated whether the exposure intervals of the camera were correct. The framing of the image is wider than the science requires, making it a record of much else besides: the plants, the folds in the makeshift backcloth, the ladder, the sunlight, the man's clothes and pose, and the very human feeling of discovery.

The question of photographic time has always been at the centre of ambitious theories of photography, and of the various attempts to define its essence as a medium. But it has eluded genuine theorization, just as it eludes the notion of what a medium is. Photography requires something beyond itself: the light that is reflected by the world. It gathers this light, and creates illusions. This means the time and appearance of the photographic image are inseparable from the time and appearance of the world, yet they are clearly not the same. By remaining an open question, photography remains fascinating, frustrating, and full of scientific and artistic potential.

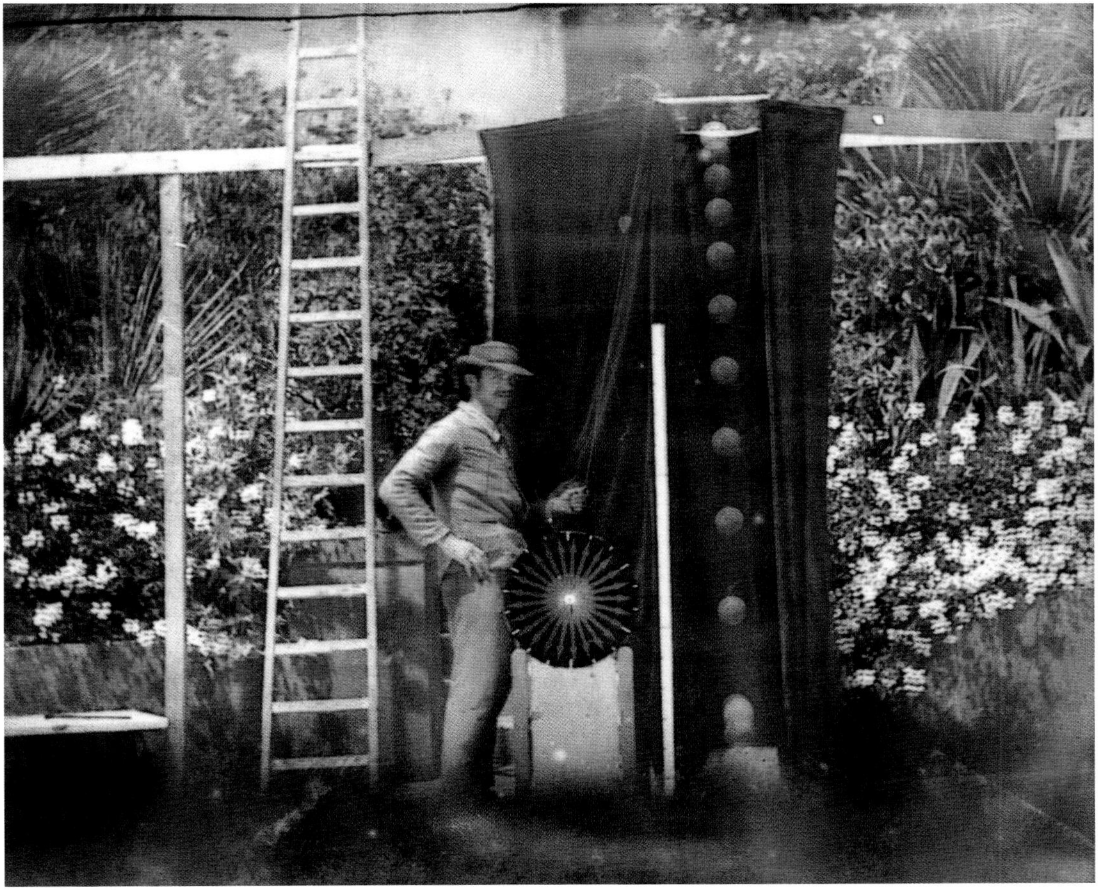

JOHN BALDESSARI

FROM THE SERIES 'THROWING THREE BALLS IN THE AIR TO GET A STRAIGHT LINE (BEST OF THIRTY-SIX ATTEMPTS)', 1973

BETWEEN AROUND 1965 AND 1975, in the heyday of what came to be called 'conceptual art', many artists in Europe and North America got involved with photography without really thinking of themselves as photographers. They had no affectionate commitment to it as a medium, but saw it as interesting because it didn't seem to carry the baggage of 'high art'. It belonged as much to the world of the common snapshot and artless document, and required no special training. This sidelong attitude opened up new possibilities. Often analytical and sometimes playful, photography within conceptual art tended to take the form of propositions, hypotheses and experiments. With its combination of mechanical standards and receptiveness to the world, photography is ideal for projects combining chance and system.

The Californian John Baldessari started his artistic career as a painter, and his first 'conceptual' gesture was to burn his paintings and begin anew. Although best known for his collage works using such pre-existing imagery as vintage movie publicity stills, he used a camera for several early conceptual works. 'Throwing Three Balls in the Air to Get a Straight Line (Best of Thirty-six Attempts)' is a fairly self-explanatory title, although it is not clear who took the photographs or who through the balls. 'Thirty-six' refers to the number of frames on the 35mm film used for the piece. It was first produced as a folder of thirteen different loose offset-lithographic prints, published by Edizioni Giampaolo Prearo and Galleria Toselli, Milan, in an edition of 500.

Baldessari made some closely related works, including 'Throwing Four Balls in the Air to Get a Straight Line', 'Throwing Three Balls in the Air to Get an Equilateral Triangle', and 'Throwing Four Balls in the Air to Get a Square'.

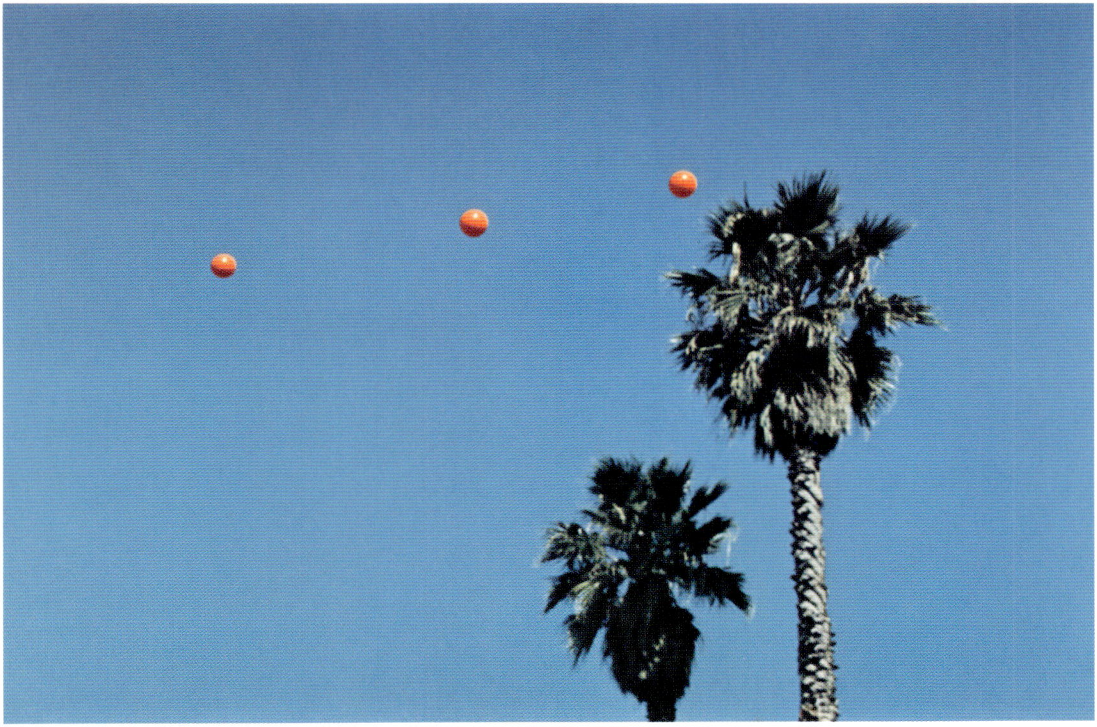

HELEN LEVITT

New York, c. 1942

THE PHOTOGRAPHER HELEN LEVITT confessed to being inarticulate, and rarely discussed the images she made in the course of her long life. Photographs do not 'speak for themselves', exactly, but their richness is often an effect of their muteness. Levitt understood this.

Born in 1913, Levitt grew up in Bensonhurst, New York. She dropped out of high school and worked for a commercial photographer. At her own pace, she came to understand the possibilities of the medium and, in turn, her own potential as a delicate observer of the world around her. These feelings were affirmed in 1935, when she saw photographs by Henri Cartier-Bresson (page 82), Manuel Álvarez Bravo (page 22) and Walker Evans (page 220) at the Julien Levy Gallery in Manhattan. The following year she accompanied Cartier-Bresson on a shoot along the waterfront of Brooklyn. His lightweight and silent 35mm Leica impressed her, and she soon bought one second-hand. Her earliest photographs were of children playing in the streets, a subject that remained central to her work. She made films too. *In the Street*, released in 1948, is regarded as a landmark of poetic observational film-making.

Street photography is both a formal photographic game and a test for anyone keen to discover what they really think about the world around them. Of all the genres, it is the most reactive, the camera equivalent to the psychoanalyst's couch. Intuitive responses can reveal unconscious thoughts. In turn, the viewer can only ever respond to the work of a street photographer in the same way: a formal game and a test of what we think about the world depicted. Second-guessing the photographer's intentions may be tempting, but it is rarely satisfying; and when it is, we have little way of knowing if our guesses are even remotely correct. Even the photographer may not know exactly why they took a particular photograph, or what it might mean.

Looking at Levitt's work, one can feel these paradoxes acutely. To spend time contemplating the apparent ease she had with her camera and her surroundings is to become disarmed. Are you looking at what she was looking at? No. She was looking at the world through a camera; you are looking at the image she made. But is what you find significant the same as what she found significant? We cannot know. Photography makes a mystery of intention.

Levitt was unassuming, and photographed primarily in African American and Hispanic communities. She barely took her camera beyond New York. This photograph was taken at 99th Street and Park Avenue, Manhattan, just seven blocks from her home. Her first book, *A Way of Seeing*, was not published until 1965, although it was planned much earlier. In 1946 the writer James Agee, a good friend of Levitt, composed an essay for it. He wrote: 'In their general quality and coherence [Levitt's] photographs seem to me to combine a unified view of the world, an uninsistent but irrefutable manifesto of a way of seeing, and, in a gentle and unpretentious way, a major poetic work.'

Uninsistent manifesto. There is the paradox again. Perhaps this is why Levitt was so often drawn to photographing children. Not because they were photogenic, or unpretentious, but because they were uninsistent manifestos – for humanity. Out of the almost nothing of us, out of the almost nothing of daily life, something emerges. A child into an adult. A photograph into a work of art.

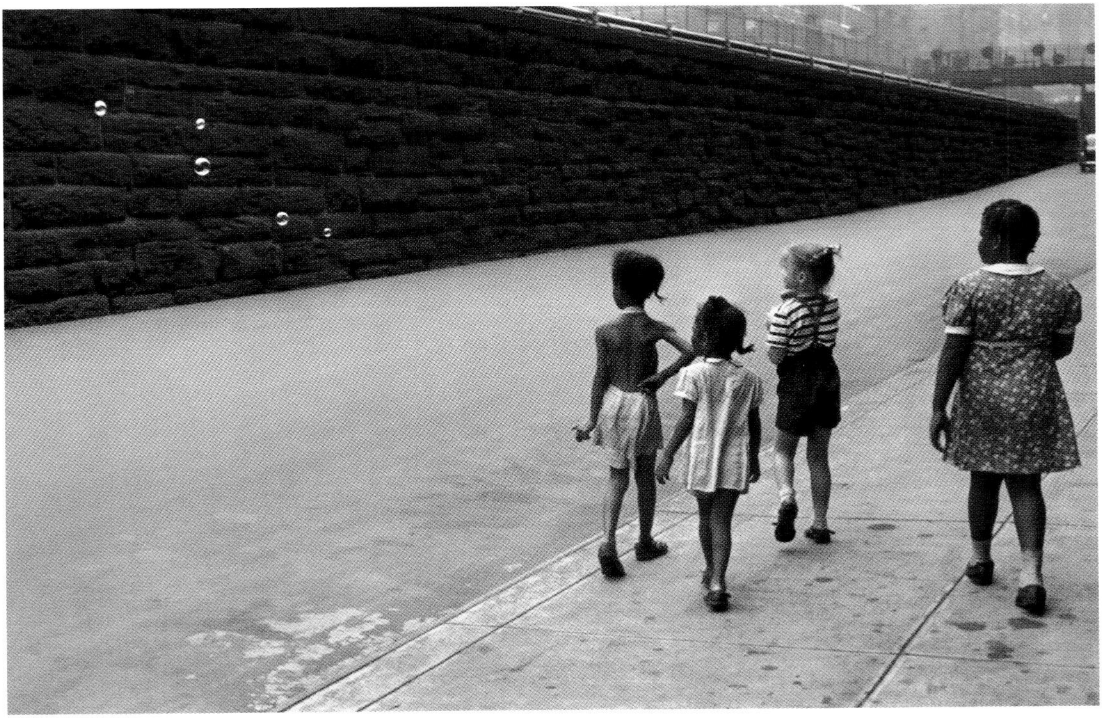

KEN RUSSELL

Teddy Girl, 1955

KEN RUSSELL WAS BEST KNOWN as an iconoclastic film-maker, but he began with a still camera, aged twenty-three, in 1951. He was therefore slightly older than the Teddy girls he photographed in January 1955. Born during the Second World War, and living through its hardships, these young people were among the first British 'teenagers'. The year 1955 was also the year of James Dean, star of *Rebel Without a Cause*. British youth looked to American culture, but had its own problems and cultivated its own rebellions. The swagger and chic of the Teddy look was a rejection of the austere post-war years. Food had been rationed by the British government right up until 1954. London's East End, a working-class area that had suffered some of the worst bombing, offered little promise. These teenagers were leaving school aged fourteen or fifteen, with few career prospects and little continuity with their parents. Looking different was a great symbolic statement.

The Teddies took their name from the high Edwardian clothing they reworked for their own, dandy look. The Edwardian era, roughly 1900 to 1914, was a moment of great style brought to a sudden end by the First World War. Teddy boys were photographed often, but the girls much less so. Russell was interested in the additional subversion going on here: these young women were re-tailoring the outfits of *men*. Their grandfathers.

Here is fourteen-year-old Jean Rayner, posing amid decade-old rubble and metalwork. From a landscape of scattered fragments, a new generation is emerging. Rayner puts herself forward, while the boys hang back. She is insouciant and bold, keen to impress her group and the photographer. To take the shot, Russell must look straight down into the viewfinder of his twin-lens Rolleiflex, held at waist level. From that angle, Rayner looks imperious. That it's only for a moment does not matter. She gazes at the open aperture and the unknown audience beyond. She has the look of studied boredom that soon became the essence of youthful rebellion. Cool, and unimpressed. But a camera picks up all kinds of minor tremors. She is also vulnerable.

In many ways, adolescence is a perfect subject for photography. It mirrors so many of the tensions within the medium: the awkward fit between appearance and deeper meaning; the limbo between past and future; the anxiety of being misread; the withdrawn silence and the wish to communicate; and the feeling that a moment could die right there, or last an eternity.

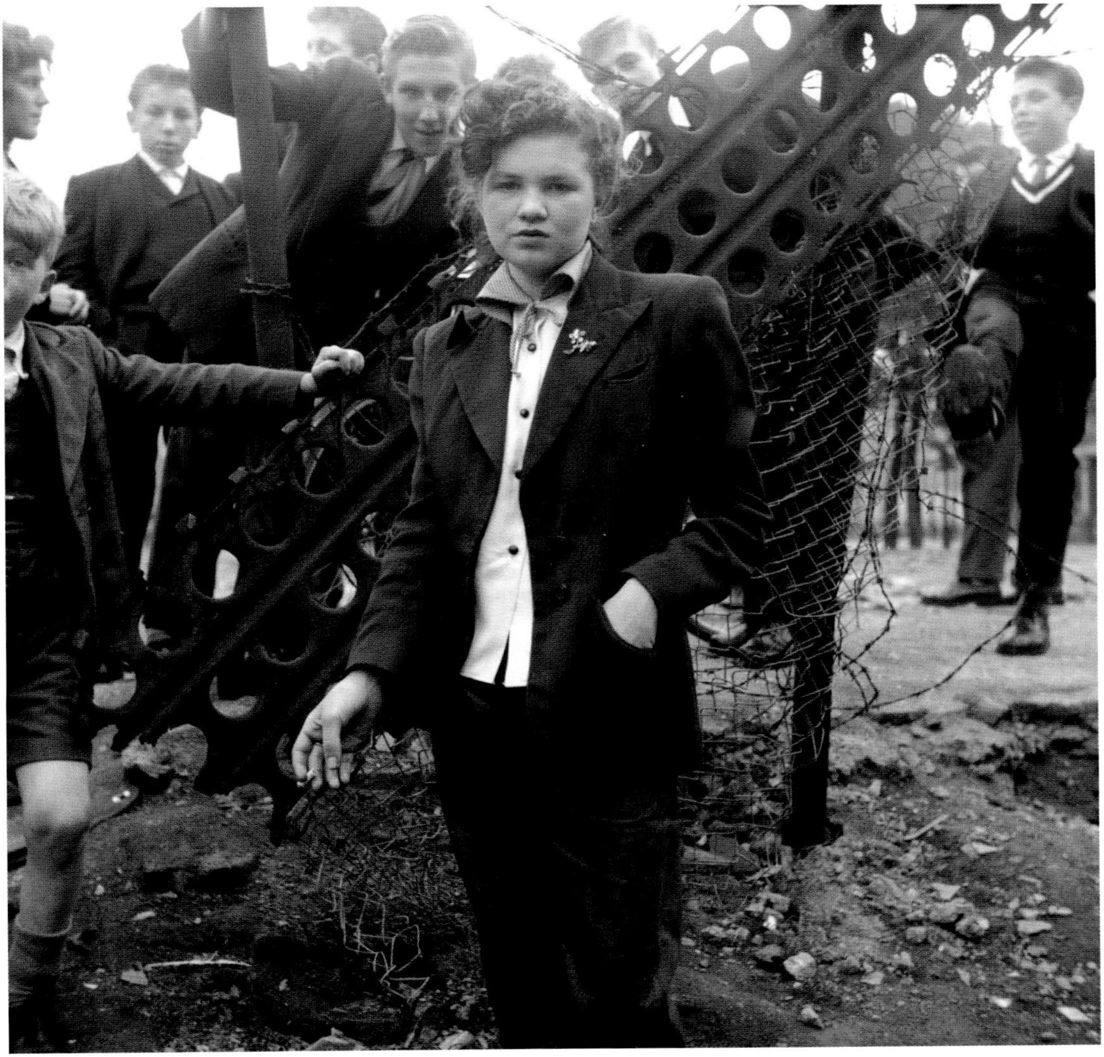

WEEGEE

Coney Island, 1940

'WEEGEE' WAS THE PSEUDONYM of Arthur (Usher) Fellig (1899–1968), a freelance photographer who worked in New York's Lower East Side. His most renowned photographs were of the city's criminal nightlife. He would hang out at the local police station, and when word came in of a crime in the neighbourhood, he would try to beat the officers to the scene and get the first photograph, which he would then sell to an agency or tabloid newspaper.

Weegee also photographed at Coney Island, the nearest seaside resort to Manhattan, and a weekend destination for the city's working-class families. His best-known Coney Island photograph shows a vast crowd on the beach one hot summer's day. There is a crowd in this one too, but it forms the background of a more intimate and disarming scene.

Weegee was famed for getting himself in the right spot at the right time. Here, his view is so optimal that the space feels almost like a stage. What is going on? It seems as though a man is being resuscitated, perhaps by lifeguards or an ambulance crew. His body has been covered in a blanket but his arm is bare. He may have been in the water, which we can see in the background of the shot. Right in the centre of the frame is a woman in a bathing suit. Perhaps she is a friend of the rescued man. Consciously or unconsciously, she has posed and smiled for Weegee's camera. As a result, she seems to belong to a very different kind of photograph. A classical portrait within an urgent news picture.

For Weegee, this kind of incongruity was something of a specialism. He was alive to irony, contradiction and counterpoint, and able work them into his hard-hitting photographs. The forceful first impression opens on to a world of rich ambiguity, and human complexity. Each of his best images is a fragment of a story. There are enough clues to draw us in, but, as Weegee seemed to intuit, photographs can never give us the whole narrative.

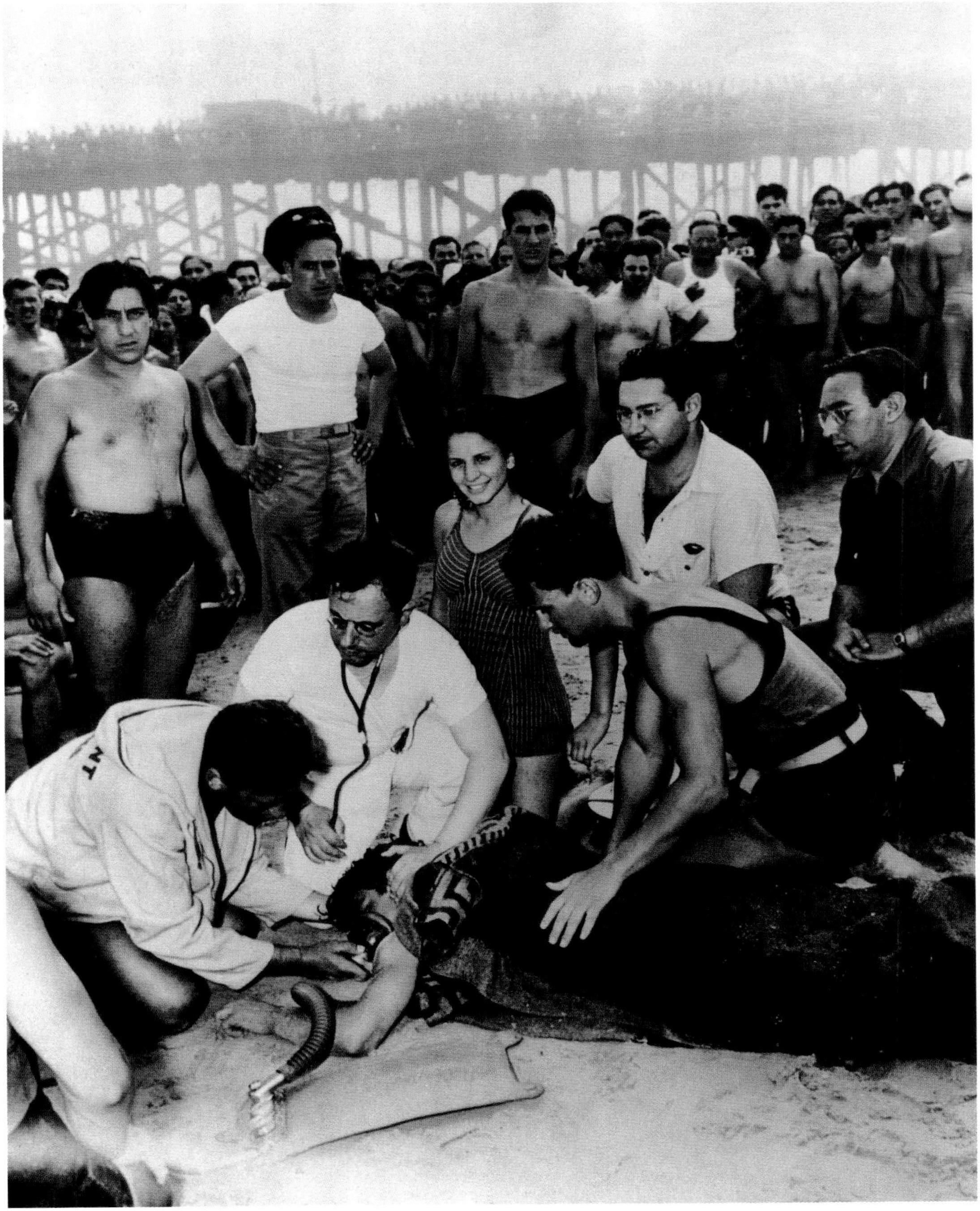

FRANCES BENJAMIN JOHNSTON

Self-Portrait (as New Woman), 1896

A PHOTOGRAPH CAN BE A DOCUMENT and an imagining, a record and a possibility, all at the same time. This is most clear in the kind of self-portrait that is also a gesture of self-actualization – putting oneself forward as one wishes to be, or wishes to be perceived. It is a practice with a long history. In 1840 Hippolyte Bayard posed as a drowned man, in melodramatic protest at the French state overlooking his contribution to the invention of photography. Throughout the Victorian era, countless photographers depicted themselves as heroes, melancholic victims, romantics, adventurers and visionaries. In today's 'selfie' culture, it is barely possible to separate self-portraiture from attempts at self-actualization.

Raised in Washington DC, Frances Benjamin Johnston was from a wealthy, well-educated, well-connected family that was very much part of the American elite. Her first camera was a gift from George Eastman, founder of Kodak. Johnston enjoyed an impressively long and diverse life in photography. Across half a century, she pioneered the emerging practice of photojournalism, made photographic studies of various institutions, worked as a commercial portraitist, photographed presidents and peace treaties, and became an accomplished architectural photographer. She was also something of a bohemian non-conformist, refusing the more demure behaviour expected of upper-class American women. She was sexually liberated, living and working with the photographer Mattie Edwards Hewitt for a number of years.

In *Self-Portrait (as New Woman)*, Johnston smokes, drinks, reveals her underskirt and flaunts her ankles. Men stare stuffily from a row of portrait photographs on the mantelpiece. Johnston's pose is strong and forthright, although her gaze has dropped slightly. Her expression is introspective, even vulnerable. She looks away, feigning disinterest in the camera, the image and the eventual viewer. It is a game, of course, playful but serious.

The year after Johnston made this image, the *Ladies' Home Journal* published her long and detailed article 'What a Woman Can Do with a Camera'. Photography, she argued, was open to women because it was not yet afflicted by the patriarchal exclusions that dominated so many fields of culture and business. She called for images of quality and distinction, not as works in their own right, but as a path to independence in the commercial marketplace. Financial self-reliance was the primary goal, although she recognized that having money to begin with was an advantage. 'Photography as a profession', she wrote, 'should appeal particularly to women, and in it there are great opportunities for a good-paying business – but only under very well defined conditions. The prime requisites – as summed up in my mind after long experience and thought – are these: The woman who makes photography profitable must have, as to personal qualities, good common sense, unlimited patience to carry her through endless failures, equally unlimited tact, good taste, a quick eye, a talent for detail, and a genius for hard work. In addition, she needs training, experience, some capital, and a field to exploit.'

Self-Portrait (as New Woman) was not made for money, and we cannot be sure exactly for whom it *was* made. Nevertheless, of all Johnston's photographs it is one with long-lasting significance, an early beacon of the struggles for emancipation and self-determination. A document of how things could be.

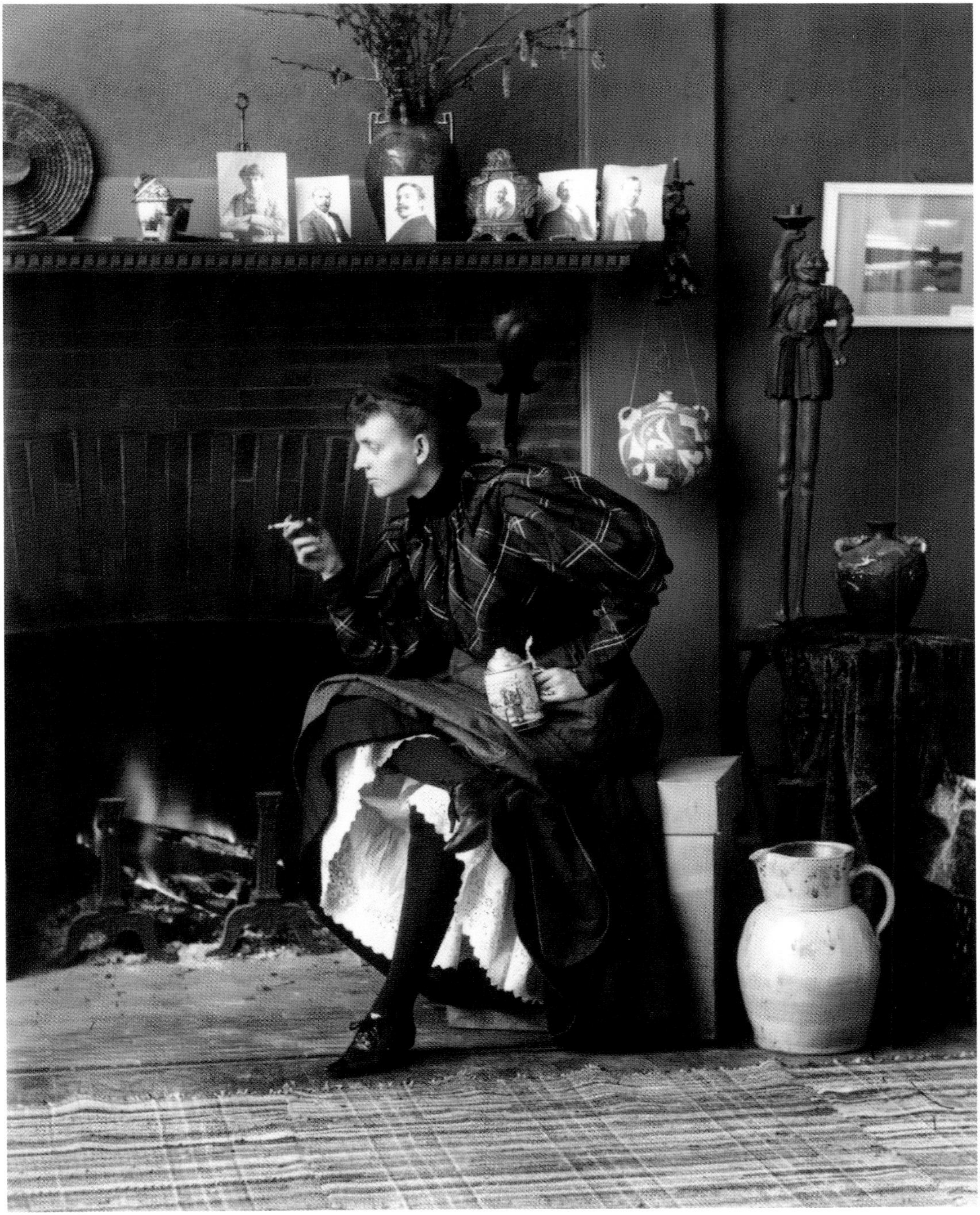

KWAME BRATHWAITE

Untitled, c. 1966

PHOTO SHOOT AT A SCHOOL FOR ONE OF THE MANY MODELLING GROUPS WHO HAD BEGUN TO EMBRACE NATURAL HAIRSTYLES IN THE 1960s

BORN IN 1938, the photographer and activist Kwame Brathwaite was a key figure in what came to be known as the second Harlem Renaissance, which ran from the 1950s to the 1970s. In the growing civil rights movement in the United States, culture was understood to be as significant as politics. Or, more accurately, culture was understood as inevitably and inherently political. Images matter, because they have social consequences. For example, ideals of beauty in Hollywood cinema, advertising imagery and fashion were (and still are) dominated by a presumption of whiteness that clearly marginalizes and often excludes non-white appearance and culture.

In 1956 Brathwaite helped to found the African Jazz-Art Society & Studios, which brought together African American artists, musicians, designers, hairdressers, writers and more. Out of this, in 1962, emerged the Grandassa Models. 'Grandassaland' was how the black nationalist Carlos A. Cooks had referred to Africa. Brathwaite adapted the name for a new kind of fashion imagery expressing the idea that 'Black is Beautiful'. The Grandassa Models kept their hair natural, and wore Afrocentric clothes and jewelry. They appeared on many jazz and soul record covers, and dynamic Grandassa fashion shows toured under the name 'Naturally'.

As much as offering a new set of positive images, the intent was to shift public perception and expand the discourse of popular visual culture. Brathwaite staged his images and events as calculated interventions, rerouting the signs and codes of mainstream white culture while also proposing new notions of beauty. As the movement grew, a sense of empowerment spread, and a new confidence in black self-expression took shape. The image reproduced here was taken by Brathwaite during a photo shoot at a school. It shows how black women were embracing natural hairstyles in the 1960s.

With the urgent and expansive energy of the Black Lives Matter movement of the late 2010s, Kwame Brathwaite's remarkable archive was rediscovered by a younger generation. They were hungry for a richer history of black representation. The first major book of his work was published in 2019. Brathwaite's ethos and imagery are helping to inspire once again.

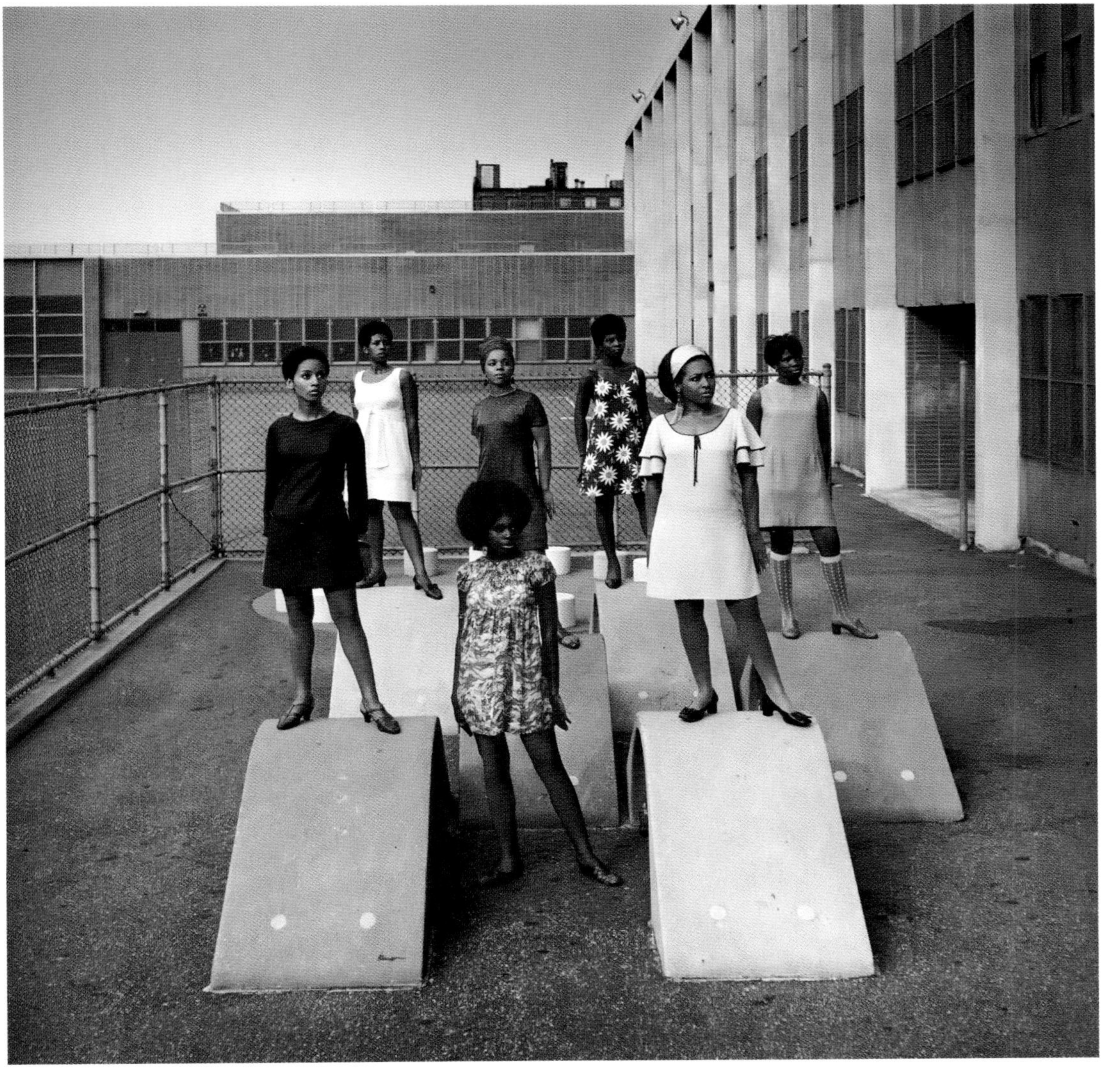

MARIANNE WEX

PAGE FROM THE BOOK *LET'S TAKE BACK OUR SPACE* (FRAUENLITERATUR VERLAG, 1984)

LET'S TAKE BACK OUR SPACE, by the German artist Marianne Wex, is one of the great unsung works of 1970s feminist history and cultural analysis. The book is subtitled *'Female' and 'Male' Body Language as a Result of Patriarchal Structures*. It is a visual survey comprised of hundreds of photographs assembled into dozens of thematic grids: 'Seated Persons – Leg and Feet'; 'Arm and Hand Positions'; 'Standing Persons – Leg and Feet'; 'People Sitting and Laying on the Ground'; 'Arm and Leg Positions'; 'Egyptian, Greek and Roman Statuary'; 'How the Men of Christianity Took Over an Old Goddess Gesture'; 'The Stultifying Effect of the Patriarchal Socialization of Men'. And so on. The images were culled from a great range of sources – advertisements, reportage, fashion magazines, studio portraits, the history of art – and many were taken by Wex on the streets of Hamburg. Wex proposes that our smallest, most unconscious gestures speak volumes about the power relations of gender in daily life.

It is an argument made with images, and, as such, it is highly dubious as science. Photographs can be chosen and sequenced to make an argument, and their evidential quality can be bent to serve almost any view. But Wex goes beyond the scientific. Her project is an intervention, and its claims to authority come less from the presentation of facts than from the flashes of recognition we might have in response to what she presents.

There is space in Wex's grand project for plenty of experiments and anomalies. When shown stereotypical photos of men asserting themselves, women can easily and comfortably imitate them. But when men are shown images of women in 'feminine' poses, either they can't or they won't imitate them, even for the sake of an experiment. The few images of children and young adolescents are very telling: we can sense how the gender- and sexuality-neutral body language of early youth is soon conventionalized into familiar patterns. Not always, but most of the time. Wex is careful not to make the argument seem absolute, or the situation unchangeable.

The approach uses heterosexuality as a kind of default, and there is little space for questions of ethnicity, subculture or the ironic adoption of the body language of the powerful. Such complexities would make updating the project almost impossible. *Let's Take Back Our Space* was first exhibited as multiple photo panels in West Berlin in 1977, but a serious illness turned Wex away from art and towards the study of alternative medicine. The book grew in reputation, but the project was not exhibited again for more than three decades. *Let's Take Back Our Space* is both a remarkable record of its time and a still-troubling reflection of ours.

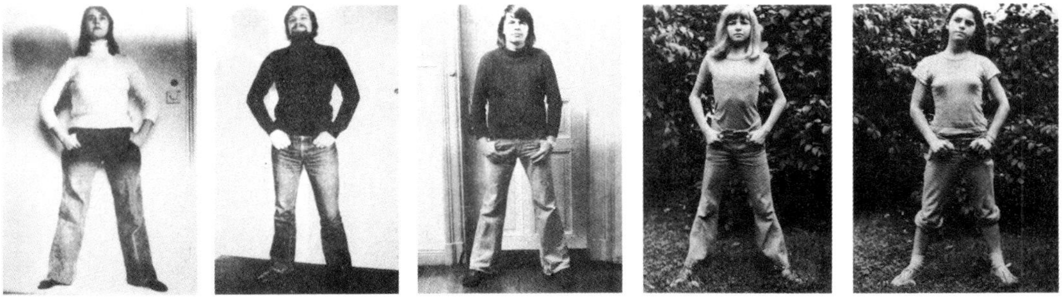

"Männlich"

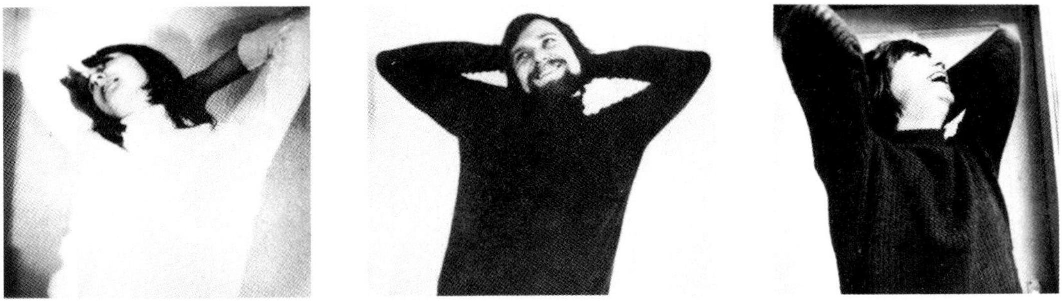

"Weiblich"

VIVIAN MAIER

Contact sheet, New York, 1954

TECHNICALLY, THE MEDIUM of photography could hardly be simpler. Even in the days of analogue photography, it was never difficult to be technically proficient. Photography is not like writing a novel or composing a symphony. One can pick up what is needed in a couple of weeks. From there, one can discover certain tricks as to how a moving, three-dimensional world can be turned into a compellingly still, mute, flat square or rectangle. The great observational photographers manage to intuit and work out their own way of doing this, one that suits and expresses their disposition towards the world. You cannot really be taught how to be good at it, but you can practise and figure something out for yourself.

All of this means that someone working in isolation, unconnected to any school or world of like minds, and with little sense of the history of the medium, can quietly go about making their own great images. This appears to have been the approach of Vivian Maier (1926–2009). While working as a nanny in Chicago, Maier took about 150,000 photographs over a forty-year period. She worked in colour and black and white, in 35mm and medium format (6 × 6 cm/2⅜ × 2⅜ in.). It was a very serious hobby, and it seems she showed her work to hardly anyone. When she died, it would have been lost to history and destroyed if her negatives and prints had not been spotted and acquired by collectors. When some of her photographs were uploaded to the image-sharing website Flickr by John Maloof, there was great interest. Today her work is widely published, held by important collections and celebrated as a great discovery. Documentaries have been made about Maier's mysterious work and life, countless newspaper and magazine articles have attempted to understand her, and several novels based on the available biographical facts have been published.

Once the cultish swirl of speculation passes, we are left with the images, and there is no clearer sign of Maier's sure vision than the contact sheets of her medium-format work. On each one, a whole film of twelve exposures can be seen in the order they were shot. Maier rarely made more than two images of any given subject that she encountered. Mostly she shot just one frame, with great precision, tender care, and an unwavering confidence in what she was trying to achieve.

In any archive of 150,000 images, there will be a few great shots. Such is the nature of wandering, observational photography. However, Maier's strike rate was prodigiously high. Her subject matter varied enormously, and her formal experimentation, particularly in her many self-portraits, was as complex and daring as that of the most celebrated and respected photographers.

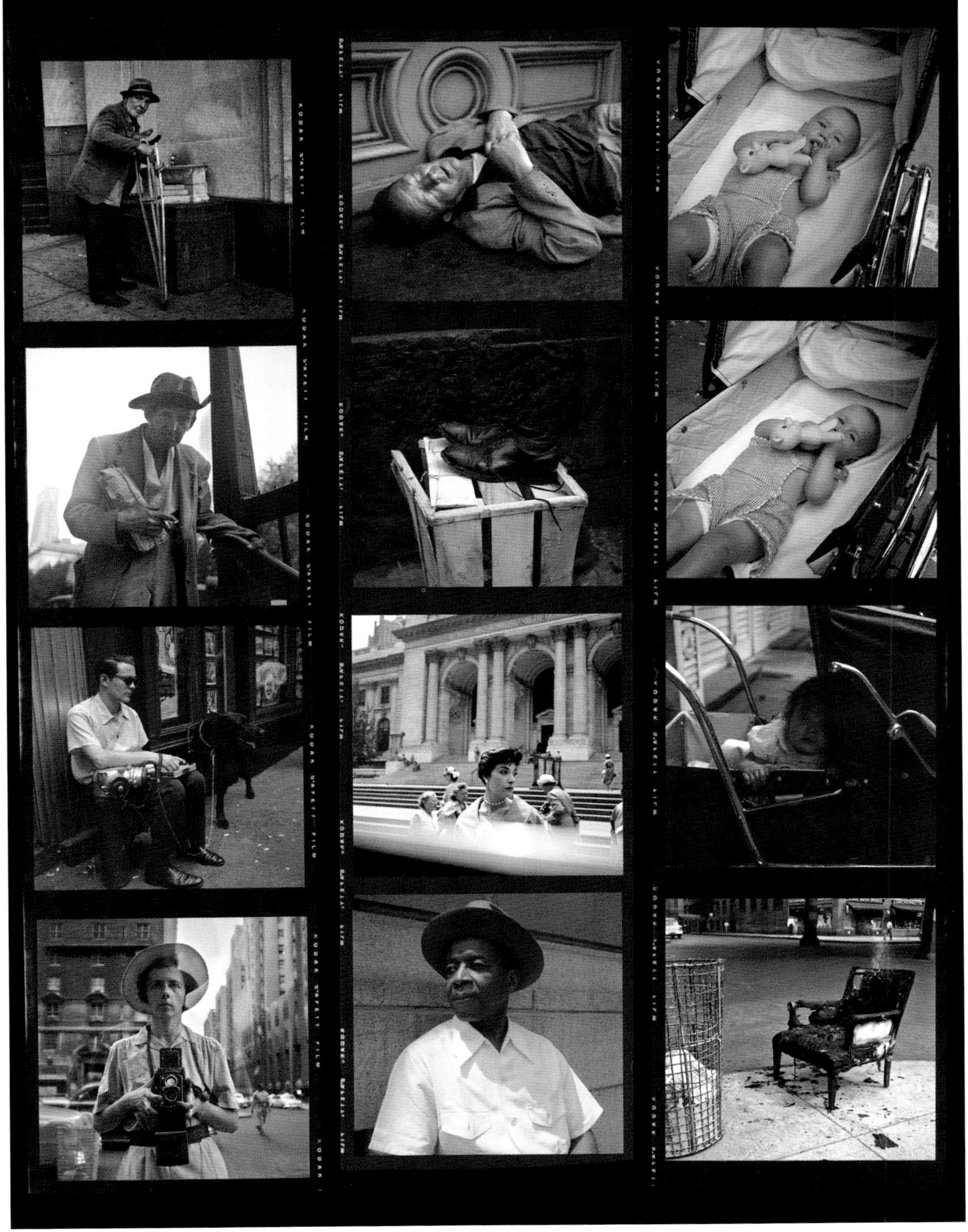
KODAK SAFETY FILM

CHRIS STEELE-PERKINS

Courtyard of the mental hospital run by the Edhi Foundation, Pakistan, 1997

IN 1997 CHRIS STEELE-PERKINS, a member of the Magnum Photos agency, was in Pakistan, working on a story about the philanthropist Abdul Sattar Edhi. Funded solely by donations, the Edhi Foundation was established in 1951 and continues to offer many services, including shelter, free hospitals, medical care and drug rehabilitation programmes. It also runs an important ambulance service and provides relief in national and international emergencies.

Steele-Perkins found himself looking through a wall into the courtyard of a mental hospital. He stood on a pile of bricks to get a better vantage point and watched the multiple views through the pattern of holes in the wall. He recalled: 'The picture was obvious. Each window had to hold an interesting fragment, and all the fragments needed to be different. The requirements of the composition and of the metaphor – fragmented lives imprisoned in darkness – were in sync. The problem was to concentrate hard enough to take the photograph that actually delivered.' Steele-Perkins shot twenty frames before moving into the courtyard.

In observational documentary photography, the pictorial and intellectual challenges (composition and metaphor) have to be thought about together, and sometimes very quickly. This is difficult enough when looking at just one scene, but Steele-Perkins chanced upon an almost impossibly complex situation – a naturally occurring composite view. By coincidence, the holes in the wall have roughly the same proportion as the photographer's 35mm film frame. This gives the final image the feeling of a contact sheet, as if we are looking at a series of exposures shot consecutively, rather than simultaneously.

STEELE-PERKINS FOUND HIMSELF LOOKING THROUGH A WALL INTO THE COURTYARD OF A MENTAL HOSPITAL. HE STOOD ON A PILE OF BRICKS TO GET A BETTER VANTAGE POINT AND WATCHED THE MULTIPLE VIEWS THROUGH THE PATTERN OF HOLES IN THE WALL.

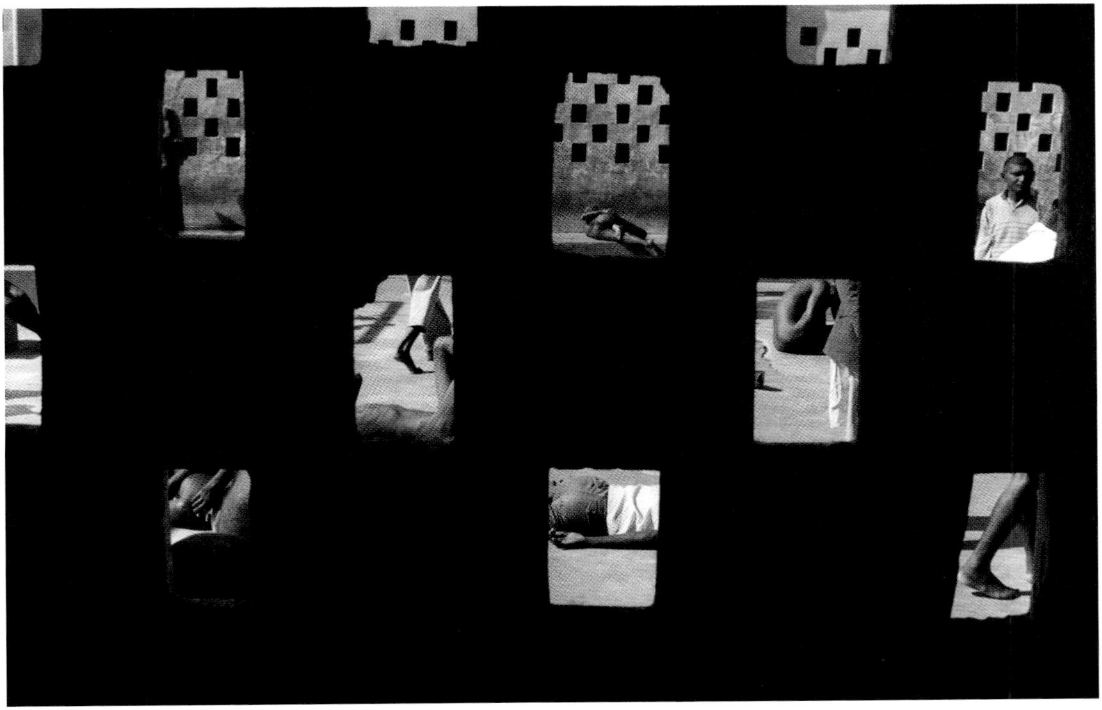

HANNAH STARKEY

Untitled, September 2008

FOR MORE THAN TWO DECADES, Hannah Starkey has been making photographs of women in city spaces. At once portraits, documents and performances, her images are also propositions about female presence. They mix the naturalism and spontaneity of street photography with preparation and collaboration. There are elements of art-historical classicism, editorial portraiture, fashion, theatre and cinema.

In contrast to the city of concrete and steel, Starkey's urban vision is often reflected and refracted. Mirrors abound, as do unnatural colours. It is a place of light and evanescence, without solidity. In part, this is a response to the remaking of London, where most of Starkey's pictures have been made. From what was an essentially Victorian city with an economy rooted in heavy industry and empire, twenty-first-century London has been reinventing itself as a hyper-fluid, free-market economy. The image it wants to project is now based on leisure and the service industries. Buildings and people are expected to be endlessly adaptable.

While this new order brings the chance to throw off old strictures, the situation is also unstable. In a precarious economy it is still women who suffer most, financially, emotionally, physically. The intense visual pleasure of Starkey's photographs is often tempered by the portrayal of mixed feelings.

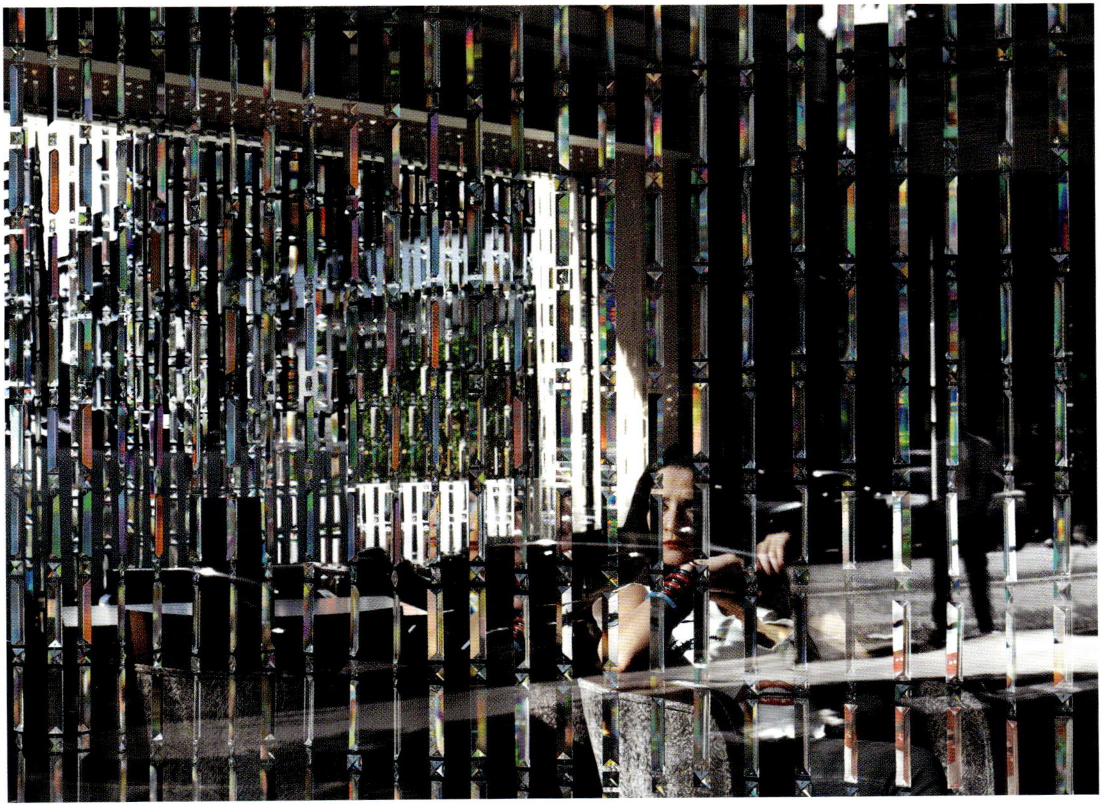

PHOTOGRAPHER UNKNOWN

Publicity still for Alfred Hitchcock's *Rear Window*, 1954

IS THERE ANY CATEGORY of photography less aesthetically pure than the film publicity still? Made by photographers working on film sets, they are rarely considered in the study of either photography or cinema. Here is one from Alfred Hitchcock's *Rear Window* (1954), one of the most celebrated films to feature a photographer. The man in the wheelchair is the actor James Stewart playing L. B. Jeffries, a New York photojournalist who has broken a leg on assignment. Confined to his apartment, he takes to watching his neighbours, and becomes convinced one of them has committed murder.

In different ways, film-still photographers and photojournalists have to solve the same two problems: visual clarity and narrative stillness. Film stills do it through the group effort of staging in a controlled situation. After the actors have performed for the movie camera, they pose for the still photographer. By contrast, the photojournalist relies on quick reactions and the speed of their equipment. Where the film still restages motion as stillness, photojournalism uses fast shutter speeds to freeze it. Both seek to secure detail and master time.

The woman is Grace Kelly, playing Lisa Fremont, who works for a fashion magazine much like *Harper's Bazaar*. The two actors/posers pretend to look intently for evidence of the murder. *Rear Window* does not quite fit the classic 1950s Hollywood pattern of the actively 'looking' male lead and the passive, 'looked at' female co-star. Although Jeffries does most of the looking, the film dwells a great deal on his weaknesses: indecision, cowardice and immobility. And while Lisa wishes to tame the photojournalist into a settled marriage, she is independent-minded, authoritative and full of initiative.

They are not quite looking in the same direction, nor are they looking into the courtyard where the action takes place. If they were, we would see only their backs. In fact, the still is a montage. Kelly and Stewart were photographed before a white backdrop in a portrait studio, and inserted later.

We can see the courtyard and the windows of the various characters from the film – two newlyweds, a lonely spinster, a dancer, an artist, a group of musicians, and a killer. The narrative of the film has been compressed so that they are all there for us at once. We can look around the picture at our own pace. It is a photograph not so much *from* Hitchcock's film as *of* it, as a whole.

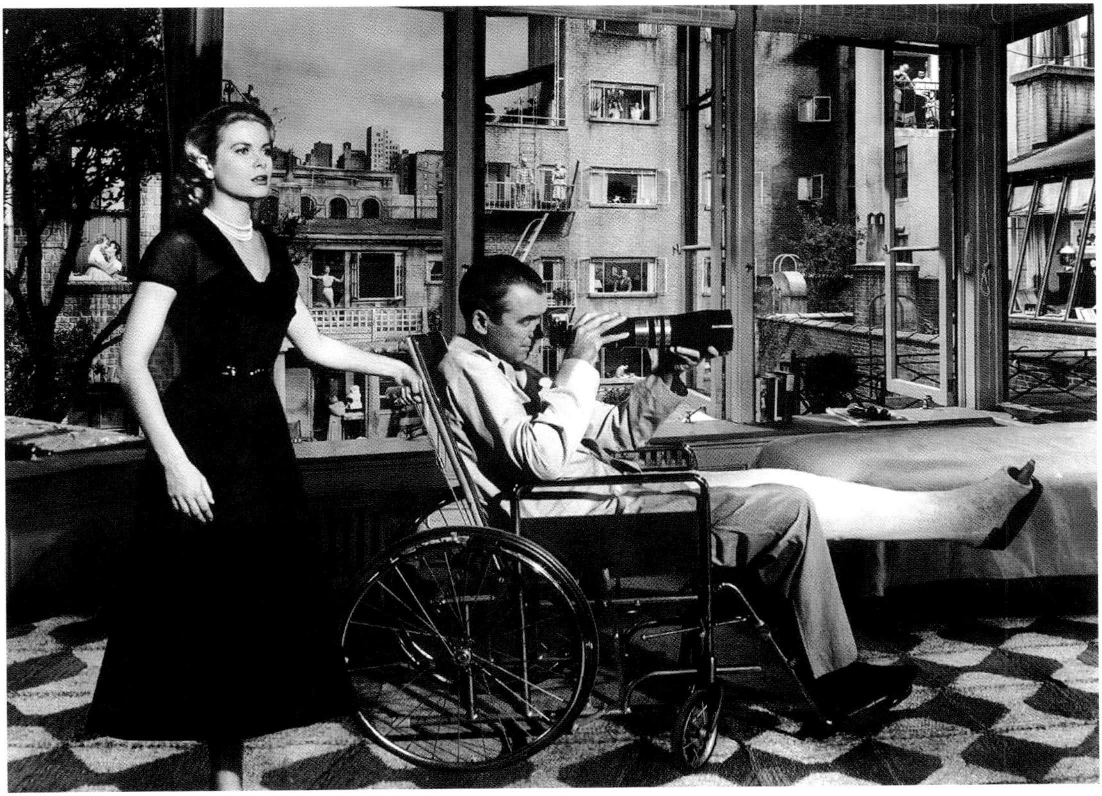

CHRIS MARKER

Photograph from the film *La Jetée*, 1962

THE WRITER, PHOTOGRAPHER, film-maker, video artist and Internet pioneer Chris Marker was one of the most exploratory and prescient figures of the last century. He published innovative books combining his photographs and writing. He was key to the development of the 'essay film', a kind of poetic and personal film-making – free-flowing, subjective and philosophical. He constructed a look back at his own work first as a maze-like CD-ROM, and then, when technology permitted, as a website. But as Marker's multi-directional creative life unfolded, one theme came to dominate: memory.

Marker made just one fiction film, the remarkable *La Jetée* (1962). Comprised of still images shot on a 35mm camera, it feels at first like a photo-novel, or a primitive filmed storyboard (directors often work out their shots with a still camera). As the film progresses, however, it becomes clear that its form is integral to its meaning. It tells the story of a group of survivors living in tunnels below Paris after a nuclear war. The ground above is radioactive and uninhabitable. Time is running out and their only hope is to make contact with the future. If they can do this they might find a way to survive. Scientists begin to experiment on a man who has particularly strong memories. First they send him into the past to test his mental resilience, monitoring his brain activity. Then they send him into the future. Marker's motionless and mute images suspend the sense of time, allowing the film to move freely between tenses while never fully belonging to any of them. With a lush soundtrack, abrupt jump-cuts and slow dissolves between photographs, *La Jetée* is a film that explores feelings of loss and hope like no other.

The grainy look and feel of the images owes something to William Klein's *Life is Good & Good for You in New York: Trance, Witness, Revels* (1956), one of the most groundbreaking and influential of all photographic books. Marker had been responsible for securing its publication in his years at the Parisian publishing house Èditions du Seuil. He was a Frenchman who had taken an English-sounding name; Klein (page 24) was an American who had settled in Paris in 1948. The two remained friends. Klein appears in *La Jetée*, helped with the English translation of the script, and provided the voiceover. It is Klein's placeless, transatlantic intonation we hear at the start of the film: 'This is a story of a man haunted by an image from his childhood. The violent scene that upset him, and whose meaning he was to grasp only years later, happened on the main jetty at Orly [airport], sometime before the outbreak of World War Three.'

Marker uses his primitive means and just 29 minutes to make a profound exploration of memory and the uncertain place that images occupy in our lives. We rely on images while distrusting them. They can aid memory but they can also replace it or even displace the need to remember at all. It turns out that the memory that had upset the protagonist of the film was a premonition of his own death. We see the boy-man as he is shot, recoiling with his arm outstretched. Marker took his inspiration for this moment from Robert Capa's much-discussed photograph from 1936 of a falling Republican soldier in the Spanish Civil War.

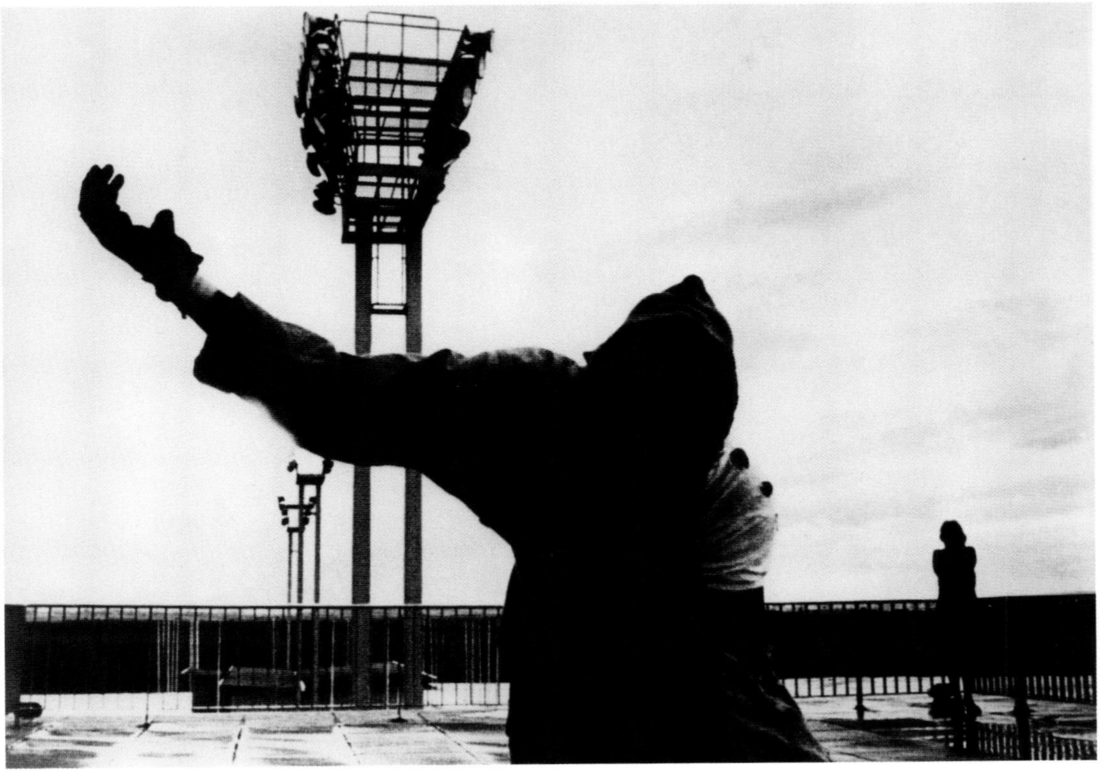

GISÈLE FREUND

Portrait of Virginia Woolf, 1939

GISÈLE FREUND WAS BORN IN 1908 to a wealthy Berlin Jewish family. She studied sociology under Theodor Adorno, Karl Mannheim and Norbert Elias, whose Marxist analysis of culture and economy would become known as the Frankfurt School. Freund became interested in photography, shot anti-fascist marches, and resolved to make her use of the camera an integral part of her socialist outlook. She befriended the intellectual Walter Benjamin, and when Adolf Hitler came to power in 1933, they both left Germany for Paris.

Freund studied at the Sorbonne, researching her doctoral thesis on photography in the nineteenth century. It was published in 1936 by Adrienne Monnier, the renowned modernist writer and bookseller. The two enjoyed an intimate relationship. Later, in 1974, Freund's thesis became the basis of her book *Photographie et société*, with an English edition appearing in 1980. In the 1930s, however, the serious study of photography was almost unheard of. The tiny handful of published books on the subject were rooted in connoisseurship, art history or technology. Freund's interest was the social consequence of photography – how it affected people's relationship to knowledge, politics, consumerism and even their sense of self. This was far more significant than photography's status as art. Benjamin's 'The Work of Art in the Age of Technical Reproducibility', published in 1935, explored similar ideas.

Through Monnier and Sylvia Beach, owner of the Paris bookshop Shakespeare and Company, Freund met the leading writers of the time. She photographed many of them, including James Joyce, Colette, Victoria Ocampo, Vita Sackville-West, T. S. Eliot and Virginia Woolf. Meanwhile, she undertook photographic assignments for the illustrated magazines that had emerged in the late 1920s and 1930s, notably the British *Picture Post* and the French *Vu*. As a pioneer of colour photography, Freund formed a long relationship with *Life* magazine, which published in colour extensively and had an international edition.

Eventually, Freund fled occupied France for Argentina and Chile, where she worked in the film industry as a stills photographer and producer. In 1947 she was invited to join Magnum Photos as one of its first members, and covered the whole of Latin America for the agency. She continued to work intensively, and in 1968 a major exhibition of her colour portraits was held at the Musée d'Art Moderne, Paris. In France, she was regarded as one of the most significant figures of twentieth-century photography. Her portraits were seen both as art and as definitive records of the key people of the era. Her thinking and writing were a major influence on the French scholarship of photography that blossomed in the 1970s and 1980s.

Freund's political leanings meant that she was refused entry to the United States until 1970. By that time, the influential English-language histories and canons of photography were well established, and Freund was almost entirely absent from all of them. Only in recent years has her contribution been recognized internationally.

Virginia Woolf disliked being photographed, and twice refused Freund's request before agreeing. This portrait was made in the novelist's London home in 1939, on the eve of war. In 1940 the house was destroyed in the Blitz; the following year, Woolf took her own life. Freund remained deeply affected by the writer and her work. In 1965 she visited Woolf's country retreat, Monk's House in Sussex, to photograph her writing desk.

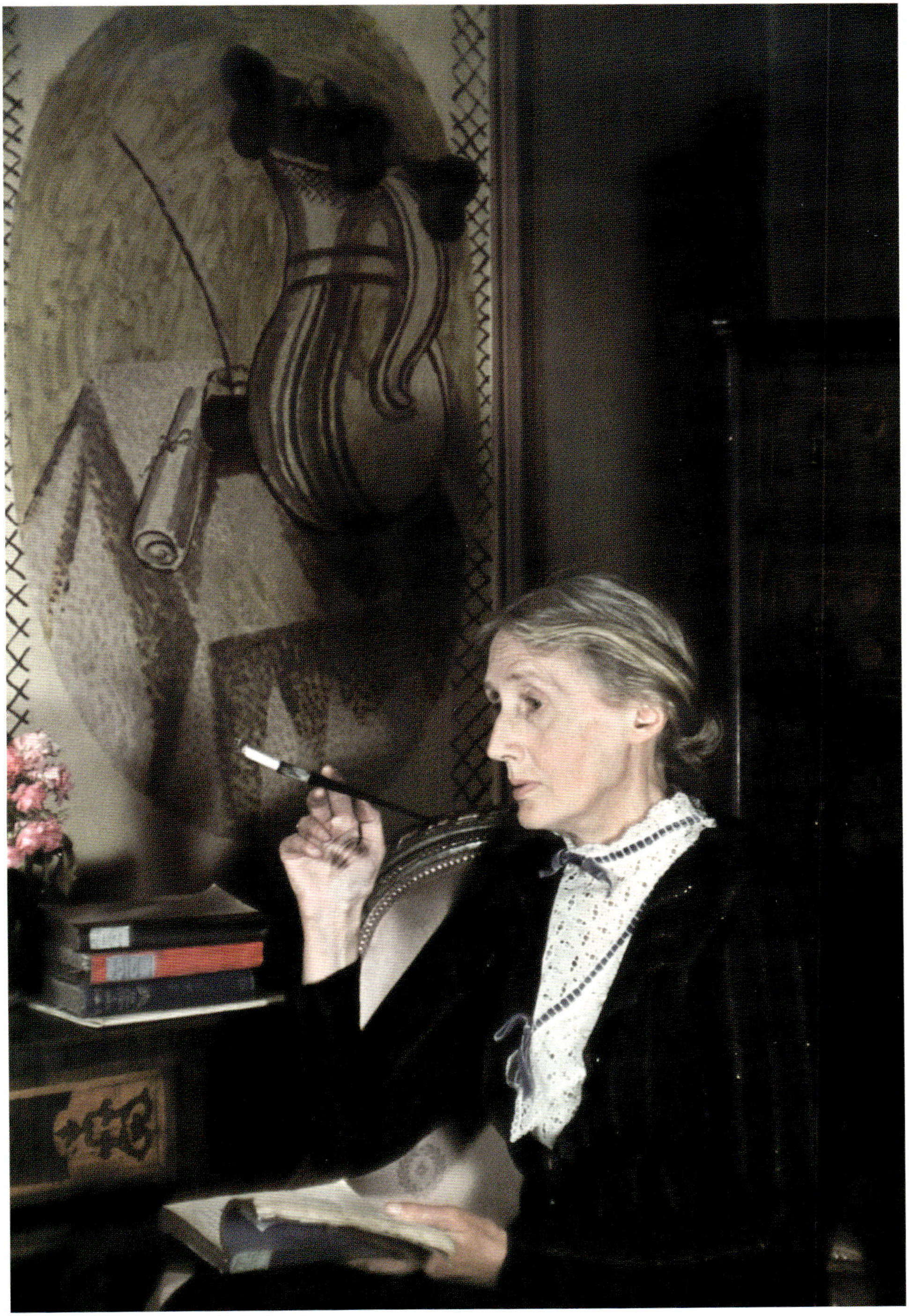

BILL BRANDT

Parlourmaid and Under-parlourmaid Ready to Serve Dinner, 1933

OVER THE YEARS, Bill Brandt's *Parlourmaid and Under-parlourmaid Ready to Serve Dinner* has acquired several roles. At times it is used to stand in for all of Brandt's work; it is regarded as a milestone in documentary photography *and* a milestone in art photography; and it has come to embody something of the stifling class system of 1930s Britain, insular and sleepwalking towards a second world war. It first appeared in Brandt's book *The English at Home* (1936), titled *Dinner is Served*.

Brandt was an outsider. Born in Germany, he came to England via Switzerland and Paris, where he worked in the studio of the surrealist Man Ray (page 154). Brandt could see clearly the ways of the English, more clearly than the English themselves, who failed to buy his book. Today, it is heralded as a classic of social observation, equal in its acuity to the novels of Evelyn Waugh.

In 1939, for the British magazine *Picture Post*, Brandt shot a 'day in the life' photo-story on this particular parlourmaid. He photographed her around the clock, from preparing the bath of the master of the house to serving nightcaps. The accompanying text tells us something the images cannot. As heads of households, parlourmaids were rare in 1939. The job usually fell to a male head butler. So the scene presented is not as typical of the time as we might imagine. No photograph can guarantee whether what it presents is commonplace or exceptional.

Even less apparent is that the parlourmaid ran two houses belonging to Brandt's uncle, a wealthy banker. Brandt frequently made use of friends and family in his photographs. He sensed right away that the parlourmaid, named Pratt, would make for an interesting subject. He had made a note about his first meeting with her in 1928: '*Fortuite ou nécessaire – qui sait – la rencontre avec Pratt m'était en tous ça fatale*' (Fortuitous or determined – who knows – the meeting with Pratt was in any case a fatal/fateful one for me).

Looking closely we can see that, in taking this shot, Brandt deliberately focused his camera on the shiny glass and silverware of the dining table. The parlourmaids behind are not so crisply rendered. Brandt was an early adopter of portable electronic flash, and with its boost of light he could have shot the scene on a small aperture to hold foreground and background in focus. Brandt chose to let the faces of the women fall out of focus. We can still see that they avoid eye contact with the camera, as if averting their gaze from their master (they 'know their place'), but the camera clearly 'sees' them, offering them a vital place in the composition. Does Brandt put us in the position of the master, keener to scrutinize the table setting than connect with the lowly maids? Perhaps, but in doing this Brandt opens up a critical distance on the whole scenario. In being invited to see the maids out of focus at a photographic level, we are by extension invited to contemplate their status as out of focus at a *social* level too. The background status of the parlourmaid and under-parlourmaid becomes part of the picture's commentary.

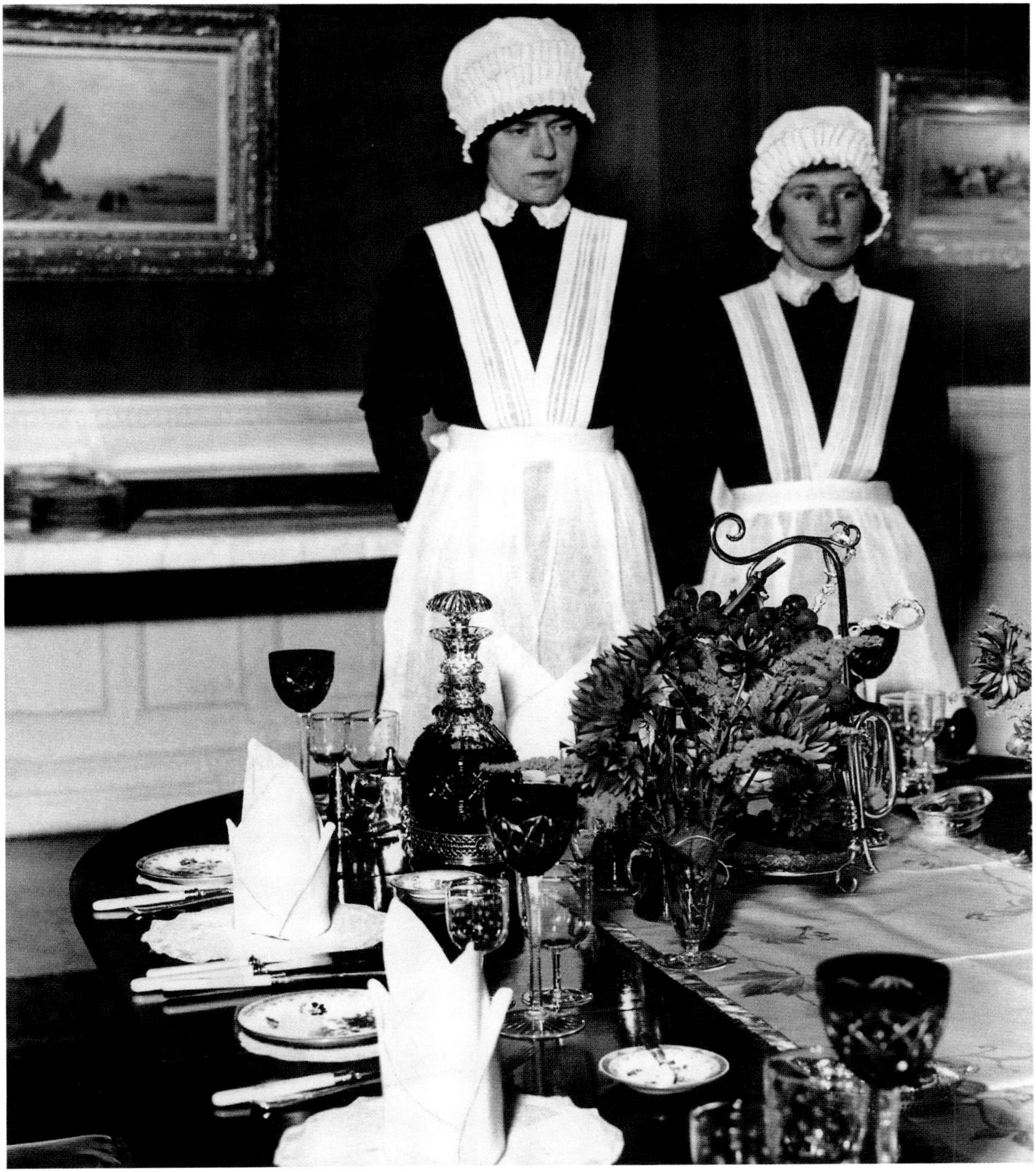

HENRI CARTIER-BRESSON

Barge Family, Bougival, 1956

WITH A PAINTER'S CLASSICAL TRAINING and a taste for surrealism, Henri Cartier-Bresson turned to photography around 1930. Almost immediately he was making remarkably agile pictures. With a lightweight 35mm Leica camera and a sharp eye, he could close the gap between noticing and picturing until they were almost the same act. Where a painter's composition is constructed, a fast-moving photographer composes reactively. Or, as the photographer Jeff Wall (page 140) put it, 'Every picture-constructing advantage accumulated over centuries is given up to the jittery flow of events as they unfold.'

The best of Cartier-Bresson's first two decades of work was published in 1952 as *The Decisive Moment*. The French title, *Images à la sauvette* (Images on the Fly), pointed as much to chance as decisiveness. Introducing the pictures, Cartier-Bresson defined his aim as 'the simultaneous recognition, in a fraction of a second, of the significance of an event, as well as the precise organization of forms which give that event its proper expression'.

Like his photographs, the sentence is beautiful but elusive. Throughout his career, Cartier-Bresson was present at a remarkable number of what we would recognize as 'events' in the historical sense, among them the coronation of George VI in London (1937); the liberation of the Nazi concentration camps (1945); Mahatma Gandhi's funeral in New Delhi (1948); and the transition of China to communist rule (1949). In 1947 he was one of the founders of Magnum, the collective agency for photojournalists. However, the majority of the images for which he is best known show no event at all. Or rather, the event is his photographic observation, his ability to seize something compelling from the flow of daily life.

As a mobile and spontaneous medium, photography clearly has a relation both to events and to non-events, but in truth the distinction is never entirely clear. At important events, Cartier-Bresson would often look for the incidental humanity, not the prize-winning photojournalistic scoop. It was as if he wanted to be present without letting the events of the world override the event of his own picture-making, which was almost always about harmony.

Few criticisms are ever made of Cartier-Bresson's photography, because his artistic achievement was so high, and because it opened so many doors. But for those committed to addressing discord, it seemed the world that was Cartier-Bresson's oyster had no grit. The photographer Robert Frank (page 248) put it most acutely: 'He travelled all over the goddamned world, and you never felt that he was moved by something that was happening other than the beauty of it, or just the composition.'

When Cartier-Bresson made this image, a little west of Paris, Frank was on the road confronting the alienation, dejection and racism of North America. But it seems churlish to deny a place to Cartier-Bresson's vision. It is not as if the world's discord is without moments of harmony. Life on a barge on the Seine was surely difficult in 1956, but it must have had its fleeting pleasures.

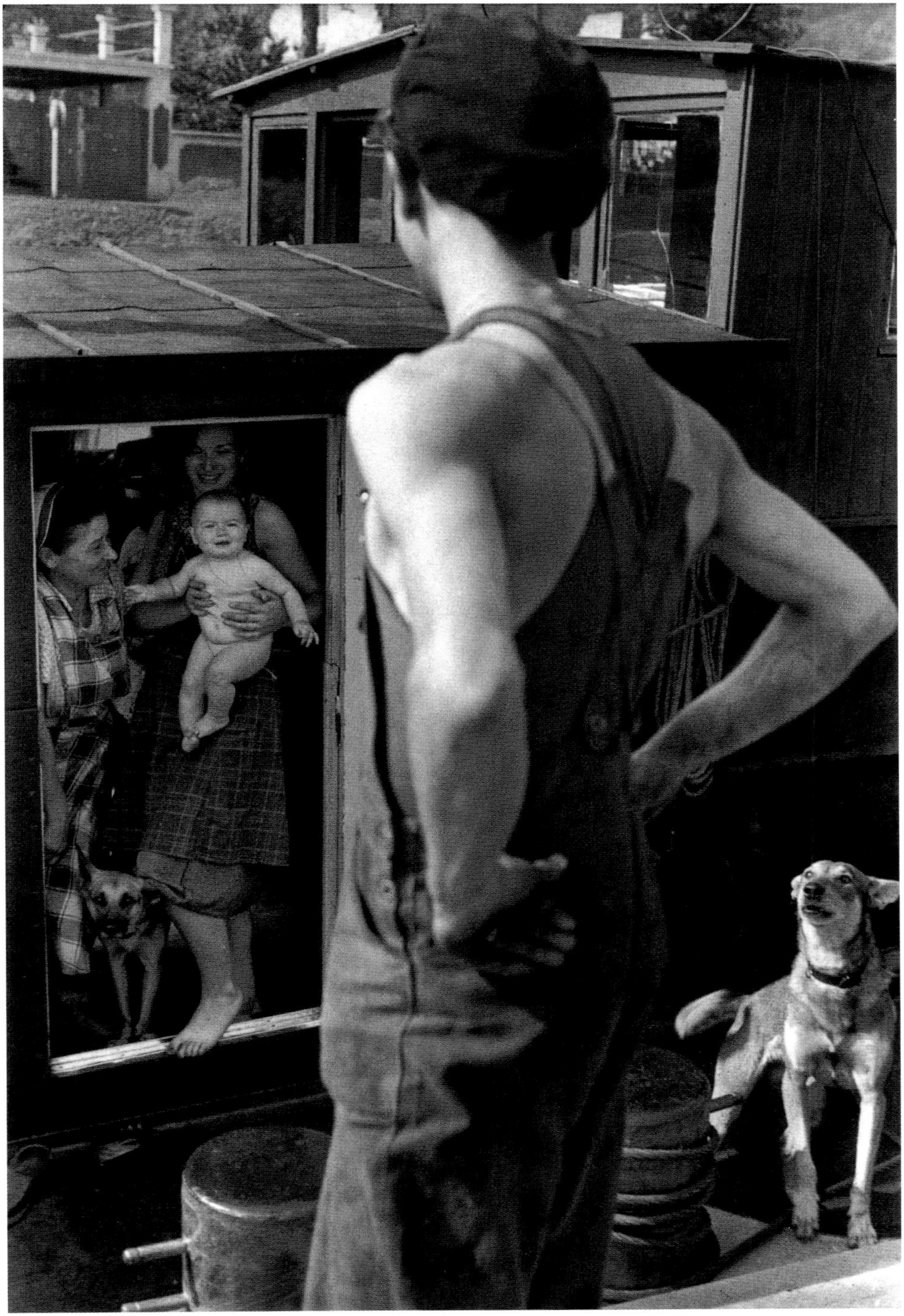

AUGUST SANDER

The Notary, 1924

THE GERMAN PHOTOGRAPHER August Sander began making the portraits for which he is well known in 1911. It wasn't until around 1925, however, that he began to formulate his ambitious project 'People of the 20th Century'. There were to be seven categories: 'The Farmer', 'The Skilled Tradesman', 'The Woman', 'Classes and Professions', 'The Artists', 'The City' and 'The Last People'. These were subdivided into forty-nine portfolios. Sander made more than six hundred portraits in total. He had a system, and thus a set of presumptions about how society was to be understood and pictured, but it is the complex humanity of his photographs that endures.

To begin with, Sander used classical portrait conventions from the nineteenth century. In the early 1920s he met the Cologne Progressives, a group of artists with links to the workers' movement. He began to see photography as an art with a social purpose. Meanwhile, the illustrated press was expanding rapidly, carrying endless photographs of people. Cameras were also becoming more common in homes. The modern relationship between identity and photography was beginning to form. Sander worked independently of the press, and his portraits became more emphatic, dynamic, even performative.

The Notary is one of Sander's most accomplished photographs, balancing the little human details with a structure that feels more like an illustration. Here is a real person occupying a position, playing a part, but he is more than the part. The notary is not working. Outside his home, he holds the leash of his Doberman Pinscher.

In 1929 sixty of Sander's portraits were published as *Antlitz der Zeit* (Face of Our Time). Although it is now celebrated as a landmark photo-book, it remains unclear exactly who bought it and how it was understood. It was one of several German publications from the late 1920s that grasped how photography belongs to many frames of reference. Was Sander's book art? Documentary? Sociology? Anthropology? Fashion? Was it a commentary? A critique? An affirmation? A mirror in which Germans might see and measure themselves? It was all these things, and inconclusively so.

In 1931 the American photographer Walker Evans (page 220) described Sander's book as 'a photographic editing of society, a clinical process'. The critic Walter Benjamin noted: 'Whether one is of the right or the left, one will have to get used to being seen in terms of one's provenance. And in turn, one will see others in this way too. Sander's work is more than a picture-book, it is an atlas of instruction.'

Sander witnessed the rise of the Nazi Party. In 1936 his book was seized and the printing plates destroyed. Did it threaten Nazi ideals? In its realism it may well have done. To a regime demanding certainty, its ambiguity was also troubling.

Sander had been convinced that, as he put it, 'people are formed by the light and air, by their inherited traits, and their actions. We can tell from appearance the work someone does or does not do; we can read in his face whether he is happy or troubled.' In profound ways, however, the experiences of war levelled appearances. In the coming years, people began to dress more similarly. Marked by trauma, shock, guilt and confusion, faces were less readable. The connection Sander had perceived between outward presentation and character had been broken.

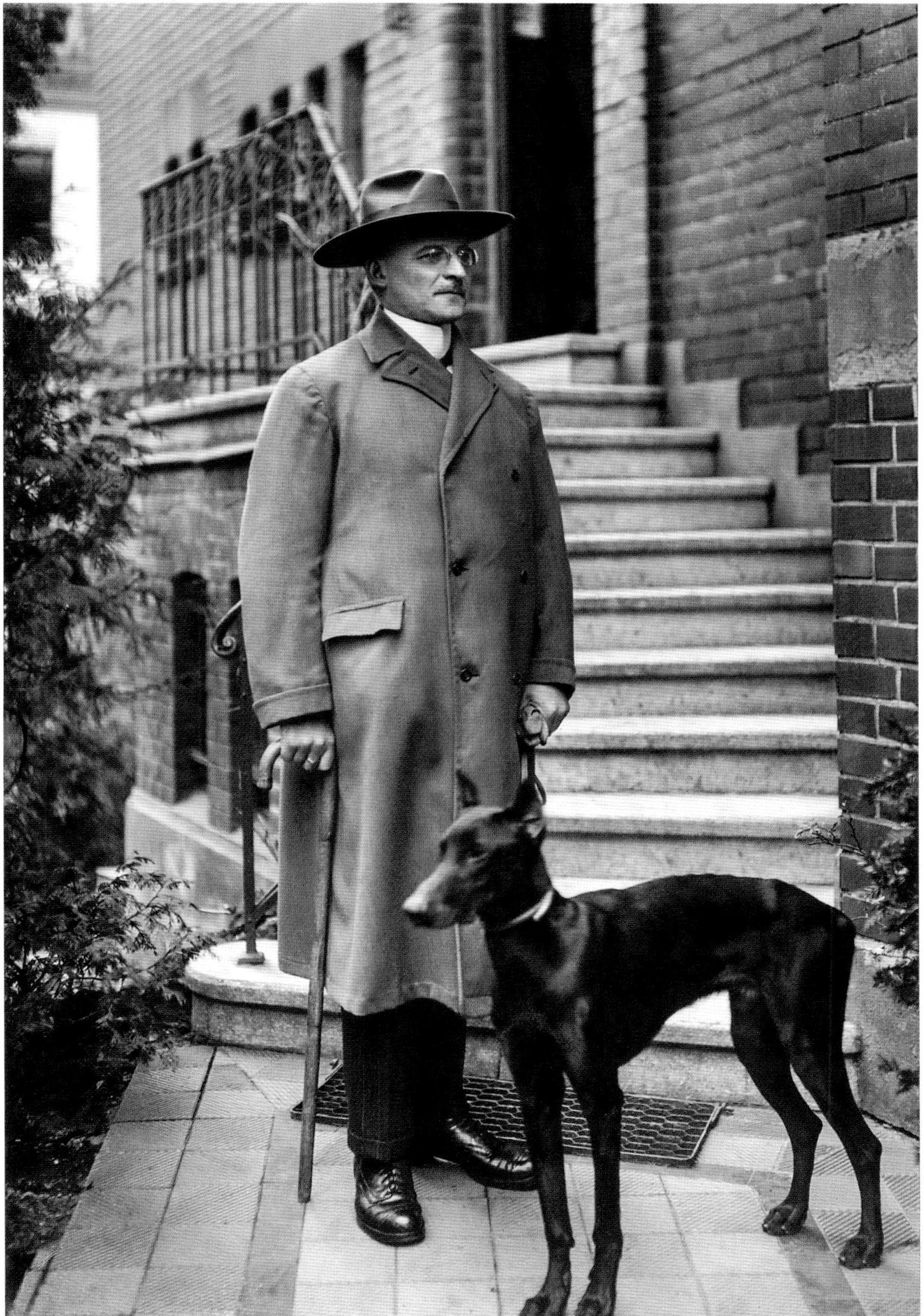

EVELYN HOFER

Queensboro Bridge, New York, 1964

HE IS IN A PARK, in Long Island City, New York. The Queensboro Bridge stretches out across Roosevelt Island in the East River, and on to the wealth and power of Manhattan's Upper East Side. Today, even that park is rimmed with astronomically luxurious apartment blocks. He wears a headscarf typical of the self-aware black youth of 1960s New York. His hands rest in his lap, and his bicycle seems to have equal poise. Its kickstand is down. This is not a hurried portrait.

All photographs are pauses, but there was never anything rushed about Evelyn Hofer's images. She worked with a slow and cumbersome 4 × 5-inch view camera, to make urban studies and portraits of great stature. Where many photographers of her generation embraced the snapshot to keep pace with the hectic metropolis, Hofer preferred a different tempo. Her photographs are monuments as much as moments, classical and grounded.

Hofer was born in Germany in 1922. Fleeing the Nazis, her family moved first to Geneva, then to Madrid, and then to Mexico. She came to New York in 1946 and worked for Alexey Brodovitch, the art director of *Harper's Bazaar* magazine. With her eye for telling detail and a sophisticated technical understanding of photography, Hofer's work became much sought after.

Beyond the images she made for magazine pages, Hofer was commissioned to photograph for what became a series of popular books about various countries and cities. Mexico and Spain; Florence, New York, Washington DC, London and Dublin. Each book paired her immaculately reproduced photographs with text by a celebrated writer. This image was first published in *New York Proclaimed* (1965), with words by V. S. Pritchett.

Throughout her long career, Hofer put her work before her own fame. The critic Hilton Kramer once called her 'the most famous unknown photographer in America'. But her images have lasted, and since her death in 2009 she has come to be appreciated as something of a quiet pioneer, not just of colour photography but also of a kind of understated gravity. She made images against which progress can be contemplated and measured.

As for the young man pictured with his bicycle, we do not know his name. There is nothing to say it won't be rediscovered at some point. This photograph belongs as much to *his* biography as it does to Hofer's.

ALL PHOTOGRAPHS ARE PAUSES, BUT THERE WAS NEVER ANYTHING RUSHED ABOUT EVELYN HOFER'S IMAGES. SHE WORKED WITH A SLOW AND CUMBERSOME 4 × 5-INCH VIEW CAMERA, TO MAKE URBAN STUDIES AND PORTRAITS OF GREAT POISE.

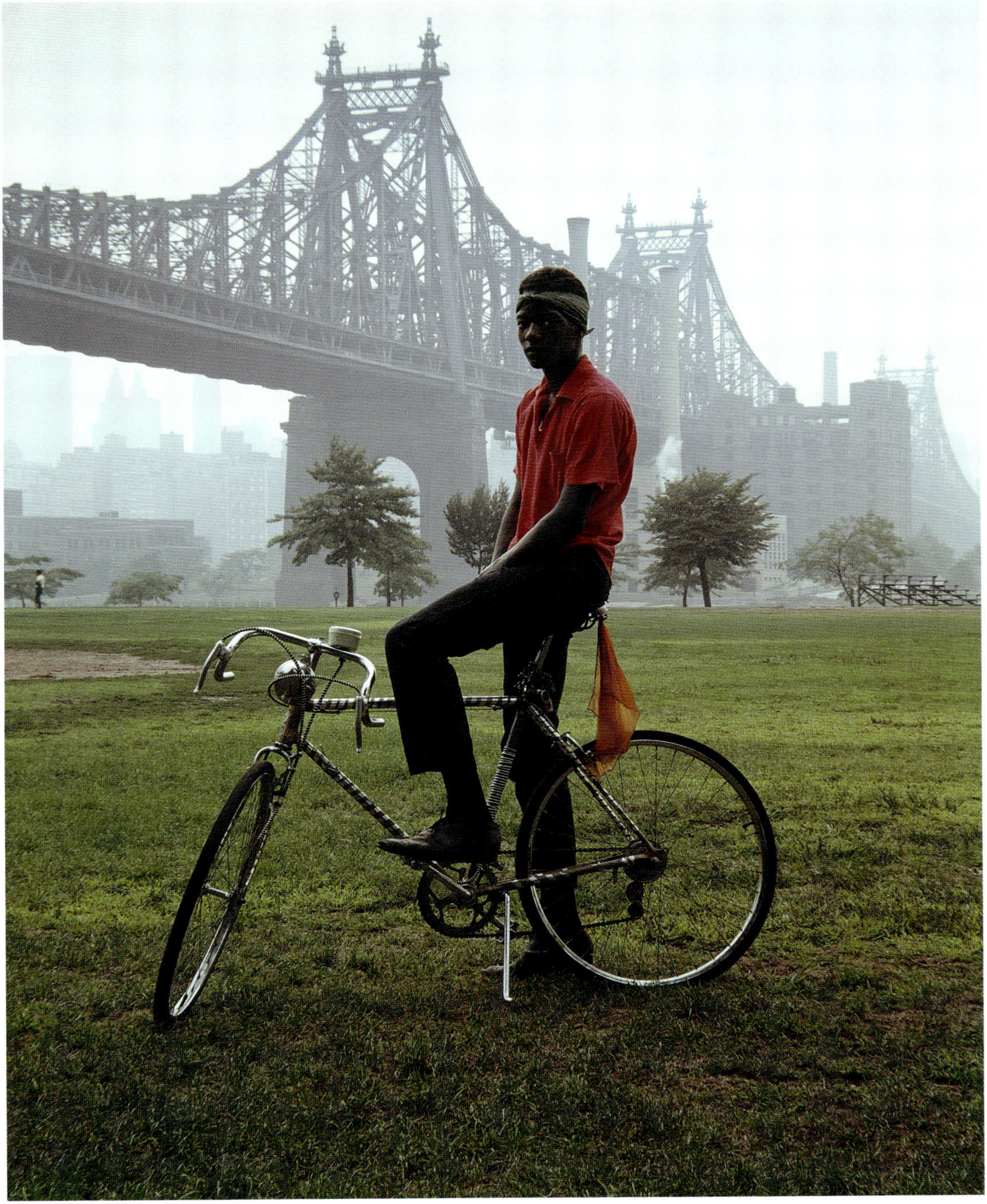

RINEKE DIJKSTRA

Kolobrzeg, Poland, July 26, 1992, 1992

FROM THE SERIES 'BATHERS', 1992–98

'BATHERS' IS AN EARLY SERIES by the Dutch photographer Rineke Dijkstra. Adolescents stand alone or in pairs, for a full-length portrait. They are on beaches. Not glamorous beaches, but real places. They might have just come from the sea.

Making such portraits is a slow process, which creates a degree of psychological intensity between photographer and subject. But intensity ebbs and flows, like waves, and Dijkstra is able to make portraits of great nuance, even vulnerability. This is not to say the images she chooses to print are definitive records of the people. No image can be. A portrait is, in the last instance, a picture, to be encountered as such.

The fill-in flash brightens the figure, making the sea and sky almost like a studio backdrop. The space and distant horizon are pulled close. With such minimal elements, Dijkstra and the viewer can concentrate on the details. The girl looks a little cold, as if she might be at odds with the air around her as much as the business of being photographed. The body under pressure is a recurring theme for Dijkstra. She has photographed exhausted mothers who have just given birth, bruised and bloodied toreadors fresh from the bullring, and partygoers straight off the nightclub dance floor.

We cannot know exactly how a photograph like this was made, and even those present could not have been fully aware of the unconscious little signals they exchanged, as we all do. 'Pose' is a very misleading word, implying self-possessed purpose on the part of the person being photographed, or the photographer. An image can result from a delicate and intuitive situation, the photographer not imposing a will, and the subject not knowing exactly what to do. But in the end it is the photograph that poses, freezing a passing moment.

Many commentators have compared this photograph to Botticelli's *The Birth of Venus*, painted in the mid-1480s. The visual similarities are as clear as the misplaced temptation to elevate photography by association with painting. Serious photography stands equal among the arts, and this portrait stands on its own. Besides, Botticelli depicted Venus as an idealization of feminine beauty, with little interest in what people actually looked like.

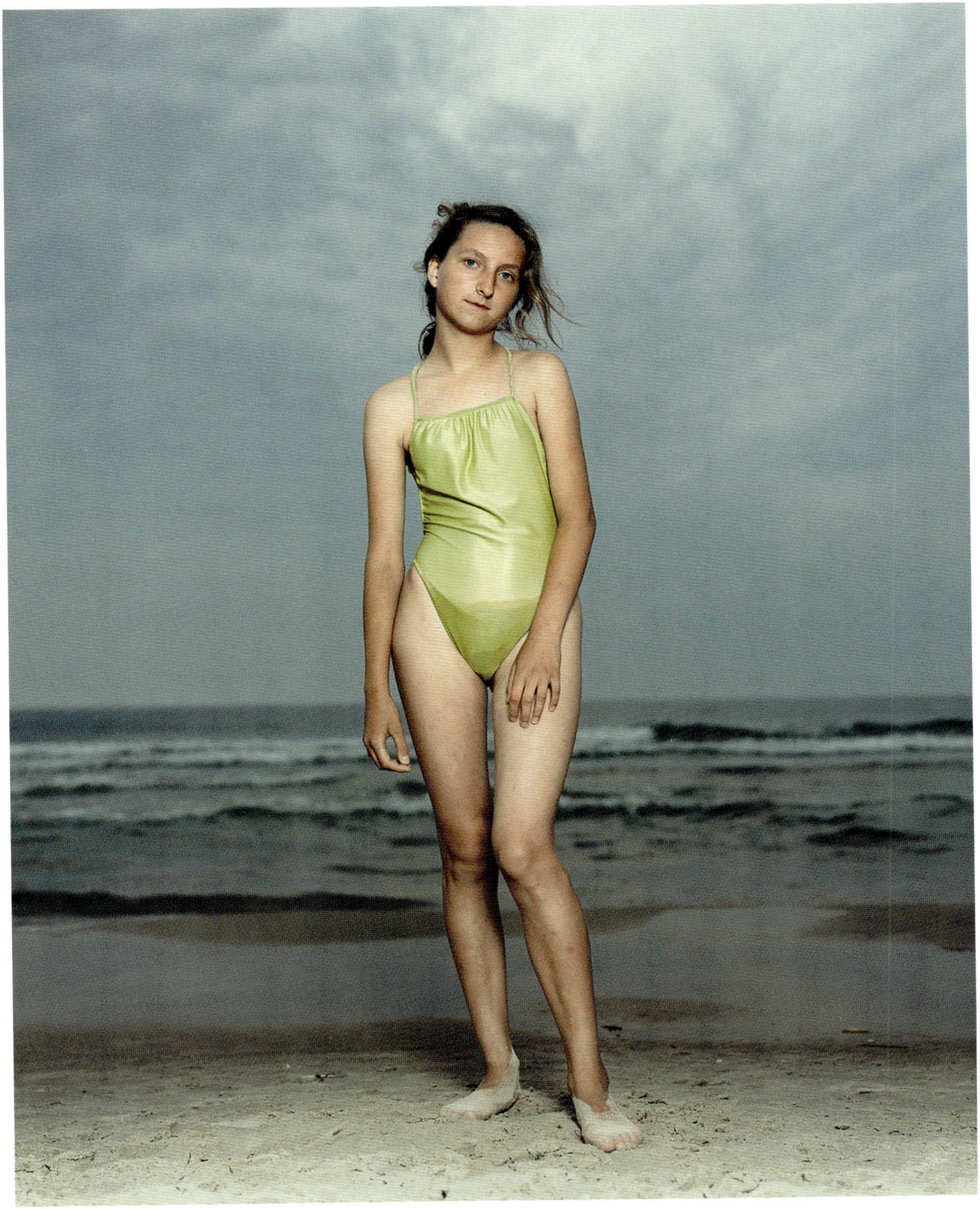

ALESSANDRA SANGUINETTI

Gauchito, 2003

FROM THE SERIES 'THE ADVENTURES OF GUILLE AND BELINDA AND THE ENIGMATIC MEANING OF THEIR DREAMS'

WHILE ATTEMPTING TO TAKE PICTURES of the animals near her parents' farm in rural Argentina, Alessandra Sanguinetti would often try to get Guille and Belinda out of the frame. But when they got to nine and ten years old, she realized that these two cousins, who were also intensely close friends, were what she wanted to photograph. She was thirty-one. The girls would play and improvise, as well as act out roles. With a little guidance, they would develop elaborate situations, re-enacting pictures from art books or moments from television.

Sanguinetti left Argentina for the United States but returned often to the cousins. She decided not to bring the project to a neat end but to keep it open, until Guille or Belinda, or both of them, no longer wanted to continue. At the start, the collaborative world shared by the three of them had been perfectly insular and somehow out of time. But children change and time passes quickly, especially through early adolescence. Sanguinetti resolved to make these changes the core of her project. The early fantasies gave way to darker themes. Sanguinetti photographed the pair for more than a decade, through psychological and emotional transitions into early adulthood.

In 2003 an early sampling of the pictures appeared in the photography journal *Contact Sheet*, and in 2010 a larger sequence was published as the book *The Adventures of Guille and Belinda and the Enigmatic Meaning of their Dreams*.

Such collaboration – intimate, trusting and evolving – is the only way to make images like this. It is also an important way to get to the delicate psychical space of young lives. Their project was a fiction in search of a truth.

SANGUINETTI PHOTOGRAPHED THE COUSINS FOR MORE THAN A DECADE, THROUGH PSYCHOLOGICAL AND EMOTIONAL TRANSITIONS INTO EARLY ADULTHOOD.

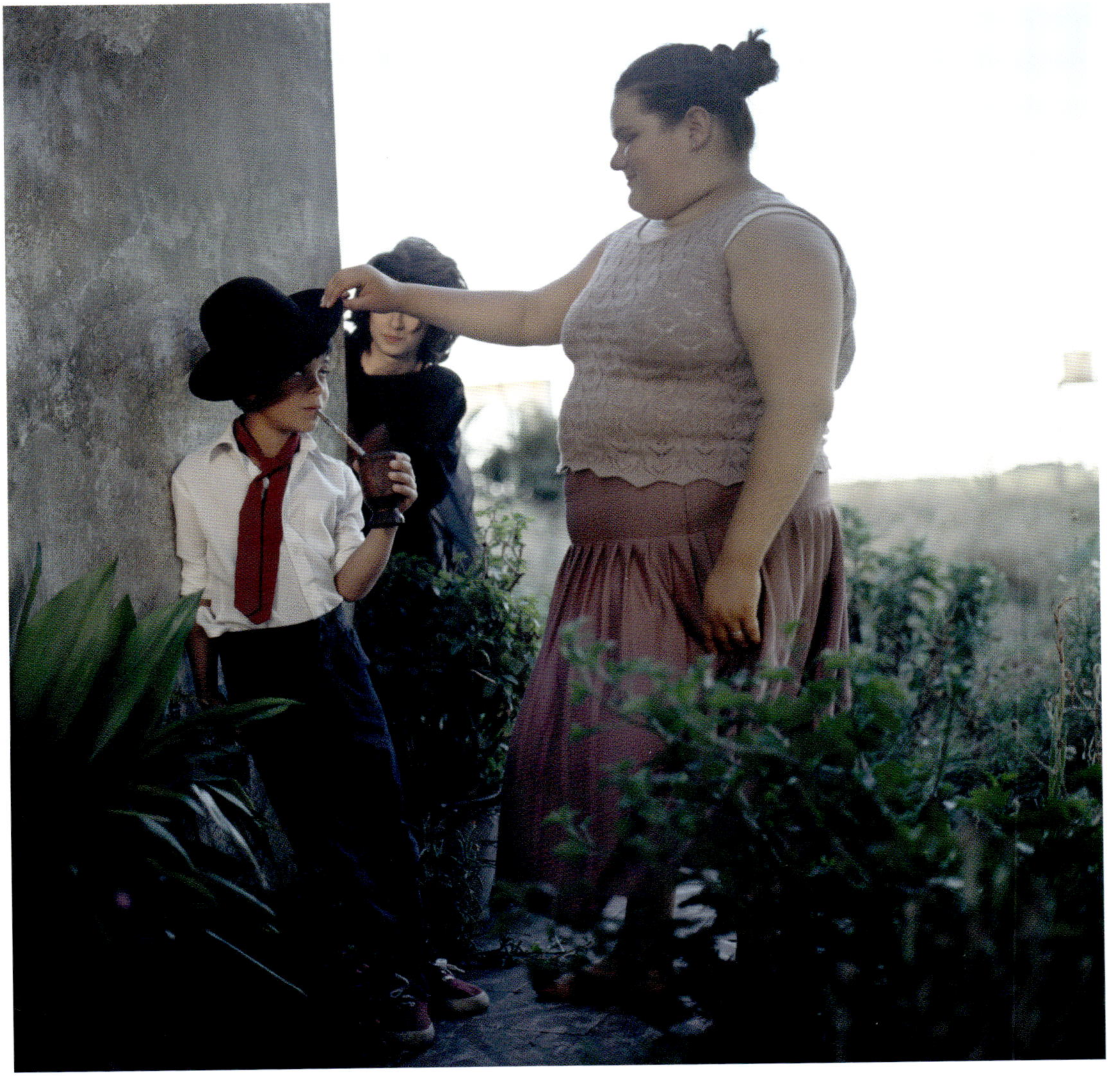

GERMAINE KRULL

Walter Benjamin, c. 1925

WALTER BENJAMIN'S WRITINGS on photography from the 1920s and 1930s are among the most widely read and long-lasting. The German cultural critic sat for several photographers, notably Gisèle Freund (page 78) and Germaine Krull, both of whom influenced his understanding of the medium's history and possibility. After the exciting experimentation of its early decades, photography slumped into commerce and kitsch, and its artistic ambitions were wedded too closely to painting and the salons of art. But in the 1920s it was becoming truly modern. In the hands of socially engaged image-makers, it was capable of deep philosophical reflection, acute cultural commentary, and could even be an agent of social change. Benjamin championed the work of, among others, Eugène Atget (page 20), August Sander (page 84), Karl Blossfeldt, John Heartfield and the surrealists.

For two slightly different reasons, Benjamin had a particular interest in the portrait. Citizens were getting used to being judged and even monitored by their appearance, but, at the same time, photography was able to capture details, 'sparks of contingency', that neither the sitter nor the photographer could fully account for. The camera can register psychological tremors beyond all intention. Benjamin called this the 'optical unconscious'.

In the mid-1920s Germaine Krull was becoming one of the most significant modern photographers, working commercially while also being involved in the progressive avant-garde. In this early portrait, Benjamin is thinking. Or he acts as if he is thinking. Or he is thinking that he is thinking. Or maybe we think that, because he is such a serious thinker, he must be thinking. We are so familiar with chin stroking, reticence and spectacles as signs of the intellectual that we might not give it much thought at all. Krull's camera is so close to Benjamin that he must surely be aware of it. There is nothing surreptitious here. He is either pretending or he is intensely self-involved. We might detect a mental activity beneath the still face and body, and a sense of melancholy too.

Melancholia was a subject central to Benjamin's thinking and it was something to which he himself was prone. It has a very particular relation to photography, being a state that exists on the threshold of withdrawal and self-performance, between absorption and theatricality. It is a condition not of the melancholic's conscious making, but it *is* experienced as a conscious condition, lived from within and observed from without. The melancholic is trapped in a kind of ongoing hyper-awareness, alone but regulated by the gaze of others, or by his or her own imaginary gaze at themselves. This might be why it is so often the subject of portraiture, particularly self-portraiture. If Benjamin had been able to photograph himself, most likely he would have done it like this.

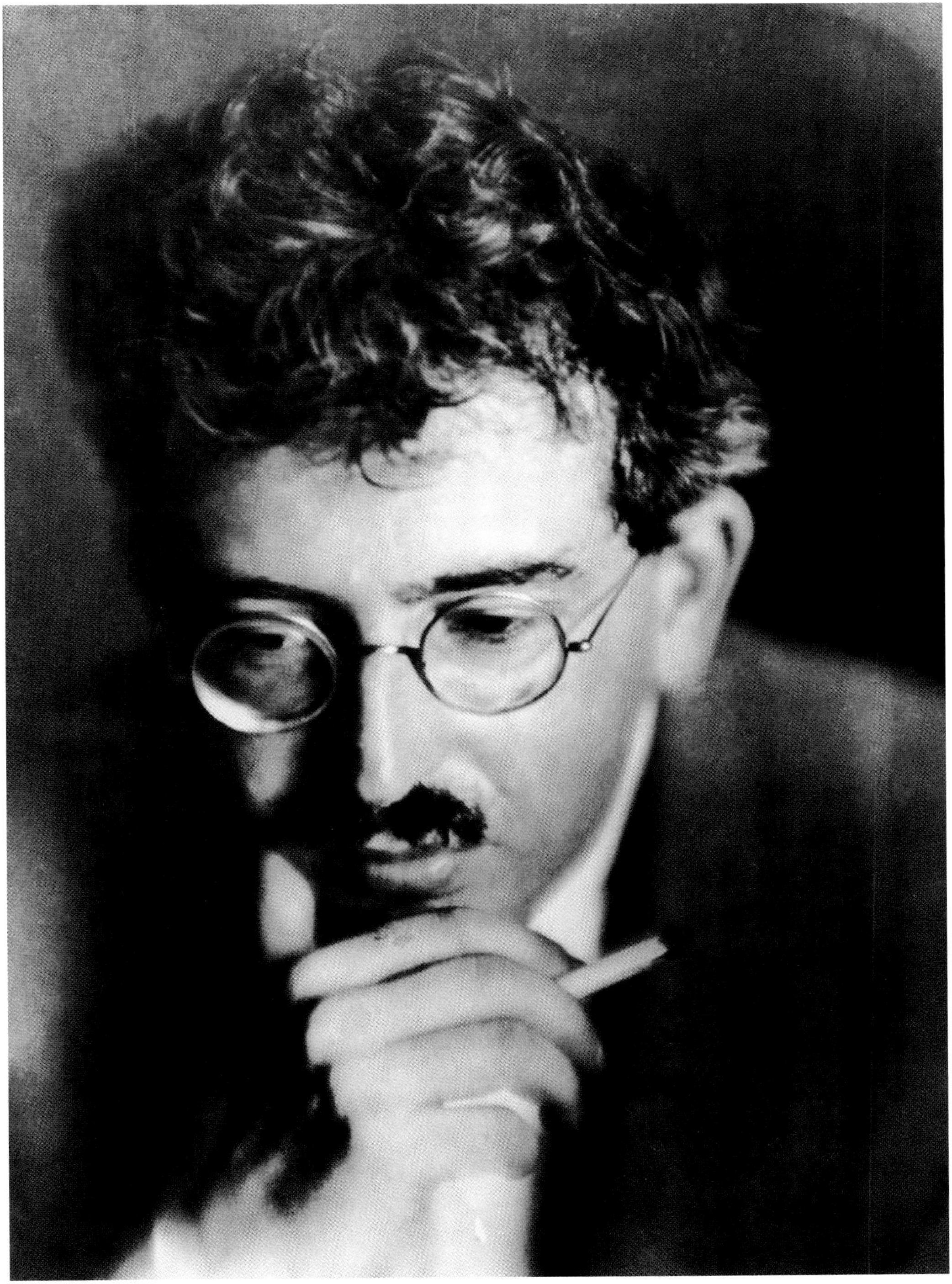

FLORENCE HENRI

Composition, Nature Morte, 1929

FLORENCE HENRI WAS BORN in New York, in 1893. When her mother died two years later, she travelled with her father, a director of a petrol company. They spent time in Paris, where she began to study music. They came to England in 1906, where her father died soon after. A poet friend took Florence to Rome, and it was there she first encountered avant-garde art and thought. By 1913 she was in Berlin, studying music again. When war broke out, she played piano accompaniment to silent films. She switched visual art, studying painting under several artists, including Vasily Kandinsky.

In 1924 she decided to go to France, but was declared stateless on the border and denied entry. Through a quick marriage, she gained Swiss citizenship and was in Paris the next year, in the classes of the painters André Lhote and Fernand Léger. Her paintings were her own version of tightly controlled cubism, both abstract and figurative, with a keen sense of colour.

In 1927 she returned to Germany, to enroll at the Bauhaus, the pioneering school of art and design. She took classes in photography with László Moholy-Nagy and befriended Lucia Moholy, who encouraged her to pursue her camera experiments. Henri worked quickly but with rigour. She took to using mirrors and prisms to make intricately framed studio still lifes that toyed with our perception of space and scale. She made self-portraits in this vein too, and explored photo-collage.

Perhaps unsurprisingly, such a restless and rootless life produced images with no particular sense of place. Henri's photographic work contains few social details that might disclose with any precision where or when it was made. Moreover, this rootlessness was also an aspect of modernist photography as it flourished in the 1920s. A 'New Vision' was taking shape that, like the International Style in architecture, seemed exciting in its disregard for the local, appealing to a forward-thinking, transnational culture.

These ideals were also expressed through photography's belonging as much to the applied and commercial arts as to the fine arts and the avant-garde. Like her contemporaries Marianne Breslauer and Laure Albin Guillot (page 96), Henri was working as a commercial photographer with her own studio while simultaneously pushing artistic boundaries. In fact, her advertising images were often simply more polished versions of the playful studio set-ups she made for herself. She published her images in many of the avant-garde journals and anthologies, and took part in several key exhibitions, notably 'Film und Foto' (1929), the great survey of documentary, art, science, fashion and advertising photography that travelled internationally.

With the coming of the Second World War, Henri stepped back from photography. Materials and commissions were in short supply and, besides, there was the risk of being denounced by the occupying Nazis as a 'degenerate' artist. In 1945 she resumed her painting career but barely picked up her camera again.

Like many photographic artists who blossomed in the excitement of the interwar era, Henri had done what she wanted in a short period of time. Few of those artists had an eye on posterity, but as interest in photography began to grow in the 1960s and 1970s, Florence Henri's work was reconsidered, exhibited and collected. She died in 1982.

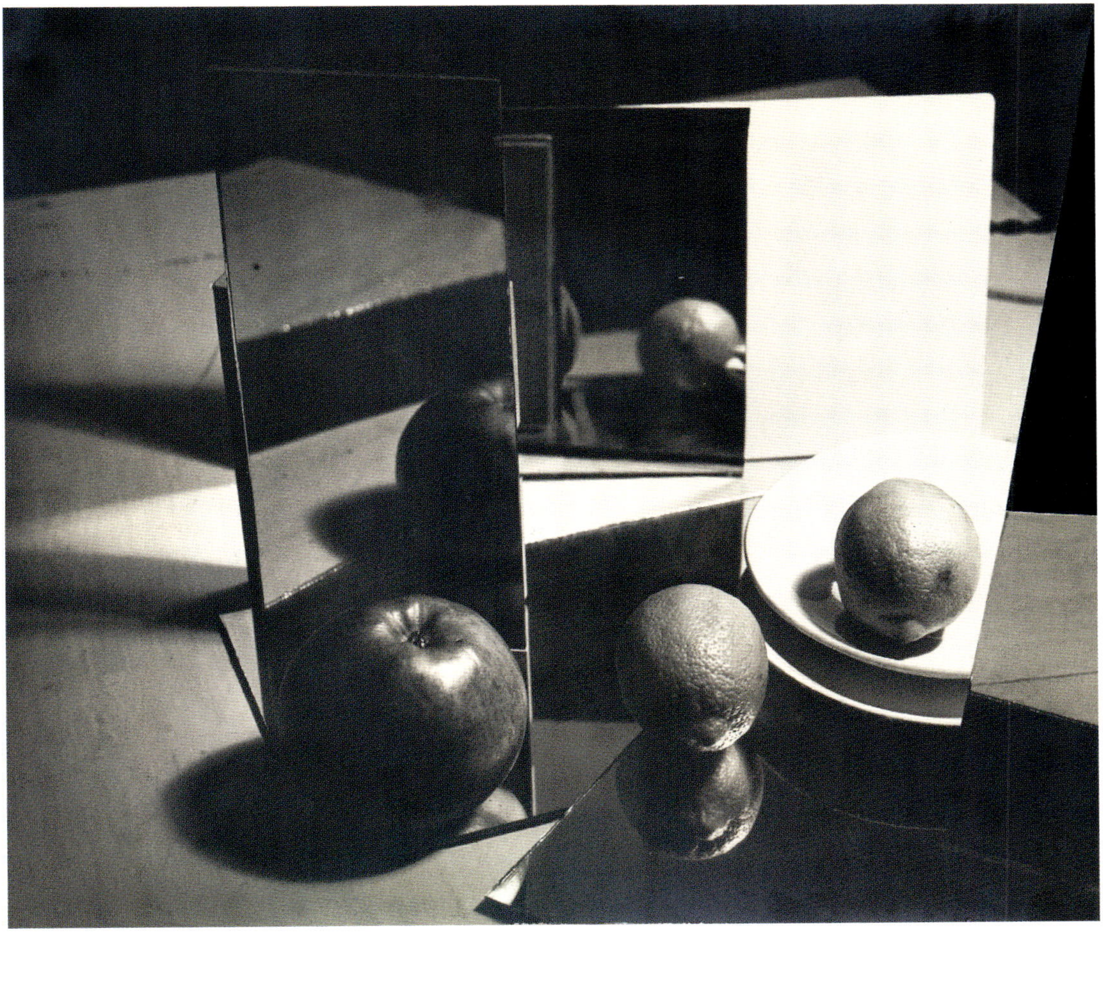

LAURE ALBIN GUILLOT

Narcisse, 1941

LAURE ALBIN GUILLOT was one of the most widely published photographers in France between the world wars, and among the most versatile. She shot fashion, portraits, still lifes, advertising, micrographic images, and more.

In Ovid's version of the ancient Greek myth, Narcissus is an exceptionally beautiful young man who disdains the rapt attention of others. One day he leans over a pool to drink, and falls in love with his own reflection but without realizing it is he. In 1941 Albin Guillot made twenty images to accompany the poet Paul Valéry's retelling of the story. It was published the following year, in a limited edition, as *La Cantate du Narcisse.*

Since Narcissus fails to recognize himself in the reflection, does this mean he is not narcissistic, or that he is extremely narcissistic? At the end of the nineteenth century, the sexologist Havelock Ellis described individuals who were the source of their own sexual satisfaction as 'narcissus-like'. In 1911 Otto Rank wrote a psychoanalytic paper on narcissism linking it to vanity, and in 1914 Sigmund Freud published 'On Narcissism', which offers an account that helps to answer this question. The narcissist idealizes and externalizes a version of the self. Freud recognizes that a degree of this impulse is present in everyone, and is necessary. In extreme cases it leads to obsessive self-interest and even megalomania, in which the self is mistaken for its idealized other.

Many photographers and writers on photography have found the story of Narcissus to be compelling, and perhaps even a metaphor for the medium. From the start, photogaphy was compared to a 'mirror with a memory', and a 'reflection of nature'. Photography transforms the world it appears to serve, and often idealizes it, but it cannot think, cannot reflect upon its actions. The camera is blind to what it is doing, and has no idea what is in front of it.

In Ovid's telling, Narcissus withers away from unsatisfied desire, and is transformed into a flower.

MANY PHOTOGRAPHERS AND WRITERS ON PHOTOGRAPHY HAVE FOUND THE STORY OF NARCISSUS TO BE COMPELLING, AND PERHAPS EVEN A METAPHOR FOR THE MEDIUM.

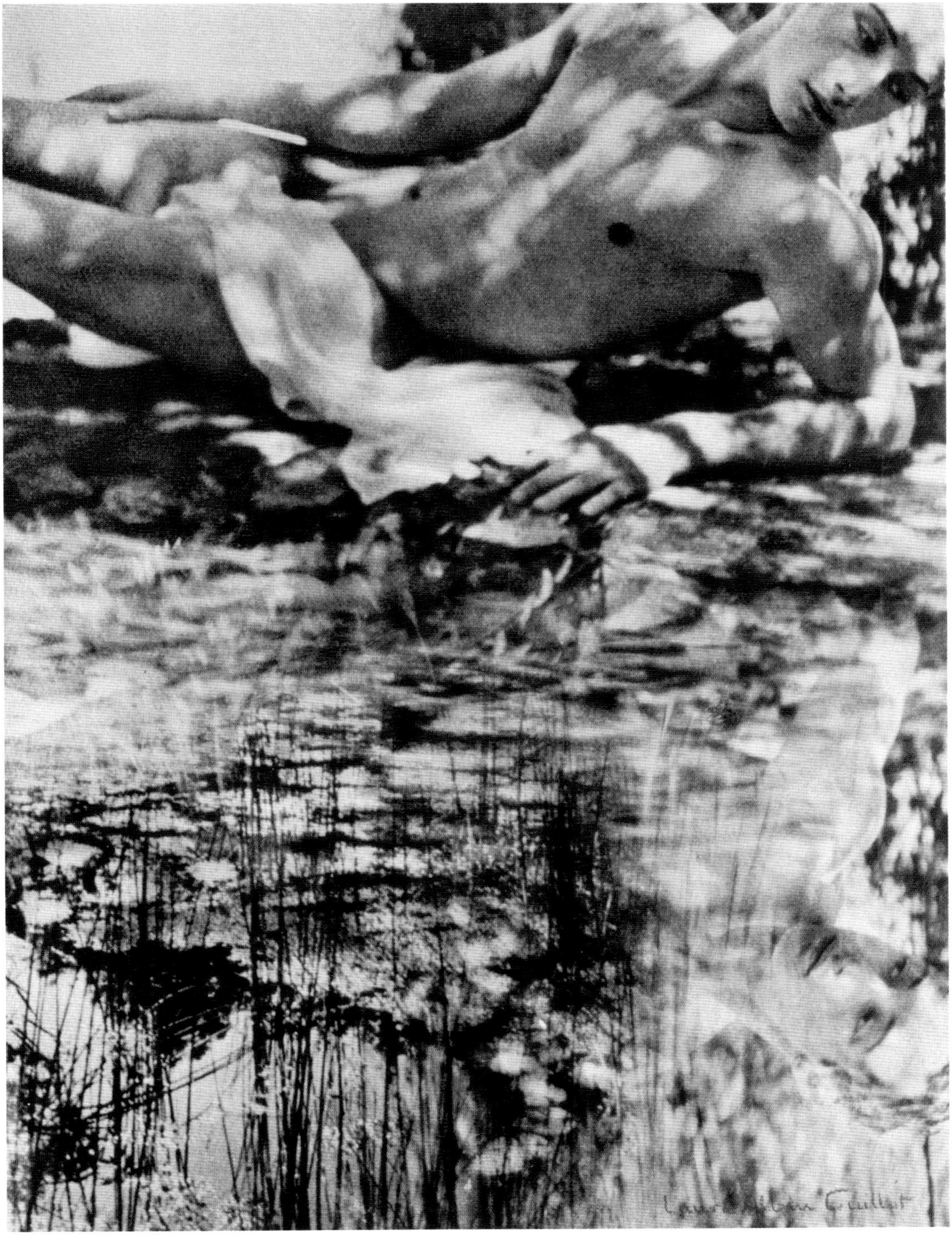

SAUL LEITER

Café, Paris, 1959

OPEN THE SHUTTER AND THE WORLD, as light, will flood into the camera. It goes from empty to full in an instant. This is unlike filling up a page of a sketchbook or a canvas with marks until it is judged to be finished. It is true that a still-life photographer can begin with an empty studio and build up what they intend to shoot. It is also true that post-production in the darkroom, or on the computer screen, can be akin to painting. These things do not negate the automatic and instantaneous aspect of photography, although they can obscure it.

If a photograph jumps from empty to full, what is the photographer looking at? They cannot look at everything, because looking is selective, and highly individual. The eye can hold on to details, or look for alignments, or it can let go, staring through the worldliness of it all to respond more abstractly to the overall composition or design. This might be why photographers shoot so many pictures. Something is always escaping attention, but the camera will seize it. Encountering a photograph, the viewer is faced with a similar challenge.

Saul Leiter's subject matter did not vary too much – street scenes, primarily in New York and abroad – and he was among the most visually distinctive of all photographers. Vertical frames with compressed compositions, often in remarkably delicate colours.

Born in Pittbsurgh, Leiter came to New York to be a painter, and had a voracious appetite for art history. He took to photography, first in black and white in the 1940s, then in colour in the 1950s. Like other photographers from what is sometimes loosely called the New York School – among them Richard Avedon (page 206), Diane Arbus and William Klein (page 24) – he was essentially an artist who found work shooting for such magazines as *Harper's Bazaar* and *Vogue*.

One often hears photographs described as 'painterly', but given that a painting can look like anything, the adjective cannot mean much. Mondrian, Morisot, Manet and Massaccio are all painterly in their own ways. If it means anything in relation to Leiter, it is to do with his two great influences, Henri Matisse and Pierre Bonnard. In their paintings, colour often threatens to untether itself from the figuration to become its own value, and its own source of visual pleasure. That is always a potential of painting, since brushstrokes of colored pigment really are abstract, and any figurative resemblance is conjured as an illusion. In observational photography, colour has its origin in coloured things in the world. A pink cake is a pink cake. Nevertheless, in some of Leiter's most consummate photographs, it feels as if he could be experiencing the colour abstractly, responding to it almost independently of the subject matter. Perhaps a colour arrangement caught his eye and he moved his viewfinder around the scene. Finding what he wanted, he then focused on something in that world. We can never know for sure. Photography has a way of covering its tracks.

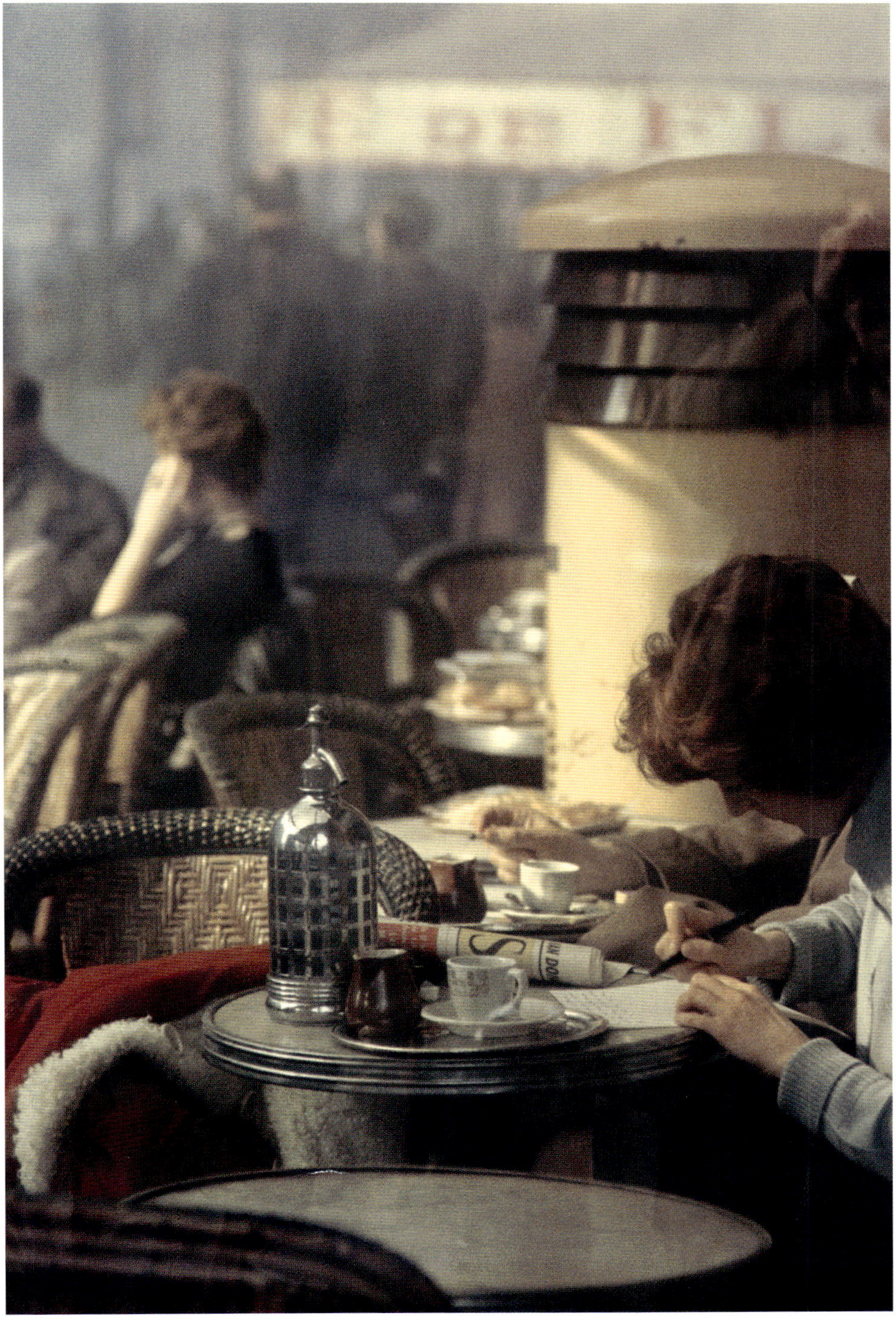

PHOTOGRAPHER UNKNOWN

Diego Rivera in his San Angel studio, Mexico City, 1940

FROM THE COLLECTION OF FRIDA KAHLO

WHEN SHE DIED IN 1954, aged just forty-seven, the Mexican painter Frida Kahlo left behind thousands of photographs. A few – of friends, fellow artists, landscapes and movie stars – have lipstick traces on the back. Only one has a kiss on the front. It is a photograph of the muralist Diego Rivera. Such an imprint will have some immediate connotations: there is, or was, love or desire here. Let us assume Kahlo held the photograph, gazed upon it, brought it intimately close, and left her mark.

The small and physically frail Kahlo first met the large, towering Rivera in 1922. He was at work on his mural *La Creación* at the Simón Bolívar Amphitheatre, in a Mexico City high school. She was fifteen, and he was thirty-six. They were introduced again, in 1928, by the photographer Tina Modotti (page 102), who was a mutual friend. Kahlo was already making her visionary and autobiographical self-portraits, and Rivera was encouraging. As their art blossomed they travelled, particularly around the United States, where Rivera took several major commissions. They married in 1929. As an artist, Kahlo was unflinching, painting so many aspects of her own experience. After a bus accident in 1925 had left her in permanent and intense pain, her body became the centre of her art. She even made a dreamlike depiction of one of her three miscarriages.

The relationship was intense but open. Both she and Rivera had other lovers, but she felt a deep sense of betrayal when her sister and he began an affair. The marriage came to an end in 1939. But they remarried in 1940, and were together until her death.

A photograph is a trace, and so is a lipstick kiss, but what is a trace, exactly? It is a presence that marks an absence, and as such its meaning can never be exact. The photograph is dated 1940 but this only deepens the mystery. Exactly when in 1940? When Frida and Diego were separated? After they had reunited? Is 1940 the date the photo was taken, or printed, or kissed? Did the kiss mean she was in love? That she once had been in love? That Rivera was somewhere else, present to her only as an image? Did she enjoy missing him, or even prefer it? In many ways the ambiguities here echo the ambiguities in their relationship. And, just as a trace and its object are linked intimately but inscrutably, so were these artists, who had made such deep impressions upon each other.

A PHOTOGRAPH IS A TRACE, AND SO IS A LIPSTICK KISS, BUT WHAT IS A TRACE, EXACTLY? IT IS A PRESENCE THAT MARKS AN ABSENCE, AND AS SUCH ITS MEANING CAN NEVER BE EXACT.

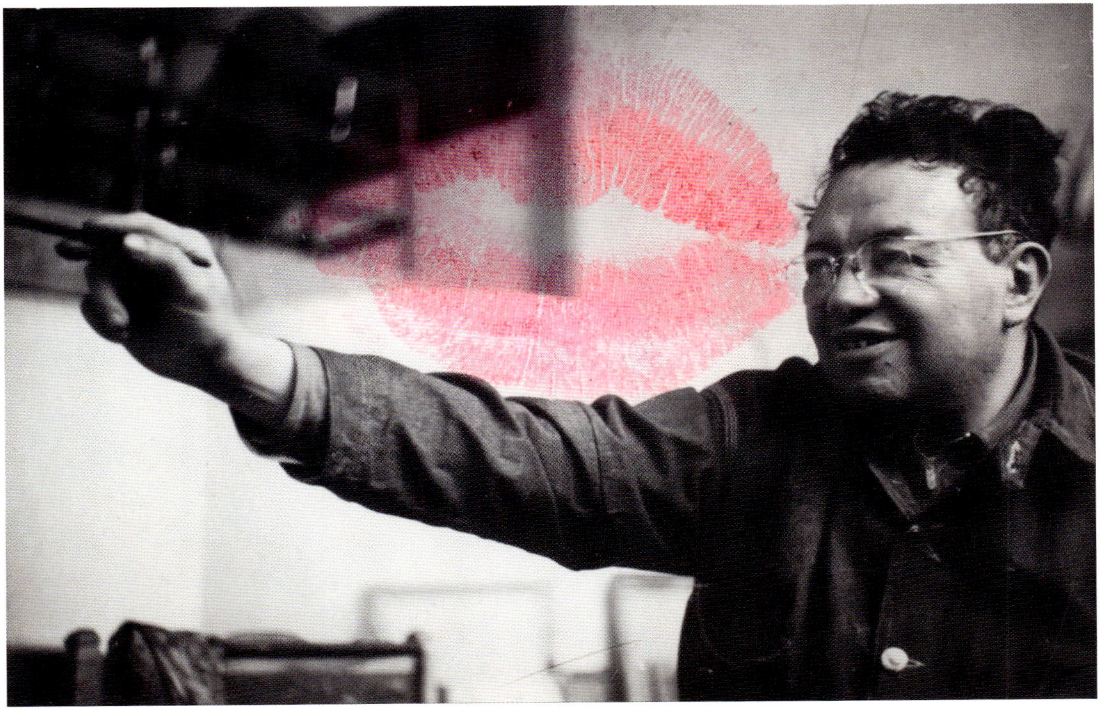

PHOTOGRAPHER UNKNOWN

Tina Modotti at an exhibition of her work at the National Library in Mexico City, 1929

ASSUNTA ADELAIDE LUIGIA MODOTTI MONDINI was born in Italy in 1896. Aged sixteen, she emigrated to San Francisco, via New York, to join her father. She was soon acting on the stage and in movies, and became known as Tina Modotti. She met and began a close relationship with the fine-art photographer Edward Weston. In 1923 the two moved to Mexico City. Modotti agreed to run their commercial studio in exchange for guidance in photography. In a matter of months, she was becoming a significant image-maker in her own right. Along with her scenes of Mexican life, she made vivid images of architectural form and new technologies, such as typewriters, telegraph wires and soaring pylons.

By 1925 Modotti was an active communist, and when Weston returned to his Californian bohemian set, she grew more committed to the revolutionary cause. Reworking Soviet iconography, she photographed a sickle with a Mexican hat, with corn, with a bullet belt and guitar. She made noble images of workers' hands, cracked and dry, and of people carrying flags. The photographs were visually striking, with a great sense of graphic economy. Often they were made for reproduction in the revolutionary journals.

However, the more politically emphatic her photographs became – carrying simple symbolic messages – the less convincing they were as art. Perhaps that did not matter. In this sense, Modotti's images from the late 1920s encapsulate a dilemma that still haunts the relationship between art and politics. What exactly is politically effective art? Perhaps exactitude is the problem. Moments of political urgency demand clarity. But ditch the ambiguity and the nuance, and the art quickly loses its richness while gaining in timely political precision. (John Heartfield, the German anti-fascist, developed a highly inventive approach to photomontage that countered Nazi media propaganda (see page 104) but gave up his claim to the status of artist altogether.)

In 1929 Modotti's name became widely known when she was linked to the murder of Julio Antonio Mella, founder of the Cuban Communist Party (they were having an affair and she was accused of a crime of passion). Modotti was absolved, and later that year she opened her show at the National Library of Mexico. Billed as the country's 'First Revolutionary Photographic Exhibition', it was extremely popular and reviewed widely. With each image on wide white mounts, the presentation resembled a modern fine-art salon. Consciously or not, however, the show presented Modotti on the cusp between formal modernist photography and her explicitly political imagery.

As Modotti's political commitment grew, she moved away from photography into more direct activism. In 1930 she was expelled from Mexico, having been implicated in the attempted murder of President Elect Pascual Ortiz Rubio. She went to Berlin and then Moscow. Italy's increasingly fascist government attempted to have her seized to face charges in her country of birth.

Modotti took no more photographs after 1931, working instead for various communist organizations. In 1936 she went to Spain to join the struggle against fascism, staying until 1939, when the civil war ended. Back in Mexico City, she died of heart failure in 1942, aged just forty-five.

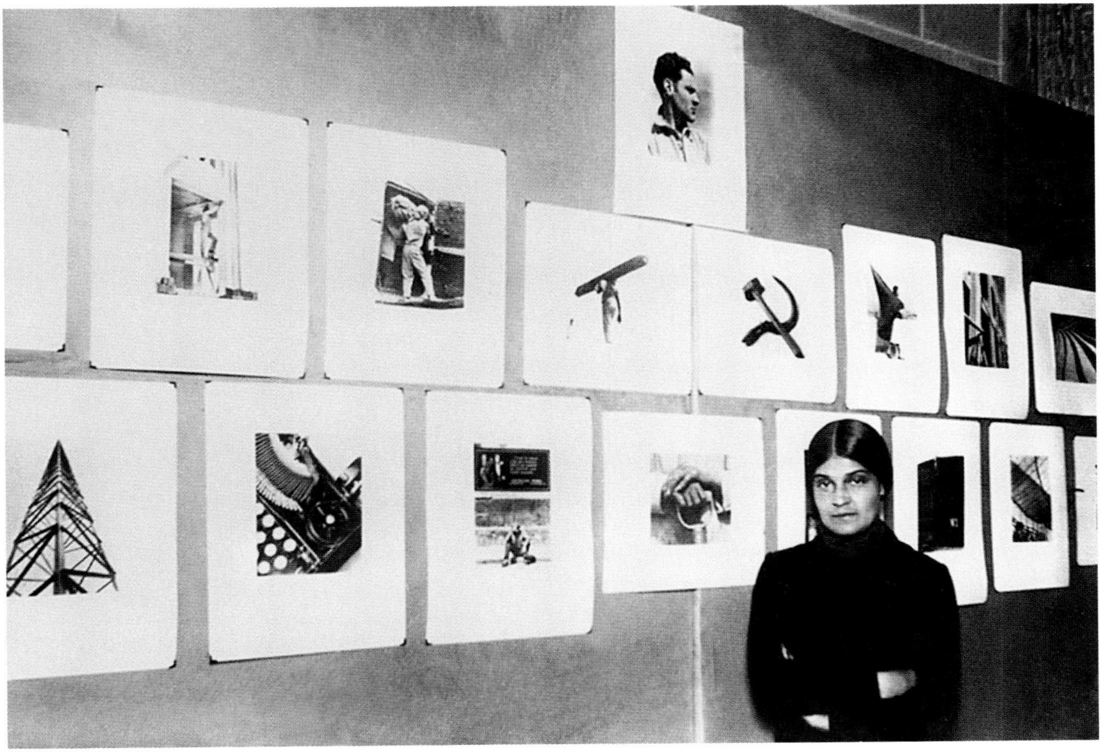

HANNAH HÖCH

Entartet (Degenerate), 1969

THE IDEA THAT THERE ARE too many images in the world has become an empty cliché, but it is not a recent complaint. There were cultural critics in the 1920s and 1930s, particularly in Germany, who warned of 'photo-inflation' – the rapid proliferation of images. Germany was also where resistance to the excesses of the new mass-media image culture was most advanced. While such writers as Walter Benjamin and Siegfried Kracauer reflected upon the social, political and psychological impact, artists developed their own responses.

Hannah Höch and her fellow German John Heartfield are the two most renowned figures in twentieth-century photomontage. Heartfield made work that countered Nazi propaganda, fashioning inventive image/text critiques for the pages of *AIZ*, or *Arbeiter-Illustrierte-Zeitung* (Worker's Illustrated Press), until he was forced to flee the country. Höch had a much lower profile, barely publishing her work at all for many years. Photographic history and art history overlooked her, but she has come to be seen as a key artist of her time.

Höch was active in the Berlin Dada group, at the heart of Germany's avant-garde, participating in the First International Dada Fair, Berlin, in 1920. She had trained in calligraphy, worked as a knitting-pattern designer, became a painter, but soon turned to photographic imagery as source material. She noted how rapidly the mass media was standardizing representations, and hence attitudes. She grew especially critical of the depictions of women and female sexuality in fashion, advertising and the news. She kept scrapbooks of cuttings and developed various cut-and-paste strategies with which to reroute stereotypes and subvert media norms. Have your way with images, or they will have their way with you.

In recent decades, Höch's work has been the subject of intense scholarship. Beyond its pioneering invention, it also offers insights into magazine culture. Höch was active between its rapid expansion after the First World War and its eclipse by television in the 1950s and 1960s. Throughout, she was a voracious but critical consumer of all kinds of imagery, German and international, mainstream and avant-garde. Her work is a map of one woman's navigation of the values and ideologies of the printed page.

As Höch continued her work, the various art movements that engaged with mass-media images came and went, from Dada and surrealism to situationism and Pop. She died aged eighty-eight, in 1978, just as a new wave of 'postmodern' artists were finding their own resistance to the spectacle of popular culture. There are distant echoes of Höch in the work of Martha Rosler, Cindy Sherman, Sherrie Levine, Laurie Simmons and Louise Lawler (page 108).

In 1969 Höch made *Entartet*, a photomontage with a telling title. It recalled 'Entartete Kunst', or 'Degenerate Art', the notorious exhibition staged by the Nazi Party in 1937 to denounce avant-garde art and artists. Nazi policy was to clear the path for the party's official art, based on ideals derived from a revisionist version of the culture of ancient Greece and Rome. Höch's work was not included in 'Entartete Kunst', but she had already suffered censorship in 1932. With a show of her paintings and photomontages planned at the Bauhaus in Dessau, the Nazi-led local council shut down the school.

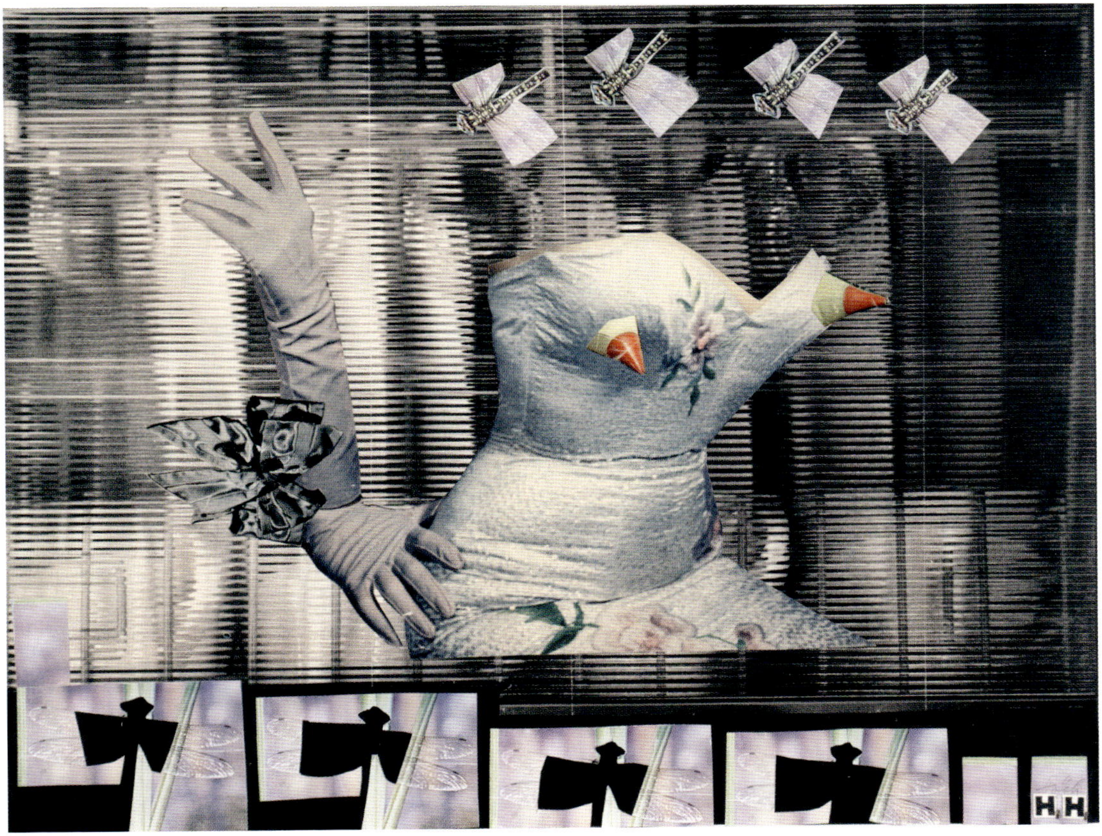
H H

ROBERT RAUSCHENBERG

Scanning, 1963

THE FASCINATION WITH printed matter shown by North American Pop artists had much to do to with the emergence of television. In the late 1950s, newspapers and magazines were starting to undergo their slow displacement from the centre of visual culture. When *Life* launched in 1936, it soon became the most popular and influential weekly magazine, and its hold on American values seemed unassailable. In less than four decades it had closed, replaced by the small screen.

If Andy Warhol was the Pop artist with the canniest relationship with the mass media, the one with the greatest appetite for its imagery was Robert Rauschenberg. Everything had the potential to end up in his work, which he made with every material and process available. Printmaking, painting, sculpture, performance, photography, projections.

Scanning is a canny title. With connotations that take in everything from radar and automated cameras to copying, it captures the idea of surveying without hierarchy, judgment or selection. Of course, humans cannot really scan, either with their eyes or with their minds. We are subjective and selective. Consciously or unconsciously, we make choices. Things 'catch our eye'. We might use machine technology to help us make images, and we hand over a lot of control in the process, but we cannot look at the results with the cold indifference of a glass lens or a photocopying machine.

Rauschenberg claimed: 'Anything that can reflect light is of some interest.' In many ways, he aspired to embody the central idea of Pop, which was to reflect an image-driven consumer society back to itself without comment; to hold a mirror up to it, silently. Yet what gives Rauschenberg's collages their charm is the way he revealed his own fascinations. *Scanning*, a giant work, may feel at first like an overload, yet these images did not choose themselves. They were selected, although very often Rauschenberg could not say why some pictures had stuck in his mind at all. Here he combines mass-media images with more personal photographs, taken of dancers. Between 1954 and 1964, Rauschenberg designed costumes, sets and lighting for his choreographer friend Merce Cunningham.

Rauschenberg printed the images on canvas as silkscreens. To these he added energetic, gestural brush strokes, and this too has a relation to scanning. With Abstract Expressionist painting, which he seems to be mocking here, the flatness of the canvas was emphasized, as opposed to the deep space of realist pictorial illusion. An Abstract Expressionist painter moves across and around the canvas, almost in a scanning motion. When Rauschenberg made this piece, Pop was usurping Abstract Expressionism as the privileged mode of North American art.

So, it seems an expanded idea of scanning is taking shape here. There is the mastering of the flat, all-over surface of the canvas, and a surveying of the all-over image-world of the mass media. Silkscreen printing a photograph is a form of scanning, a way to get a depiction on canvas without having to actually paint it. We see the image, but also the fine matrix of the silkscreen itself, not unlike the halftone screen of newsprint, or even the television screen seen close up.

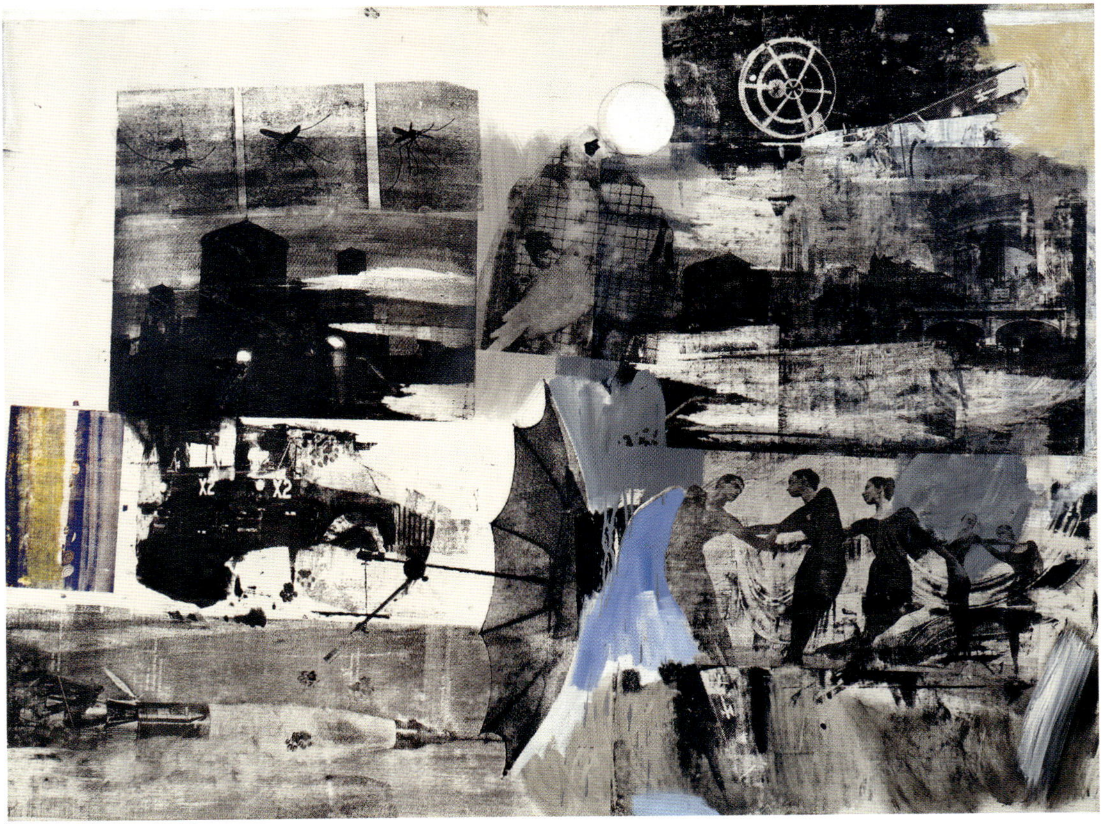

LOUISE LAWLER

Life After 1945 (Hats), 2006–07

IN HIS ESSAY 'A Small History of Photography' (1931), the German critic Walter Benjamin speculated about photography's double-relation to art. On the one hand it was an expressive medium in its own right, but on the other it was the functional means by which all the visual arts could be documented, studied and publicized. Benjamin wondered if the emerging modern art of photography was less important than the fact that all art was beginning to be experienced through photographic reproduction: 'It is indeed characteristic that the debate should have hardened most of all over the question of the aesthetics of photography as an art, while for example the so much less questionable social fact of art as photography scarcely received a glance. And yet the effect of the photographic reproduction of works of art is of much greater importance for the function of art than whether a photograph is more or less artistic in its composition.'

In practice, photography's two functions can never be kept entirely separate. In fact, in the earliest decades of the medium, the photography of art, particularly sculpture, was a minor but important genre of the art of photography. Many of the pioneers, including William Henry Fox Talbot (pages 198, 224), Louis-Jacques-Mandé Daguerre and Hippolyte Bayard, made notable images of artworks. The motivations were complex. Was it an attempt to make photography a high art by association? Was it to show that they had access to, and appreciation of, the other arts? Was the aim to use photography to serve and disseminate? It was all these things.

Artworks have continued to be subjects for photographic artists, and in many ways the motivations and meanings have become even more layered. The North American artist Louise Lawler had been making art about art and artists since the early 1970s, but came to prominence in the 1980s when she began exhibiting photographs she had taken of other exhibited artworks. She would document the work and something of its surrounding context – walls, labels, tools for hanging and installing. She also photographed artworks in the galleries of auction houses and in private homes.

Lawler's gesture raises many more questions than it can answer, and there can be no simple or single reading of it. But there is a difference between the gesture *per se* and each of Lawler's photographs in particular. In *Life After 1945 (Hats)*, we see two artworks by prominent post-war artists, the North American Andy Warhol and the German Gerhard Richter. Both works use photographic source material. Warhol's piece is one of several screen-printed canvases made in 1964 using news images of Jacqueline Kennedy, before and at the funeral of the assassinated President Kennedy. Richter's painting *Herr Heyde* (1965) is also based on a news image. In 1959 Werner Heyde, a key figure in the Nazi Party's euthanasia programme, turned himself into the authorities. Just before his trial in 1964, he took his own life. Lawler's photograph incorporates and offers for contemplation all these people and their histories, as well as their passage into artworks and art history.

Given that exhibitions are the hallowed space of originality, this is where Lawler's photographs are at their most resonant and perplexing, not on the page. In museums and galleries they hang as works in their own right, while rerouting the art around them.

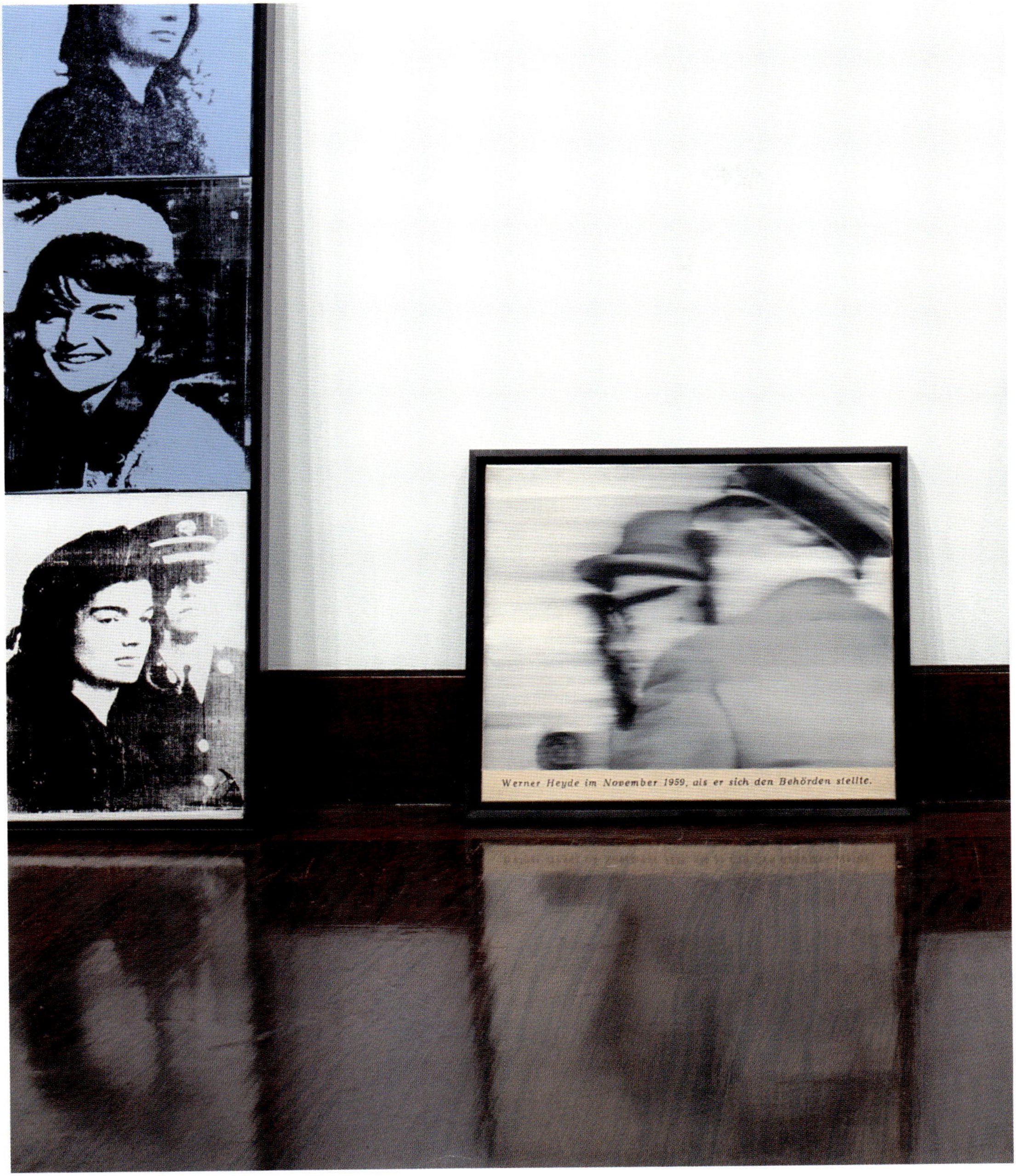
Werner Heyde im November 1959, als er sich den Behörden stellte.

JASON EVANS

Artwork for the Four Tet album
There Is Love in You, 2010

THE BRITISH PHOTOGRAPHER Jason Evans began working in fashion, advertising, portraiture and music photography in the early 1990s. He has had many exhibitions, and also works on community projects. For him, photography is an *applied* art, and no less creative or innovative for that. This understanding harks back to the 1920s and 1930s, when many of the key figures in the avant-garde also worked commercially, moving between different genres, contexts and audiences. Make good work and the 'art' will take care of itself.

Evans's artworks for albums and singles by such musicians as Four Tet are a reminder that record covers can still be hotly anticipated and dearly prized in the era of music downloads. His approach is to attempt to make some kind of visual equivalent to the recorded sound.

The image for Four Tet's album *There Is Love in You* (2010) started with Evans scavenging the test prints made each morning by the commercial digital print labs of central London. Images of colour spectrums, bright flowers and fine geometric grids will tell technicians if their printers are working correctly. Evans pinned these test prints to his studio wall and photographed them on a sheet of medium-format colour negative film. Once processed, the film was hole-punched. The tiny, rough-edged discs were arranged meticulously on a piece of glass. The glass was then placed in a photographic enlarger and a positive print was made. Look closely and you will see that the image could only have been produced this way. The analogue/digital image is a consummate translation of the electro-acoustic music. The design was also intended to function effectively for all the available music formats. The cover of the gatefold 12-inch vinyl record shows a large field of the coloured discs; the CD cover has fewer; while the online MP3 icon features just a handful.

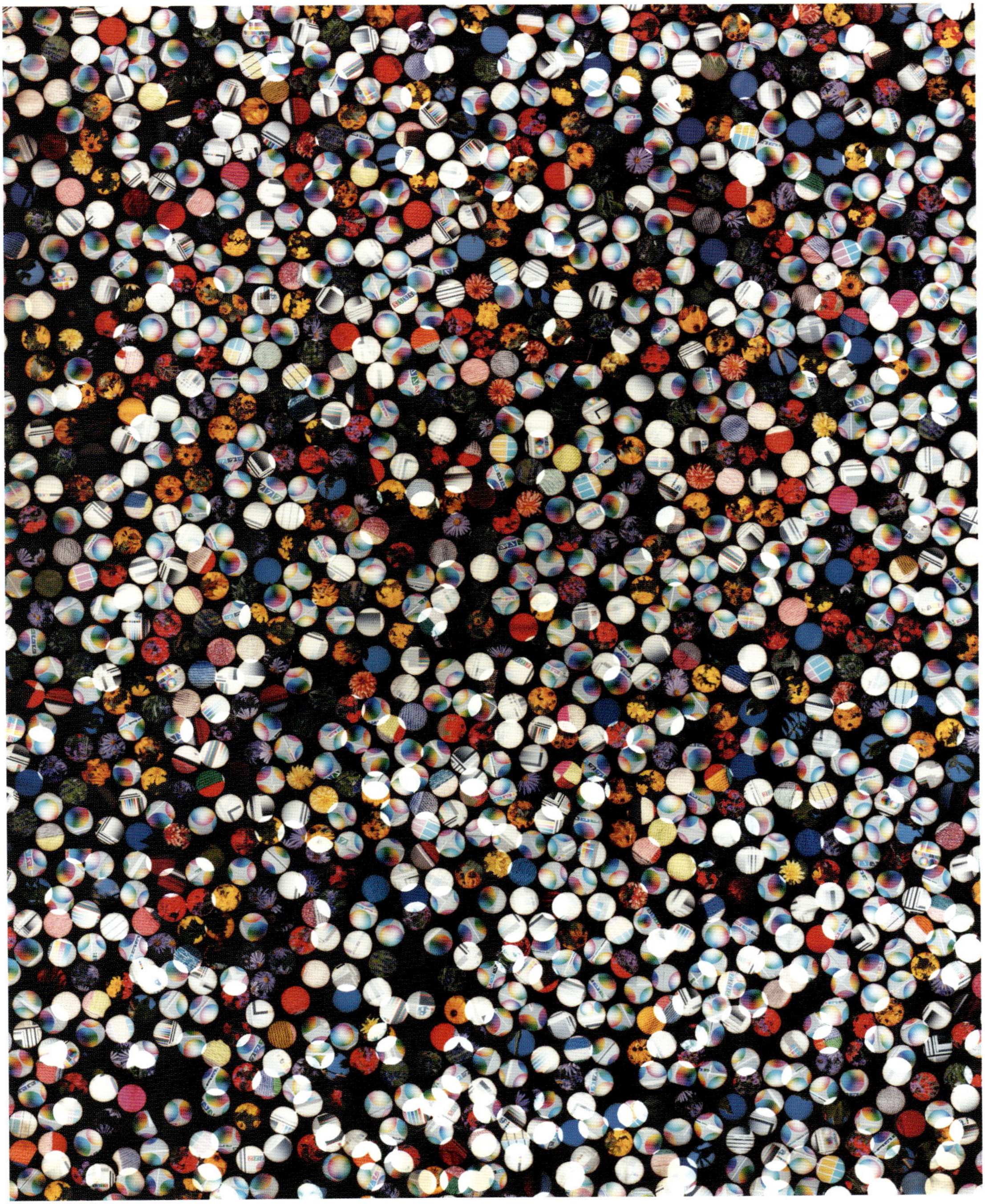

PAUL RAND

El Producto cigar box, 1952

PAUL RAND WAS ONE OF the most prolific figures in twentieth-century North American graphic design. His corporate logos for IBM, ABC Television and UPS remain among the most recognized in the world.

Along with his contemporaries – the art directors Alexander Liberman (at *Vogue*) and Alexey Brodovitch (at *Harper's Bazaar*), and the graphic designer Saul Bass – Rand shaped a visual sensibility with an influence that can still be felt today. All four took the insights and appetite for design innovation that had been developed by the European avant-garde, notably the Bauhaus in Germany and Russian Constructivism, and applied them to the intensely commercial climate of the United States. Rand also incorporated the cool elegance of mid-century Swiss graphic design, which appealed to America's more conservative corporations. But Rand was always keen to experiment too.

In 1952 the El Producto cigar company needed publicity images for magazines and billboards. Rand produced a family of more than a hundred designs. This led to an invitation to design a box. Traditionally, cigar-box graphics had been very tame, resembling the ornate labels on venerable whiskey and brandy bottles. Rejecting all that, Rand took a handful of cigars and a glass ashtray into a darkroom. He placed them directly on to a sheet of light-sensitive paper and exposed it. It was the classic way to make a photogram, as pioneered by Man Ray (page 154) and László Moholy-Nagy.

The exposure was made in stages, with cigars added at each point. In the negative tones characteristic of the photogram, the cigars left in place the longest made the whitest shapes. Printed on paper glued to the cedar wood box, the objects appear close to the actual size of the cigars inside. Rand's design ethic was always to simplify, keeping all the graphic elements as clear and efficient as possible. When told the design was radical, he replied: 'What's the big deal? I was just showing the cigars.'

TRADITIONALLY, CIGAR-BOX GRAPHICS HAD BEEN VERY TAME, RESEMBLING THE ORNATE LABELS ON VENERABLE WHISKEY AND BRANDY BOTTLES. REJECTING ALL THAT, RAND TOOK A HANDFUL OF CIGARS AND A GLASS ASHTRAY INTO A DARKROOM.

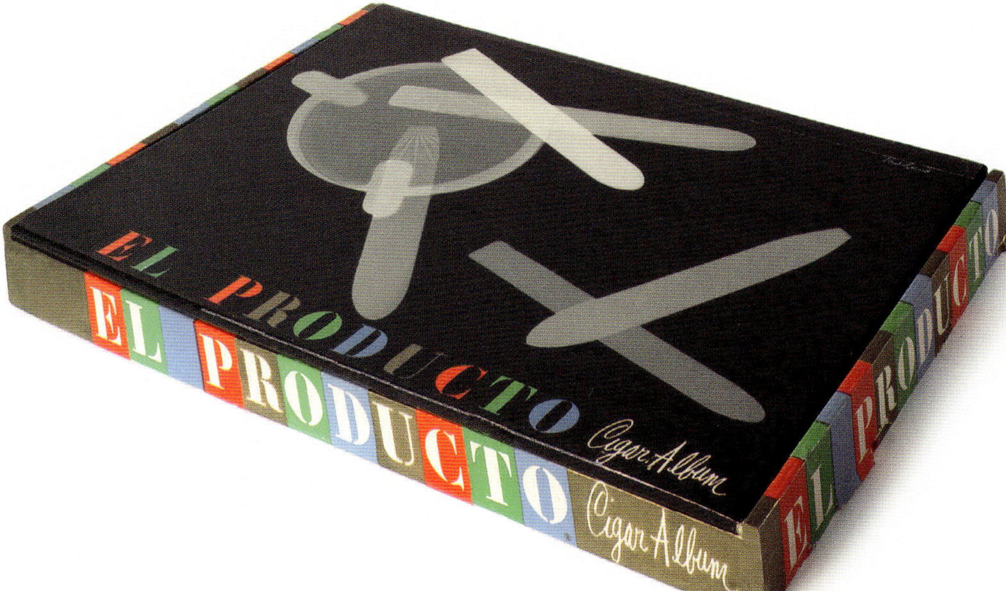
EL PRODUCTO
Cigar Album
EL PRODUCTO
Cigar Album
EL PRODUCTO

IRVING PENN

Frozen Foods, New York, 1977

FOR DECADES, Irving Penn was *Vogue*'s prime photographer. The magazine first published him in August 1943, and his last contribution was in August 2009. The work ranged from portraits and fashion shoots to elegant still-life compositions of food and flowers. Although his imagery was innovative, influential and much admired, Penn himself was a private man.

Penn's aesthetic concerns had little to do with the commercial setting in which he worked, and they had taken hold very early in his artistic career. He destroyed most of his earliest paintings and drawings, but those he preserved are precise and complex, resembling collaged amalgams of scientific instruments and organic parts, surrounded by empty whiteness. He consumed a great deal of art, in museums but also on the printed page, and from this emerged a sensibility informed by the work of Heironymous Bosch, Francis Picabia, Giorgio de Chirico, Max Ernst, Fernand Léger and Alexander Calder. Penn produced a few illustrations for *Harper's Bazaar* magazine, and with his earnings he bought a camera. He looked to such photographers as Walker Evans (page 220), Eugène Atget (page 20), Julia Margaret Cameron, Henri Cartier-Bresson (page 82), Bill Brandt (page 80), August Sander (page 84) and Nadar. It was clear immediately that photography offered Penn both the lucidity and the strange beauty he was after.

Penn was a modernist in two important senses. He was attentive to the qualities that were specific to his medium: light, description, illusionism, and the camera's way of taking a slice of the world from one place and putting it in another. Secondly, he understood that photography truly blurred the distinctions between the so-called fine arts, graphic arts and applied arts. In photography, you could simply try to make good work that might raise the standards of whichever outlet you were working for, but you could also keep to your own criteria, and the work might even last.

In July 1977 *Vogue* ran a summer feature on iced soups, complete with recipes and a slight variation of this photograph by Penn. Slabs of frozen fruit and vegetables are stripped of their packaging and arranged on a simple white backdrop. Assembled like a toddler's building blocks, the food looks familiar and yet odd, disarmingly basic but monumental. It is not advertising, exactly, although stylistically it relates to it; nor is it a self-consciously art-historical take on the still life. Instead, Penn creates an image out of looking closely for unexpected beauty. Why shouldn't unpackaged frozen food be given the same attention as fresh ingredients and fine cuisine?

Attention – be it with our eyes, with a camera, or both – transforms what we are looking at. Things in photographs become signs of themselves, but exactly what they signify is often unclear. In a magazine feature about soup, this image might have had quite specific meanings, but Penn's ability to make unexpectedly compelling images always pointed beyond mere function.

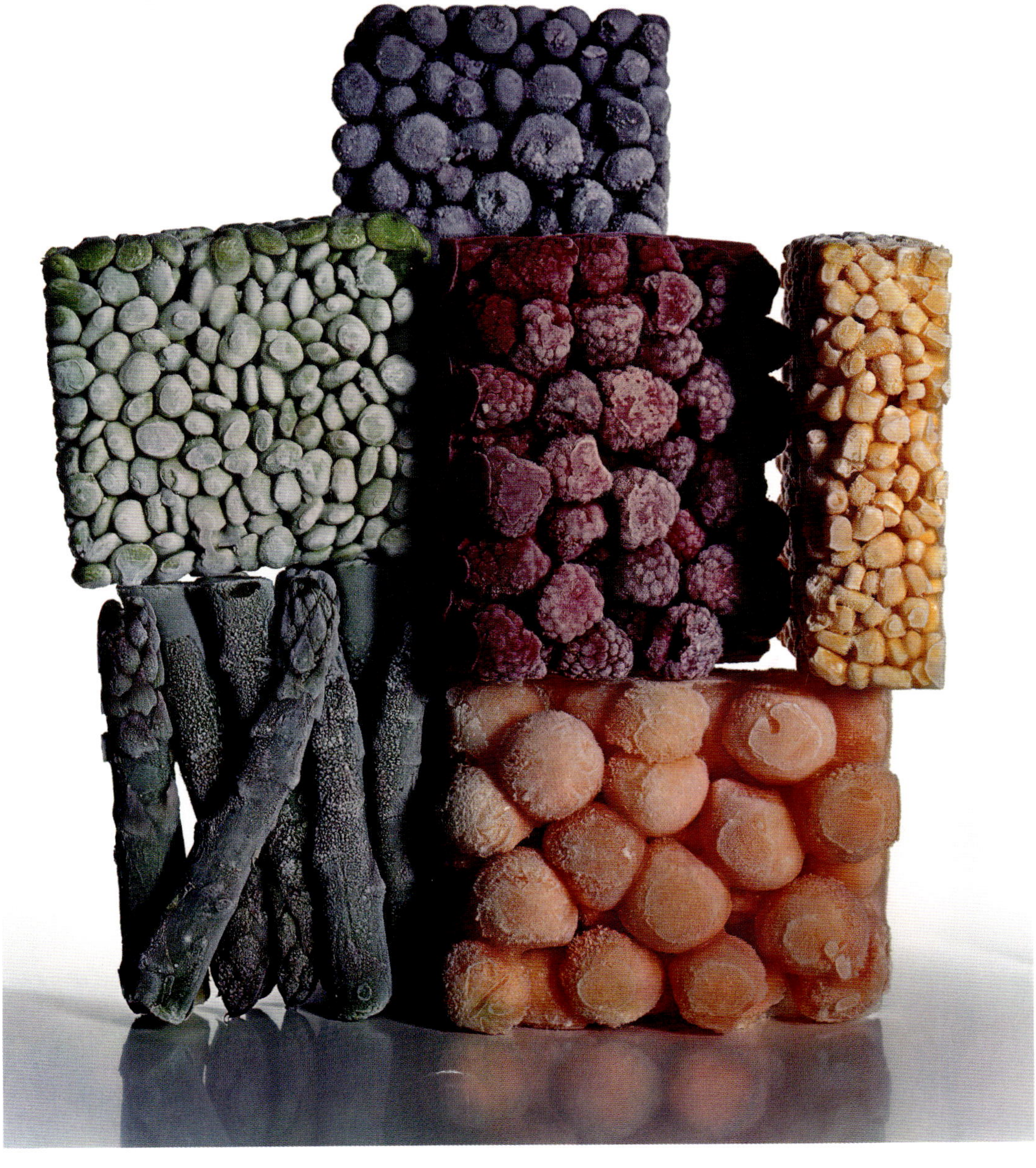

MYOUNG HO LEE

Tree #3, 2006

FROM THE SERIES 'TREE', 2006–11

PHOTOGRAPHY IS A MEDIUM of specifics. Its powers of description rest upon its capacity to record detail. In *The Pencil of Nature* (1844–46), William Henry Fox Talbot (pages 198, 224) included a photograph titled *Articles of China*. Thirty ornate objects – vases, jugs, bowls and cups – were arranged on four shelves in front a plain backdrop, and photographed face-on, as if they were being catalogued. In his accompanying text, Talbot wrote: 'From the specimen here given it is sufficiently manifest, that the whole cabinet of a virtuoso and collector of old China might be depicted on paper in little more time than it would take him to make a written inventory describing it in the usual way. The more strange and fantastic the forms of his old teapots, the more advantage in having their pictures given instead of their [written] descriptions.'

Being a medium of specifics means photography is not well suited to generalities. A photograph can record the uniqueness of an object but it cannot designate the general category to which it might belong. What makes it useful in compiling an inventroy makes it quite useless in defining the group. Consider, for example, the images found in books to be used for identifying plants. A photograph can record a specimen but not the species as such. Each individual specimen is a variation. The skill of a botanical illustrator is to look at several specimens and then produce an avergage. The average does not exist in reality but it is useful to have it. Botanical identification is much better served by drawing than by photography.

Photographs of specimens are of course extremely useful in their own way. They show not the average or the ideal, but the actuality. A photograph of a plant might be able to show an instance of mutation by which a deviation is made from the species average. It might be able to show the specific effects of the environment on that particular specimen. To ease study, a specimen is best isloated from its surroundings. This is easy enough with small plants, but more difficult with large trees, for example. Yet this is the task that the South Korean photographer Myoung Ho Lee set for himself. Behind each selected specimen a giant white backdrop was erected, turning space into a stage upon which the tree presents itself (or *performs* itself) for the camera. The framing is wide, allowing us to see not just the isolated tree but also the whole drama of its isolation. Although absurdist and comical, the series, simply titled 'Tree', can also be seen as a meditation upon the artificial terms and conventions by which photographic images can become knowledge.

A PHOTOGRAPH CAN RECORD THE UNIQUENESS OF AN OBJECT BUT IT CANNOT DESIGNATE THE GENERAL CATEGORY TO WHICH IT MIGHT BELONG.

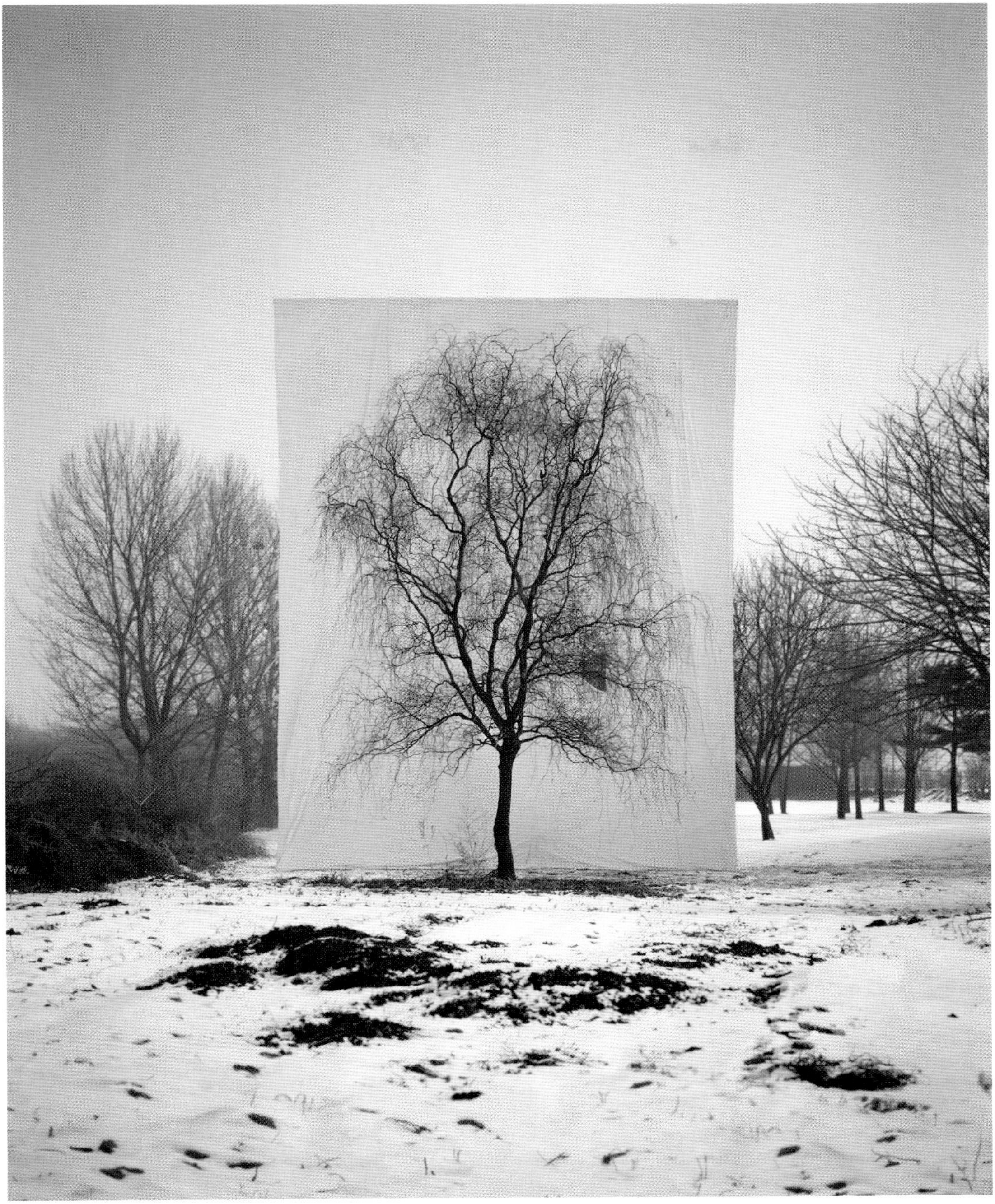

NOÉMIE GOUDAL

Cascade, 2009

IN *A STUDY OF SPLASHES*, published in 1908, A. M. Worthington offered a visual inventory of liquid forms, with 264 photographs of examples. He documented everything from milk droplets entering water to the permament 'splashes' left when a projectile pierces armour plate. But Worthington understood that science comes from simple curiosity. This is how he introduced his book: 'There will be but few of my readers who have not, in some heavy shower of rain, beguiled the tedium of enforced waiting by watching, perhaps half-unconsciously, the thousand little crystal fountains that start up from the surface of pool or river; noting now and then a surrounding coronet of lesser jets, or here and there a bubble that floats for a moment and then vanishes.'

Water has a complex relationship with photography. Flows, waves, splashes, reflections and refractions are deeply photogenic. Water must be kept away from the camera, and yet for most of its history photography required liquids at many stages of its production. We need only think of the darkroom, with its various fluid chemicals for processing film and making prints.

The unpredictable nature of water meant that it posed a technical challenge to photography while offering new aesthetic possibilities. A long exposure of a waterfall will sacrifice detail but offer a spectral impression of the total volume of space occupied by the liquid as it drops. This chaotic freedom of water was among the motivations towards faster shutter speeds and the instantaneous image. Like humans and animals on the move, liquids reveal themselves to the camera in ways the eye cannot see. The faking or imitation of water also has a long history in photography. It is often easier and cheaper to replace a fluid with something more manageable and controllable that will give the desired impression.

Water is a recurring motif in the work of the French artist Noémie Goudal. Moving between photography, sculpture, performance and temporary installation, she constructs worlds that dramatize the tensions between the natural and the man-made. In *Cascade*, a dry valley is draped in white plastic sheeting. Plastic is an oil-based product that repels water and nature in every sense, but it can also resemble them. Plastic can imitate the appearance of almost anything, but not its other properties. It cannot flow like water, nor evaporate and, as science currently stands, it will not biodegrade for centuries. Since its invention in 1907, approximately 10 billion metric tonnes of plastic have been prodced, and nearly all of it still exists in one form or another. In the same timeframe, the molecules that make up water would have found their way into lakes, seas, rivers, plants and animals, several hundred times over.

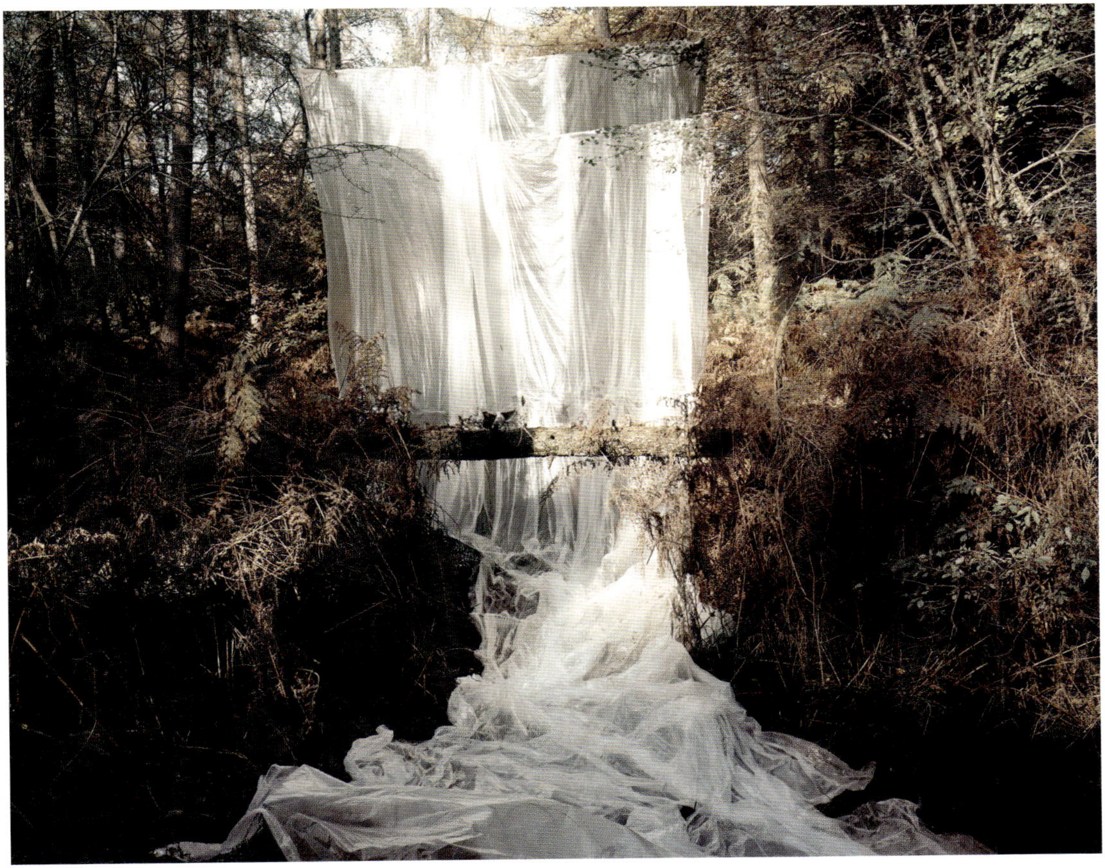

ESTHER TEICHMANN

Untitled, 2015

FROM THE SERIES 'MYTHOLOGIES'

IN GENERAL, A PAINTER DOES not paint her painting and then decide what size it will be. She does not paint and then decide what materials it will be made from. In general, scale and material are integral to painting, sovereign to it, in ways they are not to photography.

Photography is a matter of image capture, followed by image output. Capture can be made with no sense of scale in mind. The photographer can look through the viewfinder, or at the focusing screen, or at the electronic screen, or directly at the world, and make an exposure while suspending the question of what will eventually become of the image. Small or large; for wall or page or screen? This is one of the fundamental characteristics of photography.

The lack of sovereign scale or materiality means that so many things can be done with a photographic image. These things might be deemed successful or unsuccessful, good or bad, but they are all legitimate. It means also that the photographic image is at home wherever it is placed, and however it is encountered. This is what has made working with photography exciting but also disarming and perplexing.

There are exceptions, of course. For example, if one looks at the history of twentieth-century street photography, it seems it was mostly made while internalizing the book or magazine page as the eventual context and size. That is what those photographers had in mind, and when exhibited, their images were not much larger than that. Blow them up to a greater size and they often look monstrous. A different kind of photographer may make take a photograph in which significant details are very small, knowing the final outcome will be a print or projection large enough to make them legible.

And yet, it may be that in looking at any photographic image, we intuit that a choice has been made. The image could have been presented a thousand different ways, but it was presented this way.

The over-painting of photographs, a practice almost as old as the medium, occupies a complicated position in this question of scale. Here is a reproduction of an over-painted photograph by the artist Esther Teichmann. The original is 150 centimetres (59 in.) wide. The coloured paints are applied loosely, often with runs and drips. The image has received the paint by hand at that scale, and this lends a specificity to the now hybrid image-object. As a mark of the hand, the paint also pulls the image away from its emphatic reference to what was before the camera, allowing it to loosen its ties to time and place. Now the reference is as much to the psychology and site of this reworking, perhaps in the artist's studio. Teichmann's artistic concerns have much to do with longing and reverie, and the delicate balance between fantasy and memory. She often works with family and friends as her subjects, but is looking for resonances that are wider and less specific than autobiography. Over-painting is one of her ways to get to them.

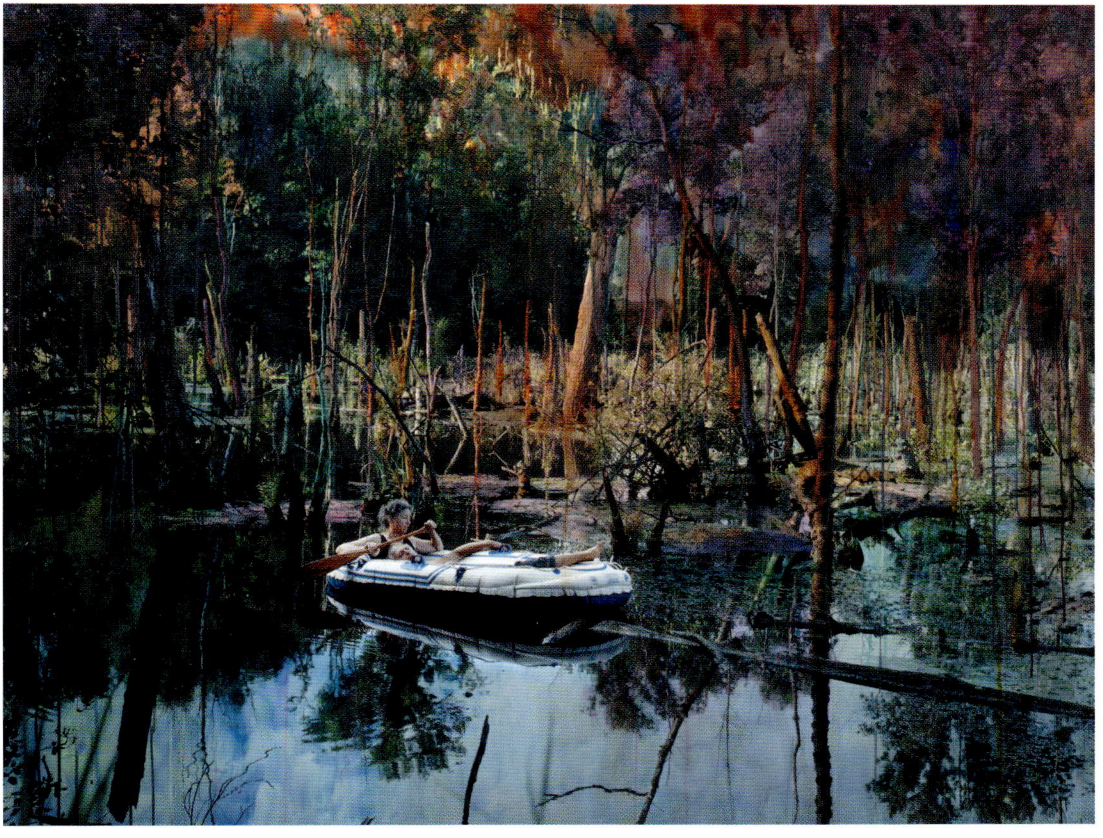

PHOTOGRAPHER UNKNOWN

Publicity still for *Lust for Life*,
directed by Vincente Minnelli, 1956

THIS IS A PUBLICITY PHOTO for the Hollywood film *Lust for Life*, Vincente Minnelli's 1956 biopic of the painter Vincent van Gogh. Playing Vincent, the actor Kirk Douglas poses at the easel, pretending to paint a portrait of his friend Dr Gachet; or rather, a portrait of the actor Everett Sloane, cast for his resemblance to Dr Gachet as Van Gogh had painted him in 1890.

For all its melodrama, Minnelli was proud of the charged realism of his film, shooting many scenes from Van Gogh's life where they had taken place in reality, notably the south of France. Dr Gachet had sat for his portrait in Auvers-sur-Oise, a suburb of Paris, but this scene was shot on an indoor sound stage at MGM Studios in California. The foreground is a set. The woodland behind is a flat backdrop painted by anonymous technicians. A Los Angeles art teacher named Robert Parker was commissioned to supply copies of various Van Gogh canvases in different states of completion. Many other paintings seen in the film are actually photographs of the originals. The garish colours of this image are typical of the crudely mass-produced movie publicity stills of the 1950s and 1960s. Perhaps inadvertently, Kirk Douglas's Van Gogh seems reduced here to a realist, merely copying the lurid world around him.

In 1990 Ryoei Saito, honorary chairman of Daishowa Paper Manufacturing Co., Japan, bought Van Gogh's *Portrait of Dr Gachet* for $82.5 million. Upon Saito's death in 1996 the painting disappeared, and its whereabouts remain a mystery. All we have at present are reproductions, or reproductions of re-enactments.

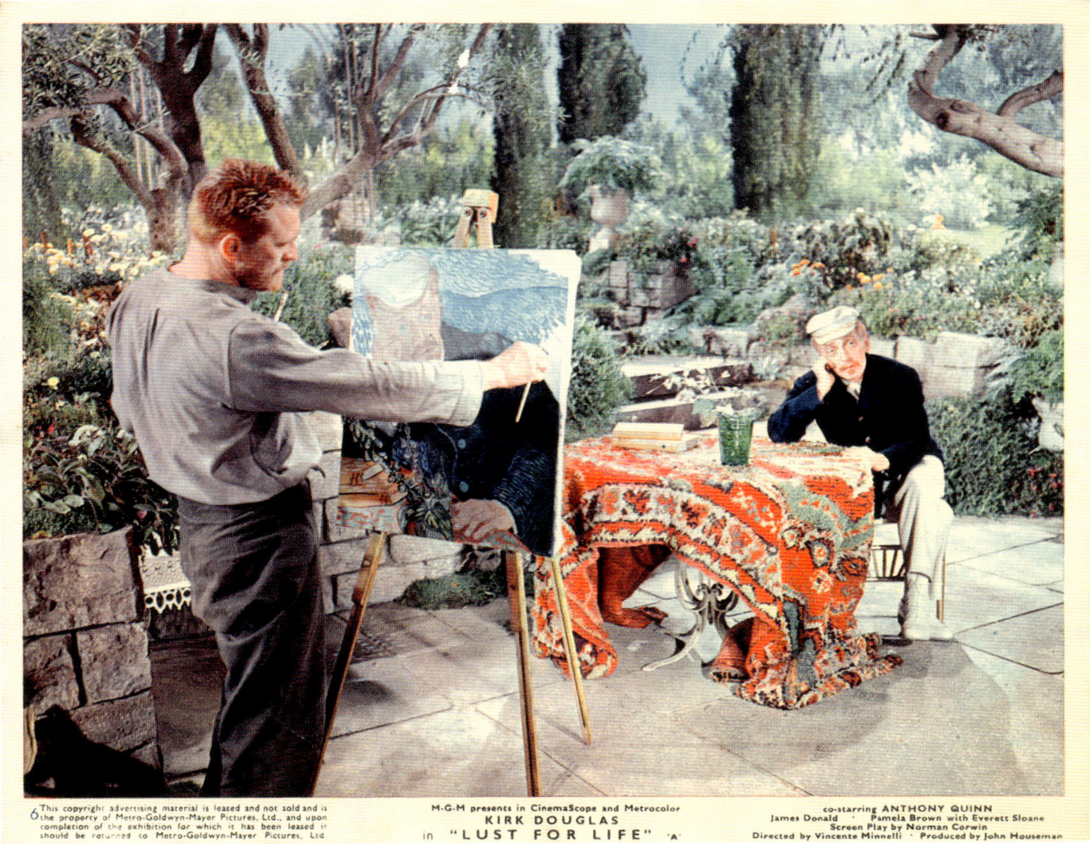
6
This copyright advertising material is leased and not sold and is the property of Metro-Goldwyn-Mayer Pictures, Ltd., and upon completion of the exhibition for which it has been leased it should be returned to Metro-Goldwyn-Mayer Pictures, Ltd.
M-G-M presents in CinemaScope and Metrocolor
KIRK DOUGLAS
in "LUST FOR LIFE" 'A'
co-starring ANTHONY QUINN
James Donald · Pamela Brown with Everett Sloane
Screen Play by Norman Corwin
Directed by Vincente Minnelli · Produced by John Houseman

LALLA ESSAYDI

Les Femmes du Maroc #30, 2006

COLONIAL AND POST-COLONIAL experience continues to redefine all of the arts. Photography's place in this process is especially pertinent, not least because of its central role in the colonial projects of the nineteenth and early twentieth centuries. The travelling camera classified, ordered, misrepresented, excluded, stereotyped and limited. And then it played its part in resistance by helping to mobilize, giving a visual presence to the marginalized, revealing suppressed truths, and highlighting representations as things to be contested rather than accepted. But perhaps what has made photography truly vital here is its inherent hybridity. There was never anything pure about photography. Not only does it borrow from all the other arts, but also it is not owned by the arts, having legitimate functions in all aspects of visual culture. Photography is a space of slippage and borrowing, of translation and fusion.

We talk of 'visual culture', but really it is 'scripto-visual', because photography and writing have been combined all along. Many photographic practices developed in full knowledge that words would play their integral part. From fashion, forensics and family albums to photojournalism and documentary. Making sense of photography should really be a matter of studying the complex interactions of word and image. And yet, photography is still thought of as purely visual. One reason is the stubborn idea that there is something universal in photography, that it knows no boundaries, geographic or linguistic. But the closer photography comes to universals, the closer it comes to empty clichés and convention.

And so, a great deal of photography's post-colonial energy has involved new forms of scripto-visuality. Born in Morocco, Lalla Essaydi has lived in France and the United States. Much of her photography has incorporated Arabic calligraphy. It is inscribed in henna upon the fabric and faces that make up her tableaux portraits of women. In its classical form, Arabic calligraphy was an almost exclusively male preserve. Essaydi's images are literally (and literarily) covered in it. But it is largely illegible. Language is present but denied its authority, rerouted into the visual design. Her iconography is a rerouting too, of the typically colonial views of North African and Arabic women as both sequestered and available.

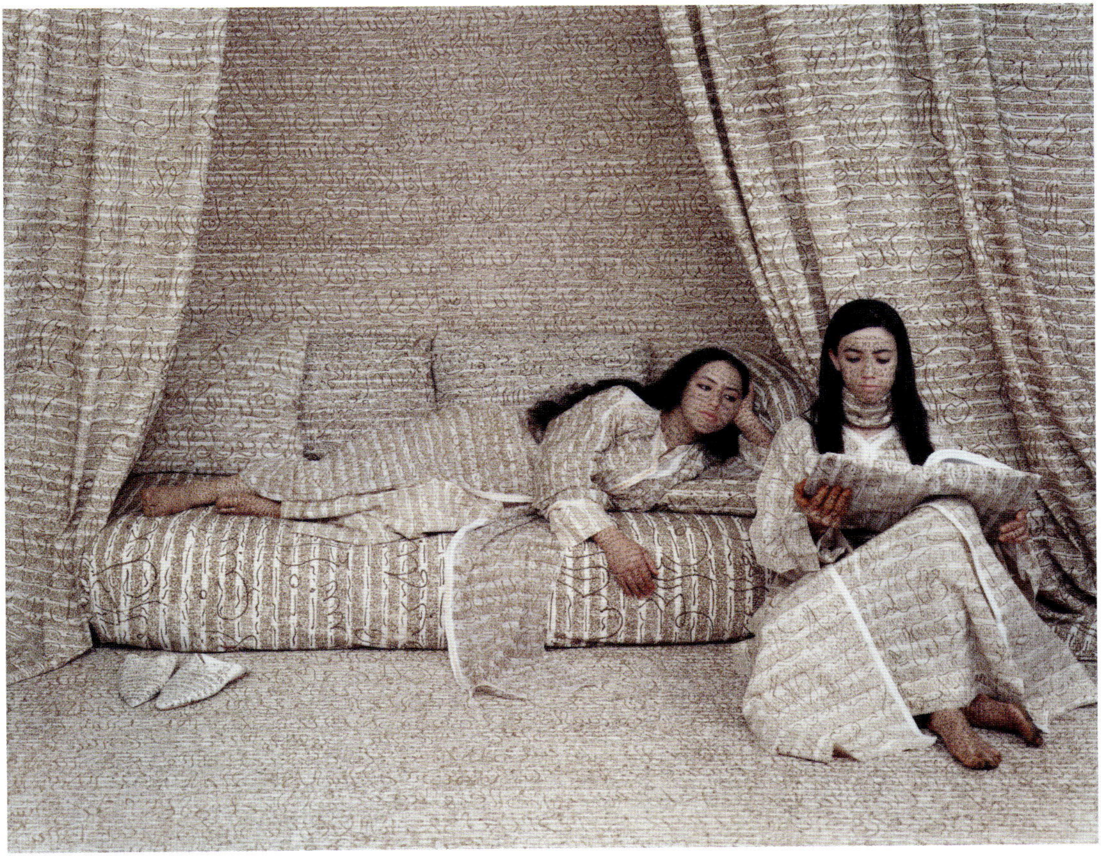

GREGORY CREWDSON

Untitled

FROM THE SERIES 'THE DREAM HOUSE', 2002

'THE DREAM HOUSE' IS A SUITE of photographs envisioned by the North American artist Gregory Crewdson. They were all shot in an empty ranch house he had come across in Rutland, Vermont. A woman who had raised a family there had died four years earlier, leaving everything behind, untouched. It was a home deprived of the life that had once animated it.

Over several years, Crewdson had already established the central subject matter and approach for his art: carefully orchestrated scenes of mildly surreal disquiet amid white, middle-class semi-rural communities. The *New York Times* commissioned Crewdson to make images in the house. He invited several film stars to collaborate, including Gwyneth Paltrow, Tilda Swinton and Julianne Moore.

If Crewdson's images relate to cinema, it is in their preparation and collaboration, and their lighting codes. The people are not caught mid-gesture, as they might be in a single frame from a film. They tend to hold still and silent poses, as if troubled or traumatized into immobility. They act as if they are posing, or pose as if they are acting. Many film actors are familiar with this, since most movie productions have a 'stills' photographer who is tasked with working on set to turn unfolding cinematic scenes into single images for publicity purposes.

This image from 'The Dream House' features Julianne Moore, an actor who has developed a measured, highly restrained and minimal kind of performance style, reminiscent of movie stars from the silent era. In cinema, when the image is moving and the subject is dramatic, the viewer's gaze is more or less trained to watch for facial expressions and bodily gestures. When the image is still and mute, the gaze is free to wander, taking in small details that would otherwise pass by. The viewer can study the image forensically. Moore's face is the focus of the composition, and its performance has clearly received a great deal of attention, from Moore herself, from Crewdson, from the make-up team, and from the lighting crew. And yet Moore's feet, parts of the body that cannot really perform, cannot act, are there to be looked at with equal attention, should you wish.

THE PEOPLE IN CREWDSON'S IMAGES ARE NOT CAUGHT MID-GESTURE ... THEY TEND TO HOLD STILL AND SILENT POSES, AS IF TROUBLED OR TRAUMATIZED INTO IMMOBILITY.

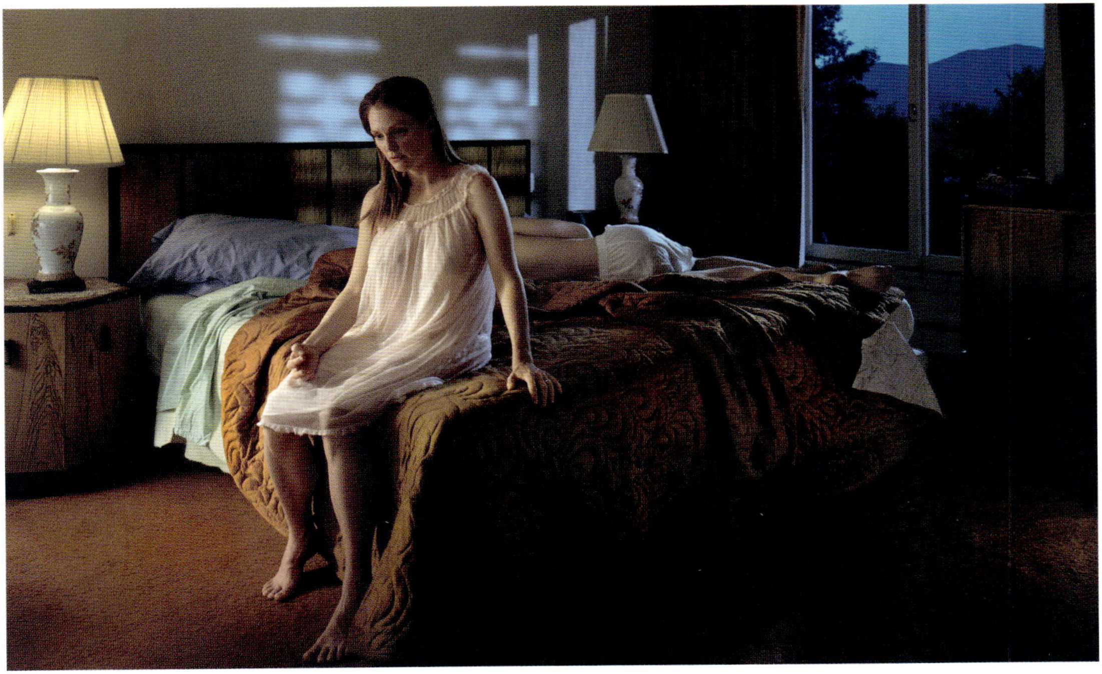

JACQUES-ANDRÉ BOIFFARD

Big toe of a man, 30 years old, 1929

IN 1924, WHILE STILL A YOUNG medical student, Jacques-André Boiffard met André Breton, the key figure in what would soon become French surrealism. Boiffard's first contribution was to co-write, with Paul Éluard and Roger Vitrac, the preface to the inaugural issue of *La Révolution surrealiste*, the movement's groundbreaking journal. He soon turned to photography, working as an assistant to Man Ray (page 154), and making the images of Parisian streets and shop fronts that punctuate Breton's experimental novel, *Nadja*. In 1928, however, Breton expelled Boiffard from the surrealists. The official reason was aesthetic differences, but it seems that Boiffard had been making photographs of Breton's wife, Simone.

The following year, Boiffard began working with another dissident surrealist, the writer Georges Bataille, who was setting up a new journal, *Documents*. Most of the photographs for which Boiffard is now known were commissioned to accompany articles in Bataille's journal. This image was made in conjunction with Bataille's provocative text 'Le Gros Orteil' (The Big Toe), which appeared in issue no. 6. One of Bataille's abiding interests was 'base materialism', the idea that no matter how sophisticated and moral human culture strives to become, and no matter how much the human body is beautified and idealized, all is squalid beneath. In standing upright, the human head is high, and a long way from the feet planted on the ground, hidden in shoes or in contact with mud. This difference, from one end of the body to the other, corresponds with a split in our self-perception: aspiring to high ideals while knowing our lowly origins. Bataille writes: 'The play of fantasies and fears, of human necessities and aberrations, is in fact such that fingers have come to signify useful action and firm character, the toes stupor and base idiocy [...] Blind, but tranquil and strangely despising his obscure baseness, a given person, ready to call to mind the grandeurs of human history, as when his glance ascends a monument testifying to the grandeur of his nation, is stopped in mid-fight by an atrocious pain in his big toe because, though the most noble of animals, he nevertheless has corns on his feet; in other words, he has feet, and these feet independently lead an ignoble life.'

ONE OF BATAILLE'S ABIDING INTERESTS WAS 'BASE MATERIALISM', THE IDEA THAT NO MATTER HOW MUCH THE HUMAN BODY IS BEAUTIFIED AND IDEALIZED, ALL IS SQUALID BENEATH.

While 'serious' photography was aiming for high art, Bataille and Boiffard understood it has as much to offer in the picturing of the things we would prefer not to confront.

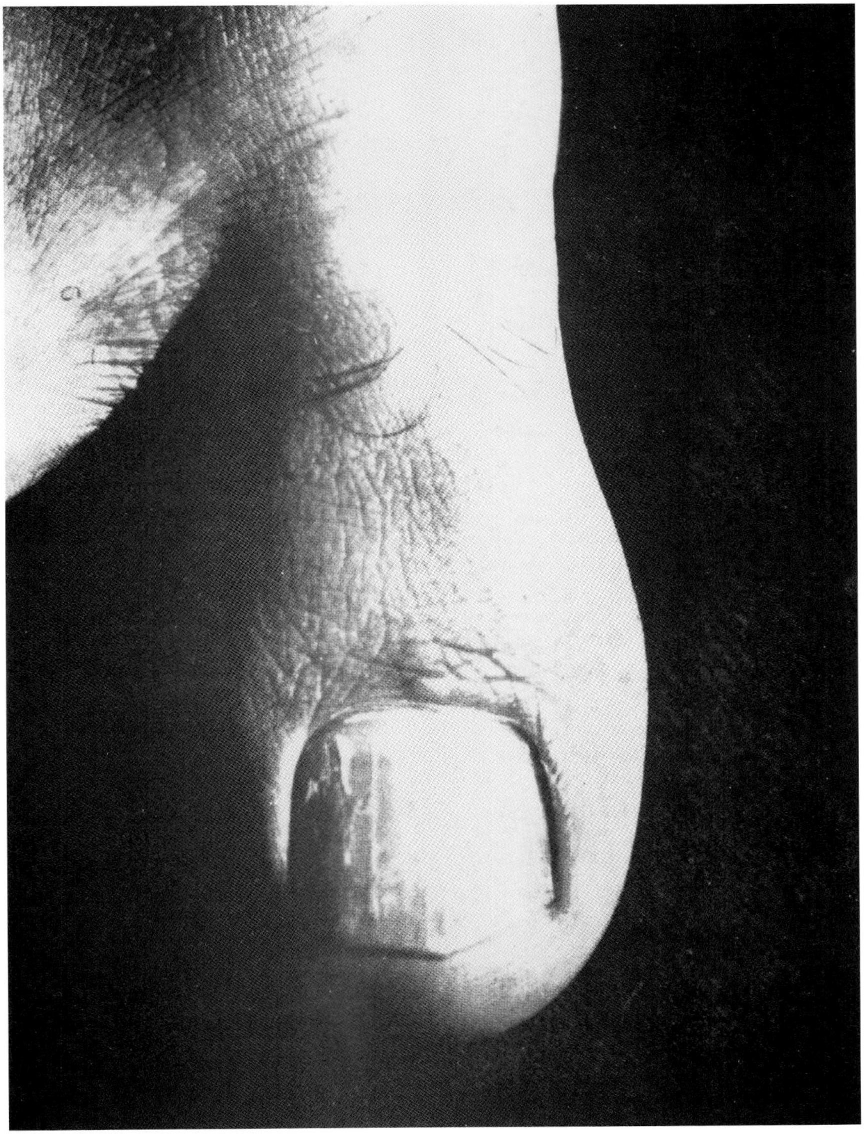

PAUL NOUGÉ

La Naissance de l'objet, 1929–30

PAUL NOUGÉ WAS A LEADING FIGURE among the Belgian surrealists, known more for his writing than for photography. This picture is one of nineteen he made between 1929 and 1930, but which were published only in 1968, as the pocket-sized book *Subversion des images*.

Several of Nougé's photographs show people transfixed or entranced by enigmatic objects. Here, a group of surrealist friends, including the painter René Magritte, await a new one. Is it imminent? Are they its midwives, or gawping spectators? And where exactly are they looking? Not into the void of the fireplace (from which Magritte would later paint a steam train emerging), but to some vague area. A woman's finger almost points, but to nothing in particular. The camera's intent is as mysterious and comic as the group's.

For decades, surrealist art was understood largely through its painting and sculpture, art's traditional mediums. Nevertheless, it was photography that gave fullest expression to the fascination with lucid dreams, broken logic and marooned facts.

Photography could charm, perplex and surprise without being arty or heavy-handed. It could float in that uncertain space between automatic document and expressive will.

Very little surrealist photography was exhibited in the movement's heyday of the 1920s and 1930s, but it was a vital component of its many magazines, journals and books. Where the gallery wall tends to turn everything it presents into art, the printed page can remain an ambiguous space: not *necessarily* art, documentation, observation or research, but a productively uncertain mixture of them all. If surrealism was about crossing boundaries in order to confuse and surprise, then photography was its ideal medium.

IT WAS PHOTOGRAPHY THAT GAVE FULLEST EXPRESSION TO SURREALISM'S FASCINATION WITH LUCID DREAMS, BROKEN LOGIC AND MAROONED FACTS.

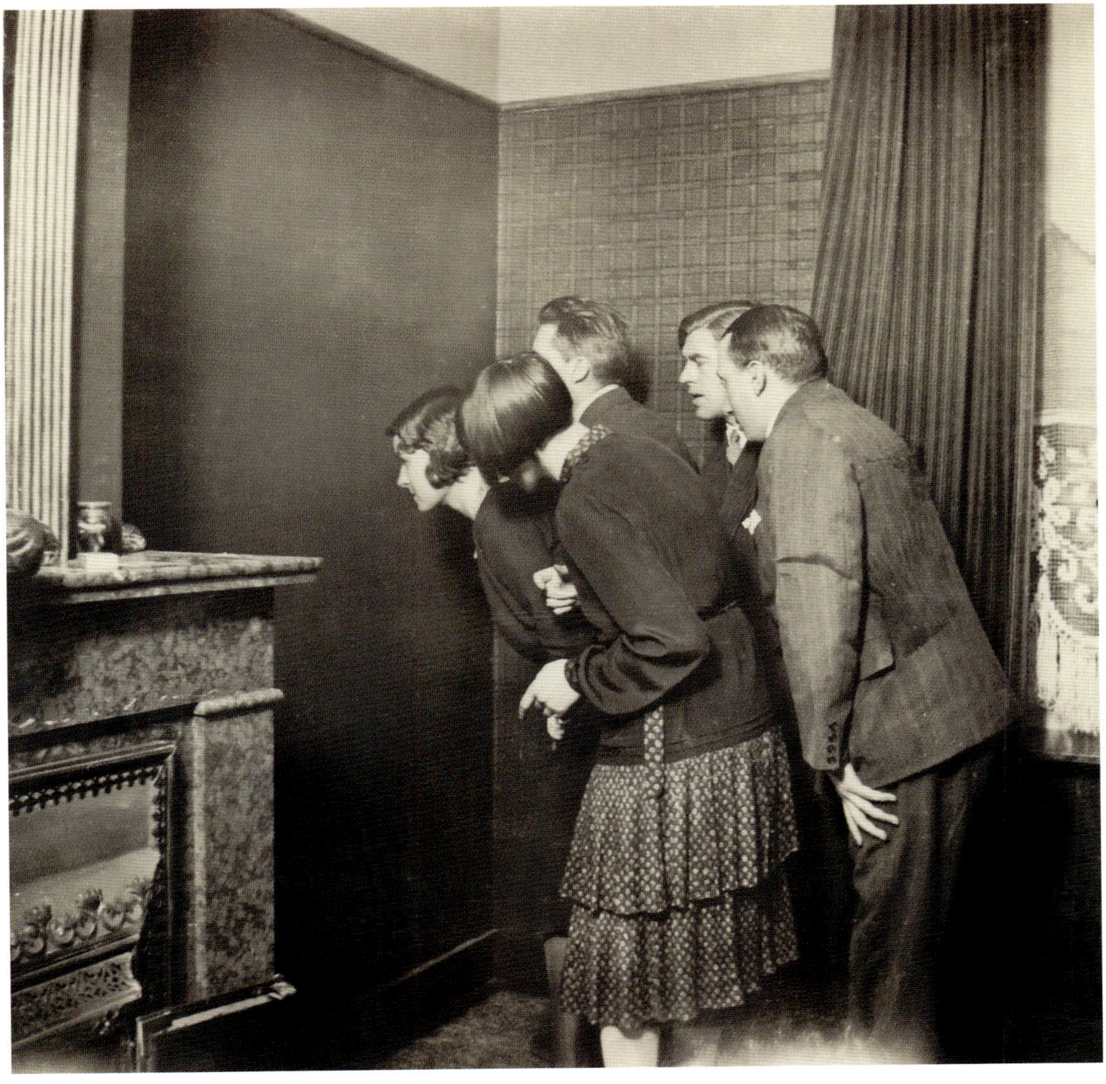

MITCH EPSTEIN

Madison Avenue, NYC, 1973

IN 1973 MITCH EPSTEIN was a student of the photographer Garry Winogrand (page 42), at Cooper Union, New York. In his first lesson on shooting in colour, Winogrand had suggested forgetting about colour altogether. This would help avoid the temptation to make obvious pictures that merely demonstrated colour.

Discussing the work shown here, Epstein recalled: 'I imagine that these well-dressed ladies were walking down Madison Avenue, window-shopping after lunch, when one of them lost a contact lens or earring on the street. What I remember is attempting to photograph over the shoulder of the woman with the polka-dotted blouse, and when that didn't work, I stepped back and incorporated the blouse into the picture. Stepping back enabled me to see the critical focal point: the red finger-nailed hand caressing the street's surface for the lost object—and include the mad array of colored fabrics and chorus of hands, one of which holds a magazine with the word "Authentic".'

Clearly all of this had to happen very quickly. Street photography of this kind relies upon intuition and quick reflexes, balancing intention and purpose with chance and opportunity. It demands a kind of hyper-attentiveness, to which the photographer has to dedicate as much of their physiology as they can. It is not just visual. Making such agile photographs is entirely embodied.

Not surprisingly, then, the best reactive street photographs have been made by younger practitioners, before the inevitable slowing of the nervous system and the encroachment of habits of seeing. Epstein's photograph, made very early in his career, could only have been made at that point.

Very few photographers sustain a long life on such a knife's edge of heightened and speedy observation. Most move to slower, more considered approaches, perhaps with a larger-format camera and even a tripod. Epstein moved in this direction, as did his New York contemporaries Stephen Shore (page 184), Joel Meyerowitz and Joel Sternfeld. Robert Frank (page 248), whose book *The Americans* (1959) became such a benchmark for street photographers, never attempted to work that way again. Only Epstein's tutor, Garry Winogrand, kept at it, prowling in search of something miraculous, like a dance around a lost object.

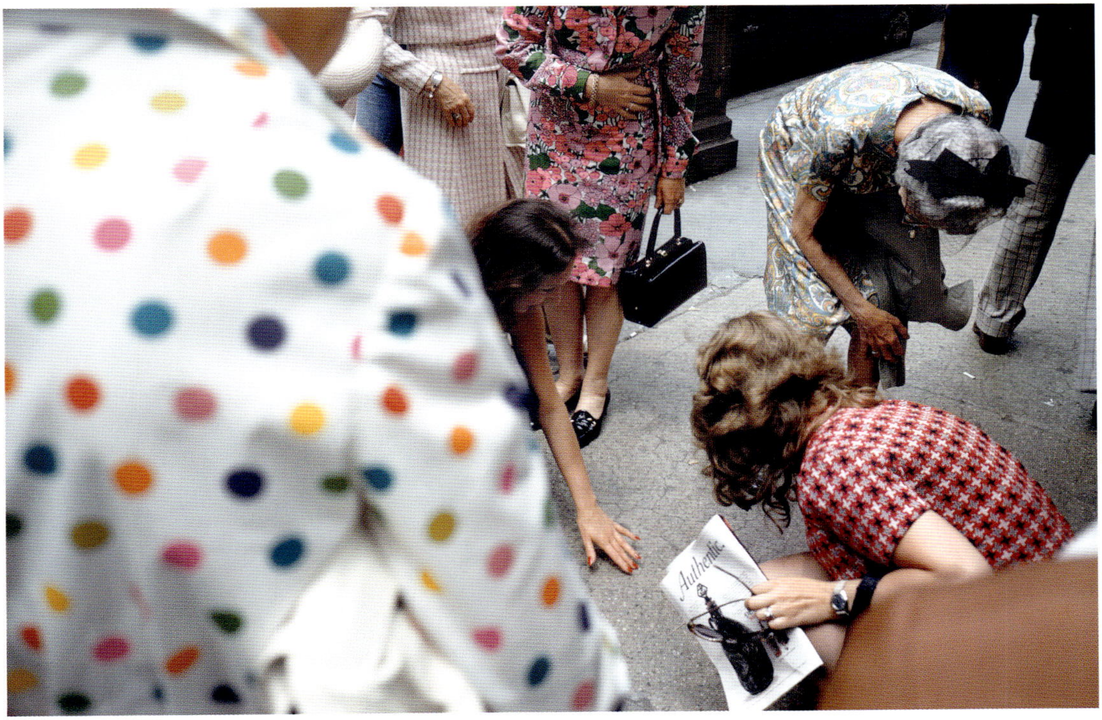
Authentic

TERRI WEIFENBACH

Des oiseaux 33, 2016

IN THE BBC TELEVISION NATURE series *The Life of Birds*, first broadcast in 1998, David Attenborough goes in search of the most complex birdsong. In a forest in South Australia, he tells us: 'There are lots of contenders but this must be one of them, the superb Lyre Bird. He clears a space in his forest to serve as his concert platform. To persuade females to come close and admire his plumes, he sings the most complex song he can manage, and he does that by copying all the songs of the birds he hears around him, such as the kookaburra [...] He can imitate the calls of at least twenty different species. He also, in his attempt to out-sing his rivals, incorporates other sounds he hears in the forest. A camera shutter. Now a camera with a motor drive. A car alarm. And now the sounds of foresters and their chainsaws working nearby.'

The scene is uncanny and disturbing. Without knowing its significance, the Lyre Bird mimics the sound of destruction of its own habitat. It is an example of what Walter Benjamin called a 'dialectical image': a social contradiction or paradox crystallized with such resonant economy that it can shift consciousness irreversibly.

Still photography is mute, so it will never record birdsong, but in itself it is a kind of mimicry. Its images are substitutes and copies that produce knowledge and pleasure. Sometimes that knowledge and pleasure derive from the photograph itself; sometimes the photograph is relaying knowledge and pleasure to be taken in the world it records. Most of the time it is a mix of the two.

Terri Weifenbach takes photographs of the birds that visit her back garden in Washington DC. Most often, she shoots with a wide aperture. This lets the most light into the camera in the shortest time, allowing her to use faster shutter speeds. However, a wide aperture also means the image has a small depth of focus. A flying bird can be shown sharply, but only if it is within that small focus range. In one sense her images feel very photographic, the result of a very particular apparatus. We can see how the camera 'succeeds' and 'fails' to capture the birds.

In another sense, Weifenbach's photographs relate to human vision, and the fact that we too cannot take in everything. Vision is also flawed. Wiefenbach balances what can be photographed and noticed with what escapes. We could read this as a kind of humility. The camera's hold on the birds is gentle. They are permitted to slip through its grasp, to elude it and keep their own secrets.

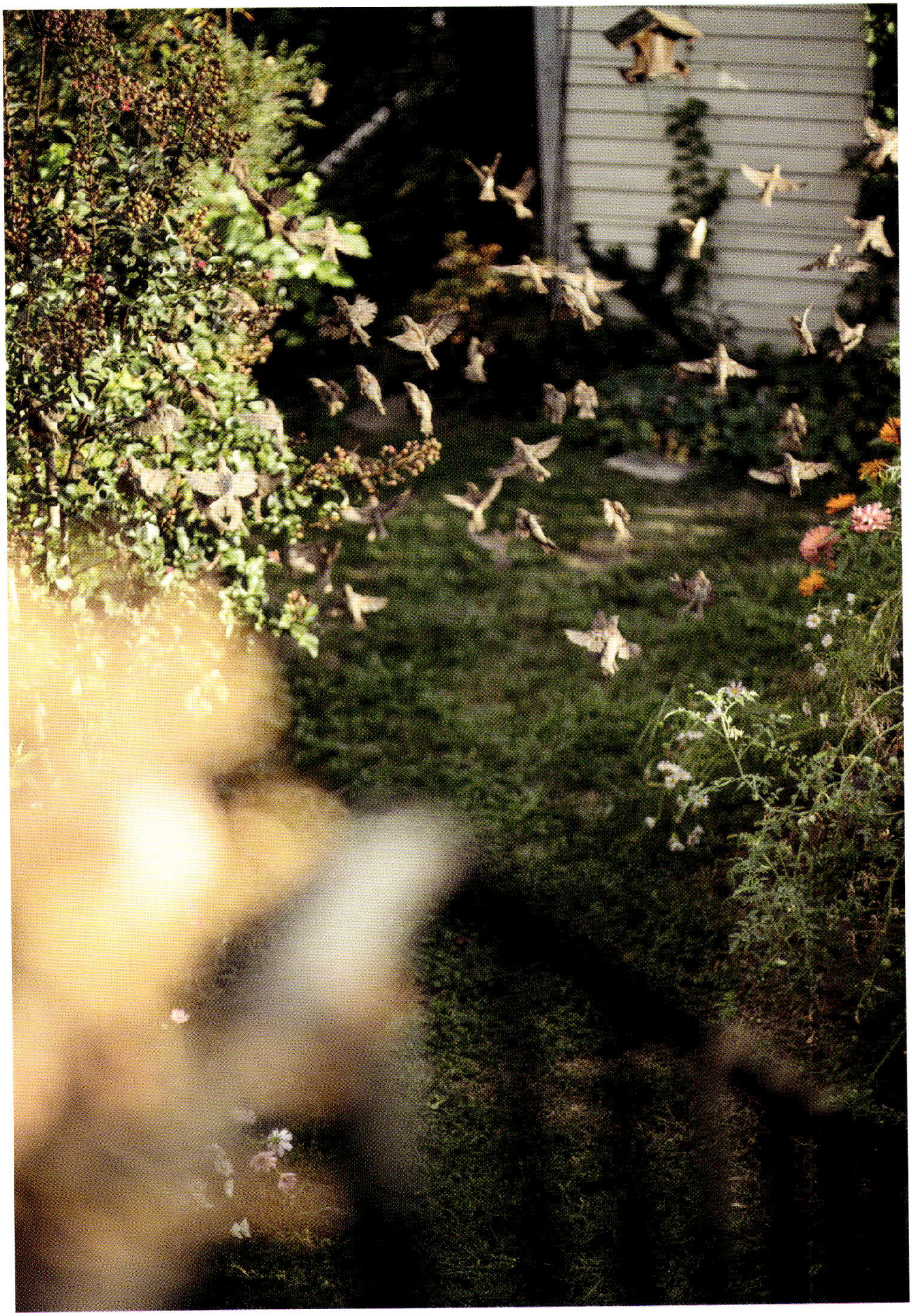

GREGORY HALPERN

Untitled

FROM THE SERIES 'ZZYZX', 2016

ASLEEP IN AN AEROPLANE OVER CALIFORNIA, Gregory Halpern was awoken by an announcement. Those on the left side of the plane would be able to see a huge wildfire below. Halpern was on the right. Landing in Los Angeles, he drove the ninety miles back to the location and made this photograph. The fire had grown and was now out of control. He was obliged to stay back in safety, but this made for a photograph in which the fire is just one element in the landscape, which is itself one part of the planet, which in turn is moving through an obscure corner of the cosmos. Telegraph cables traverse a hillside that looks both ashen and snowy. Licking around the green of the tees near the horizon, the fire is hazy in the long exposure. In that duration, the spinning earth has turned the stars into arcs of light. To Halpern, the fire seemed so vast and unpredictable that it might consume the whole of the state.

The image became part of Halpern's project 'ZZYZX'. Published in book form in 2016, the project is a response to California and the difficulties of picturing a place that has been pictured so much it is hard to see it for oneself. While working on it, Halpern wrote: 'I am interested in the contradictions of California, from its urban sprawl to its natural wonders. It's easy to separate them in our minds, but when it's all seen together—the sublime, the psychedelic and the self-destructive—there's a strange kind of harmony. Photography has a tendency to simplify, but people and places are complicated. From the moment photographers are taught about composition, we are trained to organize the chaos around us. It is sometimes said that photography is uniquely suited to reflect the world. Yet our surroundings are complex to the point of being incomprehensible. I want my photographs to reflect that.'

It is quite clear that California's fires are now more than merely expected and integral parts of the local ecosystem. Their frequency and ferocity are symptoms of our climate crisis. There is much talk of the destruction of the planet. But is not the Earth that needs saving, only our own continuation. The Earth and life upon it will go on without us, in one form or another.

Out in the heavens, beyond the portion of sky trapped by Halpern's photograph, is this planet's eventual end. The Andromeda Galaxy is on a collision course with Earth, and nothing will stop the impact in around 4 billion years. The sun will burn out in around 5 billion years. So we know categorically that a double fate for the planet is written in the stars, whether or not we avert our immediate ecological catastrophe. However, the creatures that will be around to witness whichever astronomical conclusion comes first will be as different from humans as we are from bacteria. Such is evolution. None of this was planned with you in mind, but photography can help you contemplate it.

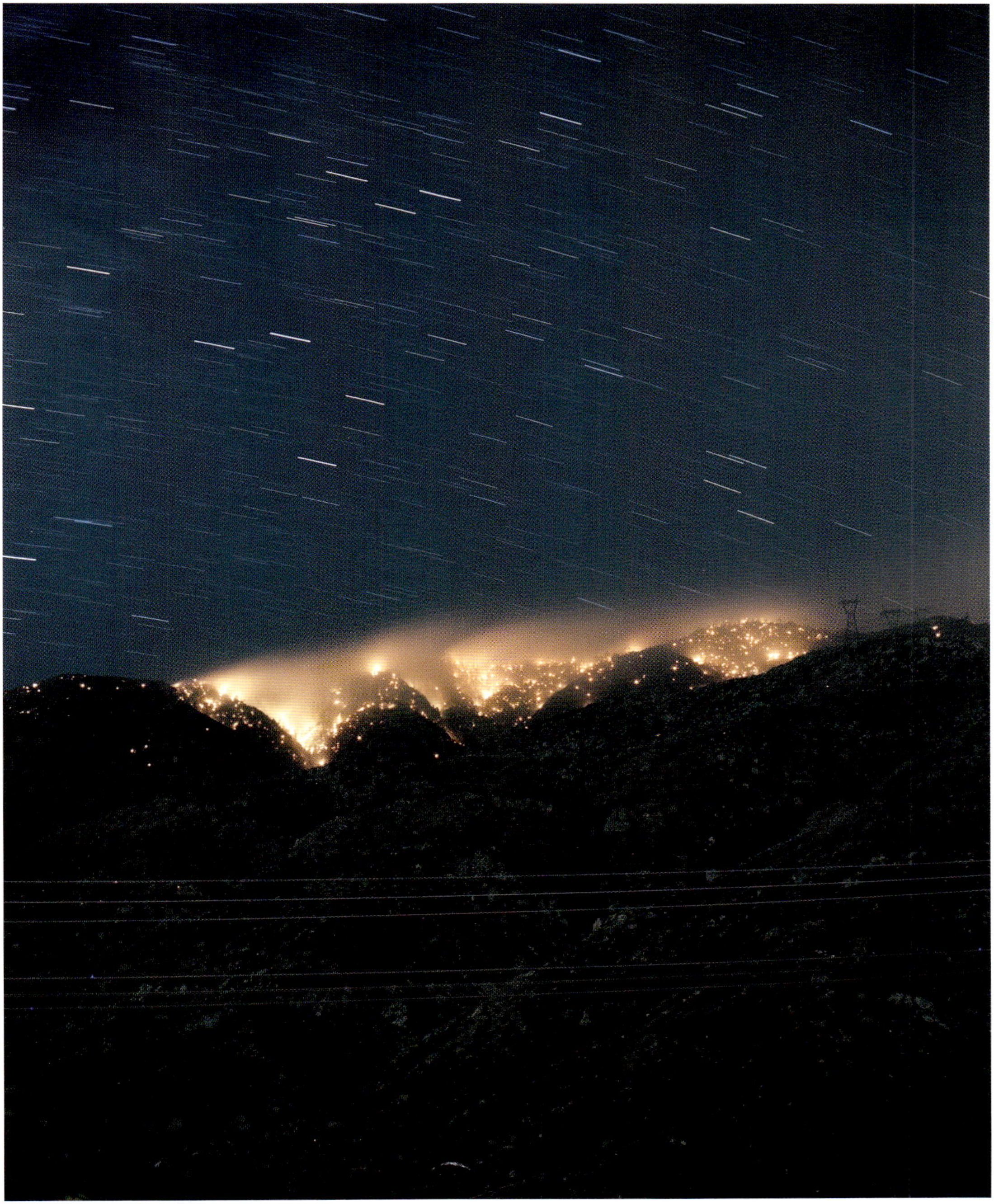

TOSHIO SHIBATA

Nikko City, Tochigi Prefecture, 2013

THE CONTRAST AND COMPROMISE between nature and man-made structures is a perennial subject for photography. In part, this is simply because most modern environments embody these contrasts and compromises. In the few instances when they do not, they are haunted by them. The experience of 'pure' nature is informed by the experience of urbanism and industry, and vice versa.

Photography can render natural and artificial forms equally well. It is a product of industrial development, but it can also be, as William Henry Fox Talbot (pages 198, 224) put it, 'the pencil of nature'. Moreover, it is a technology that harnesses and shapes the natural phenomena of light and optics, and, in the process, it can almost posit itself as natural, and almost absent itself in the face of what it offers.

When the world first saw photographs of the North and South poles, they were less significant for what they showed of the landscapes than for the fact that photography had got there. The camera had colonized those places. Whatever else they document, photographs are records of their own making. The camera is always recording its own condition, although this is rarely what it presumes to communicate. It pictures so well, so 'naturally', that it appears to disappear. The ubiquity of photography only serves to further the disappearance. In being everywhere, it is nowhere. This is why tourists insist on being in their own photographs. Without this, their images will resemble everyone else's. It is also why so many people find it difficult to think about photography with much critical distance. A fish cannot think about water.

The Japanese photographer Toshio Shibata was first of all a painter. That is to say, he moved from an additive medium to a subtractive one. He is as concerned with what is not in the frame, and not communicated, as with what is. He is looking to make images that are elemental in form and theme. Nearly all of them picture civil engineering projects in otherwise natural landscapes. His camera, placed to record and dramatize the interface of the two, suspends obvious judgment.

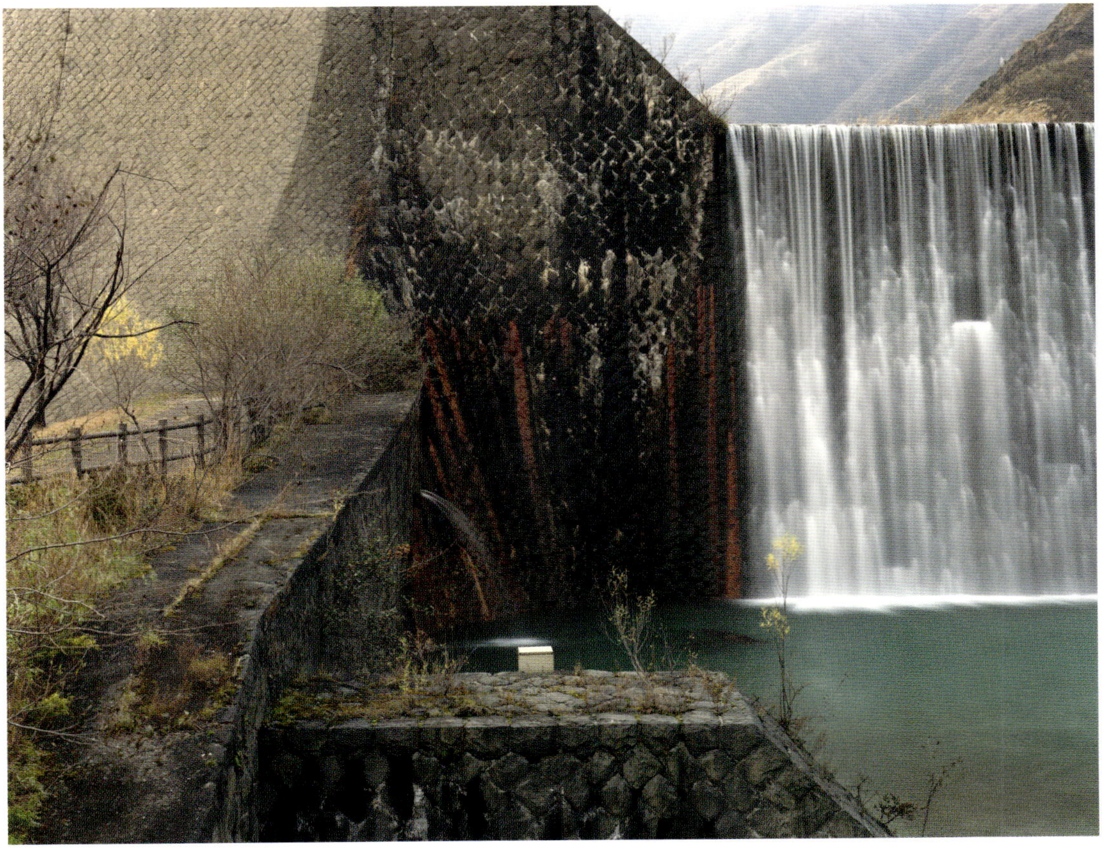

JEFF WALL

Morning Cleaning, Mies van der Rohe Foundation, Barcelona, 1999

IN 1929 THE GERMAN-AMERICAN architect Ludwig Mies van der Rohe designed a pavilion for the International Exposition in Barcelona. It has become one of the pre-eminent symbols of modernism, not least through its complicated relationship with photography.

Rather than housing an exhibit, the structure was intended to *be* the exhibit: a showcase for Mies's thinking about space and materials, and 'an ideal zone of tranquility', as he put it, set apart from the bustle of the exposition. It was also intended to be temporary, and within a year it was dismantled and removed. In its absence, the reputation of the pavilion grew, via images circulated in various publications internationally. In 1983 reconstruction of the pavilion began, using those photographs and the original plans. It reopened in 1986.

In 1999 the Canadian artist Jeff Wall photographed a man named Alejandro, one of a team of three responsible for keeping the pavilion clean. The morning routine was shot every day for two weeks, always from the same camera position. Wall's final image is a digital composite that allows all the detail of the shadows and highlights produced by the strong morning sun to be rendered correctly (a range that is beyond a single exposure).

The picture celebrates the building, but it also sets itself apart. Unlike architectural photography of the 1920s, the point of view here is offset from the pavilion's geometry. Moreover, Wall pictures the space as a site of both tranquillity and work. The cleaners must arrive and leave before the pavilion opens to the paying public. The black carpet is rucked, soap bubbles slide down the glass and the Barcelona chairs – designed by Mies for this building – are out of place. As Wall himself noted: 'These buildings require an especially scrupulous level of maintenance. In more traditional spaces a little dirt and grime is not such a shocking contrast to the whole concept. It can even become patina, but these Miesian buildings resist patina as much as they can.'

WALL'S FINAL IMAGE IS A DIGITAL COMPOSITE THAT ALLOWS ALL THE DETAIL OF THE SHADOWS AND HIGHLIGHTS PRODUCED BY THE STRONG MORNING SUN TO BE RENDERED CORRECTLY.

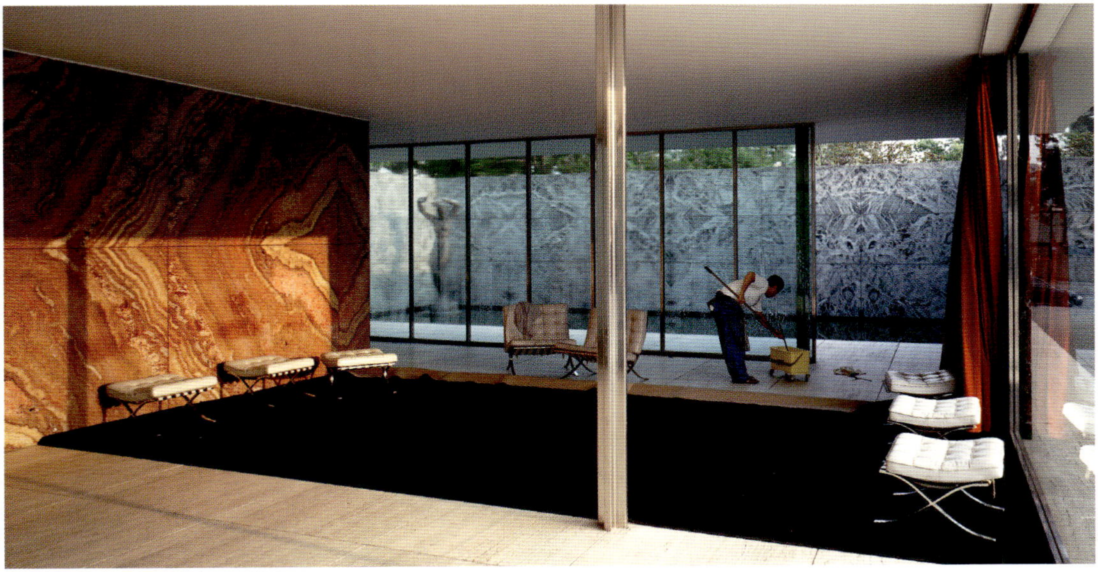

LUIGI GHIRRI

Versailles, 1985

FOR A WHILE, it seemed as though the work of the acutely perceptive Luigi Ghirri was destined for obscurity, beyond his native Italy. The story of colour photography becoming accepted as art in the 1970s and 1980s has tended to be told through the work of North Americans, notably William Eggleston (page 36), Stephen Shore (page 184) and Helen Levitt (page 56). But the lack of recognition for Ghirri was not just a matter of geography. His vision was emphatically impure, rooted in his realization that a camera was the perfect way to hold together all kinds of hybrid influences.

The basic craft of photography could not be simpler, particularly for the kind of notational images Ghirri made with his basic camera. Beyond the choices of vantage point, framing and exposure, there was not much more to his photographic procedure. What gives his images their distinctive and sophisticated character was his ability to use a camera to allow what was in front of him to meet his intellectual and aesthetic understanding. Seeing is informed by what has been experienced and learned already. In almost every photograph by Ghirri, there are echoes and resonances of other images, other times, other places, other arts.

Ghirri turned to photography and writing having first been a surveyor. In the 1970s and 1980s he produced a series of thoughtful photo-essays for the architecture magazine *Lotus International*. His now much-loved photograph of the Palace of Versaille appeared on the cover of issue no. 52. Inside, in an essay titled 'Objective Vision', Ghirri wrote of his desire for a 'holistic photography', one that was open to all artistic ideas, from painting and cinema to music, literature, poetry and architecture. He noted, too, how photography could play with time, sliding the present into the past while summoning the past to the present. Indeed, for Ghirri, photography could be honest only if it accepted all these complicated times and influences.

Ghirri recognized that photography's relation to built form could be rich, multilayered, subjective and, as a result, true to experience. There is a beguiling formal perfection here, but it is not quite the perfection of the architect's ideal view of the building and its gardens. Ghirri finds his own formality, one that recognizes the architectural ideal but also allows us to see what has happened to Versailles. The place is a living archaism, a tourist destination and a site of time travel. The milky lightmakes everything visible but also makes it strange, even uncanny. Ghirri permits us to see the place almost as a model of itself, dreamlike and suspended in time for our contemplation.

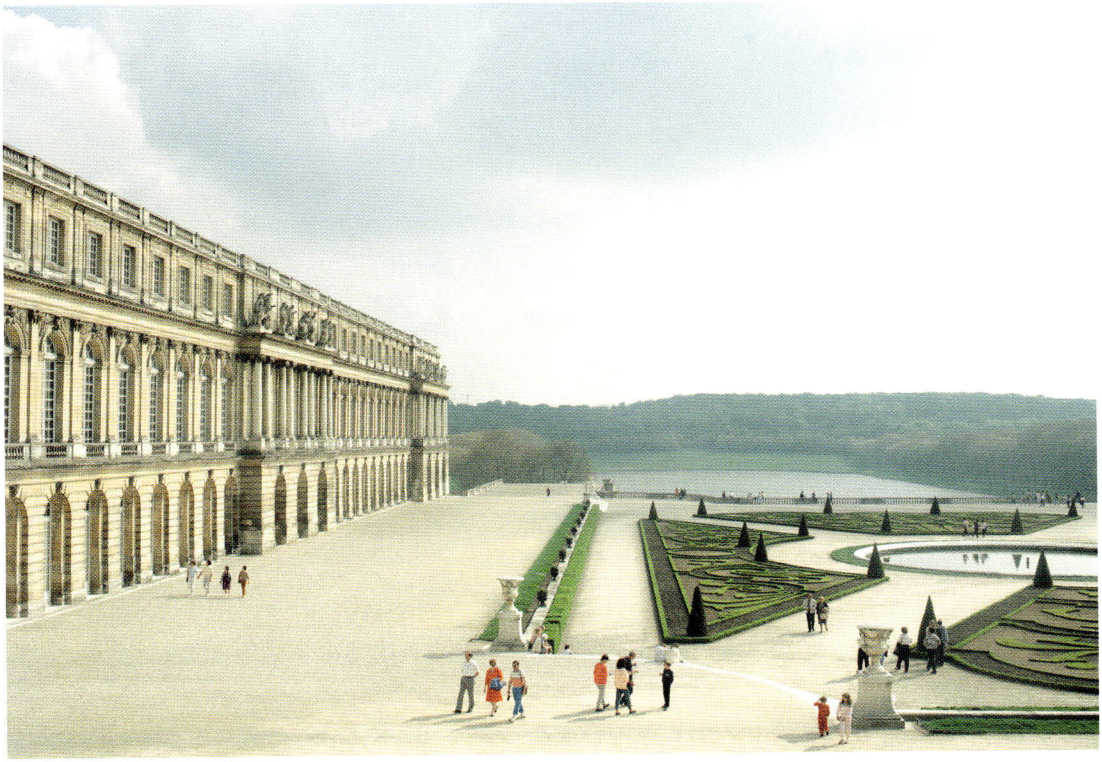

GUSTAVE LE GRAY

Vue du Salon de 1850–1851, c. 1850–51

THE PARIS SALONS WERE LARGE, state-sponsored exhibitions, primarily of painting and sculpture, held annually between 1737 and 1880. By the mid-1800s they had become important events in the French cultural calendar, visited by large numbers of the public. The Salon of 1850 opened on 30 December and closed on 6 March 1851. It included paintings by Courbet, Meissonier, Millet and Van Gogh, and sculptures by Pradier, Cordier and Barye.

Gustave Le Gray was one of the most significant French photographers of the nineteenth century. He made a great number of aesthetic and technical advances, and was also a sensitive documenter of sculpture and painting. He photographed a number of the Paris Salons, beginning in 1850. The best of these images were attempts to capture the mood and atmosphere of the galleries as much as the artworks. Photographed without visitors, the rooms appear ghostly. No human eyes fall upon the mute depictions in oil and marble. The glass lens of Le Gray's camera, itself a kind of spectral visitor, captures what was there, for viewers who were not.

Le Gray's photography was deeply sympathetic to these spaces, but he grasped how profoundly different photography was from the other arts it could picture. Its frozen realism tended to mortify the living and animate the dead. Sculptures often look livelier in photographs than they do in real life, since the medium disguises their silence and stillness.

This image was made under difficult lighting conditions, and with photographic materials that were still primitive. But great work often emerges from the struggle against limitations. Here, Le Gray positions his camera so that the outline of the liveliest and most brightly lit sculpture is picked out against the velvet darkness of the painting in the shadows behind. The contrast is even more dramatic when we know, as Le Gray surely did, that the painting was by that other great Gustave. It is Courbet's *Burial at Ornans* (1849–50), which was being exhibited for the first time.

PHOTOGRAPHED WITHOUT VISITORS, THE ROOMS APPEAR GHOSTLY. NO HUMAN EYES FALL UPON THE MUTE DEPICTIONS IN OIL AND MARBLE. THE GLASS LENS OF LE GRAY'S CAMERA, ITSELF A KIND OF SPECTRAL VISITOR, CAPTURES WHAT WAS THERE, FOR VIEWERS WHO WERE NOT.

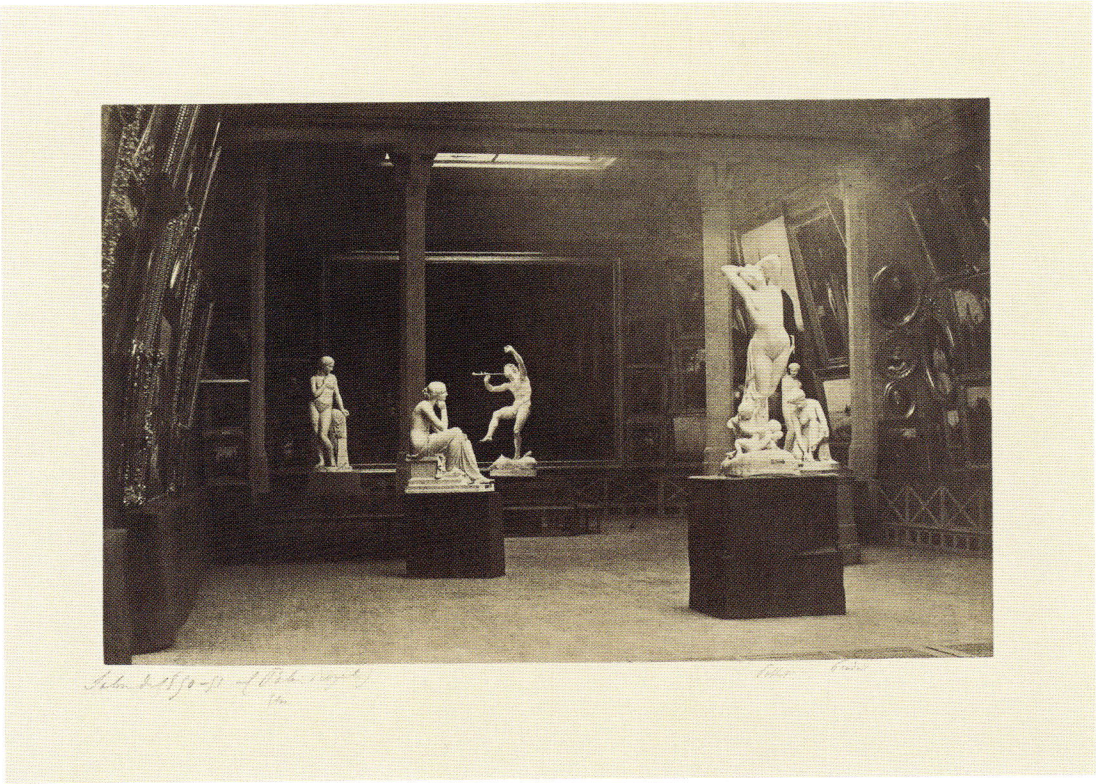

BRUCE NAUMAN

Self-Portrait as a Fountain, 1966–67/1970

UNTIL THE 1950s, there were stark differences between an artist's studio and a photography studio, if not in practice then in public perception. A photography studio was a clean space, for more or less commercial work. A photographer would come, take shots of people or objects in controlled light, clear up, and leave. Artists' studios, for painters or sculptors, were more psychologically charged spaces of creation and failure.

After the Second World War, catalogues and magazines began to carry increasing numbers of images of artists at work. Think of the photographs taken of the Abstract Expressionist painter Jackson Pollock, leaning out over canvases spread on the floor, caught in the balletic movements with which he dripped his paint. Such images emphasized process as much as the final result. The artwork was becoming inseparable from the performance of its making. Once a space set aside, the studio was becoming a kind of stage.

Emerging in the second half of the 1960s, the North American artist Bruce Nauman identified with no particular medium. He moved freely between painting, sculpture, photography, video and performance. He would use cameras to document actions he performed in his studio, and the resulting films and photographs would be exhibited. These were works in themselves, but also records of artistic activity.

Self-Portrait as a Fountain uses photography to exploit this slippage. Nauman performs as a statue, relying on the ossifying effect of the still image to render his brief action permanent. One of Nauman's lifelong influences has been the work of Marcel Duchamp from the 1910s and 1920s, which was rediscovered by a younger generation of artists in the late 1950s and 1960s. This photograph might be a reference to the urinal that Duchamp exhibited in 1917 as a 'ready-made' titled *Fountain*.

NAUMAN WOULD USE CAMERAS TO DOCUMENT ACTIONS HE PERFORMED IN HIS STUDIO, AND THE RESULTING FILMS AND PHOTOGRAPHS WOULD BE EXHIBITED. THESE WERE WORKS IN THEMSELVES, BUT ALSO RECORDS OF ARTISTIC ACTIVITY.

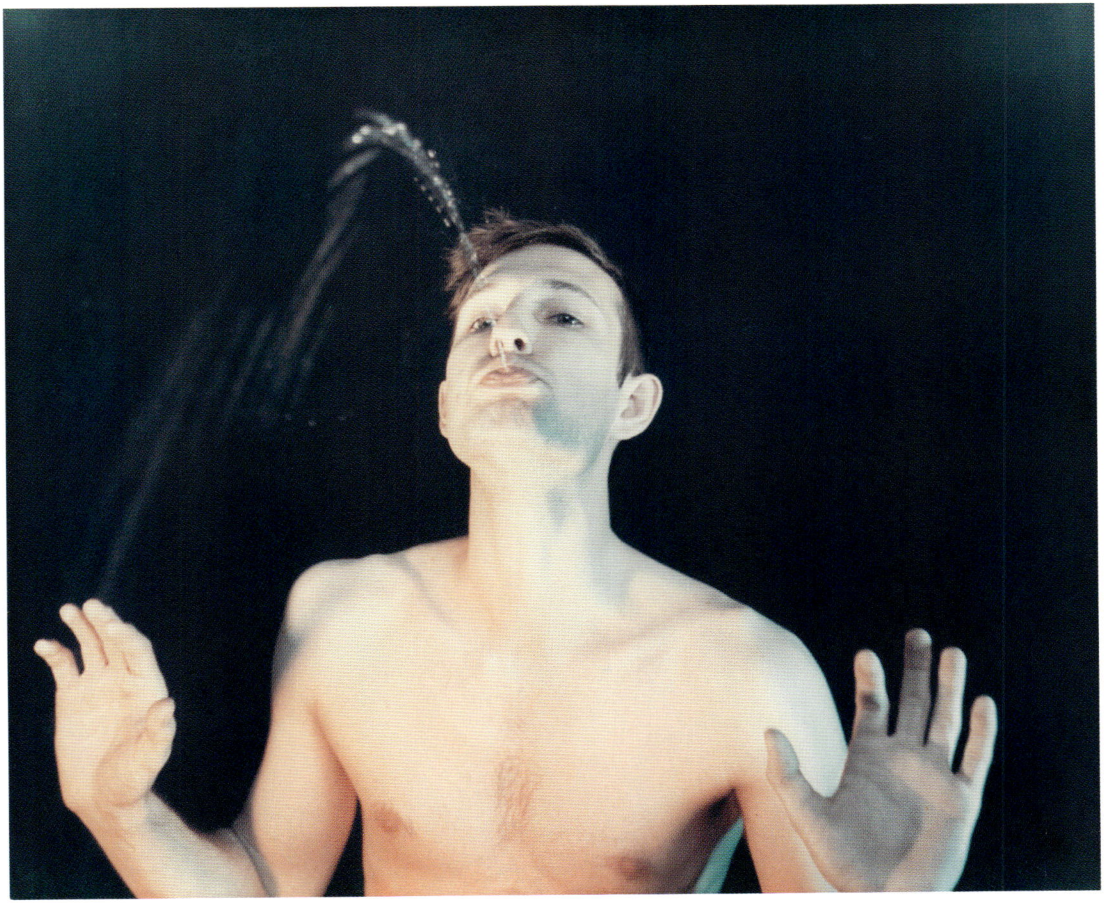

ALFRED STIEGLITZ

Marcel Duchamp's Fountain

PAGE 3 OF *THE BLIND MAN*, NO. 2, MAY 1917, EDITED BY MARCEL DUCHAMP, BEATRICE WOOD AND HENRI-PIERRE ROCHÉ

IN 1917 THE ARTIST MARCEL DUCHAMP submitted a urinal – titled *Fountain* and signed 'R. Mutt' – for inclusion in the first annual exhibtion of the Society of Independent Artists, New York. Duchamp proposed that any object could be nominated as an artwork. He called his own such objects 'ready-mades'. *Fountain* was refused by the society, and the object was soon lost, but not before being photographed, by Alfred Stieglitz. Duchamp wanted the encounter with his ready-mades to be like the flash of recognition we get when looking at a photographic snapshot. He was also fascinated by the way the reputation of an artwork could be carried by word of mouth, by statements, and through photographic reproduction.

Stieglitz was a leading photographic artist, publisher and gallerist who championed the latest avant-garde art. He documented *Fountain* on a pedestal in front of a painting. In 1917 plain white walls were more common in public lavatories than in art galleries, and it was important that the photograph placed *Fountain* in an art context.

It was taken for issue no. 2 of the journal *The Blind Man*, which aimed to publicize the scandal of Duchamp's gesture. On the page, the image is attended by three separate texts: 'Fountain by R. Mutt', 'Photograph by Alfred Stieglitz' and 'The Exhibit Refused by the Independents'.

Duchamp's urinal-as-artwork alluded to low bodily functions and was not gender neutral. Men are more intimate with urinals than women, but women were involved in Duchamp's enterprise. One of the editors of *The Blind Man* was Beatrice Wood, and *Fountain* was actually submitted on Duchamp's behalf by Louise Norton, who also wrote an eloquent defence of it: 'They say any artist paying six dollars may exhibit. Mr. Richard Mutt sent in a fountain. Without discussion this article disappeared and never was exhibited. What were the grounds for refusing Mr. Mutt's fountain:— 1. Some contended it was immoral, vulgar. 2. Others it was plagiarism, a plain piece of plumbing. Now Mr. Mutt's fountain is not immoral, that is absurd, no more than a bath tub is immoral. It is a fixture that you see every day in plumbers' show windows. Whether Mr. Mutt with his own hands made the fountain or not has no importance. He CHOSE it. He took an ordinary article of life, placed it so that its useful significance disappeared under the new title and point of view—created a new thought for that object.'

For nearly half a century, *Fountain* existed only as documentation and hearsay. The absence of an artwork may be no obstacle to its reputation or influence, especially if it is a conceptual gesture akin to a photograph anyway. Only in 1964 did *Fountain* resurface. In Italy, an architect made a steel matrix based on Stieglitz's photograph. Then a urinal company was commissioned to make an edition of eight copies, which Duchamp signed, as R. Mutt.

Fountain by R. Mutt

Photograph by Alfred Stieglitz

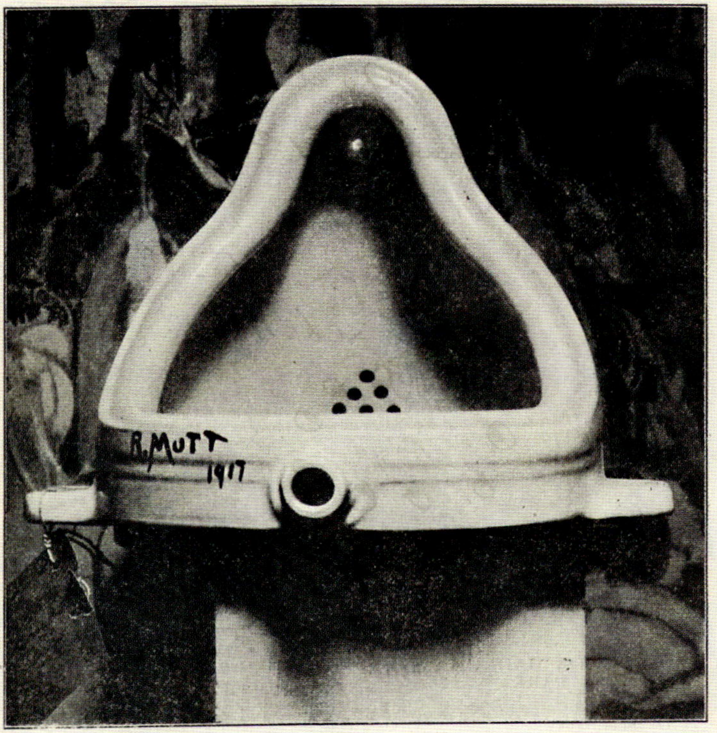

THE EXHIBIT REFUSED BY THE INDEPENDENTS

JACQUES-HENRI LARTIGUE

My Butterflies Gala, 1935

THERE IS SOMETHING A LITTLE 'Peter Pan' about photography, with its promise to stop time and put off growing up. Of course, the promise is also *deathly*, because it cannot be kept, and the arrested moment will inevitably highlight our own unstoppable passage through time.

Jacques-Henri Lartigue was the most Pan-like of photographers. As the son of a wealthy banker, his youth was idyllic, and the only expectations were that he should live well. He received his first camera in 1902, aged seven, and set about recording eight decades of extraordinary change. In 1909 he photographed his older brothers, who had got in early on the craze for manned flight. By 1971 he was on a commercial Boeing 747, photographing its wing over the Atlantic. In between, world wars came and went, architecture was totally transformed, fashion circled back on itself, and modern art went through several revolutions. But Lartigue's two passions remained constant: an adoration of beauty, and the pursuit of *fun*. He was that rare thing in the twentieth century: an artist whose prime subject was joy. Of course, pursue joy too zealously and it can start to look melancholy.

Photography was Lartigue's private passion. For decades, only friends and family saw his pictures, and only a handful were published. If he had any reputation at all, it was as a society painter and interior designer. Then, in 1963, Lartigue came to wider attention. A selection of his photographs appeared in *Life* magazine (somewhat overshadowed by images of President Kennedy's assassination), and New York's Museum of Modern Art presented an exhibition of his work. Overnight, the diminutive Lartigue was hailed as a giant of photography. Spotlit in his sixties, he now felt his great task was to organize his own past, which had never ceased to pile up around him as images. He began assembling large albums, sticking in prints and writing captions, telling his story not as it had happened but how his photographs prompted him to remember it. In the end, there were 133 albums up to 1986, the year he died.

This photograph appears in an album from 1935. For a number of years, Lartigue designed annual galas for a chic venue on the French Riviera. In this particular year, he painted giant flowers on the panelled walls and hung thousands of paper-cut butterflies from the ceiling. It was all conceived with a photographic eye. As he recalled: 'A chandelier in the big room lights up. I jump! [...] then suddenly the other chandeliers fill with light and then all the spotlights at once light my panels, the ceiling and innumerable multicolored butterflies like a cloud of confetti frozen by a snapshot.'

All the effort was for one night only, but Lartigue's pictures remain. Like bugs in amber.

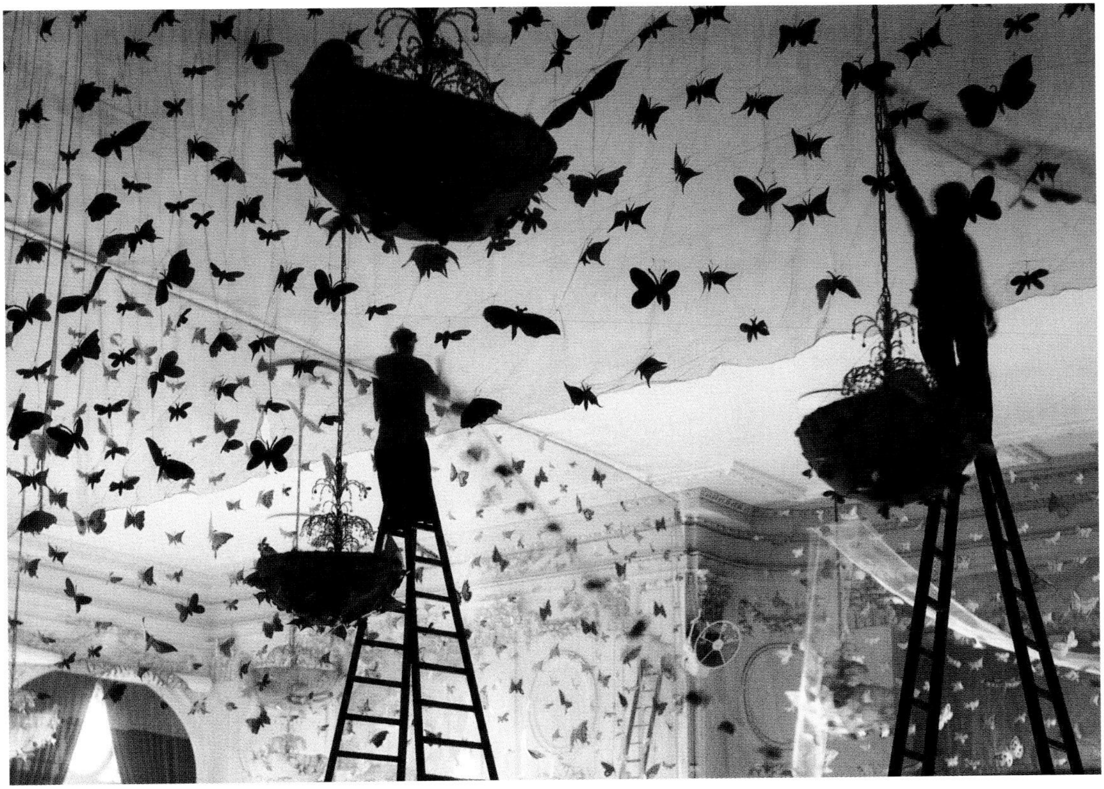

BRASSAÏ

Pages from *Les Sculptures de Picasso* (1949), with an essay by Daniel-Henry Kahnweiler

AT WHAT POINT DOES A PHOTOGRAPHIC document of a sculpture become an artwork in its own right?

For the first few decades of his career, Pablo Picasso was known as a painter. *Les Sculptures de Picasso* (1949) was the first book to present his three-dimensional work. The photographs were taken by Brassaï (Gyula Halász), a close friend of Picasso who had been shooting the artist and his sculptures since the 1930s. Early examples of these images had appeared in the first issue of the surrealist magazine *Minotaure*, in 1933.

PHOTOGRAPHY CAN MAKE EPHEMERAL THINGS PERMANENT, AND MARGINAL THINGS MONUMENTAL.

The book opens on a formal image of Picasso posing with his hand around the neck of a bronze. This is the standard way any illustrated book about a sculptor begins. It proceeds in chronological order with fairly standard photos, shot either in the studio or against plain backgrounds. Most of the works are in wood, bronze or plaster.

Then, something strange happens, and quite unannounced. The role of photography begins to change. We see a piece of wood the size and shape of a cigar, resting on a matchbox. The two objects seem less like a sculpture than a sort of sculptural opportunity, depending on how you look at them. It may have been something Brassaï chanced upon in Picasso's studio, but we cannot be sure. The camera records the arrangement but also makes it significant, and perhaps more sculptural. Photography can make ephemeral things permanent, and marginal things monumental. Opposite we see a paper flower, its stem pressed into the end of a crusty baguette. The assembly survives only as an image.

Later in the book there is a photograph of *Bull's Head* (1941), Picasso's remarkable bronze casting of a bicycle seat and handlebars. This sculpture is as effective in a photograph as it is in real life. On the opposite page we see a collision between two very different kinds of object. It is described as 'Wooden head placed on a radiator', 1943. This is not a title as such, leaving it unclear as to whether the radiator is part of the work or an addition occasioned by Brassaï's camera. The radiator is certainly a major part of the photograph.

Brassaï is credited in the book as the photographer, but not as a collaborator. We are left to encounter these playful slippages between sculpture and photography, and draw our own conclusions.

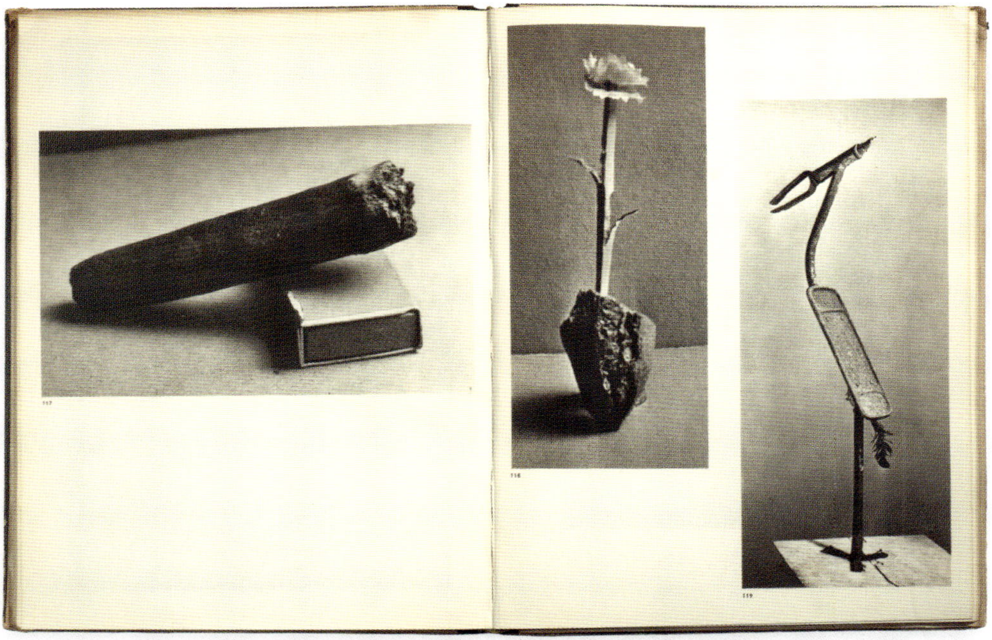
117
119

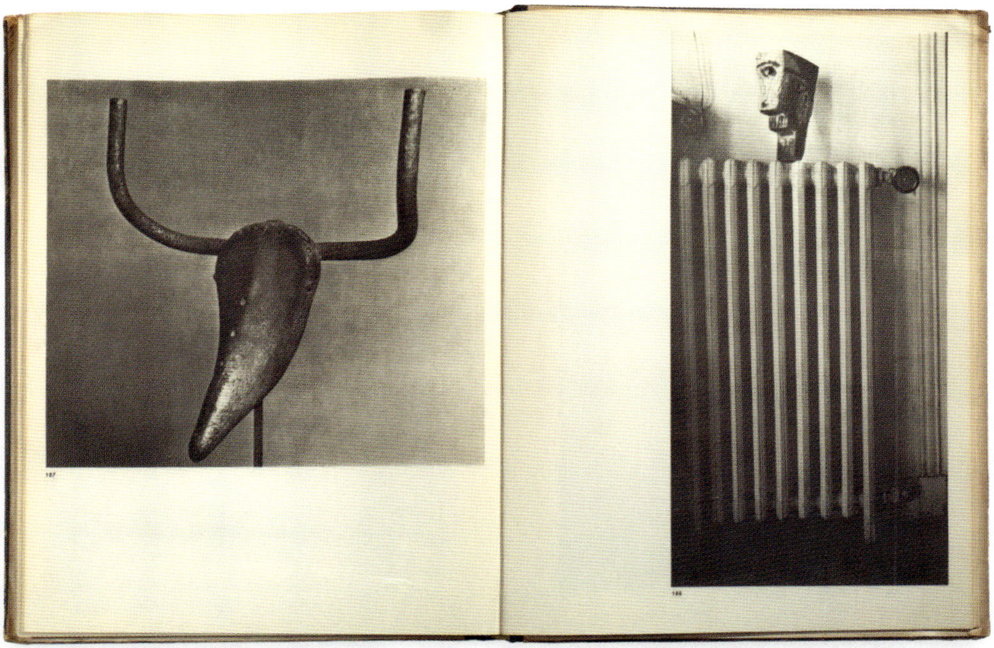
107

MAN RAY

Dust Breeding, 1920

THE ARTIST MAN RAY began as a painter and sculptor, and taught himself photography as a way to document and publicize his work. In 1920 he was asked by the influential collector Katherine S. Dreier to photograph a number of pieces in her collection. 'The thought of photographing the work of others was repugnant to me, beneath my dignity as an artist,' Man Ray recalled in his memoir, *Self-Portrait*, but he needed the money. Pondering the commission, he visited his friend Marcel Duchamp in his New York studio. The place was filthy, and in the middle of the room was a sheet of glass covered in dust. Duchamp had been letting the dust accumulate as one of the many stages in the making of his great opus, *The Bride Stripped Bare by Her Bachelors, Even* (also known as *The Large Glass*; 1915–23).

Duchamp suggested Man Ray practise his photography. The resulting image was strange: an oblique gaze at an obscure surface with no obvious subject matter or scale. It was first published in October 1922, in the Parisian avant-garde journal *Littérature*. It was captioned 'View from an aeroplane'. The same month, in London, T. S. Eliot published his great modernist poem, *The Waste Land*, which contains the line 'I will show you fear in a handful of dust'. Also that month Ernest Hemingway wrote that, having seen Paris from above, he now understood cubism. The First World War had not long passed, and the public was already familiar with aerial images of desolate and abstract landscapes.

This photograph had a curious life in and out of various journals, each time cropped, titled and contextualized a little differently. This was the period in which artists were exploring new angles, new relations of image to language, and the uncertain status of photography between document and artwork.

In 1964 the photograph came to be formally titled *Dust Breeding*, when an edition of ten prints was produced. In books and shows about Man Ray's work, it is usually presented as a visionary image by a pioneer of photographic art. In books on Duchamp, it is regarded more as an anecdotal image, a production shot simply showing his *Large Glass* in the making. Appreciating the ambiguity, both Man Ray and Duchamp signed the prints.

In the 1960s and 1970s, *Dust Breeding* appealed to mixed-media artists looking to make work at the interface of photography, sculpture, process and performance. It was even reproduced as a keynote image in the catalogue of the first major survey of conceptual art ('Information', 1970, Museum of Modern Art, New York). In 1989, when photography reached its 150th year, it was included in many of the big celebratory shows. It was there on the wall when the Royal Academy in London finally accepted photography as an 'independent art', as they called it. But how independent is it? It seems tied to so many other bits and pieces of knowledge.

Dust Breeding continues to haunt photography. It often crops up in debates about the medium's status as index or trace, in exhibitions about abstraction and marginal materials (there is nothing more marginal than dust), and even in discussions of landscape imagery.

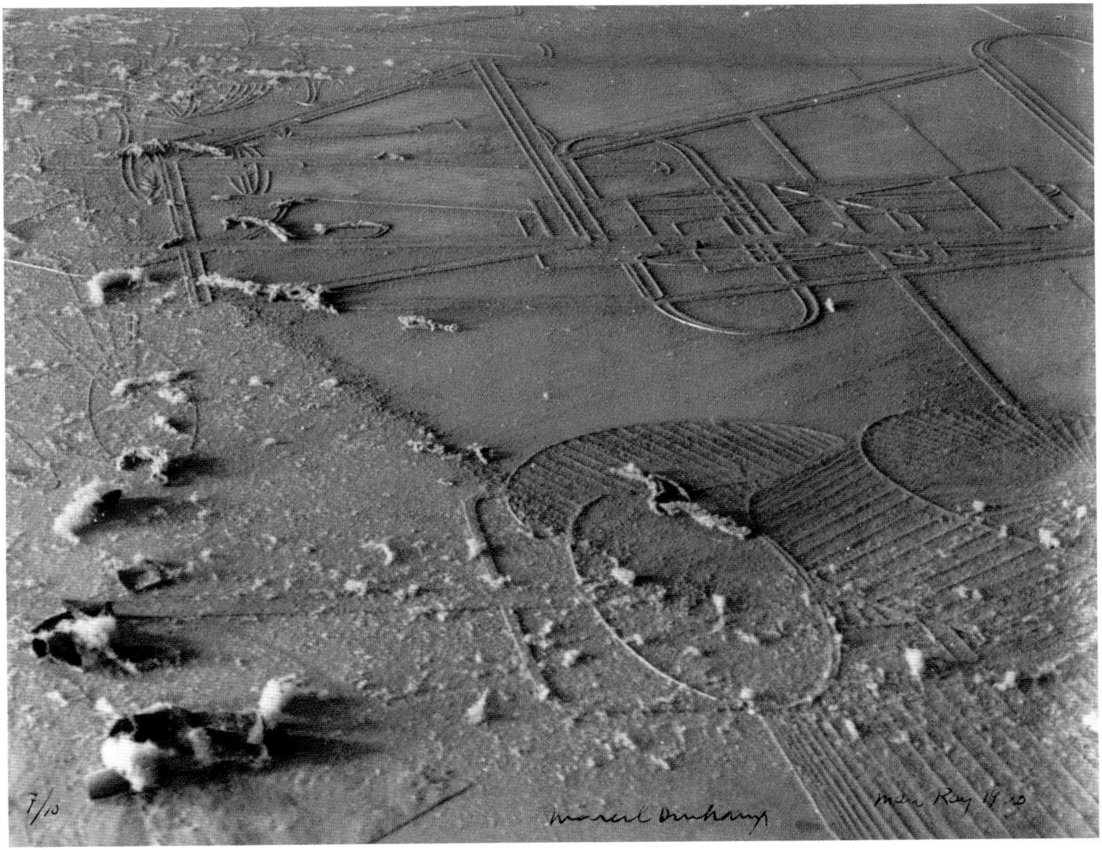

FREDERICK SOMMER

Arizona Landscape, 1943 (top); *Arizona Landscape*, 1945 (bottom)

AS REPRODUCED IN *APERTURE*, VOL. 10, NO. 4, 1962

BETWEEN 1943 AND 1945, Frederick Sommer made several photographs of the Sonoran Desert, near his home in Arizona. They show bone-dry hillsides without horizons, strewn evenly with rocks and dotted with cacti. Shot in black and white on a large-format camera, they oscillate for the eye between flatness and the receding space of incidental detail.

Photography is usually a matter of translating three dimensions into two, via an aperture. It is a medium of distances and perspectives. This means that making sense of a photograph is never just a matter of recognizing what is depicted: it also involves knowing from where it has been depicted. An unorthodox vantage point may render abstract even the most optically clear photograph. Likewise, a seemingly abstract photograph may cohere once we know its vantage point.

The more one looks at Sommer's landscapes, the more disconcerting they can become, both as pictures and as records of the world. With a poet's economy, Sommer spoke of each as a *constellation*, a word that might suggest something prosaic, like a gathering or assembly. In astronomy, a constellation is an arbitrary formation of stars perceived as a figure or design. It is the seeking of pattern that turns the chaos into order. These photographs are as carefully composed as any, yet they can ruffle our composure. We might say they are composed to show the essentially uncomposed, unnervingly brute fact of nature from which we are alienated by our very capacity to contemplate it. These are not landscapes fashioned to reflect back our wishes, our dominion, or even our physical scale. They are alien.

In 1944 two of Sommer's desert photographs appeared in the American surrealist journal *VVV*, on a double-page spread. At first glance they seemed to resemble a pair of stereoscopic images, promising the clarity of a third dimension. But each is quite singular, and their pairing only adds to their perplexing effect. In 1962 a similar layout appeared in an issue of *Aperture* magazine dedicated to Sommer's work. These were the only landscapes amid the still lifes and collages for which he is best known. Surrealist photography tended to explore claustrophobic spaces as metaphors for the dark chambers of the unconscious. For Sommer, the great outdoors and its blinding light were just as unfathomable, their beauty just as disturbing.

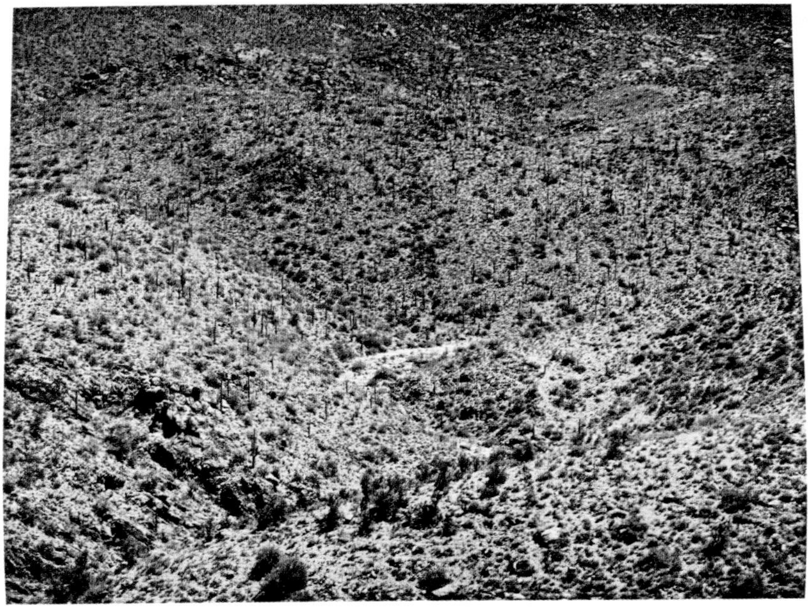

ARIZONA LANDSCAPE 1943 146

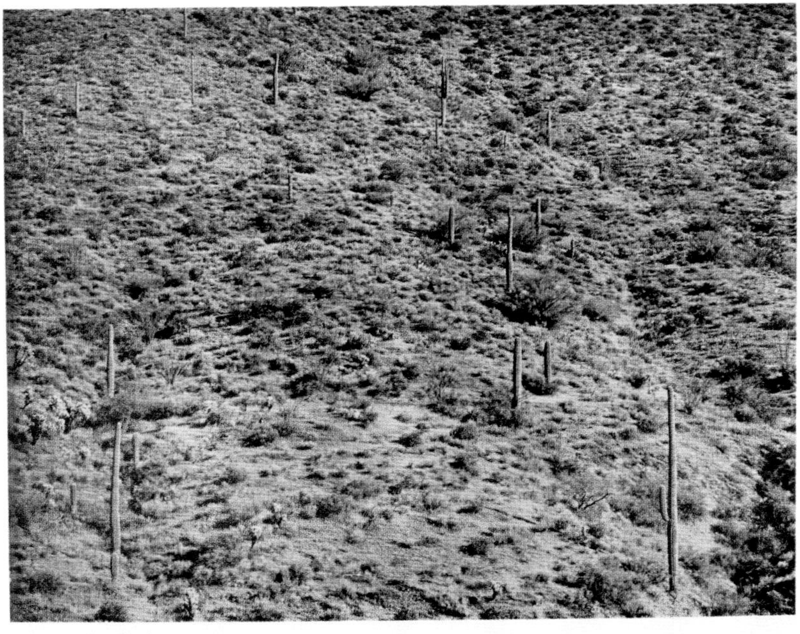

ARIZONA LANDSCAPE 1945 147

VICTOR BURGIN

Photopath, 1967–69

INSTALLATION VIEW, 'WHEN ATTITUDES BECAME FORM', FRUITMARKET GALLERY, EDINBURGH, 1985

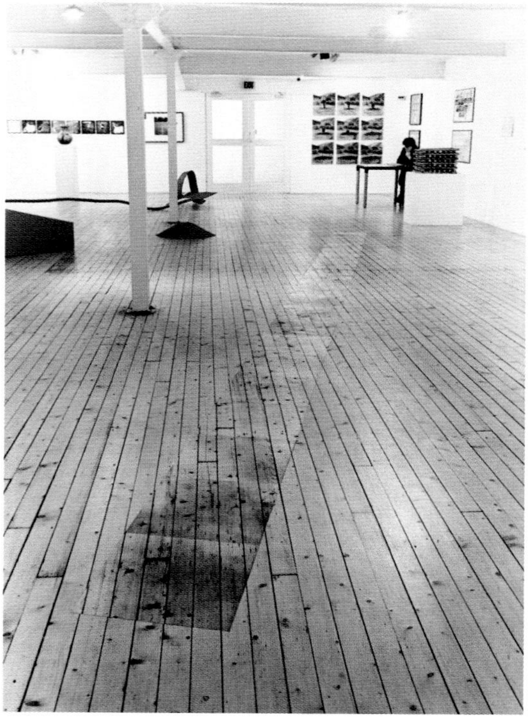

IN HIS VERY SHORT STORY 'On Exactitude in Science', Jorge Luis Borges describes a civilization that desires maps of ever finer detail. Eventually, a map is produced at 1:1 scale, covering the entire land it represents. The citizens take to living on the map, which slowly decays and dissolves back into its territory.

Most maps, like most photographs, are not made at the scale of their objects. Neither are they co-extensive with them. They are portable miniatures that relay information and impressions from one place to another. What use would there be for a photograph the size of the Pyramids, displayed at the site of the Pyramids?

Victor Burgin's *Photopath* is unique: a Borgesian image-object that seems to break every rule of photography while adhering so strictly to the medium's oldest aspiration, to substitute itself for the world.

In the spirit of 1960s conceptualism, *Photopath* is not photographic, strictly speaking. The work itself is an index file card, bearing a simple set of instructions: 'A path along the floor, of proportions 1 × 21 units, photographed. Photographs printed to actual size of objects and prints attached to floor so that images are perfectly congruent with their objects.'

Anyone can make a Photopath, and each manifestation will be a singular, site-specific instance of the idea. It can be made on any floor and at any size, although the proportions must remain 1 × 21. Burgin has made the piece several times, notably as part of the exhibition 'When Attitudes Become Form: Live in Your Head' at London's ICA in 1969, and in the rotunda of the Guggenheim Museum, New York, in 1971. In 2011 technicians made a colour version of *Photopath* for a survey show of conceptual art at the Art Institute of Chicago. It was installed in the institute's new glass-walled lobby space. During the exhibition, the new wooden floor was bleached by bright sunlight, and when *Photopath* came to be removed, it left behind a dark patch, a perfectly congruent shadow of its former self.

A PATH ALONG THE FLOOR, OF PROPORTIONS 1 X 21 UNITS, PHOTOGRAPHED. PHOTOGRAPHS PRINTED TO ACTUAL SIZE OF OBJECTS AND PRINTS ATTACHED TO FLOOR SO THAT IMAGES ARE PERFECTLY CONGRUENT WITH THEIR OBJECTS.

MASON WILLIAMS

Bus, 1967

INSTALLATION VIEW, 'STAND STILL LIKE THE HUMMINGBIRD', DAVID ZWIRNER, NEW YORK, 2012

IN 1967 THE ARTIST, writer and musician Mason Williams made an actual-size image of the side elevation of a Greyhound bus. It was 11 metres (36 ft) long, and 3.2 metres (10½ ft) high. More precisely, Williams made an edition of 200 of them. The original photograph of the bus was taken at Williams's request, by the photographer Max Yavno.

At full scale the image looks like a commercially produced billboard, but was in fact screen-printed by hand in several sections. Each *Bus* took nine hours to assemble, fold, and place in its specially made box. A warning on the box read: 'DO NOT OPEN IN THE WIND'. Williams sold them for $35 each, and exhibited them in galleries and museums. He also used one as a backdrop for his concerts. A photo of him standing in front of *Bus* appears on the cover of his 1968 LP *Phonograph Record* (a title as deadpan as the image itself). The LP won two Grammy awards, and includes the track 'Classical Gas', the most played piece of instrumental music on North American radio.

EACH *BUS* TOOK NINE HOURS TO ASSEMBLE, FOLD, AND PLACE IN ITS SPECIALLY MADE BOX.

Williams was inspired by one of his friends, the Californian artist Edward Ruscha. Since 1963 Ruscha had been making and self-publishing photographic books, each with a disarmingly straightforward title and subject matter: *Twentysix Gasoline Stations*; *Various Small Fires*; *Some Los Angeles Apartments*; *Every Building on the Sunset Strip*. The last of these, made the year before Williams's *Bus*, was a panorama that unfolded to a length of 8.2 metres (27 ft).

As well as his success as a musician and artist, Williams performed as a stand-up comic and wrote scripts for television. One of the keys to his success was his way with everyday cultural forms in imagery, words and music. This made his work easily accessible while chiming with the interest in popular culture that was central to both Pop and conceptual art. Always operating on his own terms, few cultural figures have managed to straddle the mainstream and the avant-garde as remarkably as Mason Williams.

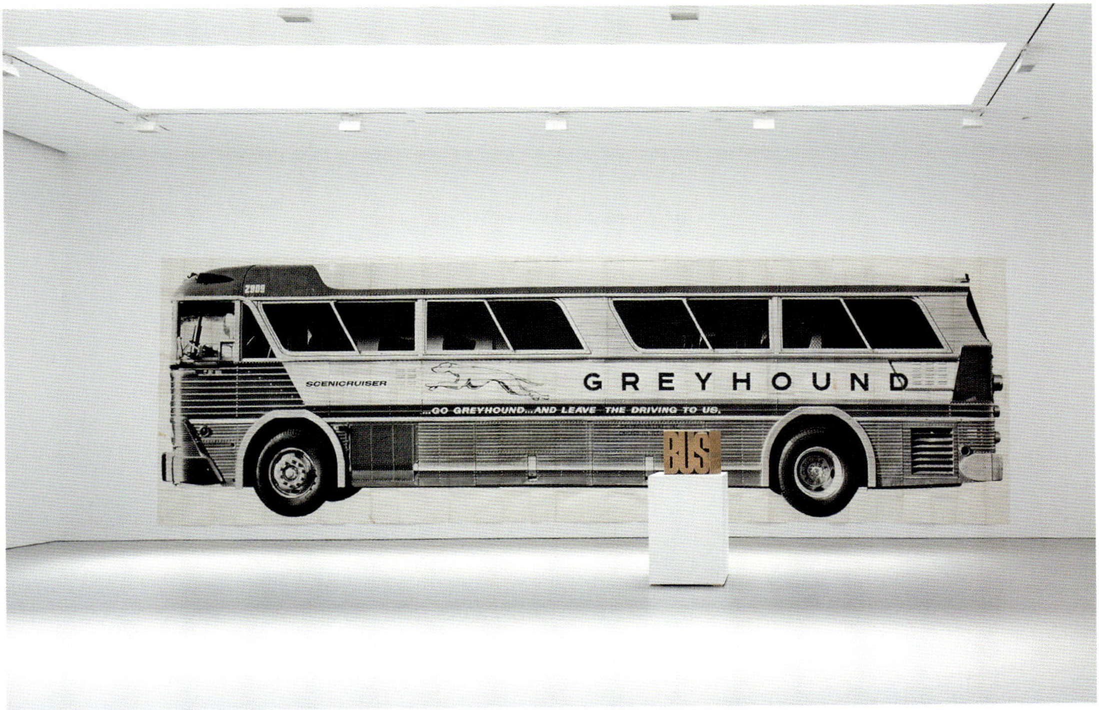
SCENICRUISER
GREYHOUND
...GO GREYHOUND...AND LEAVE THE DRIVING TO US.
BUS

SYLVIA PLIMACK MANGOLD

Two Exact Rules on a Dark and Light Floor, 1975

SYLVIA PLIMACK MANGOLD has been a stubbornly independent artist from the outset. Her work belongs to no group or movement. It seems to have a relation to photorealist painting of the late 1960s and early 1970s (most of which was made by men and understood largely in terms of nerdy masculine obsessions). In the end, however, Plimack Mangold's work is remarkably singular. Where much art of that time now looks quite dated, hers, especially the early paintings of floors and rulers, feels timeless. The insistent but obscure sense of purpose, the basic motif, along with the interest in vision, appearance, surface and reproduction, are among art's implacable concerns. For many years her work had a few dedicated admirers, but over recent decades it has come to be appreciated much more widely.

But why is the work of a painter included here, in a book about photographs? An obvious reason would have something to do with painting's confrontation with photography, not only as a medium of description, but also as a modern standard of visualization. The simplistic art-historical narrative is that photography's arrival freed painting from description, allowing it to move into abstraction and the contemplation not of worldly material things but of its own materiality – the stuff of paint and canvas. But abstraction was not the only response that painters could make to the camera image and its colonization of vision. There were in fact unlimited directions. Plimack Mangold painted the floor, not looking straight down but at a very human angle. Clearly she must have looked very intently, and we are encouraged to look intently too.

One of Plimack Mangold's earliest paintings, simply titled *Floor (1)*, was made in 1967. This was the year Victor Burgin first produced *Photopath* (page 158) and Mason Williams made *Bus* (page 160). All these works played with the detailed, actual-size replication of surfaces. Several other artists were doing this too, notably Mel Bochner. Quite why it was all happening in 1967 is unclear, although the status of both photography and painting were on many artists' minds, as Pop and conceptualism emerged as the cultural vanguard. Nothing was to be taken for granted. All assumptions about art and images were to be questioned.

Another reason for including Plimack Mangold's work here is more perverse, but also instructive. Such work does not reproduce well on the printed page. In fact, the 'better' it is reproduced, the more one realizes that it needs to be seen in person. Her paintings are not images. They are objects – unique, handmade. We are used to reproductions of artworks being offered to us as effective substitutes. This one asks you to seek out the real thing.

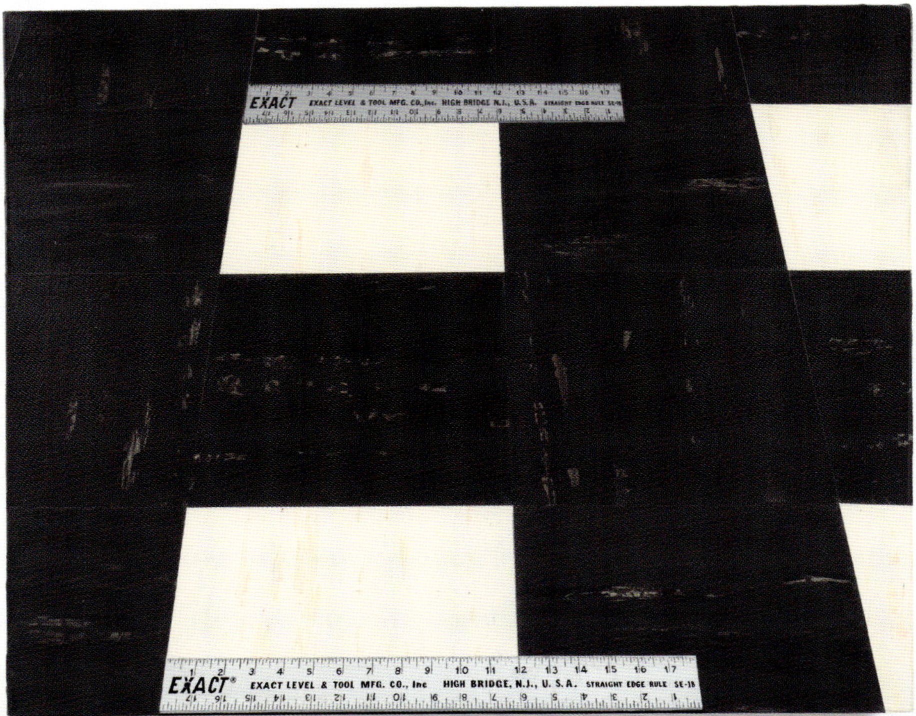
EXACT
EXACT LEVEL & TOOL MFG. CO., Inc
HIGH BRIDGE, N.J., U. S. A.
STRAIGHT EDGE RULE

GABRIEL OROZCO

Breath on Piano, 1992

IN 1952 THE AMERICAN EXPERIMENTAL musician John Cage composed *4'33"*. It was first performed by the great pianist David Tudor in a chamber-music concert hall near Woodstock, New York, as part of a recital of contemporary piano music. Tudor sat at the piano, spread out six sheets of blank sheet music, closed the piano lid, set off a stopwatch, put his hands in his lap and sat motionless. After thirty seconds he opened the lid and closed it. He did the same after two minutes and twenty-three seconds. A light wind blew, a little rain began to fall, and some of the audience got up from their seats to leave. At four minutes and three seconds, Tudor lifted the lid, stood up and bowed in the usual way. Those remaining offered a little applause.

4'33" is a score that, when 'performed', attunes the audience to the ambient noise that is always present. Absolute silence is not possible. If placed in an anechoic chamber (a room that absorbs all noise), a living person with good hearing will pick up the sound of their own heartbeat and the flow of blood around their body. Background becomes foreground. The fact that sound is always present in the world ensures that every performance of *4'33"* is unique.

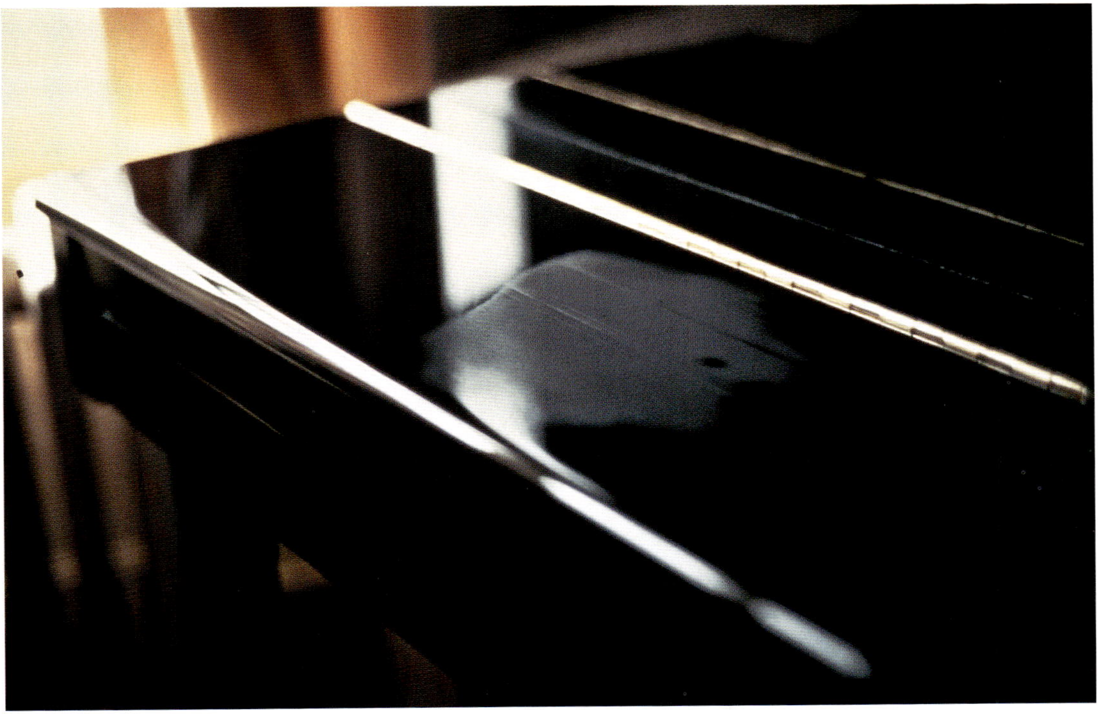

LIFE MAGAZINE

'Prisoners of War and the Sound of Peace', 26 June 1939

STILL PHOTOGRAPHY IS MUTE, and, strictly speaking, there is no audio equivalent of the still image. Recorded sound is continuous, whereas photography, even in the form of a movie made up of frames, is not. But photography does have a sonic *accompaniment*. It seems probable that we learn how photography is supposed to *sound* in parallel with how it is supposed to *look*. At an early age, television and cinema told us so. How many times have we heard the swelling chorus of paparazzi clicks and flashbulb pops that signal the arrival of the star at a movie premiere? Or the staccato motor-drive click-whirrs accompanying a series of freeze-frames, telling us the person on screen is being photographically observed by a detective or voyeur? Or a symbolic single click, perhaps with a slight echo for effect, when a famous news photograph appears in a TV documentary? An impoverished mother and her children look pensive ... click; a man leaps a puddle ... click; a man recoils from a bullet ... click. Never mind that the Leica camera that took many of those shots was prized for its unobtrusively quiet shutter.

So ingrained is the audio accompaniment to picture taking that our digital cameras and mobile phones are programmed to mimic those same sounds. As if it could not really be photography without them. As if we could not tell if we had actually taken a picture without some audible confirmation. Just as our vision intensifies at the moment we take a photograph, so does our *hearing*. We listen for the reassuring sound, real or synthetic, that says: 'Yes, the shutter did open. Rays did pass through the lens to hit the light-sensitive surface. Something was preserved, silently.'

Approximately two months before the outbreak of what would become the Second World War, *Life* magazine offered this innovative double page marking the end of the First World War. As the guns stopped firing at 11 am on 11 November 1918, the sound was recorded as an optical track. The muteness is as visible as the stillness.

SO INGRAINED IS THE AUDIO ACCOMPANIMENT TO PICTURE TAKING THAT OUR DIGITAL CAMERAS AND MOBILE PHONES ARE PROGRAMMED TO MIMIC THOSE SAME SOUNDS. AS IF IT COULD NOT REALLY BE PHOTOGRAPHY WITHOUT THEM. AS IF WE COULD NOT TELL IF WE HAD ACTUALLY TAKEN A PICTURE WITHOUT SOME AUDIBLE CONFIRMATION.

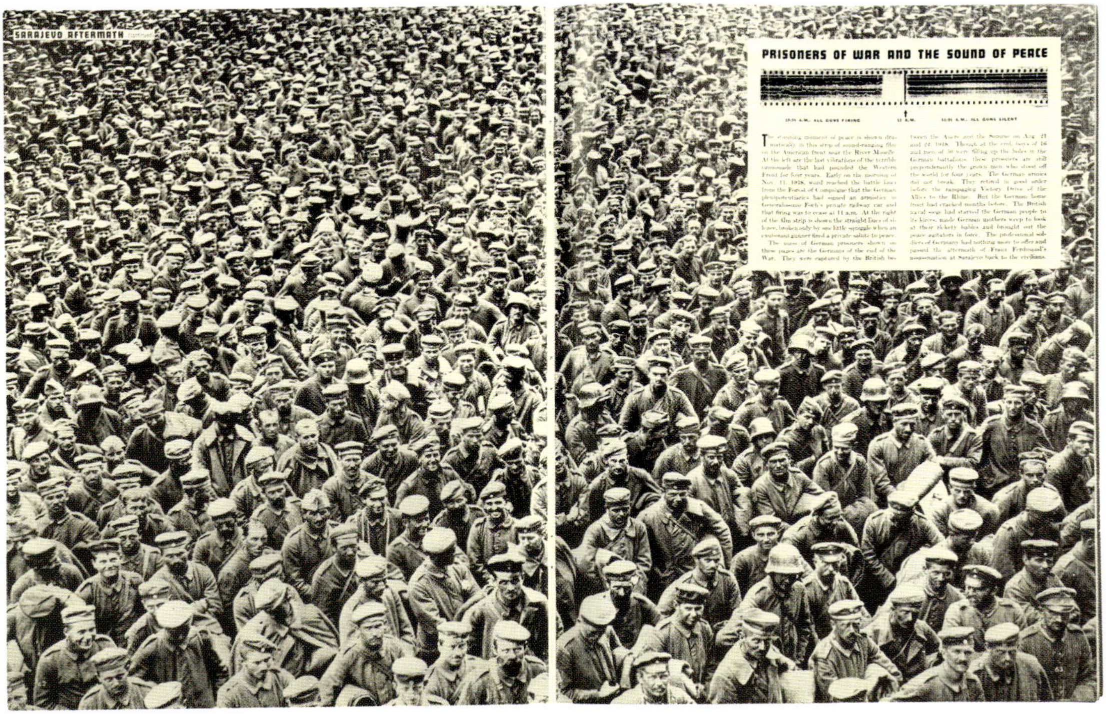

SARAJEVO AFTERMATH (continued)

PRISONERS OF WAR AND THE SOUND OF PEACE

10:59 A.M.: ALL GUNS FIRING — 11 A.M. — 11:01 A.M.: ALL GUNS SILENT

The stunning moment of peace is shown dramatically in this strip of sound-ranging film on the American front near the River Moselle. At the left are the last vibrations of the terrible cannonade that had pounded the Western Front for four years. Early on the morning of Nov. 11, 1918, word reached the battle lines from the Forest of Compiègne that the German plenipotentiaries had signed an armistice in Generalissimo Foch's private railway car and that firing was to cease at 11 a.m. At the right of the film strip is shown the straight lines of silence, broken only by one little squiggle when an exuberant gunner fired a private salute to peace.

The mass of German prisoners shown on these pages are the Germans of the end of the War. They were captured by the British between the Ancre and the Somme on Aug. 21 and 22, 1918. Though at the end, boys of 16 and men of 50 were filling up the holes in the German battalions, these prisoners are still preponderantly the grown men who stood off the world for four years. The German armies did not break. They retired in good order before the rampaging Victory Drive of the Allies to the Rhine. But the German home front had cracked months before. The British naval siege had starved the German people to its knees, made German mothers weep to look at their rickety babies and brought out the peace agitators in force. The professional soldiers of Germany had nothing more to offer and passed the aftermath of Franz Ferdinand's assassination at Sarajevo back to the civilians.

PHOTOGRAPHER UNKNOWN

The library at Holland House, Kensington, London, 1940

THE CIRCUMSTANCES OF WARTIME give rise to visions and images that are stranger, more unsettling and more lucid than any artist might invent. Remembering his experiences of the Second World War in London, the photographer Nigel Henderson said: 'Surrealism was everywhere in a sense. Houses chopped by bombs while ladies were still sitting on the lavatory, the rest of the house gone but the wallpaper and fires still burning in the grate. Who can hold a candle to that kind of real-life surrealism?' Similarly, the film editor Dai Vaughan has noted: 'In a bombed hospital, an umbrella might well encounter a sewing machine on a dissecting table. If the goal of surrealism was *changer la vie*, life was now changing before everyone's eyes ... generating imagery at a pace which left the artist no need to trawl his or her subconscious for symbols of flux and transcendence. Surrealism and the documentary imperative were united.'

From 1 September 1939, in anticipation of air raids, blackout regulations were imposed on large parts of England. No street lights, and heavy curtains drawn in all windows. Bill Brandt (page 80) ventured out alone to photograph the streets. 'The darkened town, lit only by moonlight, looked more beautiful than before or since,' he remembered. After the bombs had fallen, Cecil Beaton posed a model amid the ruin: 'Fashion is Indestructible', read his caption. In 1945 the *Vogue* model, surrealist and war photographer Lee Miller stripped off and posed in Hitler's liberated bathtub. Perhaps all images that are designed to jolt us will lack in taste. But when the events of the world itself are so jarring, there is a need for pictures that do the same. And there is no formula for the unexpected.

On 27 September 1940, two German bombs destroyed most of Holland House, a private residence in west London. The extensive library lost its roof but the shelves were left remarkably undamaged. A press photographer, whose name has been lost, took at least three shots, of which this is the most formally composed. Some newsreel also survives of these figures picking their way through the debris.

Regarding this photograph, Susan Sontag suggested: 'It is pleasing to imagine that ... these three gents were observed indulging their bookish habits in the destroyed mansion and the photographer did little more than space them differently to make a more incisive picture.' She was writing in her book *Regarding the Pain of Others* (2003). There's no physical pain depicted in this picture, and its incisiveness seems to serve a contradictory mix of urgency and distanced contemplation. Given the essential theatricality of the scene, to ponder whether the photograph was a set-up seems beside the point. Who wouldn't feel like a strolling player in such a place? And who with a camera could resist that awful tension between reality and nightmare?

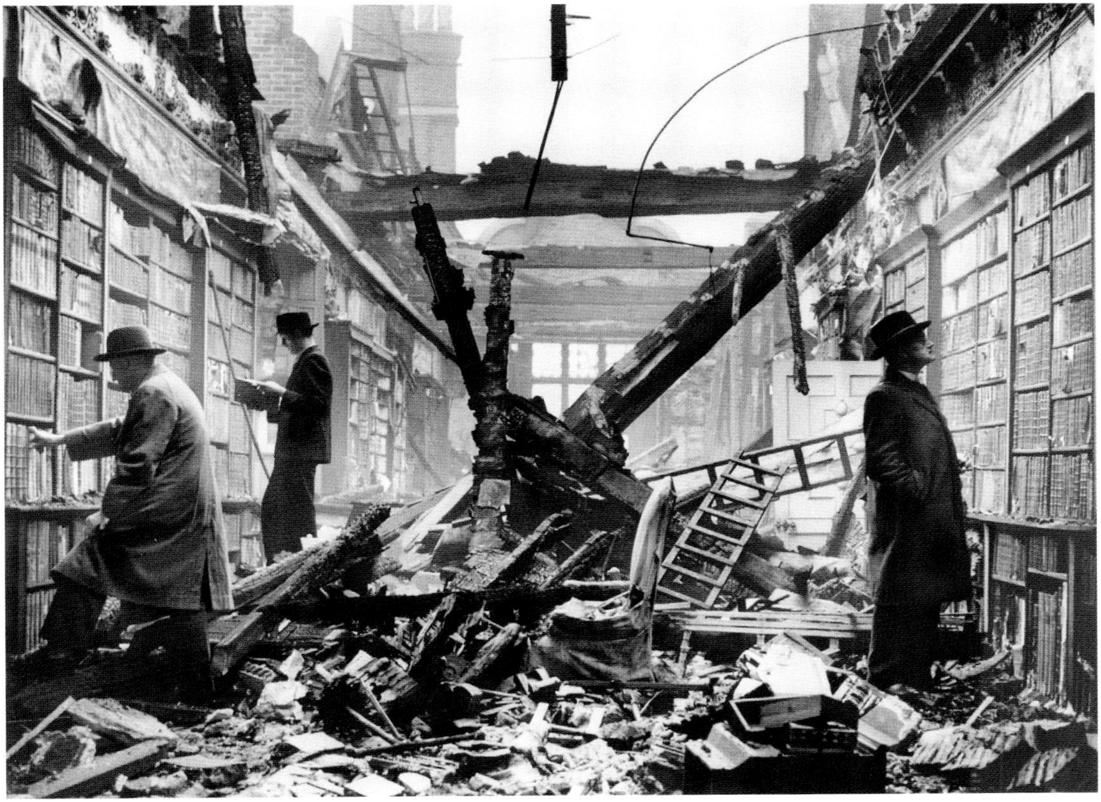

PHOTOGRAPHER UNKNOWN

The Federal Bureau of Investigation Fingerprint Database, 1943

DURING THE SECOND WORLD WAR, the Federal Bureau of Investigation (FBI) pushed hard to collate the fingerprints of all US citizens. Identifying defectors and spies was the stated aim, although the gathering of information on individuals was becoming widespread in many countries. The fingerprint database was a system of indexed cards, and the filing staff was almost exclusively comprised of women. By 1943 approximately 400,000 new sets of prints were arriving each month. This photograph shows the overflow, housed in the DC Armory in the US capital. The vast space was photographed several times, for publicity purposes.

A photograph and a fingerprint are in some ways similar. Both are traces, and each is unique yet repeatable. When part of larger systems, both can help to identify. The first criminal fingerprint identification was made in Buenos Aires, Argentina, in 1892. This was the year Sir Francis Galton published a book outlining how fingerprints were individual and unchanging. In 1901 the Metropolitan Police Service in London established its fingerprint branch. The United States created its first national fingerprint repository in 1904, and by 1924 it was under the control of the FBI.

In *The Pencil of Nature* (1844–46), William Henry Fox Talbot (pages 198, 224) speculated that photography could become 'evidence of a novel kind'. Criminals and prisoners were photographed as early as the 1850s. However, crime-scene photography was not formalized until 1903. The French criminologist Alphonse Bertillon, who had already established a system for collating photographic and other data on individuals, developed sophisticated procedures for the standardized photographing of crime scenes, and the interpretation of the images. Thus, fingerprinting and forensic photography were institutionalized around the same time and brought together as related systems.

In 1980 the FBI introduced computer-aided fingerprint searching, and by 1999 the system had been digitized. Today, the fingerprint archive of all US citizens would fit on a hard drive barely larger than a finger. News photographs like this one used to be printed 8 × 10 inches and stored for future use in filing cabinets. Now, they too are produced and stored as electronic information.

While a photograph can be used to identify, it rarely reveals the maker of the image. It would need to be a self-portrait (and we'd need to *know* it was one), or it must carry additional information as text. The name of the photographic reporter who took this image has been lost. However, there is a fingerprint in the top left-hand corner. It probably belongs to the darkroom technician, who handled the wet print too early in the rush to meet a newspaper deadline.

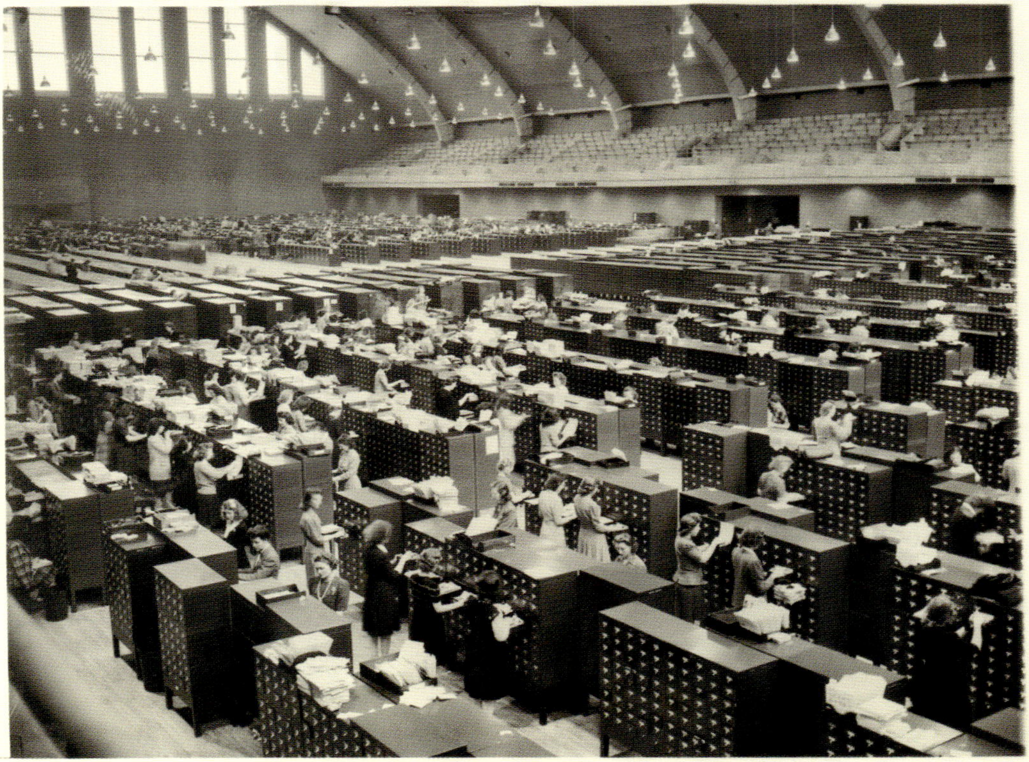

MAURICE JARNOUX

André Malraux at Home, 1954

PHOTOGRAPHY MAY BE AN ART, but it is also the means by which many of the other arts are documented, reproduced, publicized and understood. In general, the photographing of paintings is perceived as copy work, while photographing sculpture is more obviously interpretative, requiring decisions about point of view, framing, lighting and background. But the photographic reproduction of *all* art involves the profound transformation of the original.

Adventurer, novelist, politician and art historian, André Malraux produced a series of illustrated art books in the late 1940s and 1950s. He exploited ruthlessly the ways photographic reproduction can bring artefacts of different cultures, places, scales and contexts into what he accepted was a questionable unity on the printed page. For him, the destiny of all artworks was to end up first in a museum and then as photographic reproduction. This world-of-art-as-photography formed what Malraux, in his book of the same name, famously called *le musée imaginaire* (translated, misleadingly, as 'the museum without walls').

To find out exactly how the camera can transform, Malraux commissioned Gisèle Freund (page 78) to photograph a Mexican sculpture of the goddess of corn. Freund recalled: 'I photographed from different angles and in changing light conditions, which made the same sculpture appear to be several different sculptures [...] Malraux chose one of these reproductions for his book, but his choice was conditioned by his own taste and his perception of this sculpture.'

Malraux's choice was also determined by the demands of sequencing and the rhetoric of his visual argument. Images were placed side by side to force connections, and some were even flipped left to right to aid the graphic flow. Dramatic crops and details, especially of sculpted heads and faces, punctuated the sequence like powerful cinematic close-ups. The overall effect is so extreme that it is possible to read the book as a lesson in photographic transformation.

Here is Malraux, a patrician and confident figure of the European establishment, presiding over the pages of *Le Musée imaginaire de la sculpture mondiale: des bas-reliefs aux grottes sacrées* (1954). It was taken for a feature in *Paris Match* magazine. Today, Malraux's high-minded view that all art can be brought into one grand narrative is rightly regarded with suspicion. Nevertheless, photographic reproductions of works of art continue to proliferate, circulate and underpin the contemporary experience of art. What now governs the circulation is less such knowledgeable, powerful or entitled individuals as Malraux, and more the networked flow of data, statistics about market value and the algorithms of popular taste.

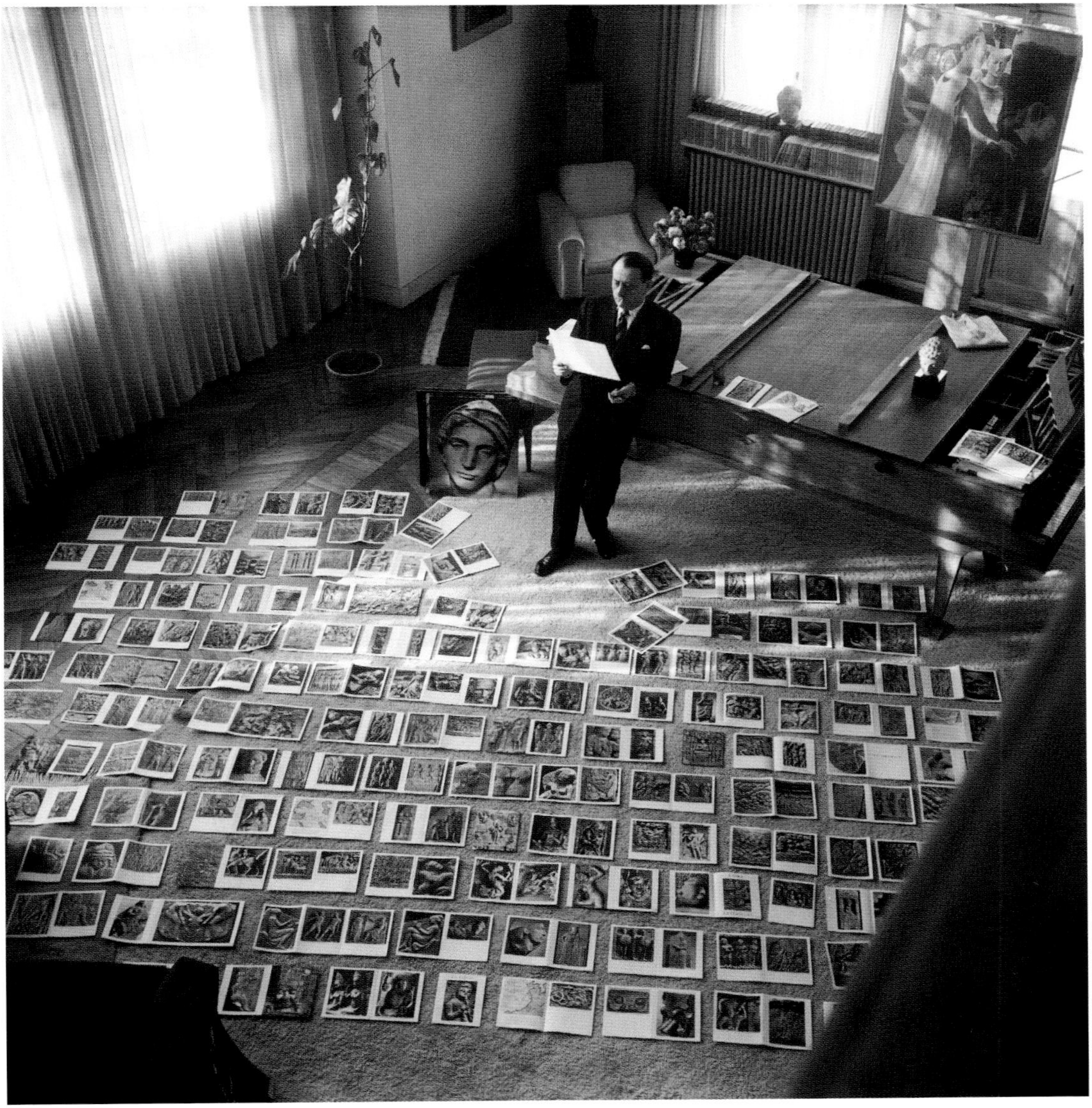

ANASTASIA SAMOYLOVA

Six Real Matterhorns, 2019

FROM THE SERIES 'LANDSCAPE SUBLIME', 2013–PRESENT

IN 2009 A BRITISH PHOTOGRAPHER won a minor prize for a photograph of a glacier floating off the coast of Chile. In 2015 a Chilean photographer claimed the image was hers, and that the British photographer had appropriated it. It turned out they had both been on the same boat and had taken nearly identical photographs.

Cruise ships and tour buses regularly pause at the optimal vantage points, knowing people want to capture the same view. Of course, such photographs are clichés, which really have no author at all. They are aggregate images: tropes, types, anonymous sets of pictorial conventions and attitudes.

In the early 2000s, the artist Anastasia Samoylova was exploring Flickr, the image-sharing website. She noticed how landscape imagery made by amateurs fell into distinct types. It was as if photographers were following an impulse not to express their feelings or experience but to show they could conform to established rules of representation. And, in the spirit of this generic aspiration, many were uploading their images without copyright restriction. Anyone could use them. Samoylova began collecting them in folders on her computer according to search keywords. Sunsets. Deserts. Beaches. Mangroves. Coral reefs. Volcanoes. Glaciers. Mountains. She would print a selection of the collected images, assemble the prints as three-dimensional sculptural forms, and then re-photograph them. These studio arrangements echo cubism, Russian constructivism (particularly the paintings of Natalia Goncharova), as well as the Pop art of Robert Rauschenberg (page 106) and James Rosenquist, but they are worlds in themselves.

Samoylova titled her series 'Landscape Sublime'. The sublime is that sense of awe one feels in a landscape of extreme beauty or overwhelming scale. The feeling often diminishes if we already know the scene from images. Today, the unimaginably vast and ever-growing number of standardized pictures accumulating on the world's hard drives is another kind of sublime. A technological sublime.

The Matterhorn, a peak in the Alps on the Swiss–Italian border, is perhaps the most recognizable mountain in the world. This is partly to do with its defined pyramidal shape, but it only looks so distinctive from the particular vantage points where most photographers stand to shoot it. Samoylova's *Six Real Matterhorns* contains seven images. One is a photograph of a fake Matterhorn in Disneyland.

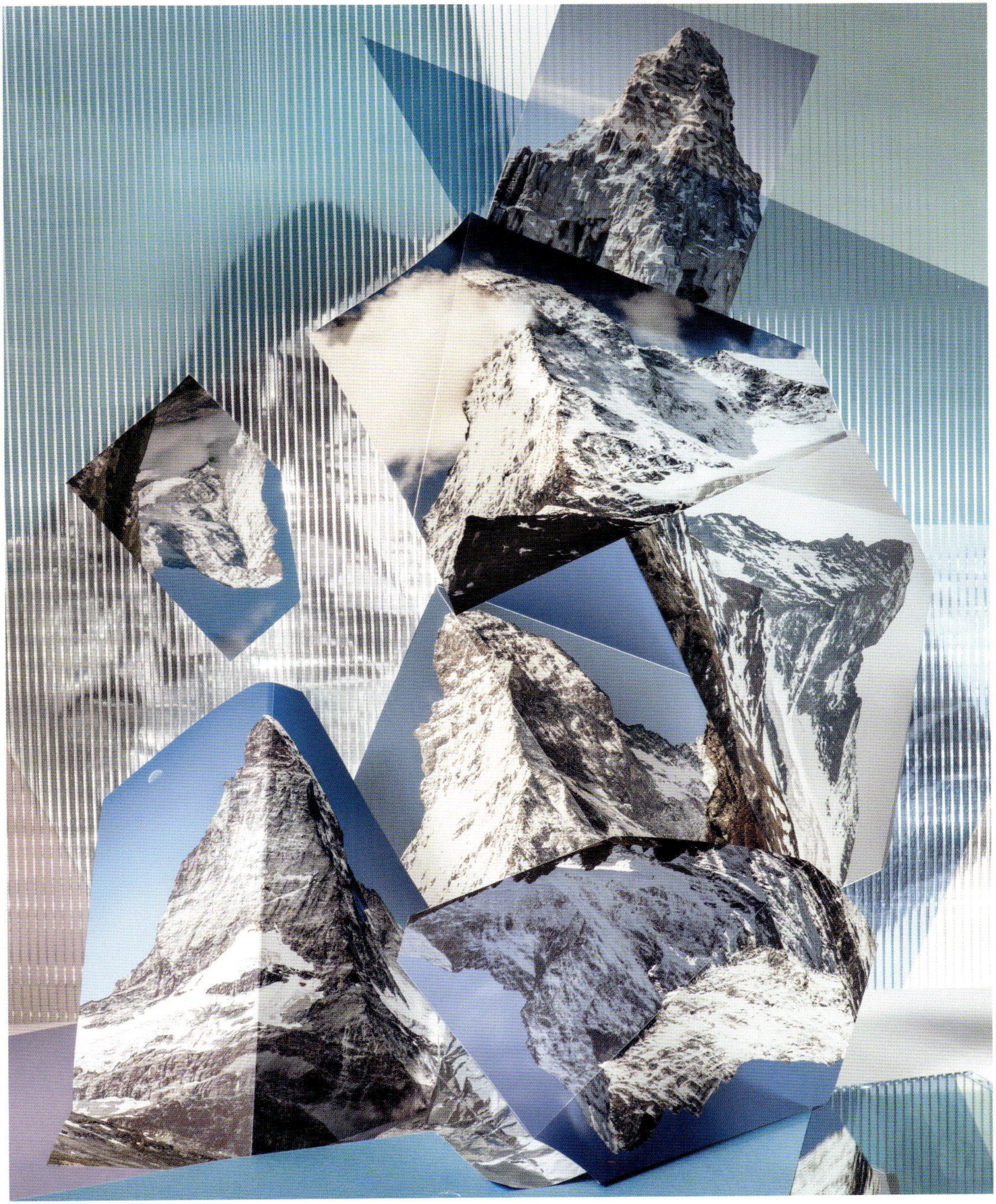

DAYANITA SINGH

Conversation Chambers: Museum Bhavan, 2013

INSTALLATION VIEW, HAYWARD GALLERY, LONDON, 2013

FOR ALL ITS ABILITY TO FIX, freeze and hold things still, photography is a shape-shifting, mobile medium. So much can be done with it, in so many forms and contexts and manifestations. This can be a source of anxiety or excitement, and, in contemporary art, both attitudes are clear. For some artists, their photographic work needs to be given a stable and unchangeable presentation. Prints are of a designated size, made with specific materials. For others, the image is simply a potential, which can manifest in any number of ways. This is how photography is encountered in daily life, but it presents something of a challenge to the traditional museum that expects its artefacts to be stable and unchanging.

Dayanita Singh's photographic work is distinctive and yet distinctively flexible. Over a number of years, she developed projects that exist somewhere between the book page, the archive and the gallery. In 2017 she published *Museum Bhavan*, a box containing nine books of photographs: *Museum of Furniture*, *Museum of Photography*, *Godrej Museum*, *Museum of* Machines, *Ongoing Museum*, *Museum of Men*, *Museum of Vitrines*, *Printing Press Museum*, and *Little Ladies Museum*. Each has twenty-six or twenty-seven images. A tenth volume contains text only, in the form of conversations with Singh. In thses small-format books, the images are printed on one side of a single strip that can be unfolded. Singh sees these mass-produced books as artworks in themselves, and has exhibited them on shelves like a portable museum.

At the same time, the project takes the form of modular units made of wood that allow various prints from the *Museum Bhavan*, all of the same size, to be exhibited in different combinations. There are more images than can be displayed at any one time, which means choices have to be made. Singh has it written into the *Museum Bhavan* manifesto that the selection and arrangement of images can be changed either by her or by the teams that install the project in museums and galleries.

Singh takes photographs serially, making groups of images of different subject matter. Each is a small visual inventory, so there is something inherently archival and categorizing about what she does. Moreover, there is a certain deathliness to any kind of collecting, especially in photographic form. Singh counters this with strategies of display and distribution that keep the work provisional. For her, the encounter with photography should be a living, breathing, improvised occasion, open to flexibility and accident.

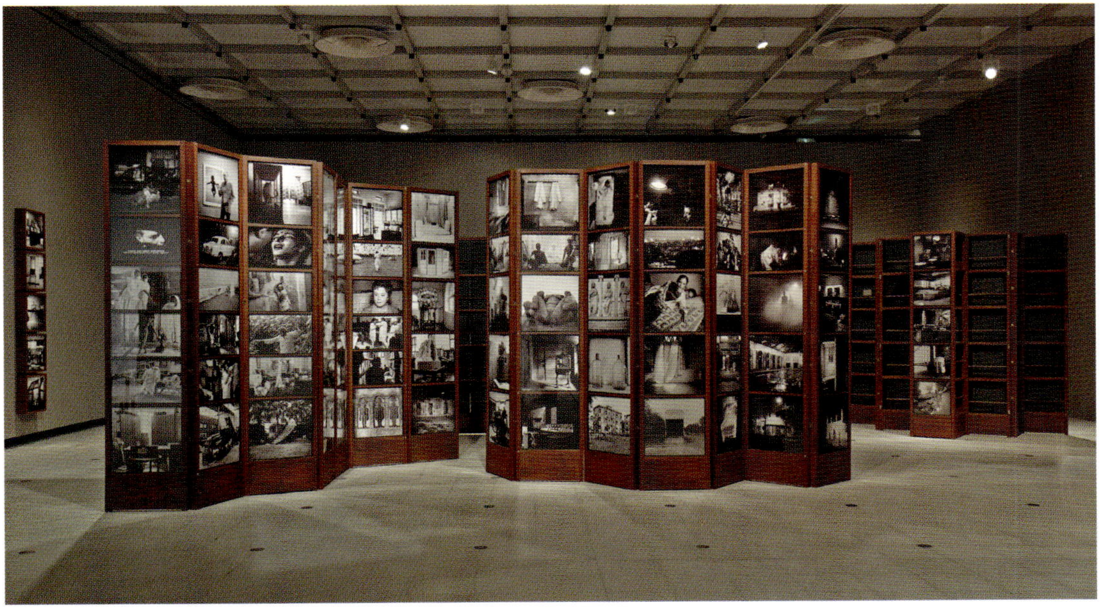

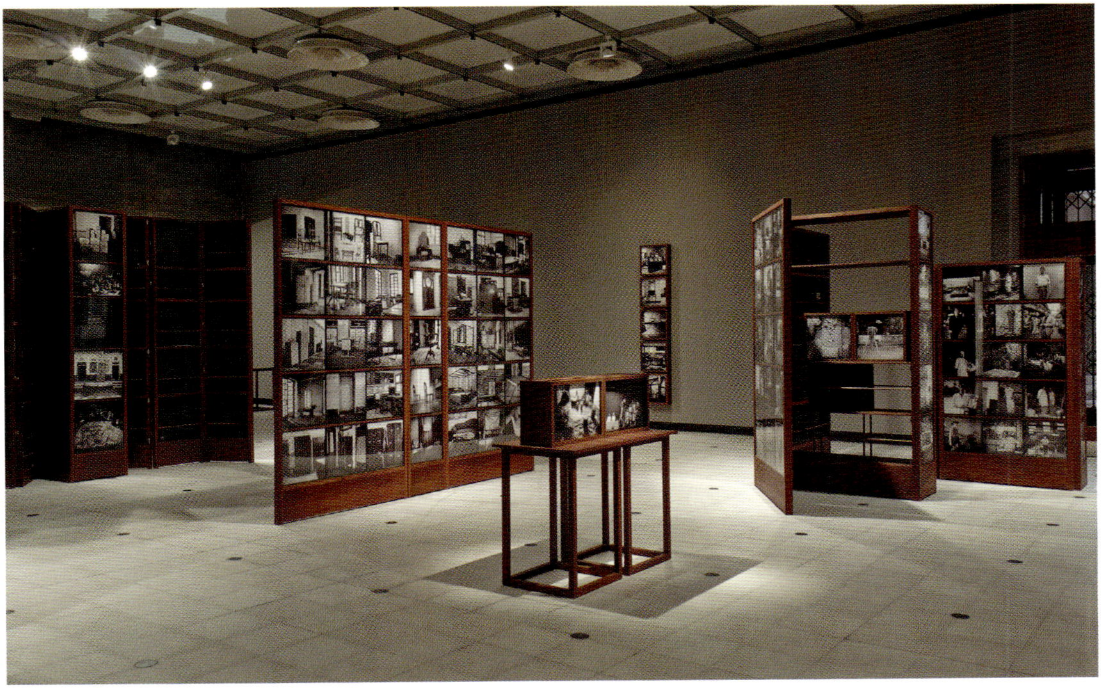

CLAUDIA ANGELMAIER

Hase

FROM THE SERIES 'PLANTS AND ANIMALS', 2004

***YOUNG HARE* (1502)**, a small painting by the German artist Albrecht Dürer, is one of the highpoints of early naturalistic art. Dürer had visited Italy in the 1490s, absorbing the Renaissance interest in proportion, realism, perspective and attention to detail in nature. We do not know exactly how he managed to make his painting. Taxidermy was not yet practised. It is possible that Dürer made sketches of hares in the wild, or kept one in captivity to study it closely. However, what makes the image so modern, after half a millennium, is the absence of symbolism or allegory. It is a painting made for its own sake. The hare signifies nothing but itself.

Although *Young Hare* is much loved, Dürer is as well known for his woodcuts. A drawn image would be cut into hard fruitwood and used as a printing block to make multiple copies. The artist Claudia Angelmaier, who is also German, is interested in different methods of image reproduction. Her photographs take as their subject matter the pages of art books and postcards.

We tend to think of photography and photomechanical reproduction as having solved once and for all the challenge of standardized imaging. The reality is very different. Reproduction technologies have never remained stable, and neither have the desires of those wanting to see reproduced images. For her series 'Plants and Animals', Angelmaier rounded up various books that reproduce the same images, including Dürer's *Young Hare*. Were we to encounter just one of these books on its own, the reproduction would probably feel more accurate and have more authority than if we saw it alongside eleven others. In seeing these twelve books reproduced together, perhaps we might begin to question the authority and accuracy of even Angelmaier's photograph, and the printed reproduction of it you are looking at now.

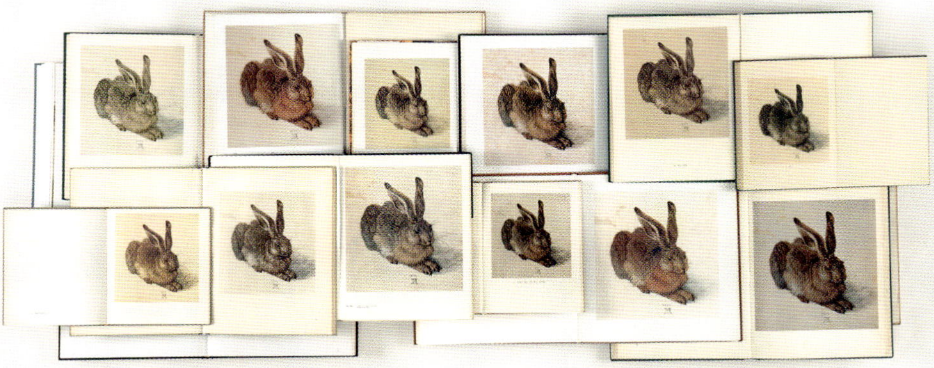

SCHELTENS & ABBENES

COS, Collections: Light Bulbs, 2012

WORKING TOGETHER SINCE around 2001, the Dutch duo of Maurice Scheltens and Liesbeth Abbenes make photographs for a range of different contexts and clients. They belong to a strong tradition of innovative practice that has been present in Dutch photography since the 1920s, in which the medium is understood as both an applied art and a fine art simultaneously. They are as comfortable making site-specific work for a royal palace as they are producing commissioned images of furniture or fabric for a catalogue or advertising campaign. For them, the printed page is no more or less significant than the fine-art print. What matters is the challenge of solving problems and making compelling images.

Scheltens & Abbenes share a deep understanding of, and affection for, the *still life*. It is a genre with a long history and flexible applications. Still-life images are found right across culture, belonging equally to all the arenas in which photography is found. It is also the genre over which image-makers can exert the most inlfuence. Scheltens & Abbenes produce highly controlled images, sometimes realist, sometimes abstract, and often somewhere in between.

This image of light bulbs emerged from an open commission from COS, the clothing retailer that has an experimental magazine. For an issue themed around 'doubling', Scheltens & Abbenes photographed collections of objects that had abstract and tangible qualities. The collections existed only in carefully constructed sets, viewed from a particular angle. In this way, the image is as much responsible for forming the collection as documenting it. Although it was made in 2012, this particular image recalls the modernist still lifes made by such photographers as Florence Henri (page 94), László Moholy-Nagy and Man Ray (page 154). They all refused easy distinctions between art and commerce.

STILL-LIFE IMAGES ARE FOUND RIGHT ACROSS CULTURE, BELONGING EQUALLY TO ALL THE ARENAS IN WHICH PHOTOGRAPHY IS FOUND. IT IS ALSO THE GENRE OVER WHICH IMAGE-MAKERS CAN EXERT THE MOST INLFUENCE.

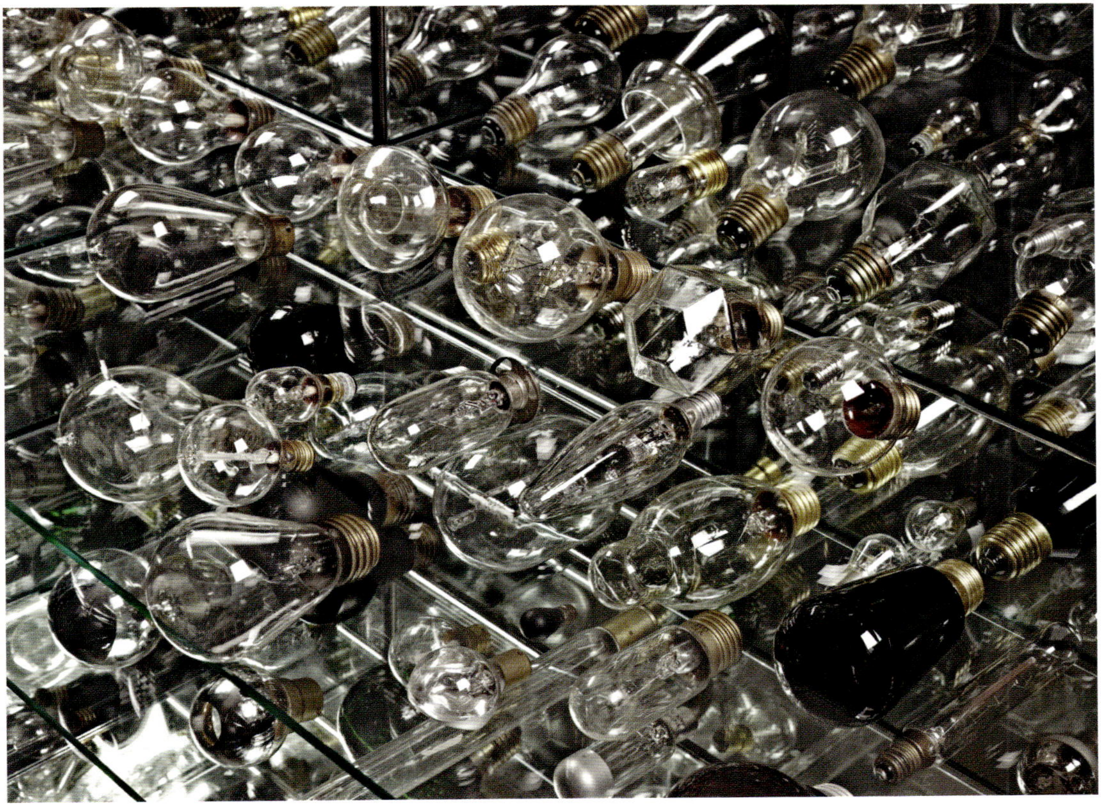

ANDREAS GURSKY

Salerno, 1990

FOR MUCH OF HIS ARTISTIC CAREER, the German photographer Andreas Gursky has made images of complex built environments. Latterly, these have involved digital montage and alteration. However, his earlier work was more or less realist photography of the observable world. His 1990 picture of the industrial port of Salerno, Italy, is among his best known.

In some respects it is an old-fashioned image, informed by the history of sublime landscape painting. The high vantage point and epic outlook imply a kind of mastery of the vista, first by the artist, then by the invited viewer. In its clear depiction of the geography, Gursky's image also echoes the practice of topographic photography as it evolved in the nineteenth century. Photographers would be commissioned by city planners, railway companies and real estate corporations to make clear and useful records of the land. The prints of *Salerno* made for exhibition measure 170.2 × 205.5 centimetres (67 × 80⅞ in.). This scale permits the image to be studied at various distances, taking in both the details and the overall view. It also permits communal viewing.

Shot with a slightly telephoto lens, the perspective of the view is compressed. This brings foreground and background into a closer relationship, while emphasizing the tension between abstract pattern and documentary record. In this way, 'abstraction' can be understood as both pictorial and social. The scene describes the abstract forces of capitalism, with its complex networks of production and trade and its modular forms, such as shipping containers. There are no workers visible (Gursky rarely shows people as more than figures in the landscape) and yet this is a thoroughly human scene. While *Salerno* now belongs to art history and photo history, it is perfectly possible to imagine it being used in a classroom. It could stimulate children to think carefully about global industrialization.

In the visual sense, the vantage point is dramatic. Does it reveal Gursky's own point of view? Does the vantage point indicate what he thought of the situation his image describes? Perhaps not. While a photograph always has a vantage point, a photographer need not have a point of view.

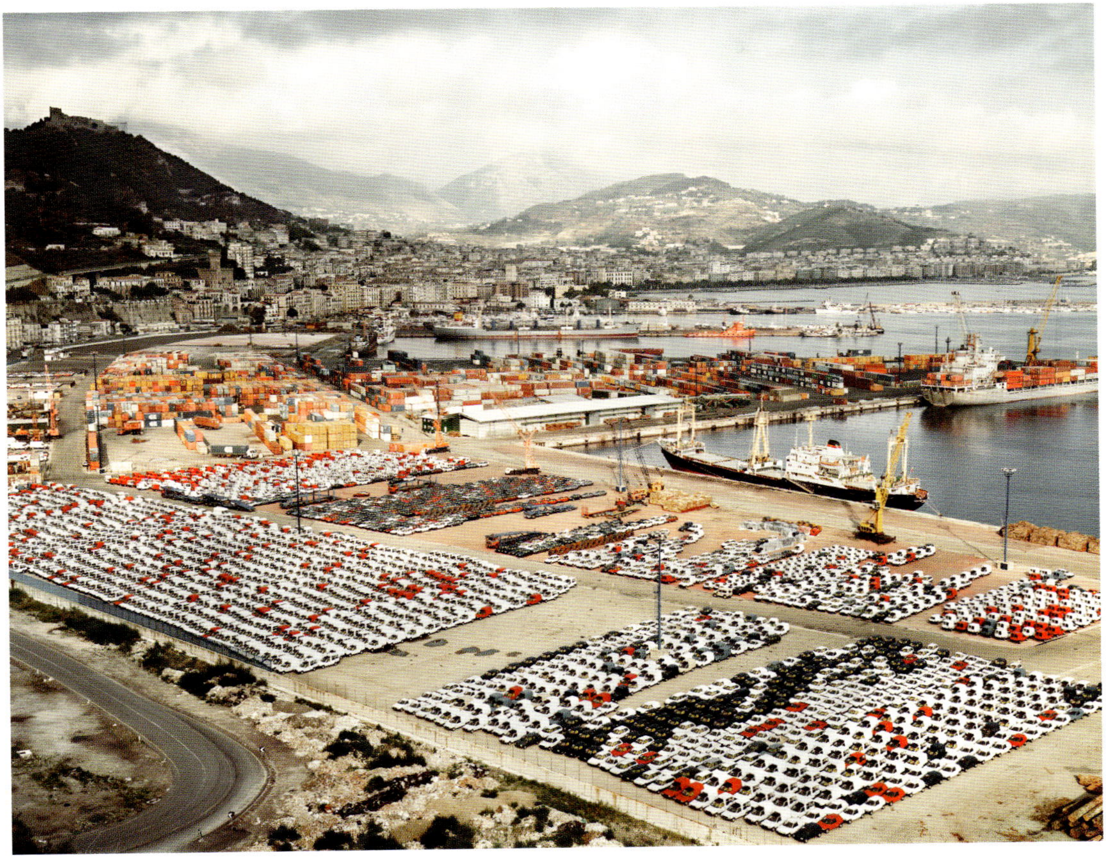

STEPHEN SHORE

Beverly Boulevard and La Brea Avenue, Los Angeles, California, June 21, 1975, 1975

THE AMERICAN STEPHEN SHORE began taking photographs at a very young age and was making serious pictures by his teenage years. The medium permits rapid artistic development, but it also means that even the best photographers often peak early and become repetitious. Shore was aware of the problem. What do you do if you want to keep your work evolving over a lifetime?

For nearly six decades, Shore has made sharp turns away from his own successes. As soon as a type of photograph or visual strategy is achieved, he is on to a new challenge. His work includes lyrical street photographs, visual inventories of food eaten and beds slept in, formally complex landscape and cityscape pictures, seemingly artless snapshots, deeply empathetic portraits, fashion photographs, rigorous sequences, groups of found images, and more. He has used just about every camera format. He is equally comfortable with the gallery wall and the printed page, with colour and black and white, analogue and digital, contact prints and large-scale photographs, postcards and print-on-demand books.

Throughout the 1970s, Shore made road trips around the United States. He would switch between making disarmingly simple pictures, almost like snapshots, and highly complex compositions, such as this one. In his 2011 essay 'Form and Pressure,' he noted: 'I was drawn to this scene because it seemed to be such a quintessential Los Angeles experience: the gas stations, the jumble, the signage, the space. I was also, for my own personal reasons, exploring visual structure [...] I was interested in how the frame of the picture forms a line that all the visual elements of the picture relate to. It is the image's proscenium, as it were. I recognized that when three-dimensional space is collapsed into a flat picture, objects in the foreground are now seen, on the surface of the photograph, in a new and precise relationship to the objects in the background. For example, look at the relationship between the "Standard" sign and the light pole underneath it [...] I was interested in seeing how many of these visual interstices I could juggle on a single image.'

Nothing man-made in this Los Angeles streetscape was built to last, and none of it has. Today, there is still a Chevron gas station on the corner, but its architecture has changed. In a token gesture to the planet, rectangles of grass the size of doormats now edge its forecourt. What does survive is Shore's photograph, a far sturdier structure.

To the extent that this image is a document of a time and a place, its value is clear. It is thick with information, all in pin-sharp focus from foreground to distant horizon. When the world finally weans itself off fossil fuels, our descendants may well look upon this image with fascination. The artistic value of a photograph may be less predictable, less definable, than its documentary value, but few would doubt formal mastery here. Whatever technological and aesthetic changes befall photography, whatever future generations make of the world it depicts, there will always be a place for pictorial structure.

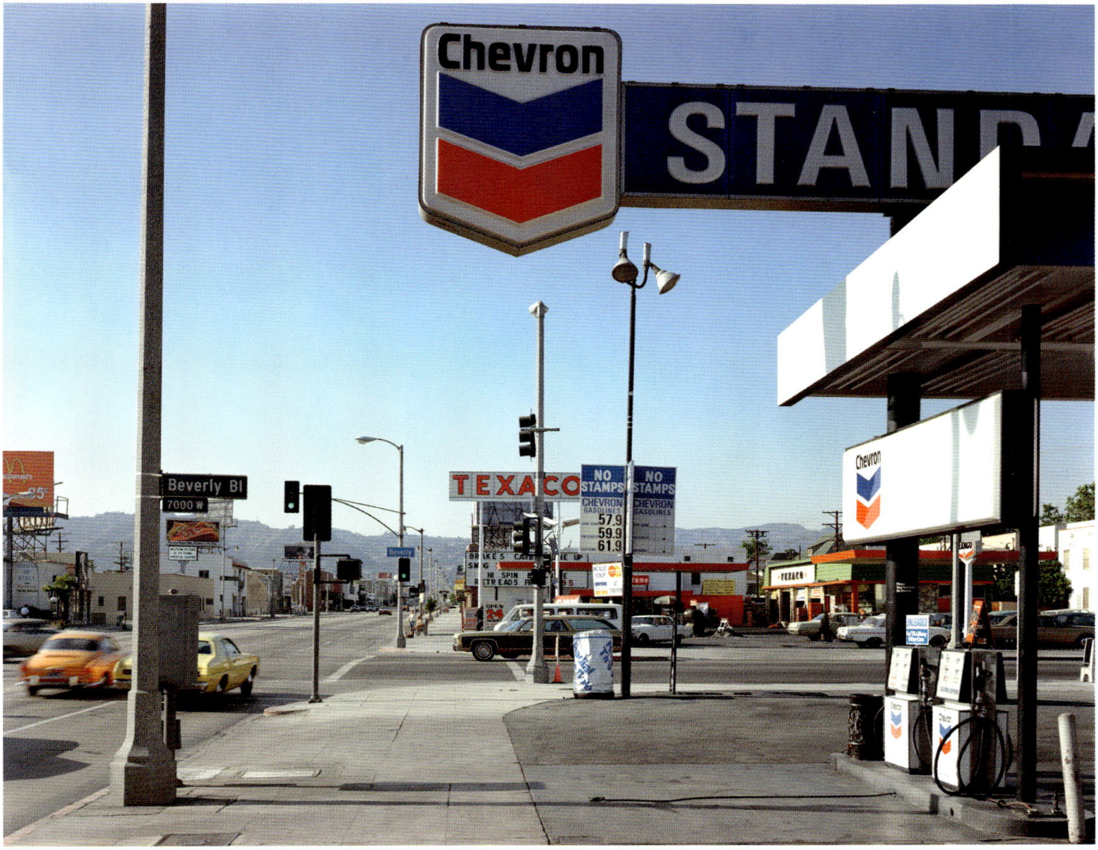
Chevron
Beverly Bl
7000 W
TEXACO
NO STAMPS
CHEVRON GASOLINES
57.9
59.9
61.9
NO STAMPS
CHEVRON GASOLINES
TEXACO
Chevron

HARRY GRUYAERT

Belgium, Waterloo, 1980

COLOUR SIGNIFIES, often forcefully, but never specifically. As the designer Ettore Sottsass once put it, 'Red is the colour of the Communist flag, the colour that makes the surgeon move faster, and the colour of passion.' That is a very mixed message, and it doesn't even account for the subtleties emanating from the ten thousand different shades we may call 'red', nor for the relation between those shades and the millions of other colours. Never trust a person who is confident they can tell you what colour 'means'.

The Belgian photographer Harry Gruyaert is, first and last, a maker of colour pictures. His choices are formal and colour is his muse. Nevertheless, for an observational photographer, there is no pure form. Shape and colour do not float freely like patches of the imagination or pigments on canvas. Rather, colour originates in worldly things, which offer themselves to the eye and the camera as light. And so, even while Gruyaert has never proclaimed any impulse to make documentary records beyond his pictorial impressions (no desire to 'tell it like it is', no deep need to communicate with anyone but himself), his pictures *are* documents. The modern world expresses itself, and often *betrays* itself, through its colour choices and its colour accidents. From carpets to cars and costumes to curtains, all that is manufactured is an expression of the values of the society that made it.

Gruyaert worked almost exclusively with Kodachrome positive transparency film, from the early 1960s until it was discontinued in 2009. The popular reputation of Kodachrome as a crude and garish film for amateurs is misplaced. It was one of the most nuanced films ever manufactured. Looked at on a light box or projected on to a screen, a well-taken Kodachrome image has a subtle beauty all of its own. Making prints that captured that beauty was almost impossible. Recently, however, digital scanning and inkjet printing have allowed Gruyaert to make the kinds of prints he had always wished for. Colour reproduction for published books has also made extraordinary progress in the last decade or so. Gruyaert's loyalty to Kodachrome has eventually paid off, and he is able to present his work as it was first visualized. But it is a cruel irony that the digital revolutions that have enabled this were what put Kodachrome out of business.

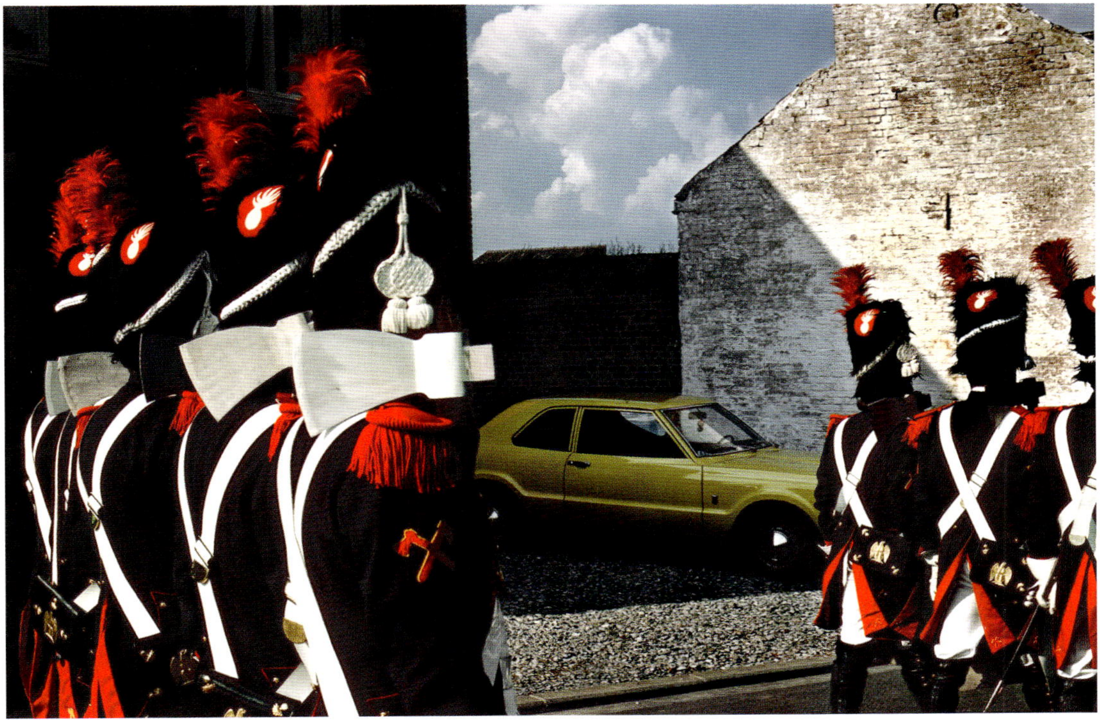

LUCAS BLALOCK

Emile, Man of the Future, 2016–17

NEW IMAGE TECHNOLOGIES tend to model themselves on the improvement of older ones, but they cannot be confined to that role. When Adobe Photoshop, the leading digital post-production software package, was launched in 1988, its tools took their names and functions from well-established analogue practices: airbrush, cut, paste, crop, slice, erase, and so on. But it soon became clear that its possibilities could, and would, exceed those of the older practices.

In its commercial applications, such as advertising, fashion and architecture, the role of digital post-production is to idealize and perfect. The never completely controllable actuality captured in a photograph is groomed and polished. The American artist Lucas Blalock pursues other possibilities. He uses Photoshop to produce gauche and absurdist inversions of commercial slickness. He shoots with a large-format analogue camera knowing that the images will be scanned and reworked on screen before being printed for exhibition. He has also experimented with augmented-reality technologies, another area in which commercial conventions are dominant.

Most often, Blalock works with the still life and the portrait. These genres are found in everything from high art to advertising, and most often they make propositions about objects and people. Blalock confuses the idea of proposition, taking the image to the point of implosion or collapse. Think of those stand-up comedians or close-up magicians whose acts are carefully crafted to feel incompetent. The conventions and expectations are unmasked, and an absurdist space of doubt opens up.

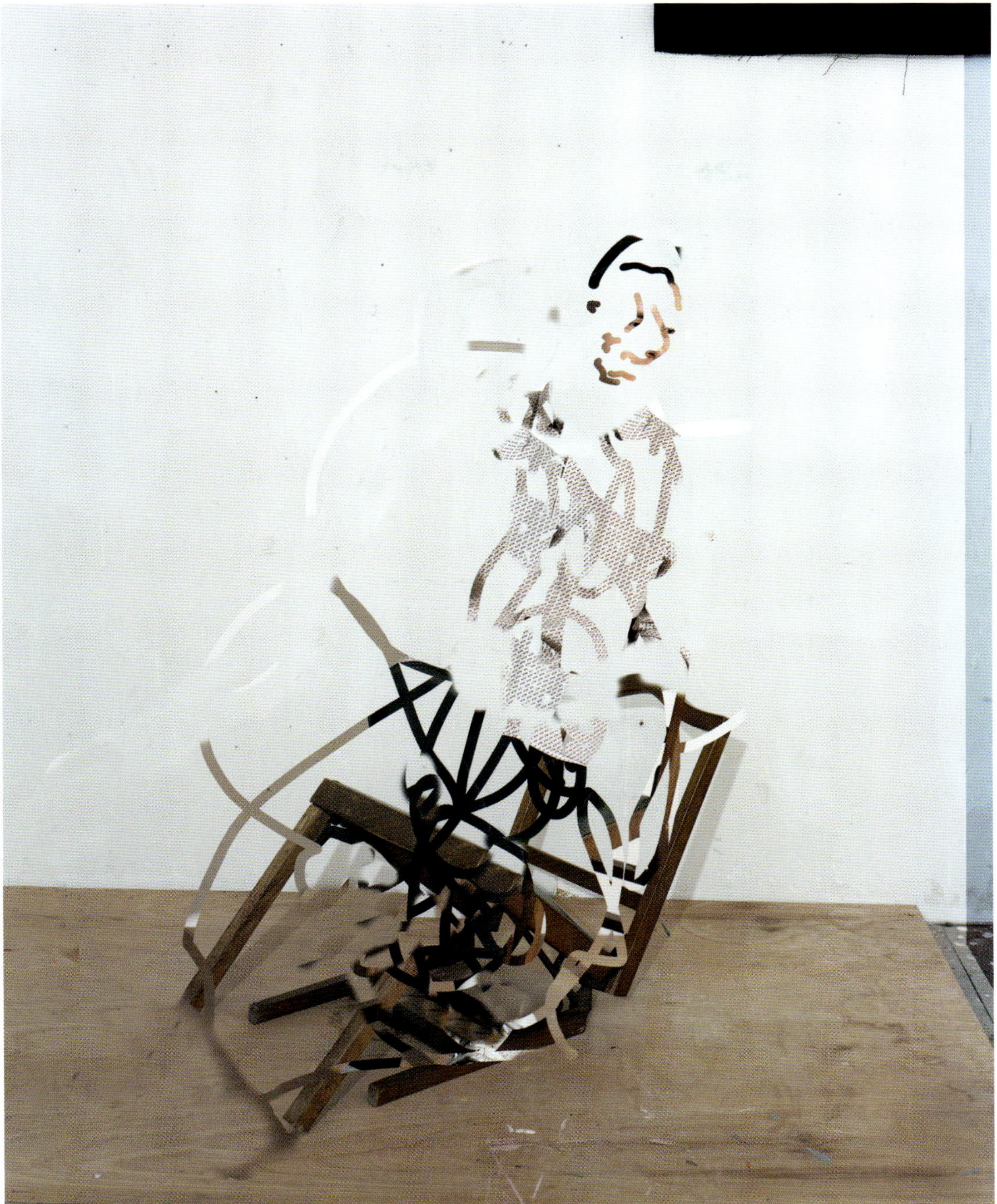

BROOMBERG & CHANARIN

The Press Conference, June 9, 2008

FROM THE SERIES 'THE DAY NOBODY DIED', 2008

IN NOVEMBER 2007 the photographic artists Adam Broomberg and Oliver Chanarin were invited to discuss with the British Ministry of Defence the possibility of making a series of portraits of soldiers in Afghanistan. They agreed to visit the territory under the sponsorship, scrutiny and supervision of the army. The military calls this 'embedding': photographers' safety is guarded, at the cost of journalistic freedom. They are taken near to the front line, but each day their digital memory cards are studied and censored. Some photographers refuse to be embedded, considering it a form of collusion.

Under escort, Broomberg & Chanarin travelled through Helmand Province, the front line between the British military and the Taliban fighters. They did not make portraits. Instead, they took with them a boxed, sealed roll of unexposed colour photographic paper, 50 metres (164 ft) long, cut into lengths of 7 metres (23 ft). At different points in Helmand, a length would be taken out briefly and exposed to the light, still rolled up. It would then be developed and fixed.

Each exposure was a *response* to a reported event, not a photojournalistic documentation of it. The titles of the exposures include *The Jailbreak*, *The Repatriation*, *The Brother's Suicide*, *The Fixer's Execution*, *The Day Nobody Died*, *The Day of a Hundred Dead*. The paper responds 'negatively' to light, so the more light it receives, the darker the marks when developed. Each length tends to be darker at the edges, and also darker at the outer end, where the bright Afghan light made its strongest impression. The colour response is also in negative, and varied unpredictably with the heat affecting the chemistry.

The work was first shown at the London gallery Paradise Row, where the other essential element of the work was a 40-minute video documenting the transport of the paper from the artists' London studio to Helmand – in and out of airports, on and off military vehicles, across the terrain of Afghanistan, and back again. The video effectively functioned as a caption, making a parallel with the way reportage images depend on supplemental information.

A degree of abstract expressivity is present in all photographs, but in these photograms we get nothing else. Think, for example, of Robert Capa's famous photographs of the D-Day landings on Omaha Beach. The expressionistic dimension – the graininess and high contrast – had very little to do with Omaha Beach that day. It was the result of Capa's film being processed and dried too hastily. But it is difficult to read the graininess for what it is. The 'look' of those images is read as a consequence of Capa's being on that beach on that day, at a certain physical, emotional and photographic limit. Likewise, it is tempting to read the marks on Broomberg & Chanarin's photographic paper as expressive of the situation in which they were made.

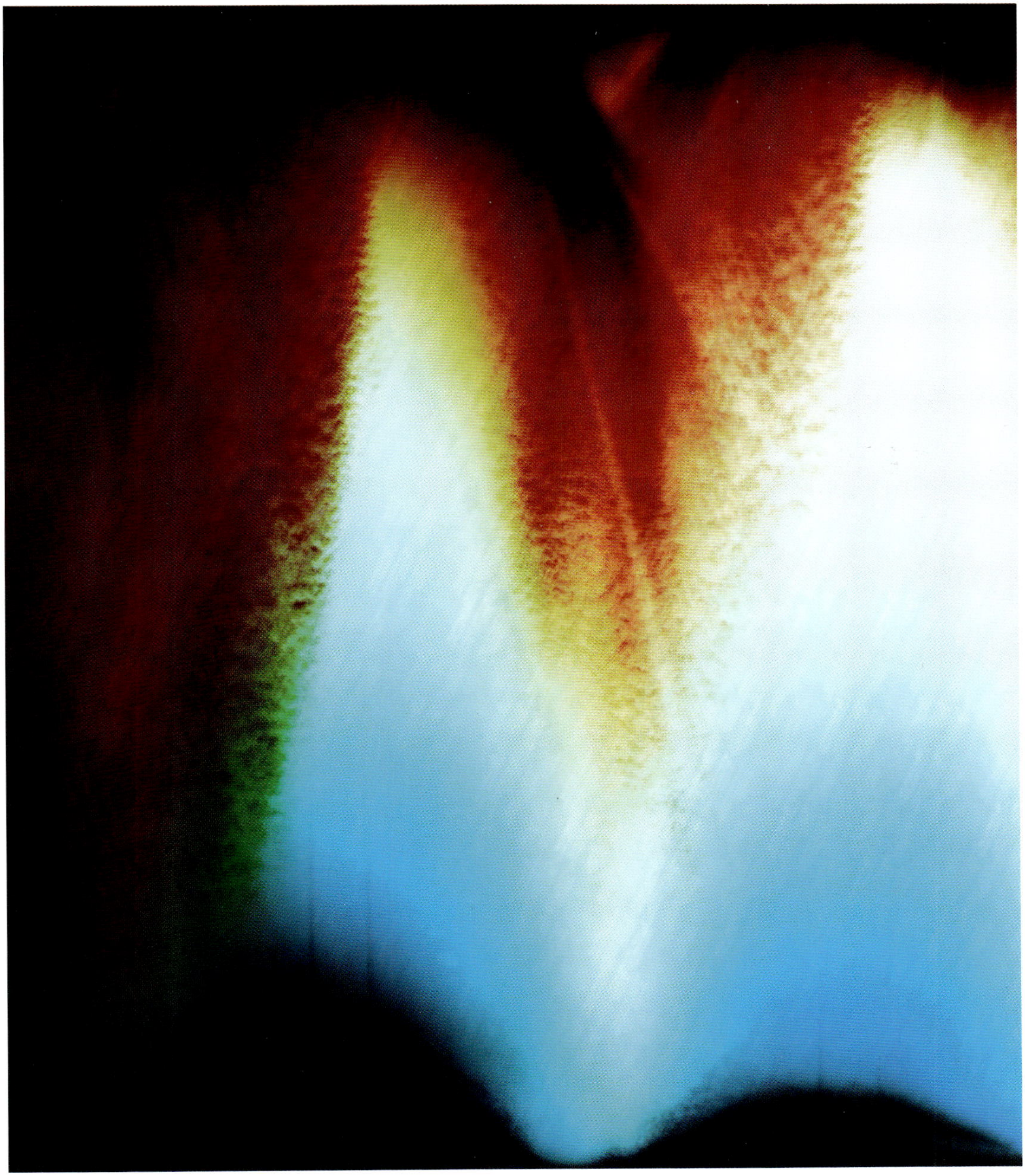

PHOTOGRAPHER UNKNOWN

Military personnel shielded from nuclear test, 1957

IN EVERYDAY LANGUAGE, light is the source of endless metaphors. They are used constantly and with barely a second thought. We talk of knowledge as *illumination.* We are *exposed* to new ideas. When we are confused, we are *in the dark*. Ignorance is a form of *blindness.* Hope is the *light at the end of the tunnel.* Intelligence is *bright.* The turn from superstition to reason was a turn to *enlightenment.* And if you understand me, you *see what I mean.*

For centuries, the coming of light has been thought of as positive, open and progressive. This changed in 1945, with the advent of the atomic bomb. Light of cosmic brightness accompanied explosions of unimaginable devastation.

The first successful detonation of an atomic bomb took place on 16 July 1945. J. Robert Oppenheimer, director of the laboratory that had researched and designed atomic bombs, recalled that it reminded him of a passage from the *Bhagavad Gita,* part of the Hindu epic the *Mahabharata*: 'If the radiance of a thousand suns were to burst forth at once in the sky, that would be like the splendor of the Mighty One... I am become Death, the destroyer of worlds.'

The following month, atomic bombs were dropped on the Japanese cities of Hiroshima and Nagasaki. In a flash, light had become deadly, heralding destruction beyond human measure. Between then and 1962, the US military conducted approximately 216 atomic tests in the atmosphere and in the sea. Then came a return to darkness. From 1962 to 1992, a further 723 tests took place underground.

FOR CENTURIES, THE COMING OF LIGHT HAS BEEN THOUGHT OF AS POSITIVE, OPEN AND PROGRESSIVE. THIS CHANGED IN 1945, WITH THE ADVENT OF THE ATOMIC BOMB.

At first, this image may look like a scene from the First World War, but this trench is protecting soldiers from the blast of a nuclear test explosion. It is night-time but the brightness is enough to illuminate the photographic plate. In reality, the light would have been too sudden and too bright for human eyes. Only the photographic image makes the situation visible, witnessing on our hehalf.

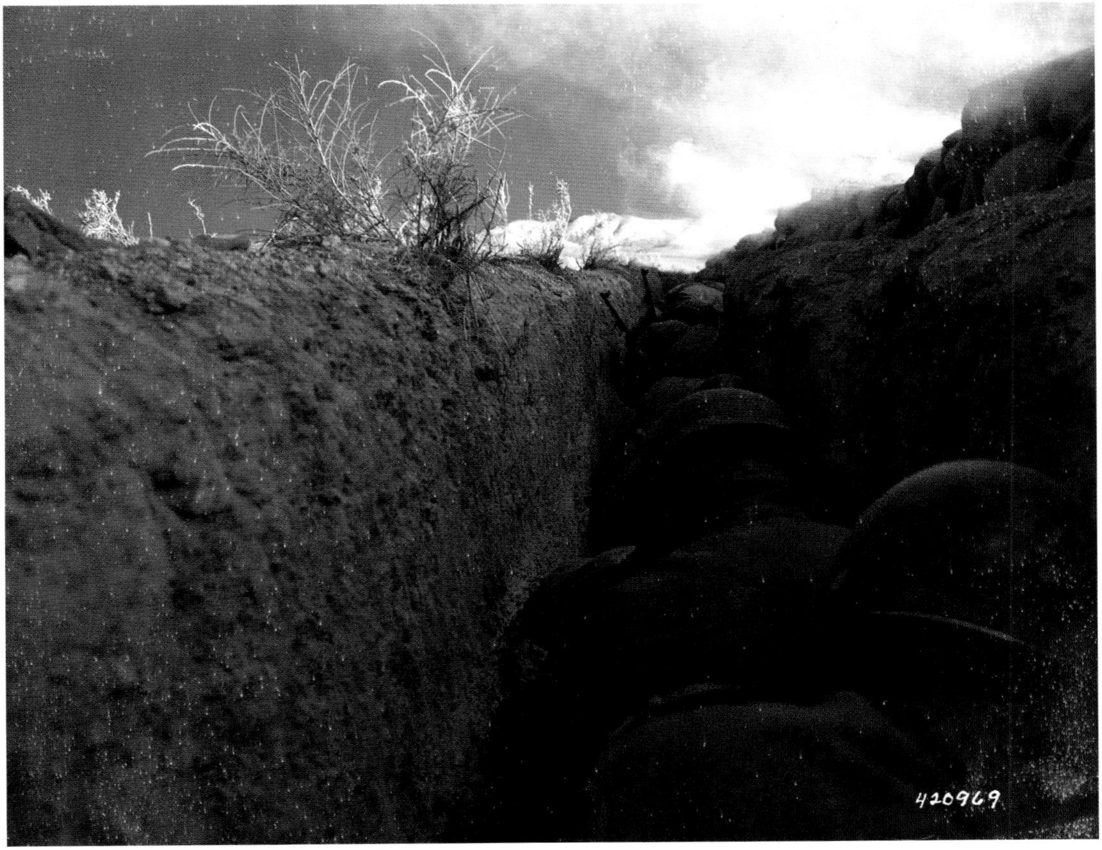
420969

CHRIS McCAW

Sunburned GSP164 (Mojave), 2007

IN 1897 THE PHILOSOPHER Charles Sanders Peirce developed a theory of communication in which he divided signs into three types: icons, symbols and indexes. An icon is a sign that resembles what it refers to. A drawing of a face that looks like a face, for example. A symbol need not resemble but it has a meaning that is culturally agreed upon. Red roses symbolize romantic love. With an index there is a causal, physical relationship. A mark in the sand is caused by a foot. Smoke is caused by fire.

With photography, particularly realist photography, icon, symbol and index combine in a highly specific way. The lens produces an image that resembles. The image may include things with symbolic meanings. The light bouncing off what is in front of the camera passes through the lens to alter the light-sensitive surface (be it chemical or electronic). Peirce was being schematic, but his theory is a suggestive way of thinking about photography. Not just realist photography, but all the deviations from it. Abstract photography, photography without a camera, impermanent photography, and so on.

In 2003 the American photographer Chris McCaw was making a night photograph in the desert of Utah. One evening, he pointed his large-format, tripod-mounted camera eastwards. With the aperture wide open, and the lens focused on infinity, he was hoping to capture a long-exposure image of the stars. He woke up the next morning, went to close the shutter, and smelt smoke. Later that day, when he was processing the film, he found it had an arc-shaped tear in it. As night ended, the rising sun had burned the film, scoring a physical line as it moved through the sky, intensifying in brightness as it climbed.

What was an accident became a technique, as McCaw found ways to refine the process. He was already adept at making simple cameras, and with a solar panel and a computer fan he rigged up an extraction system to remove smoke from the inside of the camera during the long exposures. In 2006 he switched from using negative film to vintage fibre-based paper, which burns differently. During very long exposures, film and paper solarize, the tones reversing but not completely. Thus, in a solarized image, positive and negative co-exist.

This image traces the sun as it rises over the landscape of the Mojave Desert, passing behind a tree. The burned arc varies in intensity, the result of clouds passing between the camera and the sun.

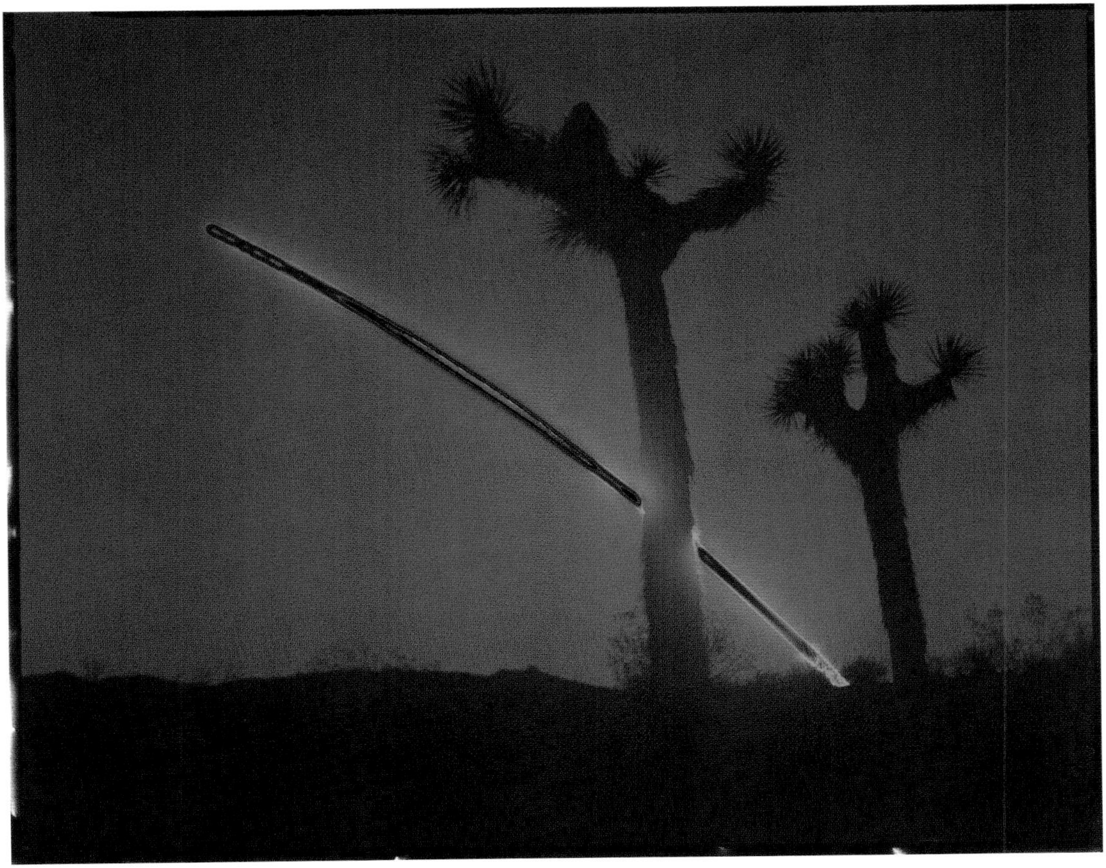

ANNA ATKINS

Cystoseira granulata

PAGE FROM THE BOOK *PHOTOGRAPHS OF BRITISH ALGAE: CYANOTYPE IMPRESSIONS* (1843)

CLAIMING A FIRST in photography is notoriously risky. New information continues to emerge that pushes dates back further and further. It is possible that Anna Atkins was the first woman to use a camera, although it might have been Constance Talbot, but no examples survive by either. What seems more certain is that Atkins was the first person to produce a photographically illustrated book. The initial volume of *Photographs of British Algae: Cyanotype Impressions* appeared in October 1843; two more volumes followed. The first of the six parts of *The Pencil of Nature*, by William Henry Fox Talbot (pages 198, 224), appeared eight months later.

Atkins and Talbot knew each other, coming from the same educated, upper-class British circle. Atkins learnt of Talbot's techniques before they had been announced officially. She made very few copies of her books, and gave them to friends and acquaintances. Talbot's publication was available via commercial subscription. Atkins' book included a short, hand-written note; Talbot's was really an image-text work, with a substantial written treatise on what photography was and might become.

Atkins didn't use a camera, instead producing photograms by laying specimens of dried algae directly upon her sensitized paper and exposing them to light. Talbot made a few images this way, but most in his book were produced with a camera. Each image by Atkins was unique, whereas Talbot pioneered the 'negative' that could be used to make multiple prints. Some copies of Atkins' book had more than four hundred images; Talbot's had twenty-four. Atkins' images, made with the distinctive cyanotype process invented in 1842 by her friend Sir John Herschel, have proved to be remarkably permanent. In the seventeen surviving copies of her book, they look as vivid as the day they were made. Talbot struggled to make his images stable, and in the forty copies of his book that remain – he produced four hundred in total – most have deteriorated.

What really unites the work of Atkins and Talbot is the way they both grasped how the photographic image was to be understood as something between art and science. This wholly new and strange genus of images had an aesthetic charge at least as significant as its practical applications.

ATKINS DIDN'T USE A CAMERA, INSTEAD PRODUCING PHOTOGRAMS BY LAYING SPECIMENS OF DRIED ALGAE DIRECTLY UPON HER SENSITIZED PAPER AND EXPOSING THEM TO LIGHT.

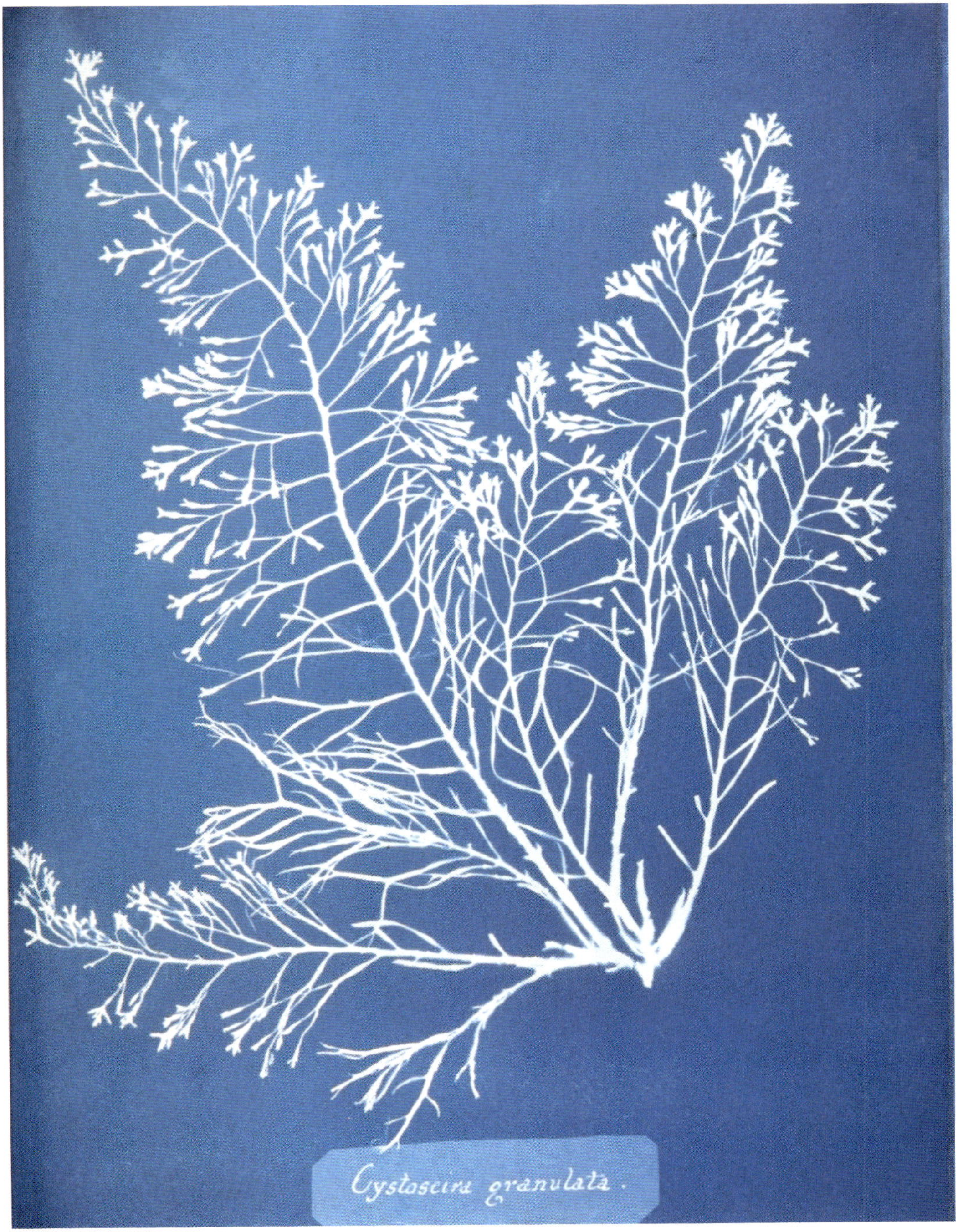
Cystoseira granulata.

WILLIAM HENRY FOX TALBOT

Lace, 1845

WILLIAM HENRY FOX TALBOT'S publication *The Pencil of Nature* (1844–46) contains a humble image of a piece of fabric. Talbot placed black lace directly on to sensitized paper and exposed it to the sun. The result was a *negative*, a term Talbot introduced to the lexicon of photography in his description of this very image. The more light the paper receives during exposure, the darker it turns when developed and fixed. The lace appears white on a dark background. It does not look like a negative, since we are as familiar with white lace as black. Neither does it look as though it's been made without a camera, since the almost flat fabric is so well rendered by the simple technique.

One of Talbot's terms for his process was 'photogenic drawing', connecting it to the idea that the photographic image is a semi-automatic stencil of the world. Indeed, Talbot confessed that the key impulse that drove his experiments was his inability to draw. The image of lace is a simple but effective demonstration. The not-yet standardized mechanism of photography takes as its subject a piece of not-quite-standardized lace. We can see pattern and repetition but also unique idiosyncrasies – the tears, fraying and undulations. The image is scientific and cold, yet intimate and gentle.

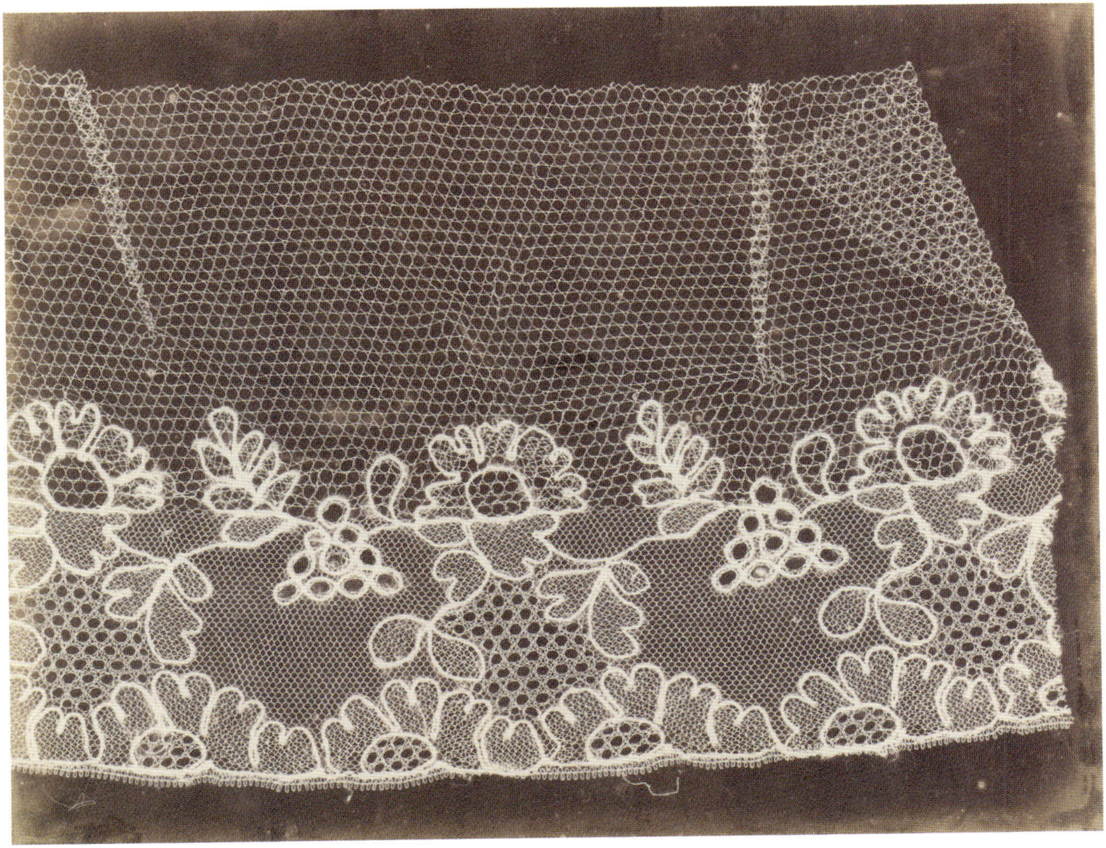

HELEN SEAR

Inside the View 17

FROM THE SERIES 'INSIDE THE VIEW', 2004–08

SEAR USES A 'PEN' ON AN ELECTRONIC TABLET. IT IS AN ABSTRACTED MODE OF DRAWING WITH WHICH WE ARE ALL FAMILIAR. WE MOVE OUR HAND IN ONE PLACE – USING A MOUSE, SAY, OR A TOUCH PAD – AND ITS EFFECT IS REGISTERED SOMEWHERE ELSE.

THE BRITISH ARTIST HELEN SEAR came to photography from painting. In the transition, the work of the hand had to be rethought. Her output is remarkably varied, but much of it makes innovative virtue of what the hand might mean to photography.

'Inside the View' is a suite of montages. In each, a portrait photograph and a landscape photograph are combined, and in the process a third image is produced. The two images are brought together on a computer screen in Photoshop. On to the image of a woman's head, Sear 'draws' a lace-like network of lines, within which emerges a photo of a landscape. In painting and drawing, the line is usually there to form an image. In Sear's work, the line *is* the image. The network becomes a lace-like veil to look at and to look through.

Sear uses a 'pen' on an electronic tablet. It is an abstracted mode of drawing with which we are all familiar. We move our hand in one place – using a mouse, say, or a touch pad – and its effect is registered somewhere else. Making 'Inside the View' involved painstaking, immersive work that demanded an inner intensity. Perhaps this is why Sear takes as her subject women contemplating landscapes. A landscape is always in some sense a mindscape, not least when we are immersed in it. But the women we see were never really in these landscapes. The effect is seen spatially but constructed on our mental screen, so to speak. It is we who are 'inside the view'.

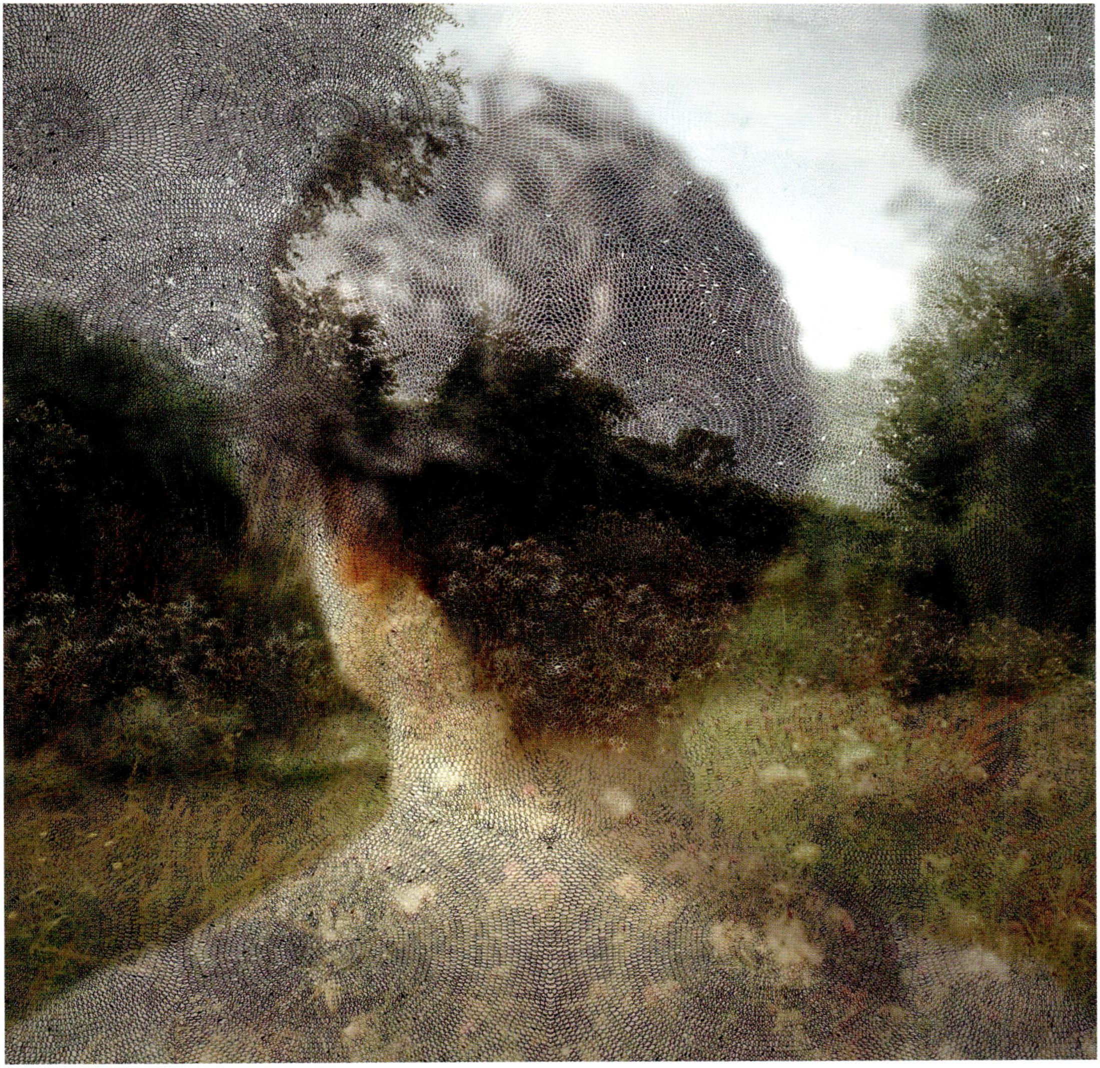

THOMAS MAILAENDER

Untitled

FROM THE SERIES 'ILLUSTRATED PEOPLE', 2014

PHOTOGRAPHY ELUDES EASY DEFINITION as a medium. As soon as one attempts to define it, exceptions and anomalies come to mind. Part of the difficulty is that what we commonly think of as the photographic apparatus – the camera – is itself comprised of three mediums: the lens or hole through which light passes; the shutter or other means of regulating the exposure; and the light-sensitive surface, whether chemical or electronic. This does not even take into account the further apparatus needed to make the image permanently visible, nor the fact that, in the digital era, all the various apparatuses have converged, and are networked to the point of being inseparable.

Thomas Mailaender's series 'Illustrated People' appears to take photography back to some kind of basics, if in a lurid and eccentric way. Mailaender applied negatives of archival images to the bodies of twenty-three volunteers and exposed them to the rays of a UV lamp. The result was 'suntans' of positive but impermanent images. Any images would have sufficed, but photography is a medium of specifics, so choices had to be made. Mailaender was invited to choose images from the misleadingly named Archive of Modern Conflict, a huge private collection of photographs with diverse subject matter, little of which is to do with conflict in any immediate sense. It is not exactly clear what governed the choices, but subject matter is bound to steer the viewer's interpretation of the process. In this image, lovers kiss – a metaphor, perhaps, for the contact between image and skin.

Mailaender's photography itself also shapes our response. Shot in flashlight as anonymous body parts against a blank wall, the images relate to medical or even criminal photography. The unforgiving harshness seems to underscore the strangely ritualistic burning of images on to human flesh. If there is a 'basics' of photography here, it comes with all manner of complications.

MAILAENDER APPLIED NEGATIVES OF ARCHIVAL IMAGES TO THE BODIES OF TWENTY-THREE VOLUNTEERS AND EXPOSED THEM TO THE RAYS OF A UV LAMP. THE RESULT WAS 'SUNTANS' OF POSITIVE BUT IMPERMANENT IMAGES.

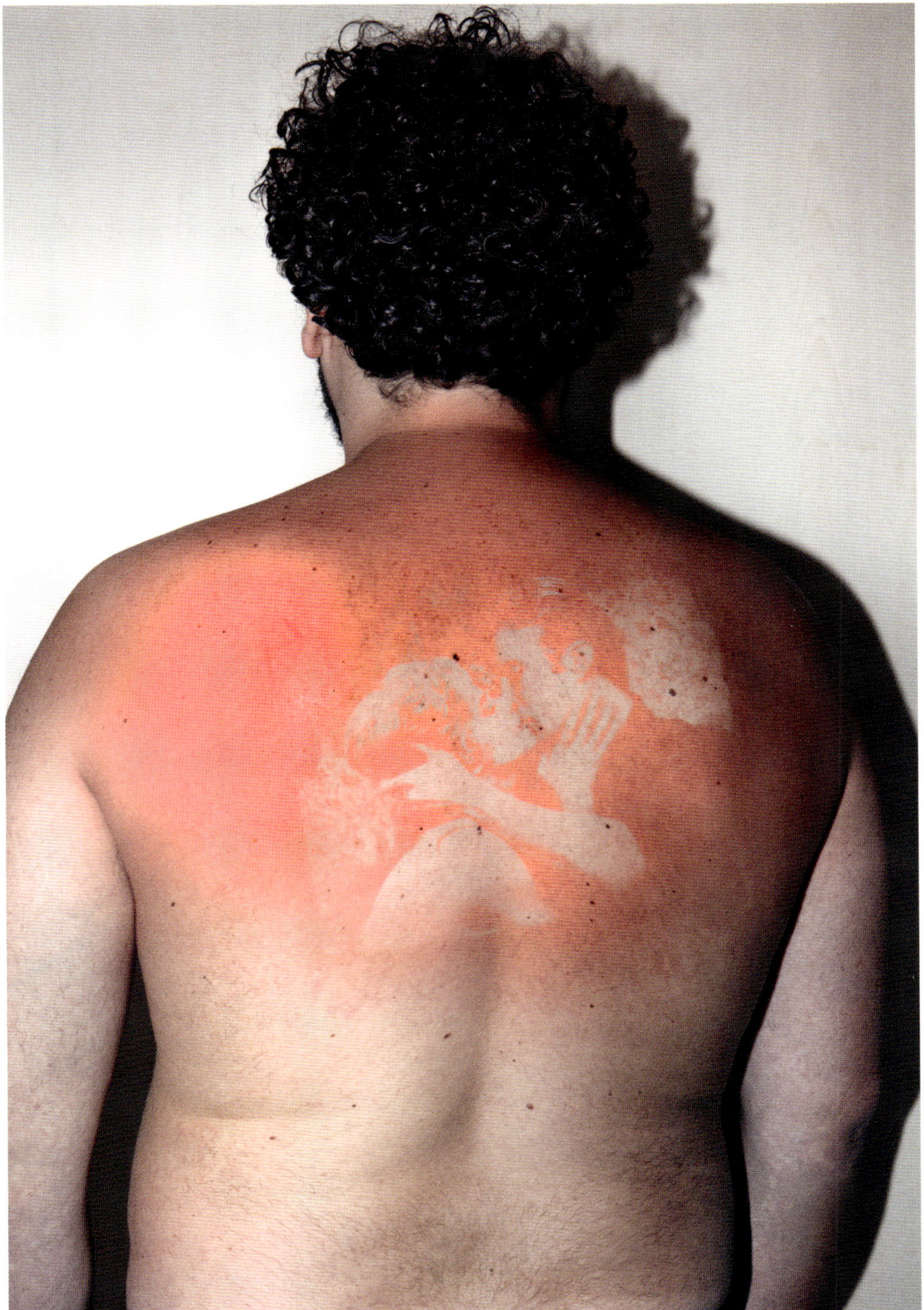

FLIP SCHULKE

Cassius Clay training in a pool at the Sir John Hotel, Miami, 1961

IT IS OFTEN SAID that Cassius Clay (Muhammad Ali) was sport's first global superstar. A world-champion boxer, he was witty, smart, clownish, ironic, serious, an outspoken opponent of North American imperialism, an advocate for civil rights, and a philanthropist.

Aged eighteen, Clay won gold at the 1960 Olympic Games. The following year he was in Miami for a fight. *Sports Illustrated* magazine assigned Flip Schulke to photograph him. To impress Clay, Schulke showed him some underwater photographs of waterskiers he had published in *Life* magazine. Clay said he often trained in a pool. Schulke fetched his scuba camera.

Confused by the idea of a boxer in water, *Sports Illustrated* turned down the photos, but they were eventually published by *Life*. The magazine quoted Clay: 'Not to be bragging or anything like that, but they say I'm the fastest heavyweight in the ring today.' Training in the pool built up strength and pace, he claimed. 'You try to box hard, then when you punch the same way out of water you got speed.' *Life* reproduced five images of Clay demonstrating his technique, but not the one that has since become well known. Perhaps it felt too posed, too static. (Many famous photographs that are now celebrated as 'iconic' did not seem so at first. Most are not born iconic – they achieve that status slowly.)

Three years after the shoot, Clay (who had just changed his name to Muhammad Ali) confessed to Schulke that he and his trainer had invented the whole thing. He never trained in a pool, and was actually a lousy swimmer. Bluffing, duping and toying with expectation came as naturally to him with journalists as with opponents.

The way in which Clay/Ali boxed was a kind of performance, aimed as much at pleasing an audience as at defeating his rivals. His startling switches in tempo, taunting expressions, flamboyant gestures and showboating were integral elements of his strategy as a fighter. Undoubtedly he was a supreme athlete, but what made him so disarming and difficult to fight was his bewitching sense of play. The blurring of boundaries between opponent and audience, boxing ring and media circus, is what made him so famous.

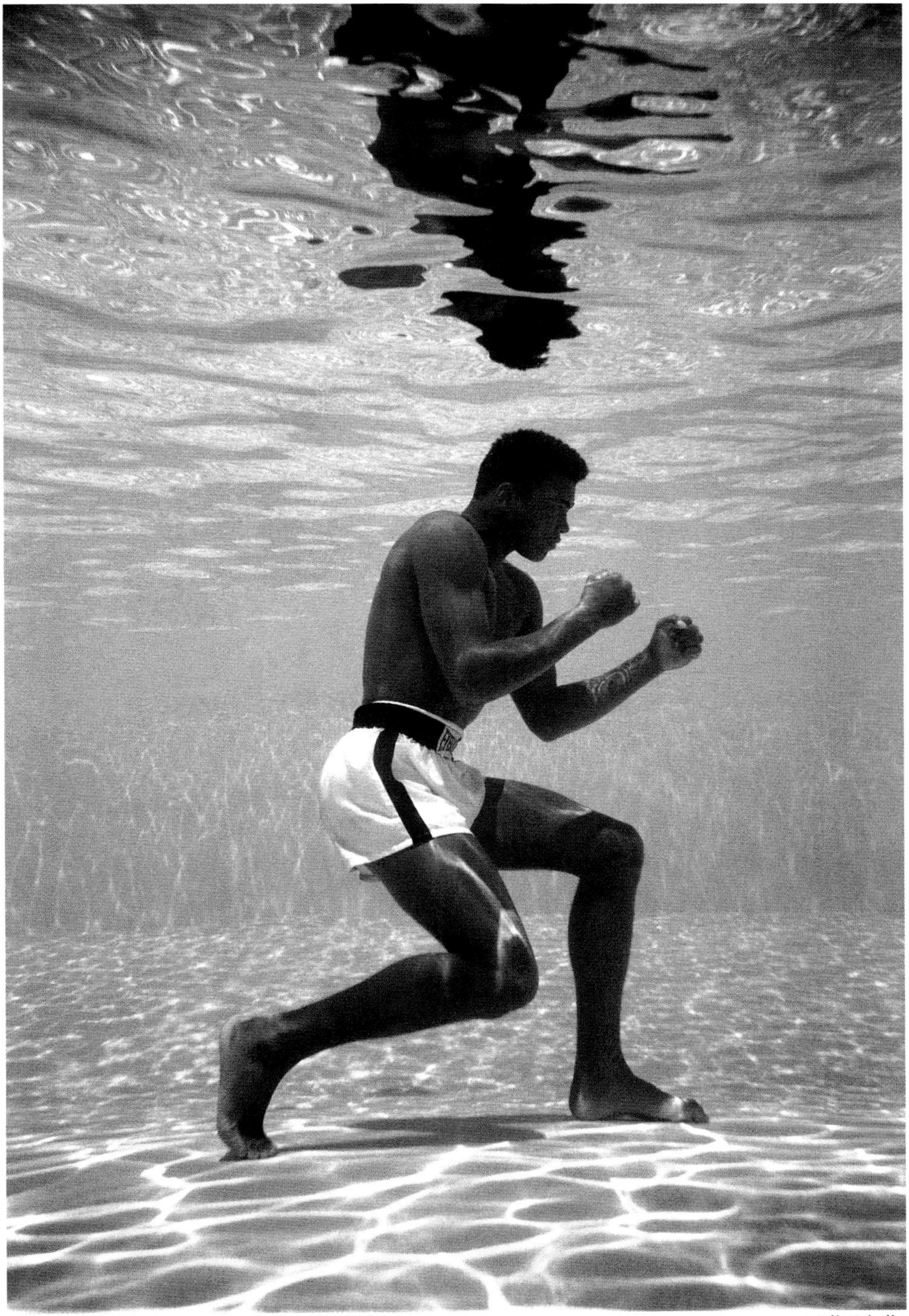

RICHARD AVEDON

Marilyn Monroe, Actress, New York, May 6, 1957, 1957

'THERE WAS NO SUCH PERSON as Marilyn Monroe. Marilyn Monroe was an invention of hers. A genius invention that she created like an author creates a character. So when Marilyn Monroe put on a sequined dress and danced in the studio ... for hours she danced and sang and flirted ... she did Marilyn Monroe ... And then there was the inevitable drop, because she was someone who went very high up and went very way down. And when the night was over she sat in the corner like a child with everything gone. But I wouldn't photograph her without her knowledge of it, and as I came with the camera I saw that she was not saying "no".'

Richard Avedon was for decades one of the pre-eminent portrait photographers working in North America. Whether made for magazines, record covers, books or exhibitions, what unites his finest images is an acute awareness of the fragility of the self, and of the camera's disarming way of getting to it.

Avedon's account of this shoot with the actress Marilyn Monroe is remarkable for what it reveals and what it leaves open. What might his tantalizing last lines tell us? Does 'like a child with everything gone' mean Monroe was pretending to be a child? And if she was not saying 'no', had she let her mask slip, or was it another mask?

The photographer Eve Arnold gave a similar account of Monroe's understanding of her public persona: 'She would say to me, "Let's make a Marilyn" ... She adored the still camera, more than the motion picture camera, because with the still camera she was in charge.'

By 1957, when this image was taken, Monroe was approaching the height of her fame, but her inner life and public image were both in profound transition. Celebrity was taking its toll on her already fragile psyche. In her next movies, notably *The Prince and the Showgirl* (1957), *Some Like it Hot* (1959) and *The Misfits* (1961), she would play characters who were similarly troubled by their image and the expectations of others.

In 1956 the psychologist and social scientist Erving Goffman had published his groundbreaking study, *The Presentation of Self in Everyday Life*. What interested Goffman, and what caught the wider imagination when the book became a bestseller, was the realization that selfhood is always a matter of performance, primarily for others but also for oneself. This performance can be an enormous burden: 'As human beings we are presumably creatures of variable impulse with moods and energies that change from one moment to the next. As characters put on for an audience, however, we must not be subject to ups or downs. A certain bureaucratization of the spirit is expected so that we can be relied upon to give a perfectly homogenous performance at every appointed time.'

Monroe knew this well. Part of her way of coping was to play characters that were struggling to cope, and occasionally to present herself as struggling. That is to say, to present the struggle that presentation demands. Was this what Monroe was doing for Avedon at the end of that day in his studio? We shall never know exactly what went on, and that is part of the compelling appeal of this photograph.

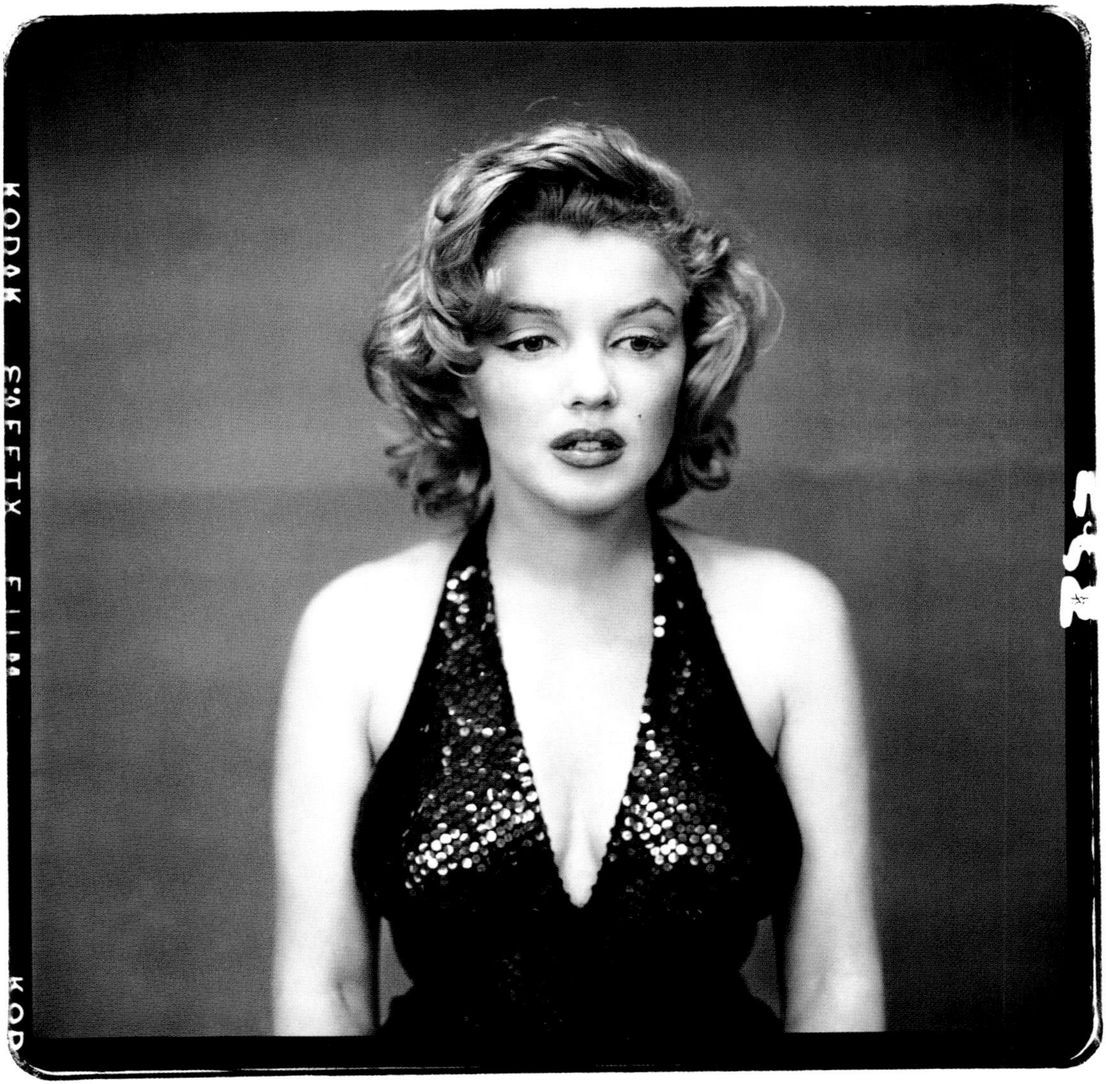

MARCELLO GEPPETTI

Anita Ekberg confronting the paparazzi, 1960

IN 1960 THE SWEDISH MOVIE STAR Anita Ekberg was in Rome to act in Federico Fellini's *La Dolce Vita* (The Sweet Life), a film about the increasingly cynical and narcissistic culture of the city.

Ekberg plays a Swedish actress who has arrived in Rome to star in a movie. *La Dolce Vita* unfolds as a series of set-piece scenes in which characters lose their sense of reality and purpose in a world seduced by media images and reputations. Ekberg's character gets involved with a shady but charming journalist (played by Marcello Mastroianni), who writes for the newspaper gossip columns.

Famously, *La Dolce Vita* also describes the emerging group of freelance photographers in Rome who would stop at nothing to get images of celebrities, which they would sell to the trashy magazines. They were working-class men who had come to the city to find a new living. In the film, one of these photographers is named Paparazzo, and it is from him that the term 'paparazzi' derives. One of the real-life photographers that inspired Fellini was Marcello Geppetti. Among his 1 million photographs are many famous images of celebrities. This one, of a shoeless Ekberg confronting Geppetti and his colleagues with a bow and arrow, is his most surreal and self-reflexive.

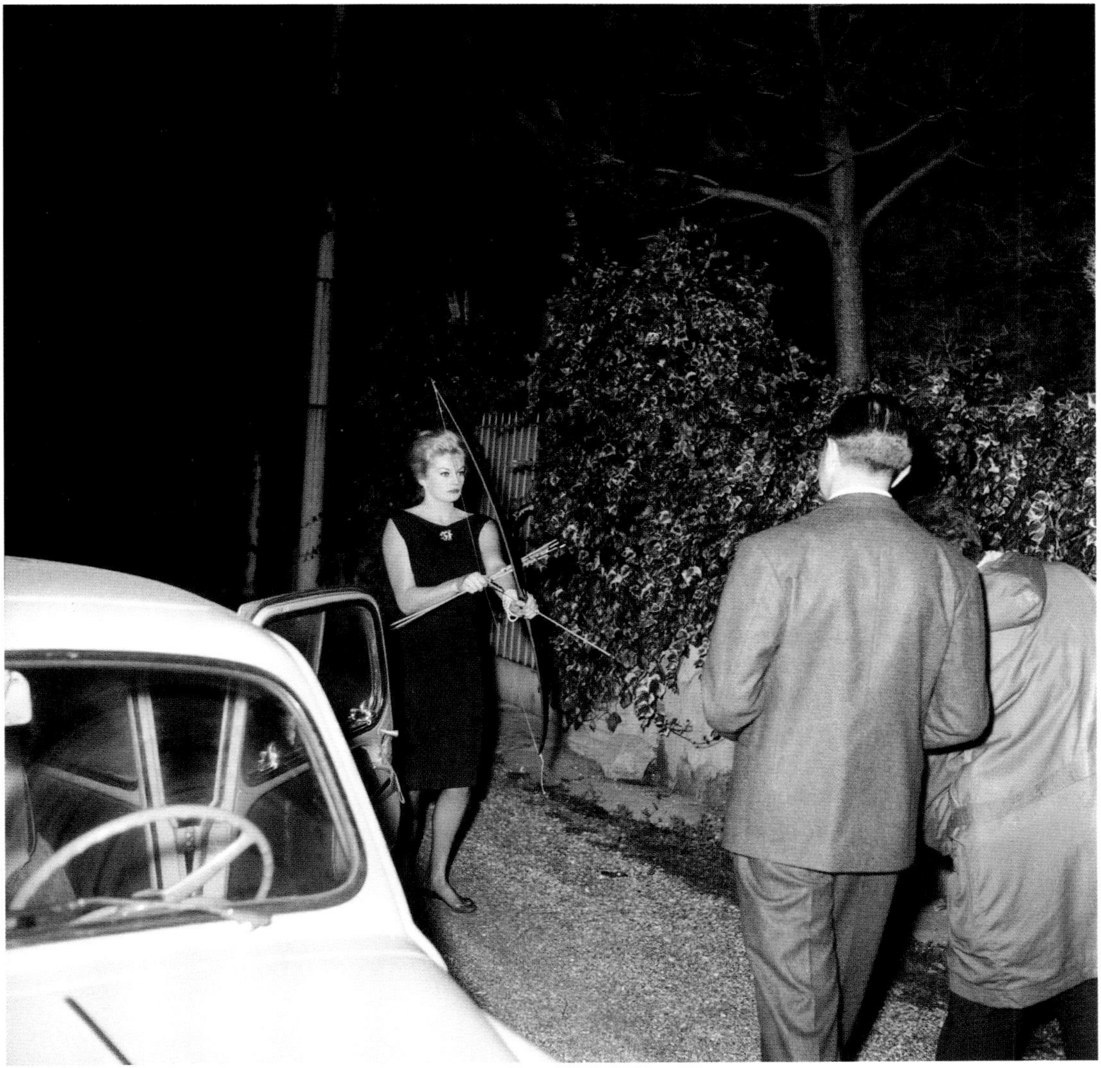

EVE ARNOLD

Army Manoeuvres, Fort Bragg, North Carolina, USA, 1967

ON 24 MARCH 1968 the *Sunday Times Magazine* carried, among other things, 'This Is How it Is', one of the British photojournalist Don McCullin's most celebrated photo-essays about the war in Vietnam. It included a photograph of a man throwing a grenade, and another of a man lying dead with his possessions spilling out around him. They are among the most reproduced images of the conflict.

A few pages further on in the same issue of the magazine there was a second photo-essay. Eve Arnold travelled to North Carolina to document one of three fake North Vietnamese villages constructed by the American military for training purposes. Recruits would be sent to these 'villages' before being shipped to the war zone. Arnold's opening spread showed young men who had been asked to attempt to camouflage themselves. In the mock hospital, one smears his face with white cream and ties a pillowcase around his head. In the bushes outside, another puts leaves in his hair and rubs grass into his cheeks. The caption for this photograph, from Arnold's third spread, reads: 'Two marines are backed by red signal smoke which indicates U.S. troop positions to prevent their air force bombing them by mistake.' Two innocents, encouraged to enter the fantasy of war, before they encounter the 'real thing'.

The contents page of the *Sunday Times Magazine* paired the photo-essays by McCullin (page 212) and Arnold under the heading 'America in Vietnam, Vietnam in America'. Thus, readers were given two very different but equally valid ways to represent that war. McCullin's pictures have been republished and exhibited many times, while Arnold's are all but forgotten. Why is this? Is it because McCullin's work fits the narrow idea of how classical photojournalism should look? Is it because Arnold was a woman, and one with little eye on posterity? Is it because Arnold's subject here was artifice, the stage-set prelude to the real 'theatre of war'? The range of work made in the name of photojournalism is much wider than the established history of photography would suggest.

TWO INNOCENTS, ENCOURAGED TO ENTER THE FANTASY OF WAR, BEFORE THEY ENCOUNTER THE 'REAL THING'.

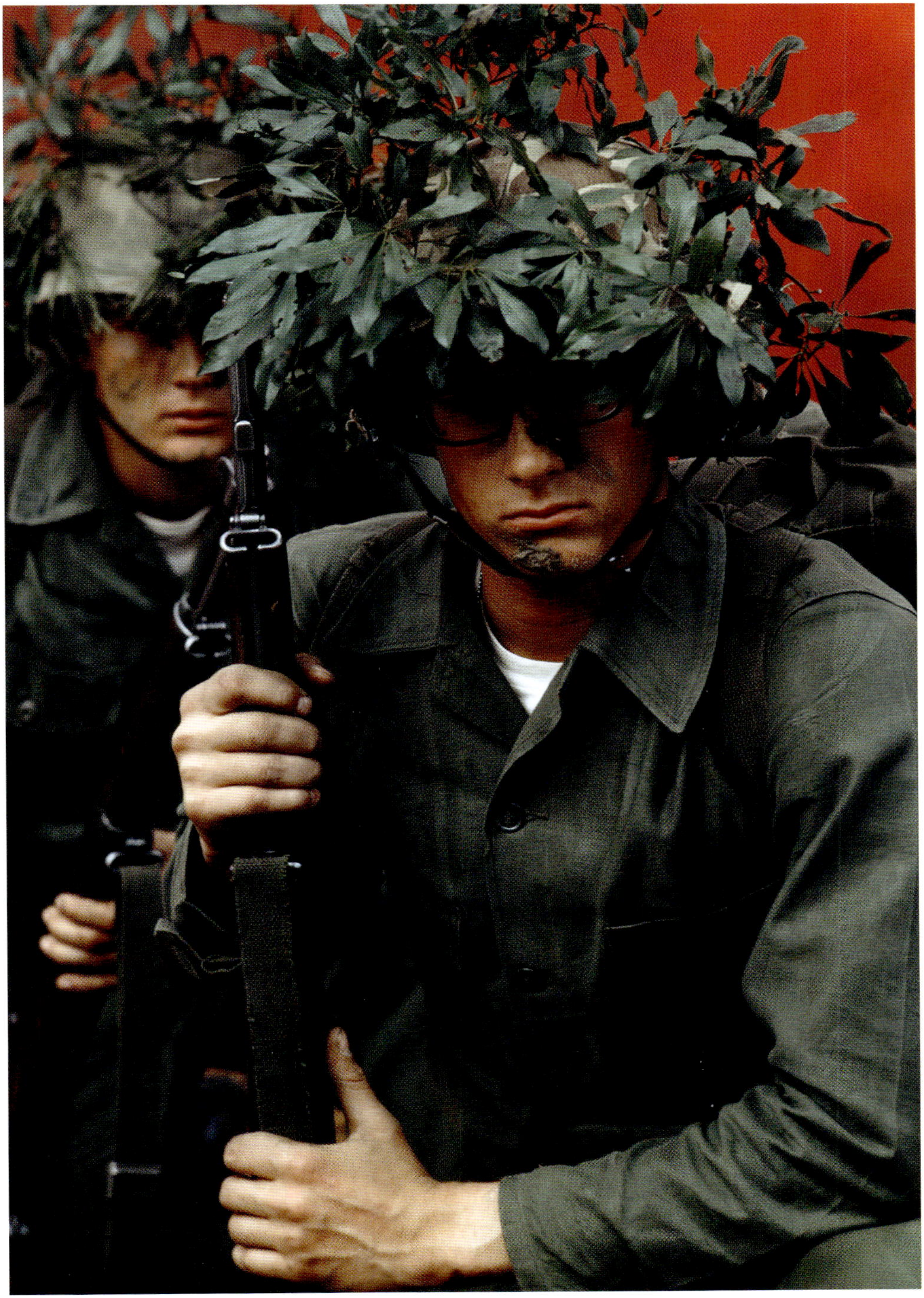

DON McCULLIN

Turkish defender leaving the side entrance of a cinema, Limassol, Cyprus, 1964

ALTHOUGH PHOTOGRAPHY MIGHT be regarded as a distinct medium, its borders with the other arts have never been, can never be, clearly defined or policed. There will be overlaps. This can be confusing or liberating, but it is inevitable. Moreover, the same permeability exists *within* photography, between the various social functions it has been given.

There is a strong desire to prevent documentary photography and photojournalism from straying and overlapping with other kinds of photography. This is because of the inherent tension between what an artwork is and what a document is. The tension is in part institutional (art demands authorship and expression, while documentary photography and photojournalism demand records and reports), but it is also internal to the medium. Each and every photograph is both an artwork and a document, and making sense of them often involves coming to terms with our conflicted responses.

In 1964 Don McCullin made an image of a Turkish gunman running down a street in Limassol, on the coast of Cyprus. The light, gestures, setting and composition were all so 'right', so pictorially precise and formally harmonious, that they worried McCullin. He told the newspaper editor Harold Evans that he felt the photograph was too much like a film still – staged, theatrical, artificial. (By coincidence, the image's caption tells us the gunman has just left a cinema.)

What does McCullin's apprehension suggest about photojournalism? That if its images are too pictorially perfect, the realism and urgency will be undermined? That it cannot risk association with fiction, even though the world sometimes looks that way in photographs? That photojournalism should follow conventions that distinguish its images from all other kinds of pictures? That a photojournalist must not confuse the audience by appearing to mix crisis with pictorial contemplation?

Photojournalism is often described as a practice in crisis. With the waning of the mass-media magazines in which it first flourished, and the spread of amateur cameras, the crisis is usually seen in economic and professional terms. However, this is only half the explanation. The real crisis stems from the constantly shifting relationship between image and reality.

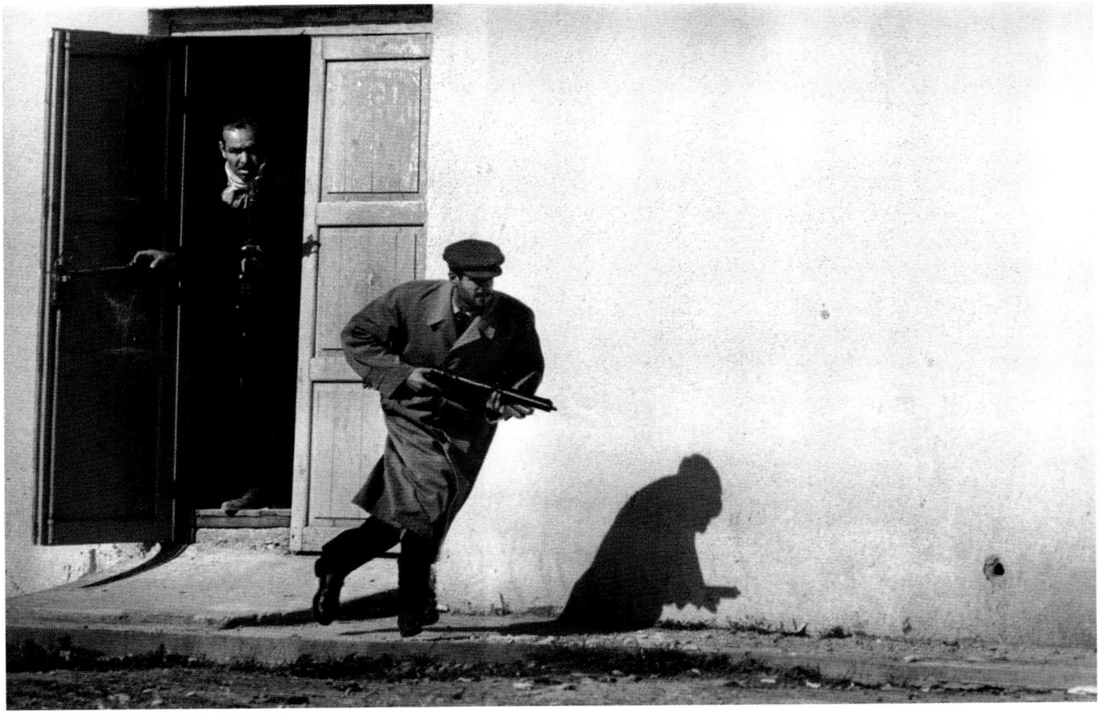

LUC DELAHAYE

Les Pillards (The Looters), 2010

ON BOULEVARD Jean-Jacques Dessalines in Port-au-Prince, Haiti, a few days after the devastating earthquake of 12 January 2010, the French photographer Luc Delahaye made this photograph of looters. He was not firing off a digital camera to make several shots from which he might later choose one, or construct a sequence. Rather, he was hand-holding an old-fashioned 4 × 5-inch view camera, exposing a single negative with no chance of quickly taking another.

The image captures the urgency and chaos of the situation. It also has an unlikely formal unity, and there is great clarity in the depiction of the drama. The red, blue, green and yellow are balanced. Every figure, gesture and face seems to reveal different aspects of the psychologically charged moment.

Delahaye began his career working in the institutions of photojournalism, but soon found the formulas expected of the profession to be obstacles, both to his own development and to the fullest expression of how photography might be able to encounter and respond to situations and events.

Photojournalism had begun as an experimental practice. Nobody knew for sure what it could or should be. But in the hands of the mass media, especially the large-circulation newspapers and magazines of the twentieth century, conventions were established. Through their repeated use, the media cemented its authority, and the authority of that kind of photography's account of reality. Eventually, those conventions wore out, losing their hold over popular understanding.

Photography has been returned to its necessarily open condition, where no single way of representing is dominant. Such a situation can be worrying, and there is much talk today of a supposed chaos of competing truth-claims. But, at root, photography has no single or superior relation to the world it can describe – not just one approach to the truths it might be attempting to access. The moment it, or its audience, presumes it does is actually a moment of cultural and political danger. As the critic and playwright Bertolt Brecht put it in 1938: 'With the people struggling and changing reality before our eyes, we must not cling to "tried" rules of narrative, venerable literary models, eternal aesthetic laws. We must not derive realism as such from particular existing works, but we shall use every means, old and new, tried and untried, derived from art and derived from other sources, to render reality to men in a form they can master [...] Our concept of realism must be wide and political, sovereign over all conventions.'

Delahaye is often described as a photojournalist who shifted position – institutionally, aesthetically and philosophically – to being an artist. This misses the point. Every serious image-maker who is interested in describing the world and their place within it must experiment.

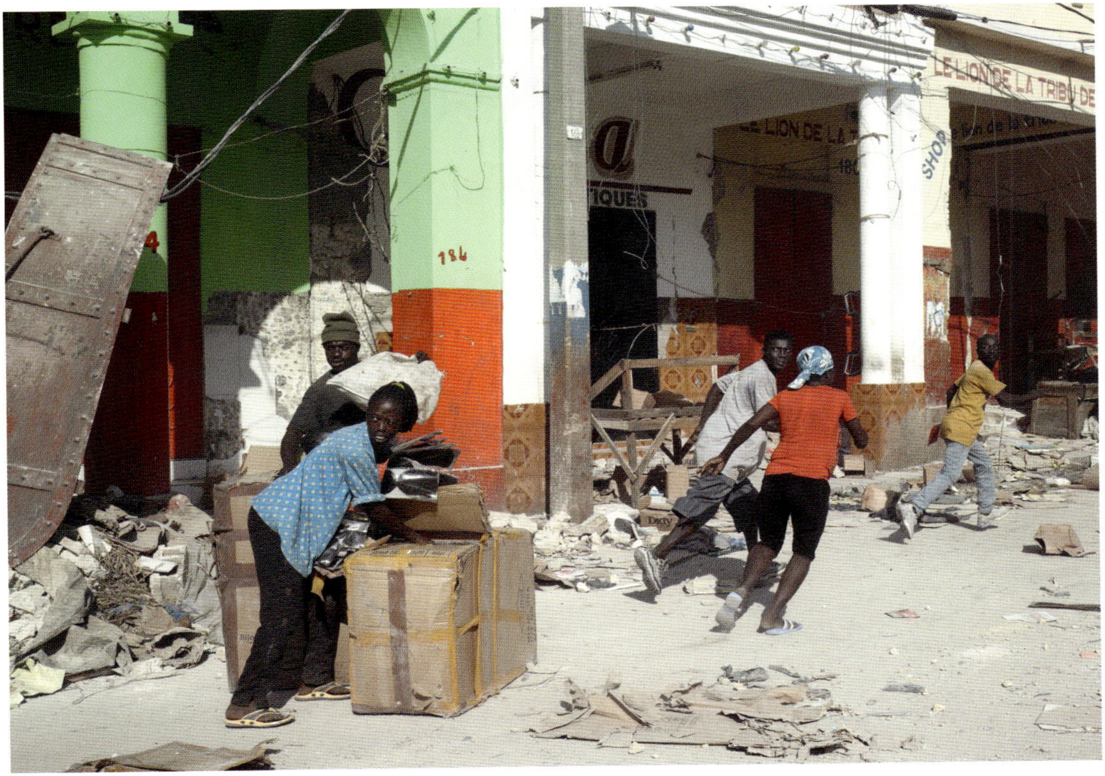
186
LE LION DE LA TRIBU DE
LE LION DE LA
SHOP
TIQUES

ALEX MAJOLI

Scene #3781, 2017

SHOT ALL OVER THE WORLD over eight years, Alex Majoli's project 'Scene' (2011–19) resulted from a particular kind of photographic procedure. Entering a situation, he and his assistant would slowly go about setting up a camera and flashlights on stands. Beginning to shoot, Majoli offered no direction to the people who happened to come before his camera. Sometimes they would refine their gestures in anticipation of an image. Sometimes they would be too preoccupied with the intensity of their own lives to even notice. Majoli photographed political demonstrations, humanitarian emergencies and quiet moments of everyday life.

Majoli's flash is much brighter than sunlight, illuminating what is near but plunging the surroundings into darkness, or something resembling moonlight. Spaces appear as dimly lit stages, and, regardless of the ambient light that existed, everything seems to be happening at the sunless end of the day. Just when the world should be preparing to sleep, it offers a heightened, twilit performance of itself.

We never really see people or situations 'in themselves'; we see only the light they reflect, and the character of that light affects how we respond and understand. In itself, light has no meaning, and yet it is a source of endless meanings. It comes to signify through pictorial conventions, which are present in everything from photojournalism and advertising to cinema, painting and theatre. We learn what kind of light is 'appropriate' for a passport photo, a wedding photo, a news photo, a war photo, a royal portrait, and so on. Moreover, it is because light has no intrinsic meaning that pictorial conventions are so strong. They repeat through visual culture endlessly, giving the impression that there is a natural correspondence between any given subject matter and the way it is to be represented. To bend or break these conventions, to experience a situation or a photograph of it in unexpected light, can be disturbing and revelatory.

Majoli's points of departure for 'Scene' came from experimental theatre, in particular Luigi Pirandello's play *Six Characters in Search of an Author*, first performed in 1921. Its 'plot' concerns a theatre director and actors who, while rehearsing their play, are interrupted by strangers. The presence of these strangers, with their complicated relationships and difficult histories, forces the director to rewrite the play in order to accommodate them. The layers of theatricality build up, and the audience has to adjust constantly. But the play would be little more than an empty game about theatre, were it not for the fact that Pirandello has deep moral questions to pose to the audience. What is our relation to the demands of others? What adjustments are we obliged to make? How do we reset the 'plot' of our life, our society, in our new relation to strangers? Like Pirandello's play, Majoli's 'Scene' offers no simple answers.

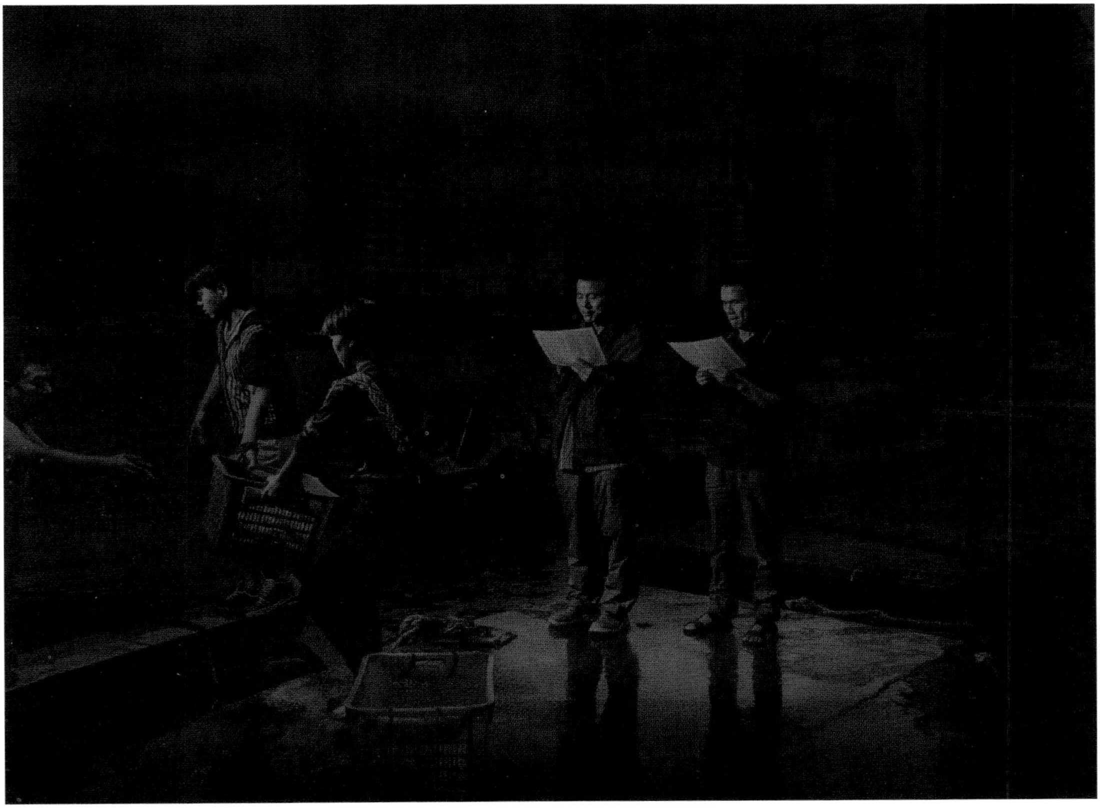

PETE SOUZA

President Barack Obama sits in the famous Rosa Parks bus at the Henry Ford Museum after an event in Dearborn, Mich., April 18, 2012, 2012

ON 1 DECEMBER 1955, in Montgomery City, Alabama, the seamstress and civil rights activist Rosa Parks refused to give up her seat on a bus to a white person. She was in the 'coloured section', and the 'white section' was full. Parks was arrested for civil disobedience. At the time, she was the secretary of the Montgomery division of the National Association for the Advancement of Black People, which considered her best placed to make a court challenge. She was fired from her job and received death threats. The event triggered a widespread, year-long boycott by the black community of the privately owned Montgomery Bus Line, which lost around 70 per cent of its revenue.

A year later, Parks returned to the bus and was photographed sitting, looking out of the window. In 1956 a federal lawsuit ruled that 'the enforced segregation of black and white passengers on motor buses operating in the City of Montgomery violates the Constitution and laws of the United States.'

In 1971 the bus was retired. The parent company of Montgomery Bus Line suggested it should be destroyed, but it sat in a field outside Montgomery. It was then bought by Roy H. Summerford, a spare-time mechanic and stock-car racing enthusiast. Looking for some extra space for his activities, he stripped out the seats. Meanwhile, Rosa Parks's defiance, the boycott and the change in the law had become important landmarks in the post-war civil rights movement.

Interest in the rusting, seatless, engineless bus also began to grow. When Summerford died, his descendants put it up for sale on eBay. It was acquired for $492,000 by the Henry Ford Museum in Dearborn, a suburb of Detroit, Michigan. Restoration cost in excess of $300,000. The bus finally went on display on 1 February 2003.

On 2 November 2008, three years after the death of Rosa Parks, Barack Obama became the first African American to be elected to the office of President of the United States of America. In 2012 he visited the Henry Ford Museum, and spent a few moments in Parks's place on Montgomery Bus Line vehicle no. 2857. He recalled: 'I just sat in there for a moment and pondered the courage and tenacity that is part of our very recent history, but is also part of that long line of folks who sometimes are nameless, oftentimes didn't make the history books, but who constantly insisted on their dignity, their share of the American dream.'

The photograph, which resembles the one of Parks from 1956, was taken by Pete Souza, the official White House photographer for Obama's presidency. Was Obama alone on the bus? Yes and no. Souza must have been there too, and no doubt there was a sizeable entourage of security and museum staff just beyond the frame. Is Obama thinking he is alone? Perhaps. All presidents are somewhat alone, and, as the first African American president, Obama was certainly in a category of one. He may have felt alone if he was imagining the bravery of Parks that day, or perhaps not alone if he was imagining her surrounded by the white faces of passengers and an arresting officer.

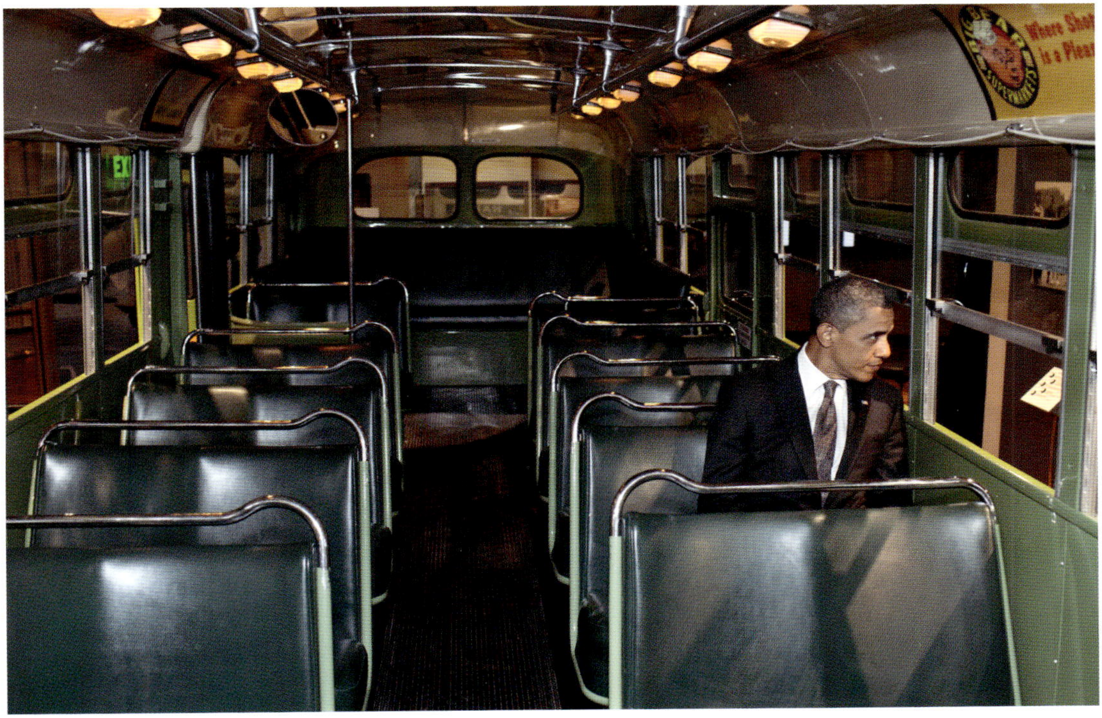

WALKER EVANS

Opening pages of 'Along the Right-of-Way', *Fortune*, July 1955

WALKER EVANS ONCE REMARKED that there are only four ways for a photographer to survive economically. They can be independently wealthy to begin with, although this will show itself in the work produced (Alfred Stieglitz was Evans's example); they can be paid to take pictures (a commercial photographer, with whatever intelligence and autonomy this allows); they can be paid *for* pictures (as an artist, for example – something that was possible only towards the end of Evans's life, when a market for art photography began to emerge); or they can be a serious amateur, protecting their photography by earning money elsewhere.

Based in New York, Evans worked for a living. On commission in the 1930s, he photographed Victorian architecture, African sculpture for the Museum of Modern Art, life under the Machado regime in Cuba, and the effects of the Depression on the rural southern states of America. He also sold a few pictures to magazines but never joined an agency or had his work syndicated. In 1934 he began his relationship with *Fortune*, the lavish business and industry magazine launched in the wake of the 1929 stock market crash. As Evans recalled: '*Fortune* didn't really know what role it should play during the Depression. They didn't know what they were doing since they were founded to describe in a stimulating way American business and industry, and that was falling apart.' With the coming of the Second World War, *Fortune*'s position was, if not contradictory, then at least sensitive to the social and cultural uncertainties of that fraught period. But with few commissions in wartime, Evans wrote urbane and witty reviews of books, art and film for *Time* magazine.

Evans had no defined political allegiance, but he waged his own personal war against the smug values of the middle class from which he had come; against the juggernaut of modernization that threatened to flatten the past in the name of progress; and against the crude commercialism of mass culture. With a reputation for all this, and proven talents as a writer and a photographer, *Fortune*'s bosses made him Special Photographic Editor in 1948. For seventeen years he set his own assignments, shot the pictures, edited them, wrote the text, and devised his own elegant layouts. He enjoyed a level of freedom unprecedented in magazine culture. Moreover, Evans had long understood that to control the meaning of one's photographs, one has to control the editing and the accompanying words.

'Along the Right-of-Way' shows Evans's characteristic resistance to the efficient use of time demanded by big business. It is a celebration of the pleasures of idle gazing from moving trains. Across the country, he had the various railroad companies clean his cabin windows. He travelled at leisure for weeks, running up his expenses, shooting the views in black and white and colour. Back in his small office, he laid out an eight-page sequence. The opening image is as good as any railroad painting by Charles Sheeler or Edward Hopper. Evans added a black border, which evoked both the edge of the film frame and the train window. He crafted his introductory texts tirelessly, and this example is one of his best: a minor miracle of reported fact, remembrance, allusion, flight of fancy, and even physics. All in three sublimely short paragraphs.

Along the Right-of-Way

In Roomette 6, Car 287, the light has not yet been switched on. For an hour the train has swayed and rattled across the land. This rented steel cubicle, with its solemn and absorbing printed directions of how to work those basic gadgets, is the harassed man's haven of detachment. The captains and the kings depart. Now if ever, in this place and in this mood, the traveler can abandon himself to the rich pastime of window-gazing.

Along the paths of railroads, the country is in semi-undress. You can see some of the anatomy of its living: a back yard with its citizen poking into a rumble seat for a trusted toolbox; an intent group of boys locked in a sandlot ball game; a fading factory wall; a lone child with a cart. Out on the plains, the classic barns and the battalions of cabbages . . .

To some, these sights gain meaning because men like Mark Twain and Sherwood Anderson and Thomas Wolfe have, in a sense, laid hands on them. For others, one fleeting landscape can flush the mind with images of the enchantment a child feels with train trips: waking at dawn to see a cool cornfield cut by a rutted road; a farmer in his wagon drawn up at the crossing; the *TING TING TING TING TING TING TING* of the warning bell—that heart-rending tinny decrescendo which is an early lesson in relativity of the senses. *W.E.*

Seven photographs by Walker Evans of middle-western and eastern landscapes seen through train windows

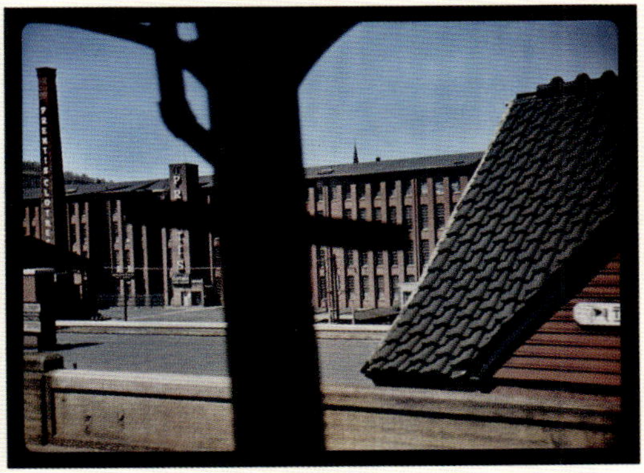

From the Sunday A.M. local, winding through the New Jersey factory towns

JÜRGEN SCHADEBERG

Drum Magazine Office, Johannesburg, 1954

THE SOUTH AFRICAN MAGAZINE *Drum* was established in 1951. It was aimed primarily at a black audience, and is best known for its coverage in words and photographs of life in the country's townships during the 1950s and 1960s. At its peak, 240,000 copies of each issue were sold, distributed nationwide and across seven neighbouring countries. South Africa's population was becoming increasingly urban, and increasingly literate. Despite the oppressive apartheid regime, there was great energy and a feeling of optimism. *Drum* played a key role in this.

The journalists pictured here – all men, and known as 'the *Drum* boys' – include Henry Nxumalo, Esk'ia Mphahlele, Casey Motsisi, Can Themba, Arthur Maimane, Victor Xashimba, Dan Chocho and Bob Gosani. Their gung-ho ethos was 'live fast, die young and leave a good-looking corpse'. *Drum* did have female journalists as well, notably Bessie Head and Jenny Joseph. Beyond *Drum*, all these figures published significant books in their own right. The magazine also pioneered the publication of fiction writing, which dealt in different ways with the magazine's main themes of crime, sex, forgotten lives and sport.

This image was taken by Jürgen Schadeberg, one of the key figures in the history of South African photojournalism. It is a theatrical collaboration, and everyone in the office is in on the fun. All the poses are ironic, stereotypical depictions of reporters at work. It is a knowingly artificial image, in contrast to the journalistic ideals of truth and objectivity.

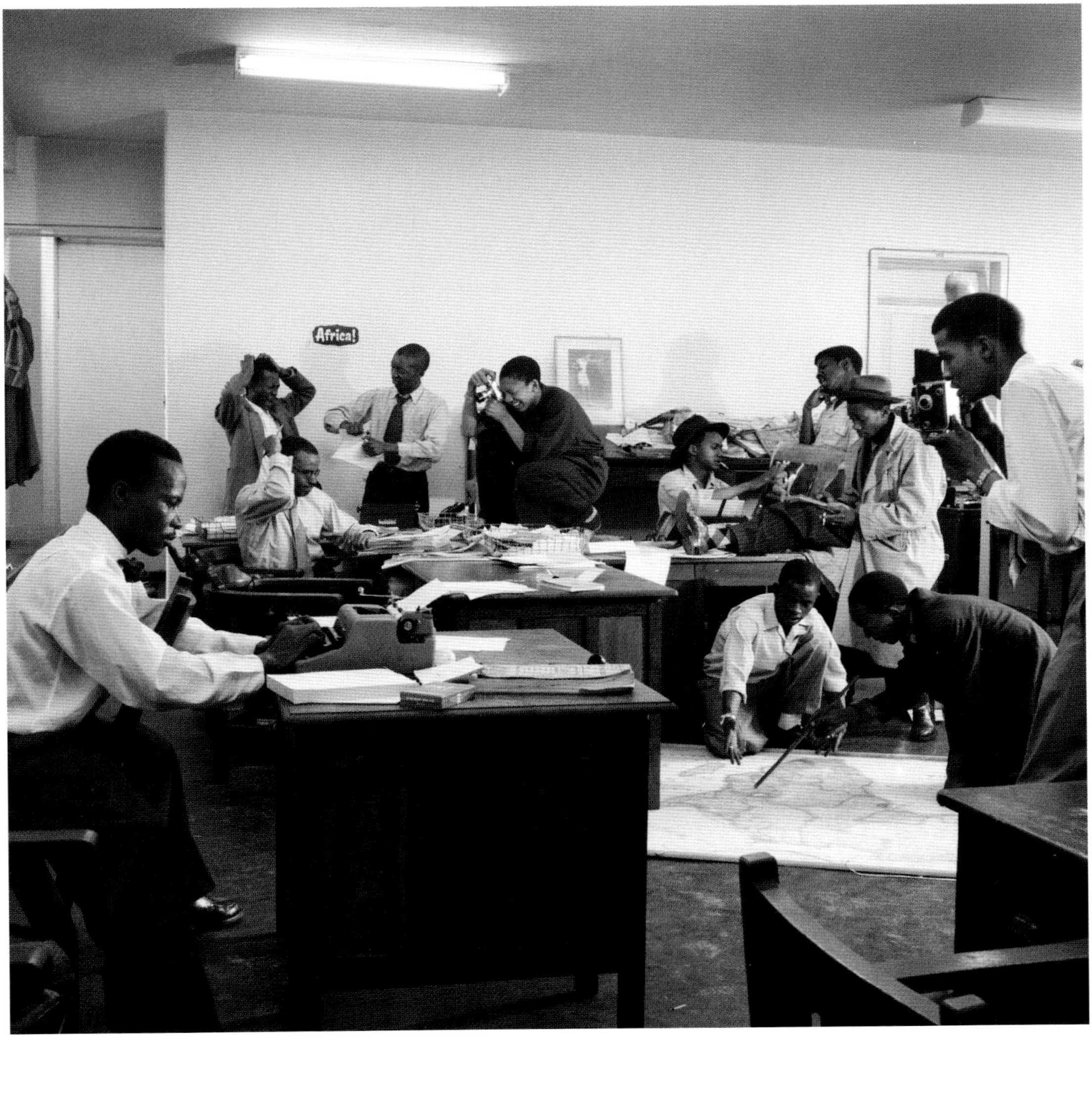
Africa!

WILLIAM HENRY FOX TALBOT

The Reading Establishment, c. 1845

WILLIAM HENRY FOX TALBOT'S calotype process involved the making of a 'negative' print that could then be used to make positives. This was profoundly different from the French daguerreotype process, for example, which produced a single, unique image on polished metal that was virtually impossible to copy. In late 1843, Talbot's close associate Nicolaas Henneman set up the world's first facility for the mass production of photographic images. It was located in the town of Reading, between Talbot's home at Lacock Abbey, in Wiltshire, and London.

In this staged, two-part panorama, we see various activities at the Reading Establishment, as Henneman's facility became known. On the far left is a wooden box camera, with a timer for making accurate exposures. The camera had no shutter, and exposures were made by removing and then replacing a lens cap. Behind is a glasshouse where light could be regulated in the preparation and application of photosensitive chemicals. An assistant is emerging with a wooden negative carrier, which would be placed in the back of the camera ready for exposure. The camera is set up to photograph what is probably a lithographic print of Anthony van Dyck's painted portrait of Cornelis van der Geest, a wealthy Dutch arts patron and collector. A second camera is being used to make a portrait of a seated man. His head rests against a metal contraption, which helps him remain still during the exposure of several seconds. The exposed sheet would then be removed and taken inside for developing, fixing and drying.

In the second panel we see portable racks angled towards the sun. These hold frames, each containing a negative paper print pressed flat by glass against a photosensitized sheet of paper, to produce a positive print through the action of light. A third camera, operated by Henneman himself, photographs a small plaster model of the popular sculpture *The Three Graces*. In the lower right-hand corner is a focimeter, a device to help ensure correct focus.

Henneman pushed hard to make the venture financially viable, but often the result was an inferior product. Talbot already had problems making his calotypes permanent, and the shortcuts taken made matters worse. This image was probably made both as a celebration of the new business, and for promotion. It is likely that Talbot was not present. As a wealthy man of public standing, he kept his distance from the monetizing of his invention. Nevertheless, in *The Pencil of Nature* (1844–46), Talbot wrote excitedly of photography's commercial potential.

Across the diptych there is an illusion of spatial continuity, and this seems to imply a temporal simultaneity. It looks as if everything is happening at once. This would be the case only if the two parts had been photographed with two cameras, exposing together. It is likely that one camera was used, and that the exposures were made at different times. The ambiguities here, between the simultaneous and the consecutive, between one image and the next, hint at the indefinable relationship between photography and time. They also point towards the photo-sequence and photo-essay. Meaning derives not only from the images, but also from the implied relations between them.

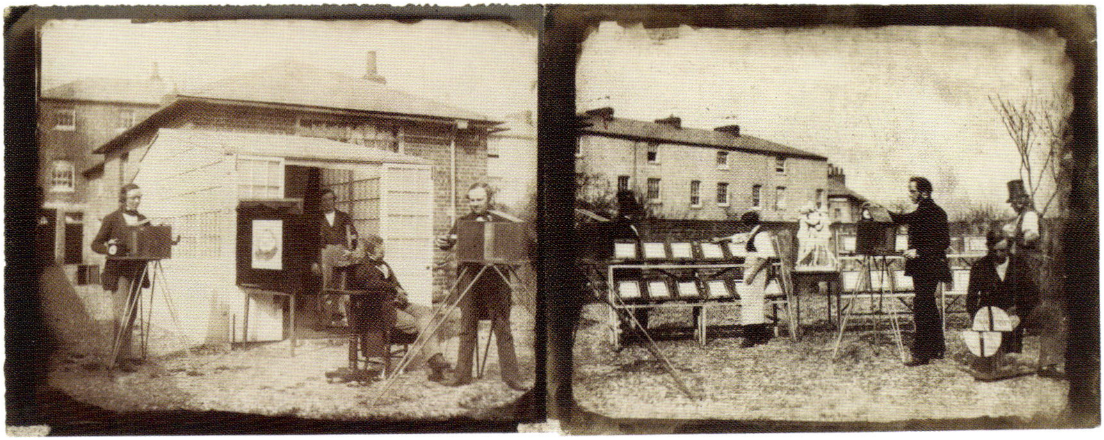

NAOYA HATAKEYAMA

River Series #4, 1993–94

ACROSS VARIOUS BODIES OF WORK, the Japanese photographer Naoya Hatakeyama has married the factual character of photography with its ability to render familiar things strange and revelatory. His subjects are often very straightforward. They include underground tunnels, water droplets on windows and explosions in quarries. However, as well as being documents, the images he makes often function as metaphors for photography itself.

One could argue that every photograph ever taken must be a metaphor for photography. They are all instances and demonstrations of what the medium can do, and it can do a disarmingly large array of things. Nevertheless, it is possible to make images that strike a viewer as more emphatic than others in how they embody the medium, or at least aspects of it.

In the compact urban density of Tokyo, river water is forced to flow along concrete channels. There are endless ways to photograph this, but Hatakeyama chose one specific way. When the water level was low, he placed his camera on a tripod in the middle of the river, with its lens at the exact height of the lip of the channel. Photographing horizontally down straight sections of the river, the perspective and vanishing point are dramatic. The image seems to split into two halves, when in fact it is one. The water in the lower half reflects and distorts the buildings and sky of the upper half.

Hatakeyama made nine photographs like this, each different but composed the same. Shot at night, they are illuminated artificially from all around, rather than the sun. All these elements seem to belong to the world, but really they belong only to the world of Hatakeyama's images, which govern our perception as much and as little as the channels govern the water.

Mirrors, doublings, reflections, inversions, one image appearing as two, many appearing as one, dark chambers, flatness, depth, flows of light and flows of liquid. The photographic metaphors abound, and compound one another.

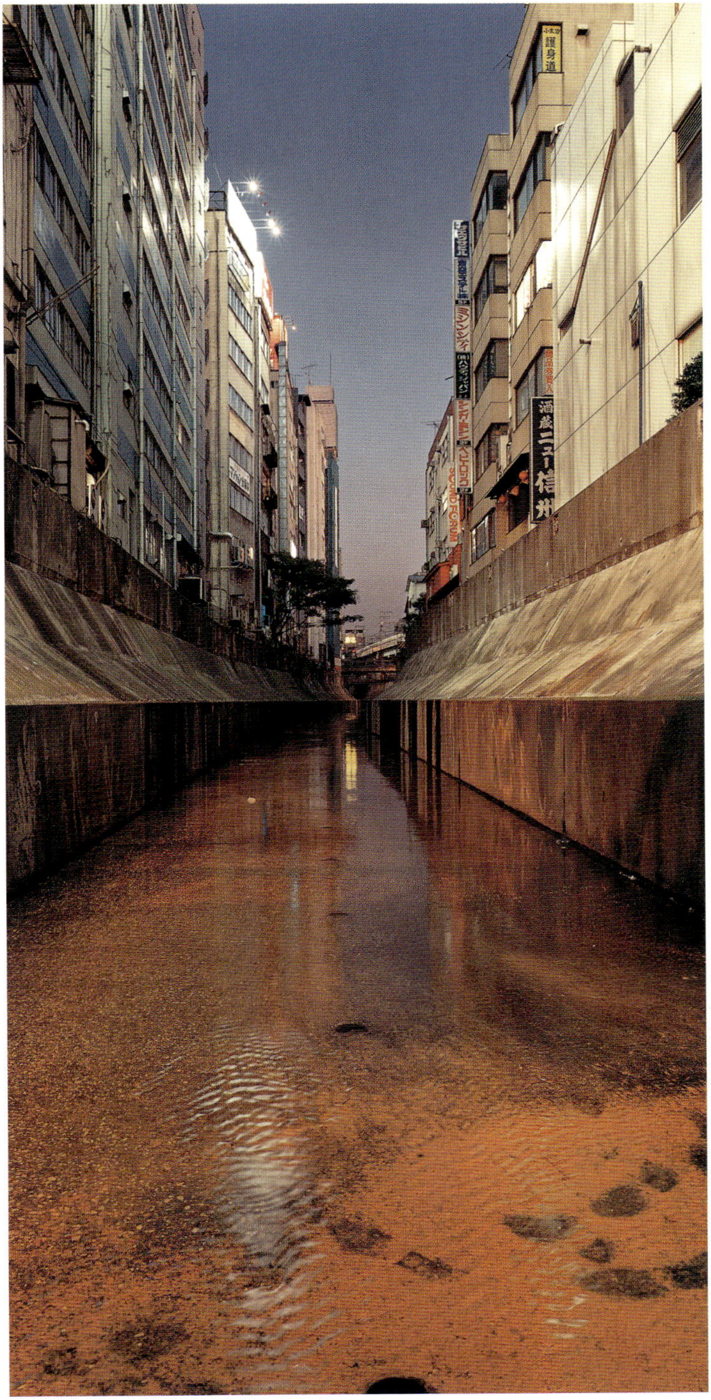
護身道
ミシンシティ
酒蔵ニュー信州
SOUND FORUM

LORRAINE O'GRADY

Art Is (Girlfriends Times Two), 1983

IN 1983 LORRAINE O'GRADY made a performance intervention in the African American Pride Parade, in New York. It was a response to the feeling that high art often had little to do with black people and black lives. O'Grady entered a float into the parade. On the side, in large letters, were the words 'ART IS ...'. On top was a 2.7 × 4.6-metre (9 × 15-ft) gold picture frame. O'Grady played the role of Mlle Bourgeoise Noire, a persona she had been using to intervene in art-world events. A group of fifteen African American and Latino performers walked around the float with empty gold frames. Sometimes they framed their own faces and gestures, sometimes they invited members of the crowd to picture themselves, to imagine themselves as legitimate subjects for high art.

Various people took photographs of the performance, and O'Grady gathered the images together. They document the event but have also been exhibited. In this way, a public, non-art event enters the traditional space of art. The photographs may prompt other questions too, which are also to do with framing. Generally speaking, art photography is not presented in gold frames. O'Grady's photographs are presented with white card mounts in plain wood frames. Moreover, the people photographed strike attitudes typical of photographic culture (smiling, playing, enjoying the moment). They don't adopt the kind of formal poses that get painted and framed in gold.

VARIOUS PEOPLE TOOK PHOTOGRAPHS OF THE PERFORMANCE, AND O'GRADY GATHERED THE IMAGES TOGETHER. THEY DOCUMENT THE EVENT BUT HAVE ALSO BEEN EXHIBITED. IN THIS WAY, A PUBLIC, NON-ART EVENT ENTERS THE TRADITIONAL SPACE OF ART.

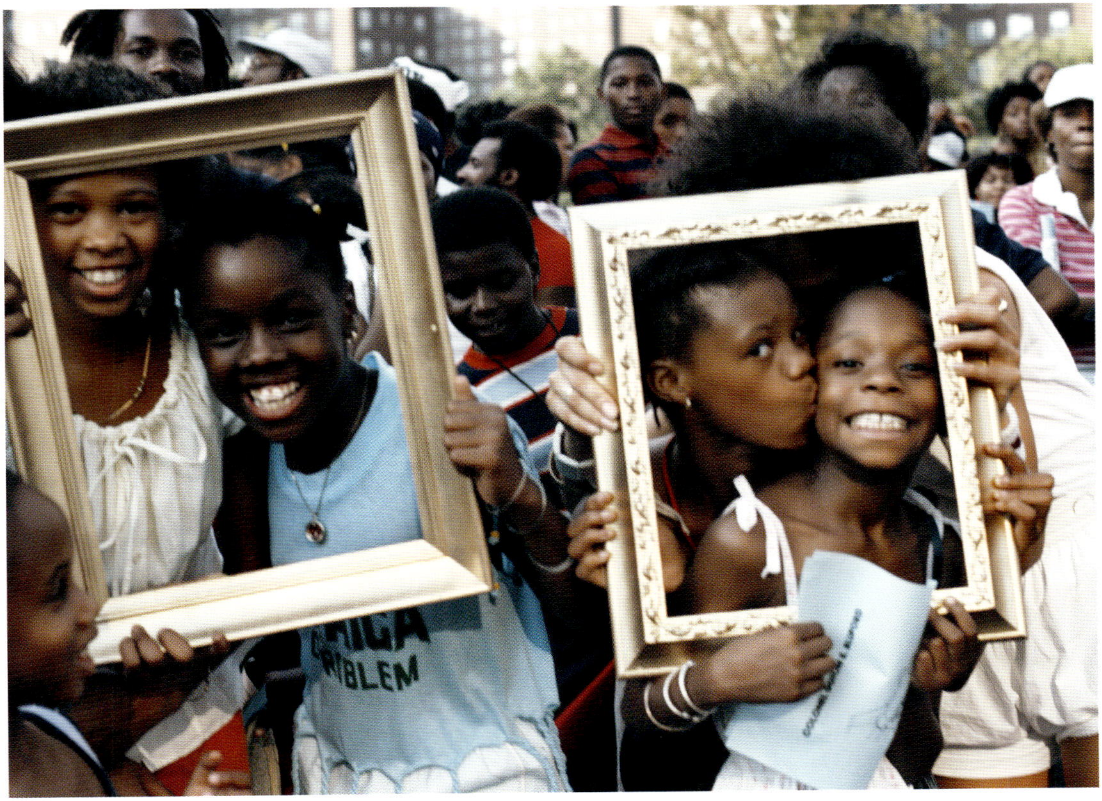

BARBARA PROBST

Exposure #137.5: N.Y.C., Broome & Crosby Streets, 05.01.18, 3:21p.m., 2018

FOR *WALLPAPER** MAGAZINE, JUNE 2018

TO EXPERIENCE A MOMENT from different vantage points at the same time is an inhuman idea. We cannot be in two places at once, and yet we know different viewpoints exist.

It is a condition explored well in literature and cinema, through parallel narration and cross-cutting. We have all seen films in which different witnesses give their accounts of the same sequence of events. Each has their own perspective, literally and figuratively, and the viewer is invited to piece them together, weighing up the different points of view. The work of the artist Barbara Probst owes something to this idea, although her attention to the split second, the instant, places it firmly within still photography.

This is the fifth of a series of six diptychs made over the course of a day on the intersection of Crosby Street and Broome Street in Soho, New York City. It was produced as part of a fashion editorial for *Wallpaper** magazine. Only the models in animal-print outfits are staged, while everyday life flows around them. Probst's cameras are connected to a radio-wave receiver and are triggered to shoot simultaneously. The artistic ideal of the single 'decisive moment', which was for so long the central dictum of street photography, is reconceived for our age of camera saturation and surveillance.

If something significant happens in a major city, we may not expect it to have been caught by an automated camera or two, but we are not surprised when it has. For good or bad, all city dwellers exist as subjects to be photographed from different angles.

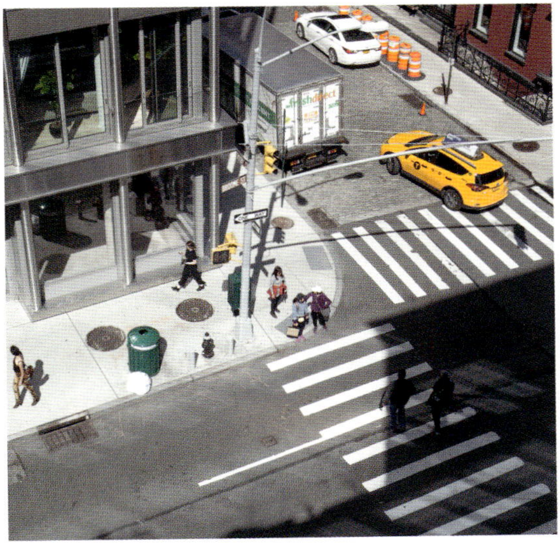

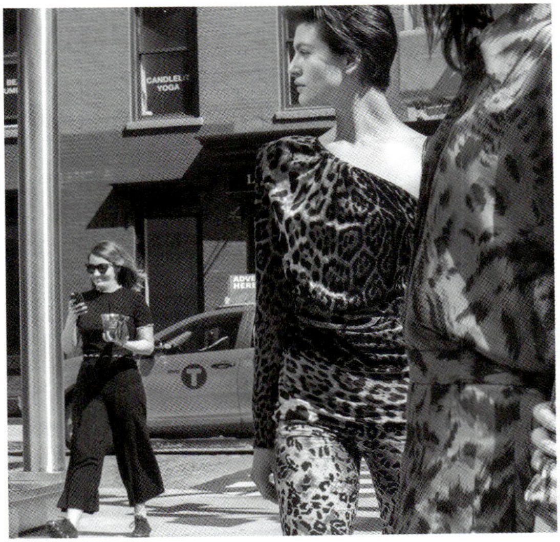
CANDLELIT
YOGA

MARK NEVILLE

Donna pregnant (Ancient Order of the Hibernian Social Club), 2005

FROM THE PORT GLASGOW BOOK PROJECT, 2004–06

IN 2003 THE BRITISH ARTIST Mark Neville made a proposal for an unusual and highly ambitious public art project. He would live and photograph for a year in Port Glasgow, a working-class town on Scotland's east coast. It was once a major centre for shipbuilding, but little had replaced the collapsing industry. Neville knew the town. He would shoot daily life in various photographic styles – classical documentary, staged collaborations with citizens, naturalistic images and carefully composed tableaux made with flashlight, in both black and white and colour.

Socially concerned photographic projects often end up as expensive coffee-table books, made for audiences far from the subjects in the pictures. And when such projects *are* made for those in the pictures, the production standards are often very low, because funding is scarce. Neville proposed to make a high-quality hardback book that would be given to each of the 8,000 citizens of Port Glasgow. It would not be available commercially. His entire budget for the project was £106,000. Of that, £14,000 was set aside for Royal Mail to deliver the books. However, in the spirit of giving back, the money was passed to the Port Glasgow boys' football team, which delivered all the books on foot.

Neville had regular work-in-progress exhibitions in the town, involving residents wherever possible, but in the end the book was his creative decision, and his to stand by. Meetings and a website were set up to gather feedback. In general, the project was very well received, although the end product did create some suspicion. Neville recalls: 'Not everyone liked the book. The most extreme reaction I had was from the residents of Robert Street, who had a meeting and decided there were too many photographs taken in Catholic pubs and clubs and not enough taken in Protestant pubs and clubs. It's still a sectarian town in many ways. They decided to burn their copies of the book. I got a call from the fire station telling me a pile of my books was on fire. I looked at the book again: there were nine photos taken in Protestant pubs and clubs, and seven in Catholic pubs and clubs [...] The book began to get a wider reputation and copies starting selling on eBay, sometimes for up to £500. So if you hadn't burned your copy you could sell it. The book cost £12 per copy to make.'

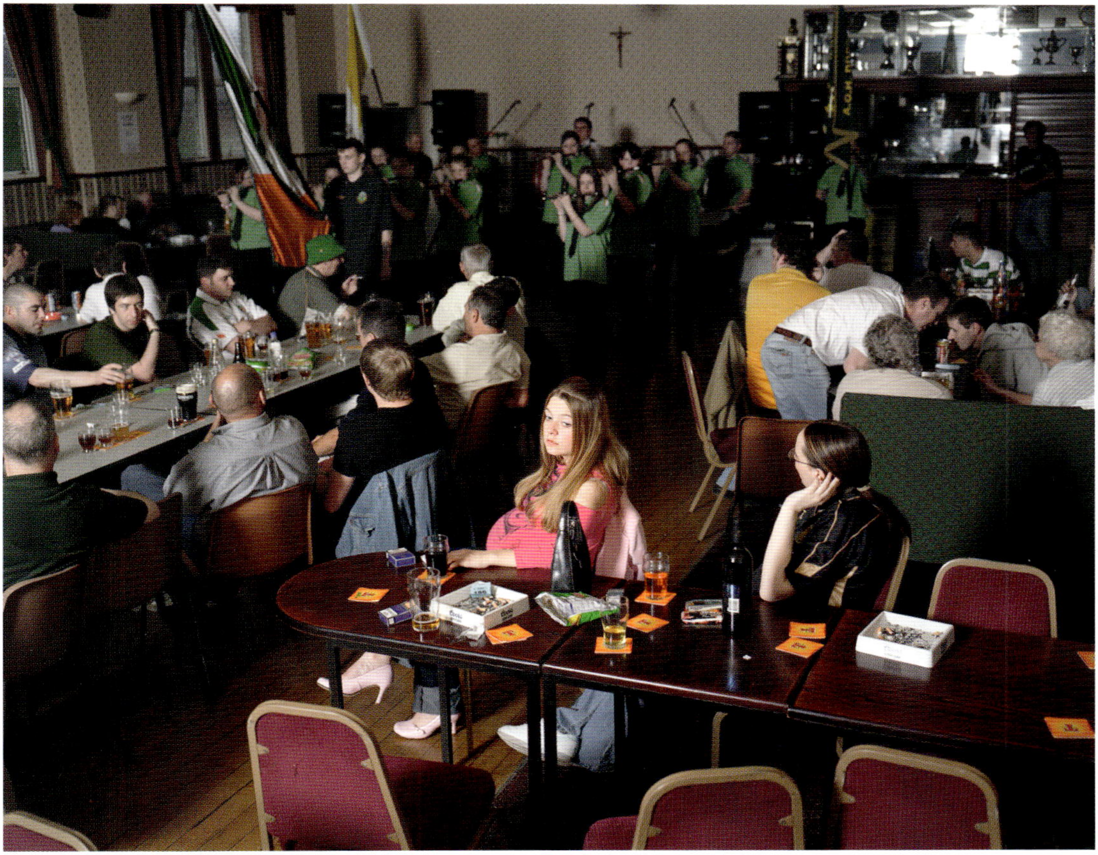

HUMPHREY SPENDER

Planning Observations at 85 Davenport Street, 1937–38

IN 1937 A SOCIAL RESEARCH project was established with the high ideal of encouraging the British to look closely at their own daily lives and come to know themselves more deeply. It was to be called Mass Observation. The three founders, who had all studied at Cambridge University, worked in a variety of fields. Tom Harrisson was an anthropologist, Charles Madge was a poet, and Humphrey Jennings was a film-maker. Further collaborators included painters, novelists and critics. Their early photographer was Humphrey Spender.

In part, the project was motivated by a suspicion both of the established mass media's way of reporting daily existence, and of government modes of information gathering. The goal was that, eventually, millions of untrained observers would contribute to Mass Observation.

In the early years there was no set programme. Mass Observation looked not to statistics but to informal data – casual conversation, anecdotes, and the minor but telling details of typical days. It established its first base in Bolton, a working-class town in the north of England. In this photograph by Spender, we see some of the group deciding what they will do that day. They often consulted newspapers for small stories that might indicate what to study. Spender was using a lightweight 35mm camera that allowed the making of unobtrusive pictures, almost like a spy.

Mass Observation knew the commitment to the minutiae of life had enormous potential to reveal profound truths, but their methods created a whole new set of problems. It was far from clear how to make sense of all the information they gathered. Indeed, scholars and researchers are still interpreting the Mass Observation archive, housed at the University of Sussex.

Moreover, there was always a fine line between observation and invasion, between the promise of self-knowledge and the gathering of facts for the purposes of control or commercial exploitation. Today, digital data mining – the accumulation of thousands of small pieces of information about our habits, interests, friends, communications and purchases – is a major source of corporate wealth and power, and a potential threat to democracy.

After the Second World War, and with the founders having left, Mass Observation shifted its focus to Britain's commercial habits. By 1949 it had become a private market-research company, which later merged with an advertising agency.

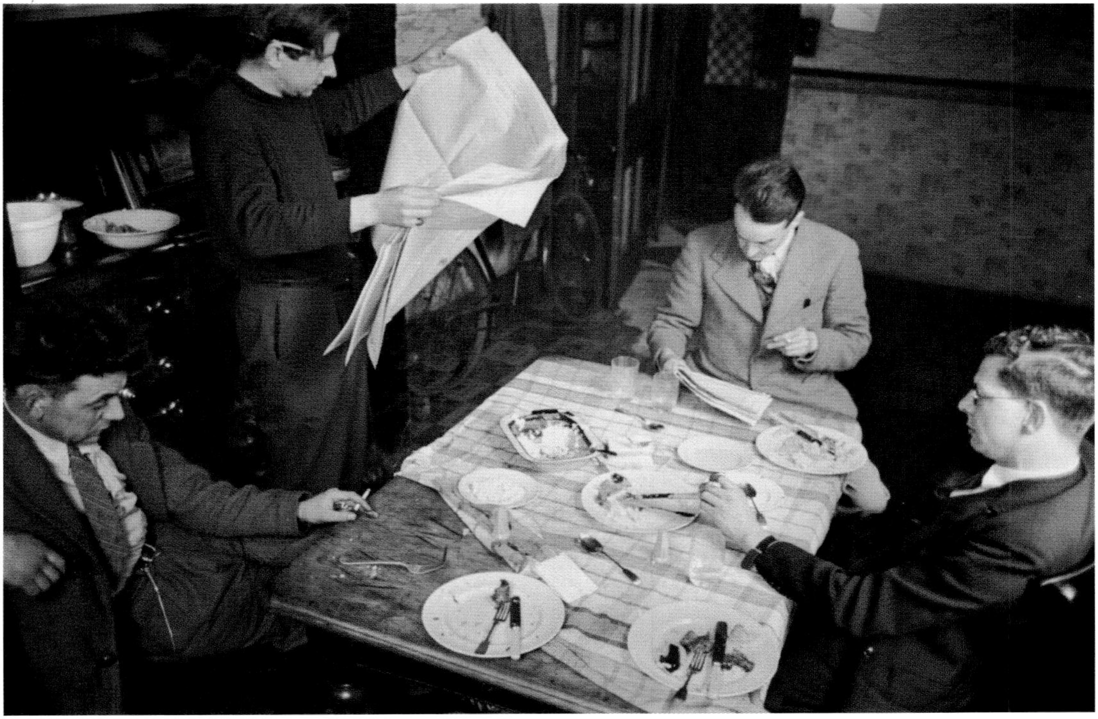

DOUG RICKARD

#96.766076, Dallas, TX (2009), 2010

FROM THE SERIES 'A NEW AMERICAN PICTURE', 2006–10

DOUG RICKARD'S 'A NEW AMERICAN PICTURE' is an archive of colour street photographs. They were not exactly taken on American streets but derive instead from Google Street View, the vast photographic map of the environments surrounding the world's network of roads. Street View is navigated by moving on-screen through a series of 360-degree panoramas stitched together to produce a virtual environment. Rickard explored a large number of American towns looking for possible pictures. The choice of subject matter and compositions is informed by the work of the many photographers, film-makers and painters that have made the picturing of daily life such a vital part of North American art. William Eggleston (page 36), Stephen Shore (page 184), Edward Hopper, David Lynch.

Mounted on a vehicle, the Street View camera takes its images at systematic intervals, all from 2.5 metres (8 ft 3 in.) above the ground, a height that is neither human eye level nor the dispassionate 'overview' we associate with surveillance. Rickard used a 35mm film camera, the classic equipment of the wandering street photographer. He placed it on a tripod in front of his large computer monitor, selecting his Street View locations and framing, but working with the pre-given moments of exposure.

Rickard's locations are small, working-class, overlooked towns far from the big cities. These often feel like places from the past, in which the Street View camera car would have looked quite out of place to those observing it. The photographs are also records of a very particular moment in image technology, with their patches of poorly rendered detail and areas where the digital seams between images are less than perfect. Street View imaging is improving all the time, and Rickard's project has become a document as much of a particular moment in the history of digital imaging as of the places it depicts.

Much of the important culture of the last century was premised upon the chance encounter, the dangerous excitement of getting lost, or the desire to disappear into the world. Around the advent of the mobile phone, there was a profound change in our relation to spaces and places, and it was irreversible. Whatever else it is, Rickard's 'A New American Picture' is about the impossibility of getting lost. Even the lowliest backstreet has a grid reference. Vanishing is all but impossible.

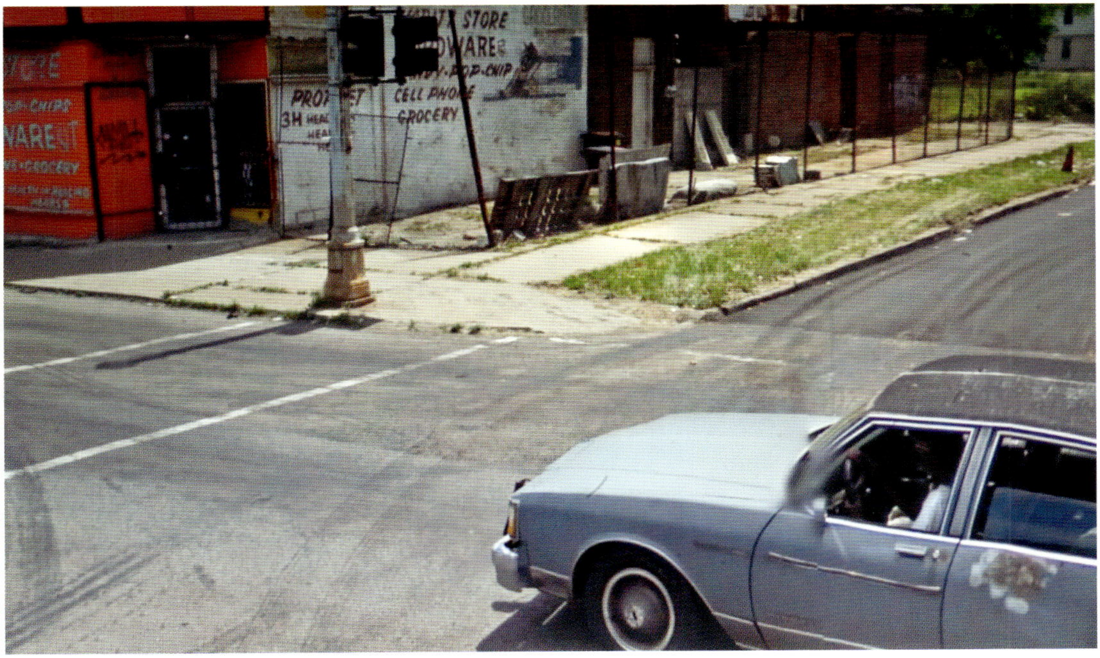
STORE
CELL PHONE
GROCERY

TIM DAVIS

Colosseum Pictures

FROM THE SERIES 'THE NEW ANTIQUITY', 2009

THE ARCHITECTURE OF ANTIQUITY has fascinated photographers since the medium's invention in the 1830s. The Victorian cult of the ruin took hold during the intensity of the Industrial Revolution. The camera, a technology born of that revolution, could render the cracks, patina and decay of old buildings in a detailed and vivid way. It emphasized the history of the ruins and the bold, pristine modernity of photography itself. As the medium spread through society to become a mass amateur and tourist pursuit, certain ruins in Europe came to be photographed so extensively that they became national symbols for the media age, recognized around the world. The Colosseum in the Italian capital was one of them.

Let us presume that the North American photographer Tim Davis saw the Colosseum being photographed by many tourists and decided to charm several of them into placing their cameras on the ground for him to photograph. The Colosseum is somewhere outside his frame, but within it too. This was in 2009. Davis's photograph was already destined to become a historical artefact in itself. It is a document, a relic, of a very short-lived moment: within a year or two, tourist photography would be absorbed by the smartphone camera.

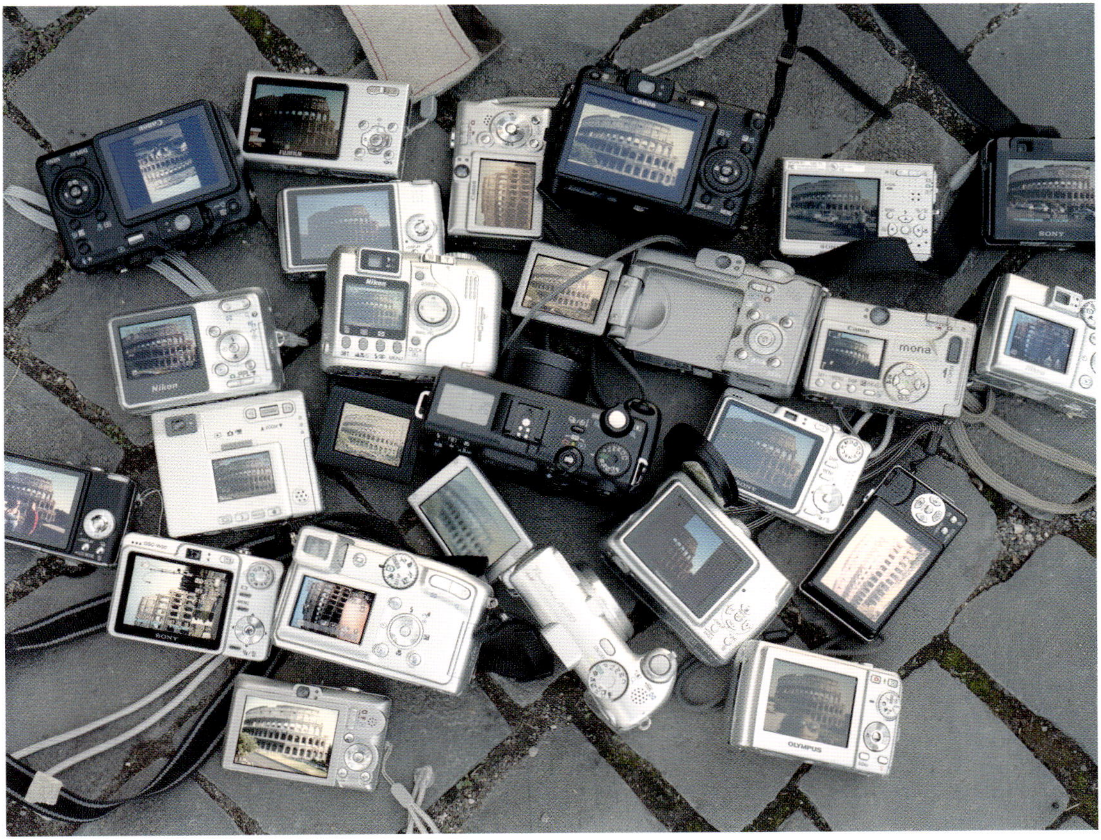
Canon
Nikon
Nikon
mona
SONY
SONY
OLYMPUS

MISHKA HENNER

Coronado Feeders, Dalhart, Texas, 2012

ON 7 DECEMBER 1972, a photograph was taken of Earth by the crew of the Apollo 17 spacecraft as it made its way to the Moon. Seen as a whole, against the blackness of deep space, the planet looked perfect and harmonious. The image, which became known as *The Blue Marble*, remains one of the most widely reproduced photographs.

Twenty-nine years later, in 2001, Google Earth was launched. It is a computer program that creates a 3D representation of the surface of Earth. Primarily, the representation consists of images taken by satellites and aircraft, which are then composited by software into a continuous, photographic planetary skin. The satellites orbit at around 35,000 kilometres (21,750 miles), which is further out than Apollo 17 was when *Blue Marble* was shot.

What does a photographic artist do when it seems as though the entire surface of the planet has been photographed? Mishka Henner is one of a number who have put their own cameras aside in order to rework and reinterpret the wealth of visual data generated by automated imaging and data systems. His work includes projects about parking lots, oil fields and military sites. What interests Henner are the very human effects upon the planet of modernity, capitalism, industrial development and ideological rivalries. These are precisely what *The Blue Marble* does not make visible, although they made that image possible.

Exploring Google Earth, Henner came across areas of land in the United States that are used for the intensive rearing of cattle. Grids of rectangular pens hold the cows. Silos mix up the grain for feed. There are tracks for trucks to deliver the feed, and there are giant ponds for the cattles' faeces and urine. It is a hyper-rationalized system, designed to extract the most profit from the least resources, and the least land.

At first glance this image appears abstract, but it is perfectly realist. Look closely and you can see it all; indeed, a view from above is the best way to comprehend it. The camera is as dispassionate and calculating as the activity it pictures. These 'feedlots', as they are known, were probably planned with diagrams that looked very similar.

Henner exhibits the work as large-scale photographs. The shift in context and presentation produces a shift in perception and understanding. Although these sites were there to be seen on Google Earth, Henner's gesture was enough to draw considerable attention to them. Most of these feedlots are in America's central hinterland, often known as the 'flyover states', between the east and west coasts. Many Americans simply did not realize that this was how their beef was reared. Of all Henner's projects to date, this one has reached the widest audience. His exhibitions of the work generated intense interest and discussion online, which is where the artist derived the Google Earth images in the first place. The feedlots had been hiding in plain sight.

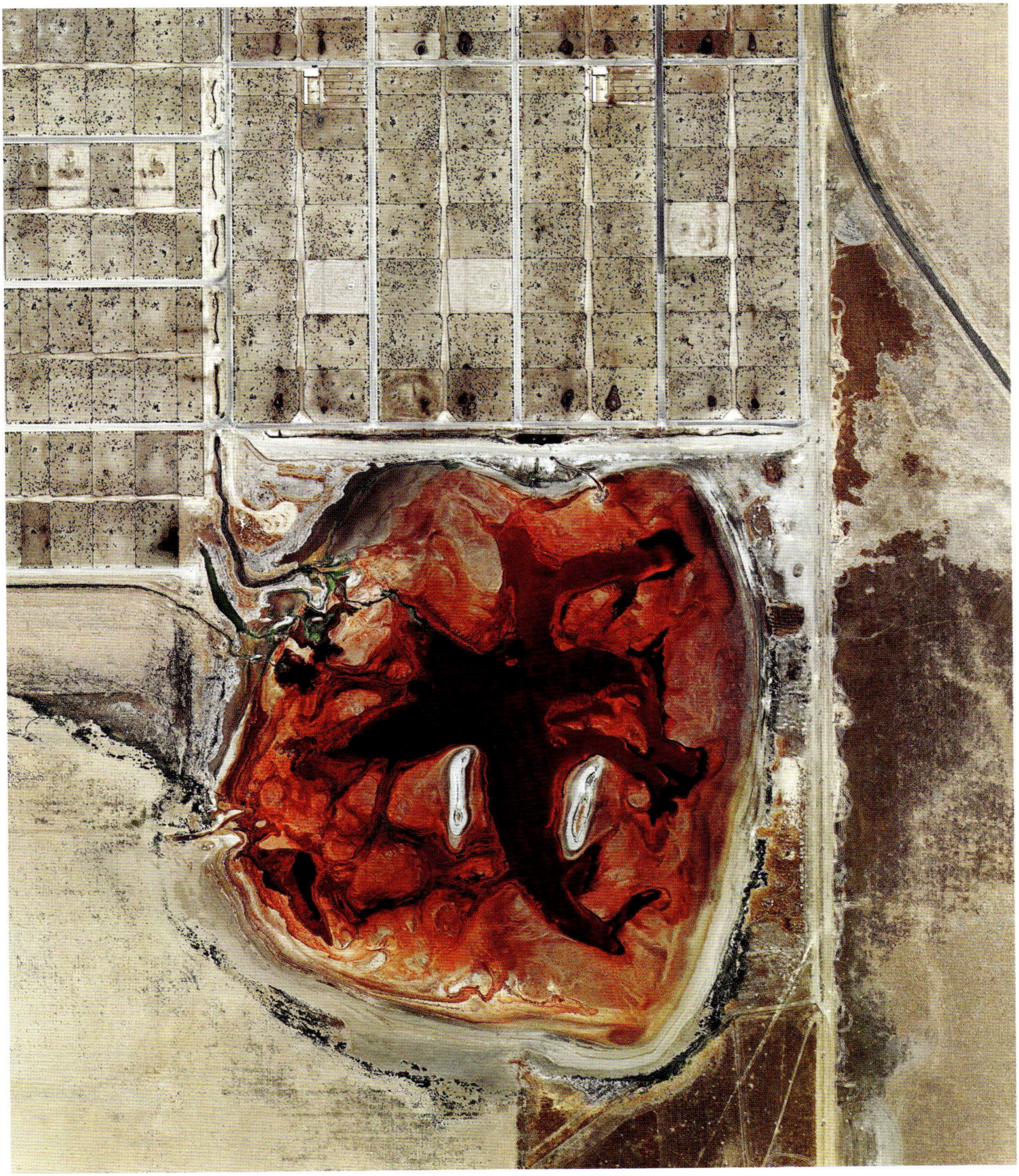

JULES SPINATSCH

Vienna MMIX – Panorama portrait of a society:
7000 Participants, 10008 Images, one every 3 seconds, 2009

INSTALLATION VIEW, RESSELPARK, KARLSPLATZ, VIENNA, 2011

SINCE 1935 THE VIENNA OPERA BALL, held annually at the Vienna Opera House (Wiener Staatsoper), has had an international standing as a rather smug and self-congratulatory dressing-up party for that year's dubious mix of politicians, businessmen, debutants and imported celebrities. In the long and luxurious evening, attendees prop up their reputations and grease the wheels of power with an appeal to 'tradition'. At the ball, there is no need for a performance: all the seats in the stalls are covered over by a ballroom floor, while tiers of extra boxes are erected on the stage to complete the narcissistic, self-gazing circuit.

In 2009 Jules Spinatsch suspended two interactive digital cameras in the centre of the Vienna Opera House. They were programmed to track incrementally, taking in the entire space, ceiling to floor. One image was recorded every 3 seconds between the start of the ball at 8.32 pm and its conclusion at 5.17 am the following morning – a total of 10,008 photographs. While doing so, the cameras together completed two full rotations, so every spot in the opera house was covered exactly twice during the evening.

Once Spinatsch's apparatus is set in motion, there is no predicting precisely what human activity will be captured or how it will be framed. The scene is trawled systematically. The cameras record gestures, form compositions and propose information. We can draw a line from Spinatsch's project back through the 'time and motion' photographic studies of the early twentieth century, all the way to the pioneers of 'chronophotography', Eadweard Muybridge and Étienne-Jules Marey, in the 1870s and 1880s. And the same ambiguity is present: is an imaging system a guarantee of some kind of objectivity, or is it simply a new technological aesthetic that is compelling?

Spinatsch has presented his photographic data in several forms, including grids on gallery walls and books. In 2011 the images from the Opera Ball were installed as a 360-degree panorama in Resselpark, Karlsplatz, Vienna. They were arranged as a chronological grid, the start of the ball wrapping around to meet its end. But instead of placing the spectator at the centre, surrounded by the view, Spinatsch faced the panorama outwards, inverting the space of the Opera House to allow viewers to encircle it. The socially exclusive interior is exposed to a democratic exterior. The private elite is put on display for all to see.

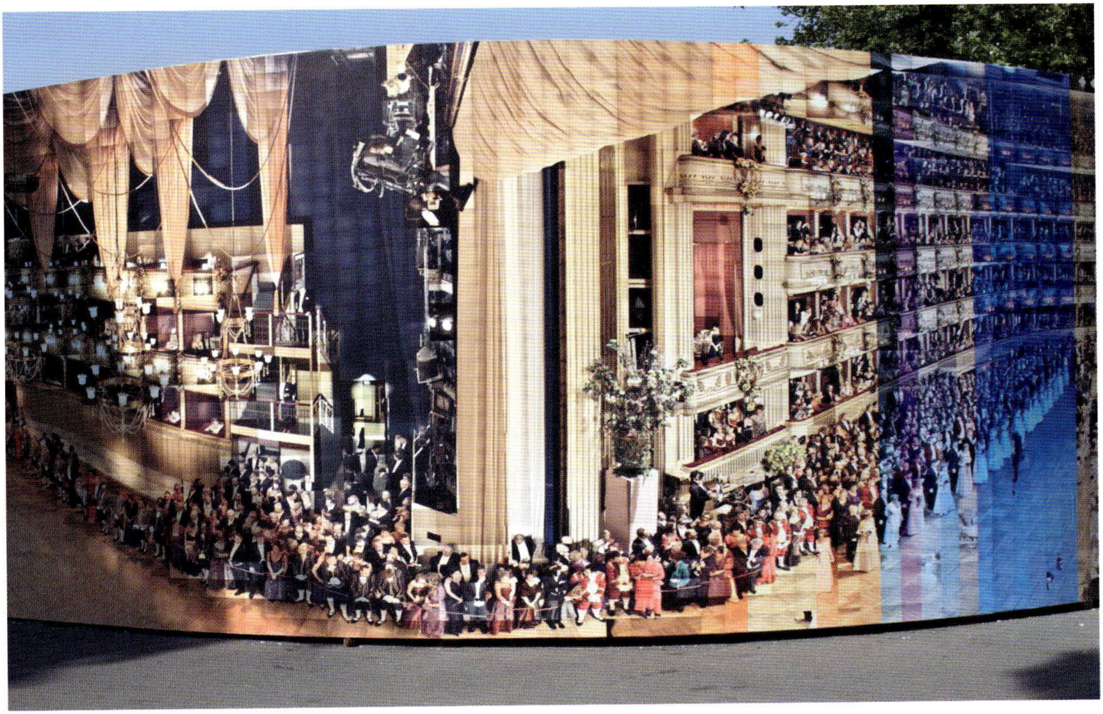

JOHN DIVOLA

Untitled

FROM THE SERIES 'AS FAR AS I COULD GET (10 SECONDS)', 1996

FOR NEARLY FIVE DECADES, the Californian artist John Divola has conducted his own offbeat, existential exploration of marginal spaces, overlooked themes and unlikely actions. He has broken into disused buildings to vandalize them artily before photographing his activity. He has made infinitely detailed mural-size photographs of banal landscapes in which he is the sole figure. He has photographed dogs chasing his car in the desert. He has even made photographs in response to Jean-Paul Sartre's book *Being and Nothingness*. It could easily be a melancholy body of work, were it not for Divola's endearing sense of the absurd and his disarming knack for getting at complex philosophical ideas about images and human experience.

'As Far as I Could Get' is Divola's simplest and most affecting work. He puts his camera on a tripod, frames a vertical landscape, and sets the aperture, shutter speed and focus. He then sets the self-timer to ten seconds, presses the button, sprints towards the horizon and ... shoots himself in the back.

We can presume Divola has to run for what feels like more than ten seconds, just to be sure. We can presume he then stops, recovers his breath, and trudges back to his camera. Perhaps he repeats the action for another attempt. Shooting on film, he cannot see the result there and then. Back in the darkroom, the film must be processed and the prints made (there are twelve in the series, shot in different locations). Only in the prints can the artist see the evidence of his lonely auto-humiliation. However fast he runs, however far he gets, the camera will always stop him in his tracks.

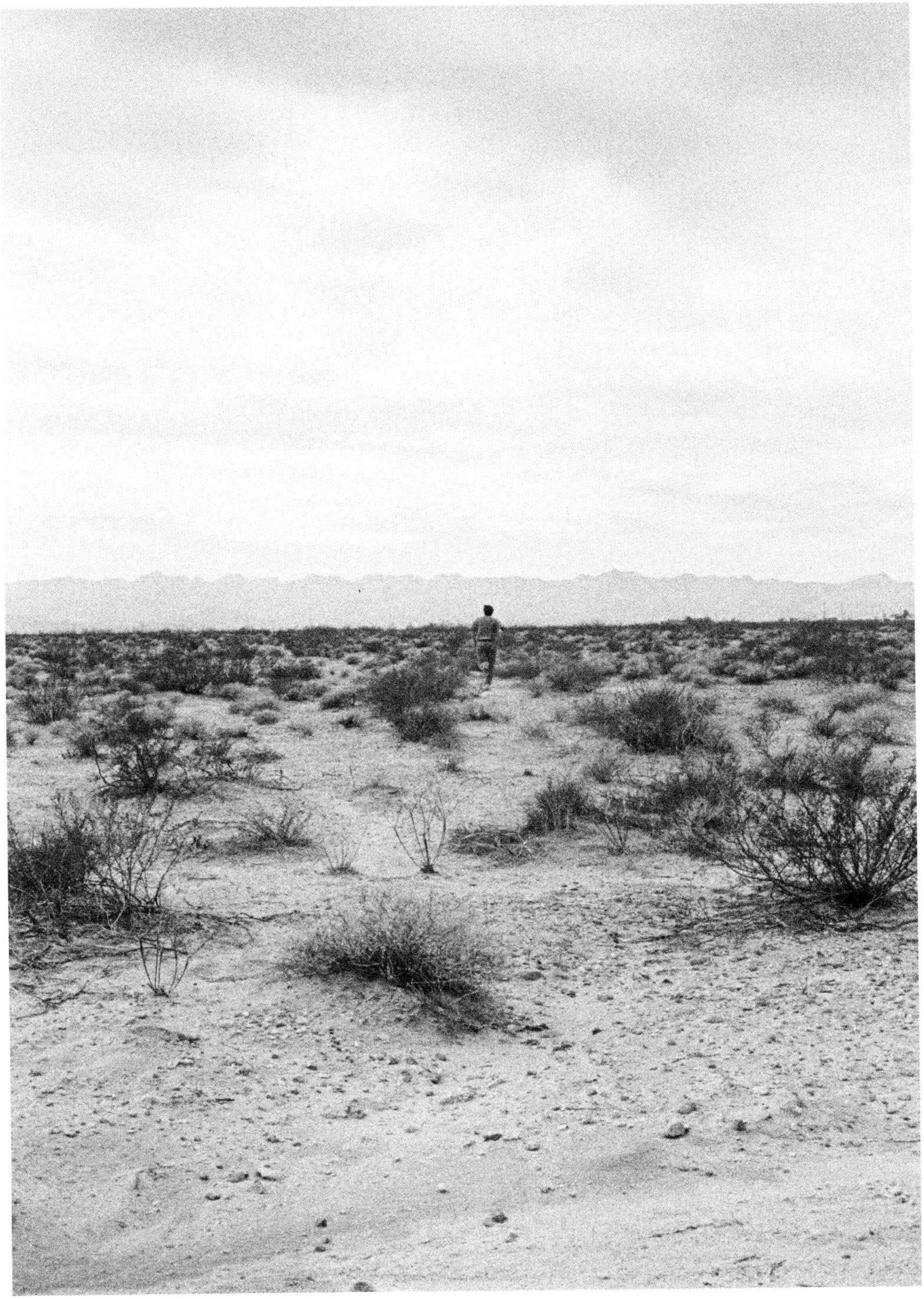

FRANÇOIS AUBERT

The Shirt of Emperor Maximilian of Mexico, 1867

IN 1864 NAPOLEON III, the last monarch of France, appointed an Austrian, Maximilian I, as Emperor of Mexico. In February 1867 the French withdrew from Mexico, abandoning their support for Maximilian. With two of his generals, Maximilian awaited the army of the Mexican nationalist Benito Juárez. Once captured, the three men were charged with treason. They were tried and convicted, and, on 19 June 1867, faced a firing squad. From a distance of five steps, they were shot, by eight riflemen.

François Aubert, a French painter and photographer, had come to Mexico in 1864. He soon became the official photographer of the court of Maximilian, and documented the ruling class of Mexico. Aubert was not permitted to photograph the execution itself, but he drew sketches of the event. He *was* permitted to photograph the firing squad, the site of the execution, the graves, the dressed corpse of the emperor in an open coffin, and the white shirt he had been wearing.

Within two weeks, news of the execution had reached Paris. Various accounts were published in the coming months. The artist Édouard Manet read these, and saw some of Aubert's photographs. His painting *The Execution of Emperor Maximilian* (*c*. 1867–68) was a response to the event, but was also a pointed reworking of another painting, *The Third of May 1808*, Francisco Goya's 1814 commemoration of Spain's resistance to Napoleon's occupying army. Manet's political allegiance was clear, and his painting was not exhibited in France.

In Aubert's photograph, Maximilian's shirt is pinned to the wooden frame of a door. It resembles a crucifixion, and, like Christ, Maximilian had in a sense been betrayed. Beyond this association, however, the photograph and the shirt say nothing about Maximilian's beliefs, nor about the presence of France in Mexico. The open meaning of the photograph meant that it became the site for the projection of differing political views. Aubert surely had his own feelings about it all, but the image does not declare them. It makes no attempt to tell the viewer what to think.

Photography is more easily, and perhaps more truly, a medium of 'what' than of 'how' or 'why' or 'whether'. It can show more readily than it can explain or comment. As photojournalism developed across the twentieth century, it could not avoid this paradox. Was it more effective if it withheld the temptation to persuade and simply attempted to show?

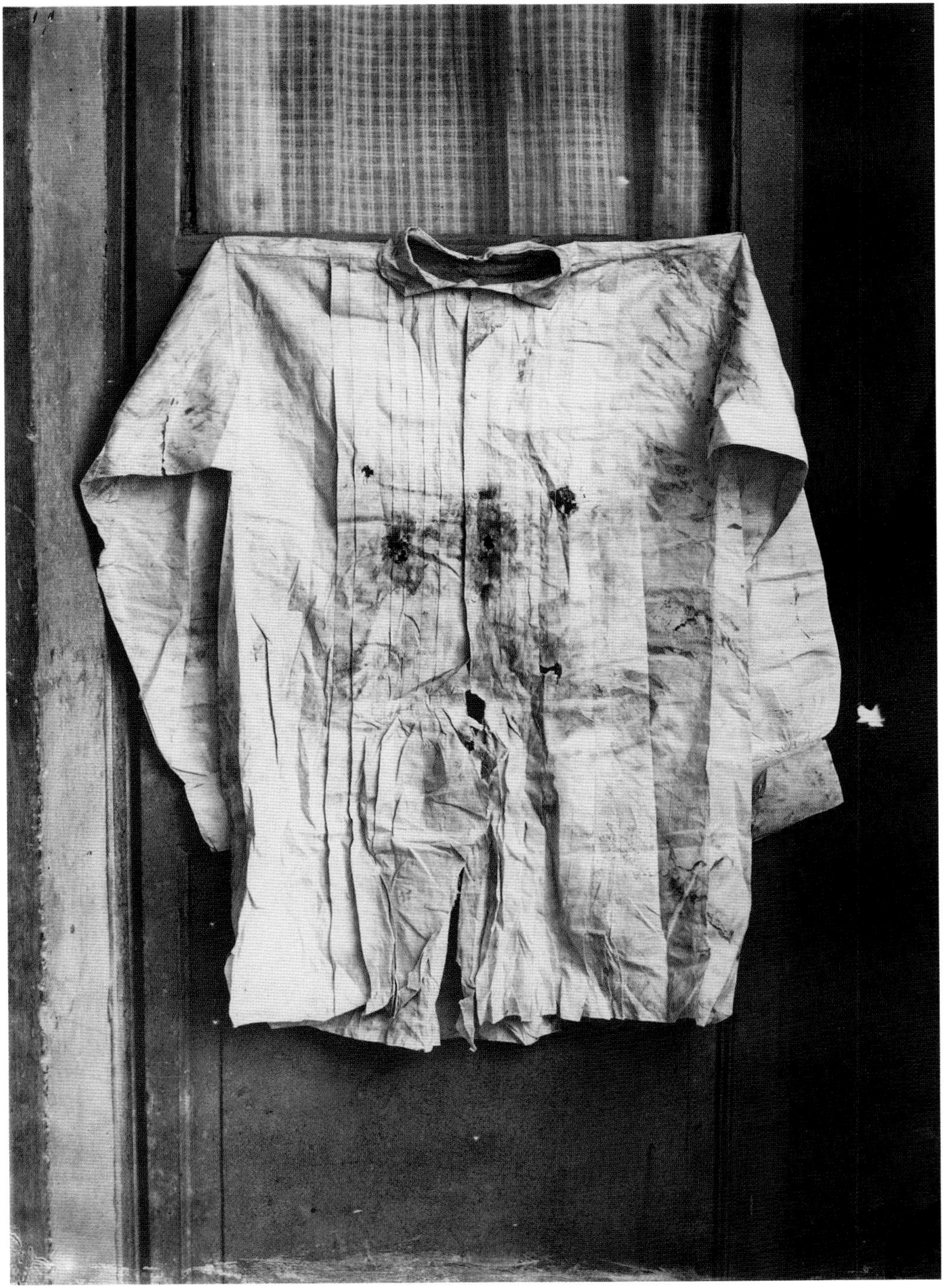

ROBERT FRANK

Mabou, 1977

IN 1954–56 ROBERT FRANK was on the road in America, making the photographs for what would become *The Americans*, perhaps the single most influential book by a photographer. Swiss by birth, Frank came to the United States in 1947. Politicians and the mainstream media were full of post-war optimism fuelled by consumer culture, television and Hollywood. All Frank could see was disappointment, alienation and systemic racism.

Published first in France in 1958 as *Les Américains*, the book included an anthology of quotes from various writers about the United States. When it appeared in America the following year, the quotes had been replaced with a foreword by Frank's friend Jack Kerouac. The publisher was Grove Press, the primary outlet for the Beat generation poets.

Frank's images were willfully subjective. They were also highly sophisticated redefinitions of the nation's iconography. The Stars and Stripes recurs, but it is either tattered or obliterating people's faces. Movie stars look uneasy; manual workers look dejected. Passengers on a trolleybus arrange themselves by race, while motels and gas stations are bleak and forgotten. But through the metaphor and allegory there was also a romantic and angry longing for something better. After all, Frank had given his photography and the country his fullest attention. Much of the best of North American culture has been critical of the country, examining the gap between its promise and its failures.

Modern America is a restart, an experiment, and its keenest observers, in photography, film, painting, literature and theatre, have been monitors of the experiment. *The Americans* divided opinion, but its reputation, particularly among other photographers, grew rapidly. For some, Frank had opened a rich new vein of image-making; for others, his achievement could not be surpassed. Different directions would have to be taken. Frank himself left photography almost immediately, and took up film-making. In 1971 he moved from New York to Mabou, in remote Nova Scotia, Canada. He returned to still photography but not in pursuit of singular, iconic images. He made collages, mixing photographs and writing in different ways. As he pushed onwards, he looked back from time to time. *The Americans* was becoming something of a counter-cultural monument. Museums and collectors were beginning to want prints.

In this photograph we see prints hanging on a washing line, on the coast of Mabou. There is an image of people on a boat. Frank shot it on the SS *Mauretania*, the day before he arrived in the United States. There is also a photograph taken at a political rally in Chicago in 1956. Three people, no faces. It is one of the best-known images from *The Americans*. On the right is the word 'Words': a substitute for an image, and a placeholder for a language to come.

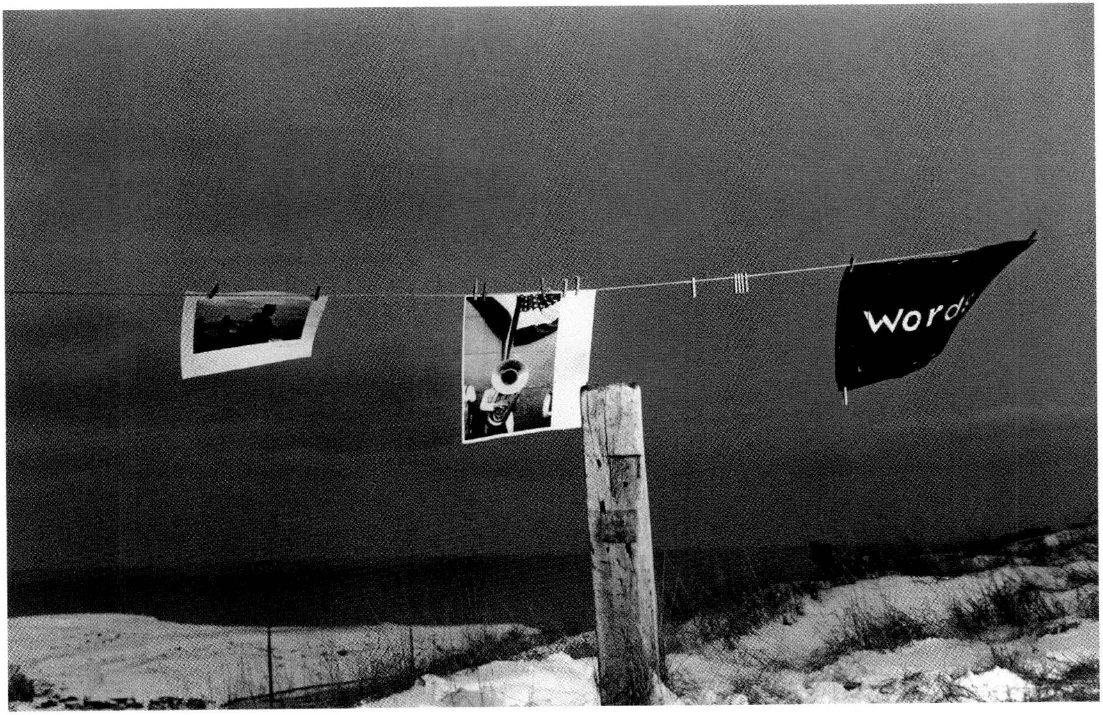
words

CONSTANCE TALBOT

The First Four Lines of Thomas Moore's 'The Last Rose of Summer', 1843

WHY END THIS BOOK with a picture of text? Is this not a perversion of what an image can be? Yes and no. Writing has long, deep and unexpected connections with photography. In 1834 a French-Brazilian by the name of Antoine Hércules Romuald Florence invented a method of copying flat documents by the action of light, laying them on photosensitive paper and exposing them to the sun. He called his process *photographie*, four years before Sir John Herschel coined the English equivalent. In fact, many of the various inventors of what we call photography made images of words, including Nicéphore Niépce, Hippolyte Bayard and especially William Henry Fox Talbot (pages 198, 224). None was aware of the others' work.

Talbot became interested in the copying of handwriting, typed text, legal documents and literature. Examples appeared in his image–text publication *The Pencil of Nature* (1844–46). There he noted: 'To the Antiquarian this application of the photographic art seems destined to be of great advantage. Copied of the size of the original, by the method of superposition.'

A man of letters, with a substantial library, it is fair to say that Talbot was surrounded by paper. His negatives and positive prints were also made of it. He was intimate with its texture and fibre, its weight and flexibility, and he understood that paper carried pictures just as well as words. When his wife, Constance, became curious about his invention, it was not the camera that interested her so much as the contact-printing of flat documents. The very first photographic image to be made by a woman was, as far as we know, her print of a typeset stanza of poetry. Its author, Thomas Moore, was a close friend of the Talbots.

The poem's reference to fading has a certain irony, since William encountered many problems making his paper prints permanent. But this one by Constance survives. Now, it is digitized and reproduced here, a strange hybrid work, not one thing or another.

I am writing these words on a smartphone, knowing you will read them on a printed page, opposite a faithful reproduction of Constance's image of text. I switch applications, and see her image glowing in the place of my words. Were she or her husband able to see this, little of it would come as a surprise. They had friends who were pioneers of what eventually became computing, where all data – words and images – are reduced to ones and zeros. The Talbot version of photography was based on the principle of infinite copies of variable sizes. William presented his images on pages, on walls and in vitrines, and knew that, in time, there would be no place they did not belong. Photography could be art and document and everything in between, and every area of human activity would be touched by it, including writing. It was all there at the beginning.

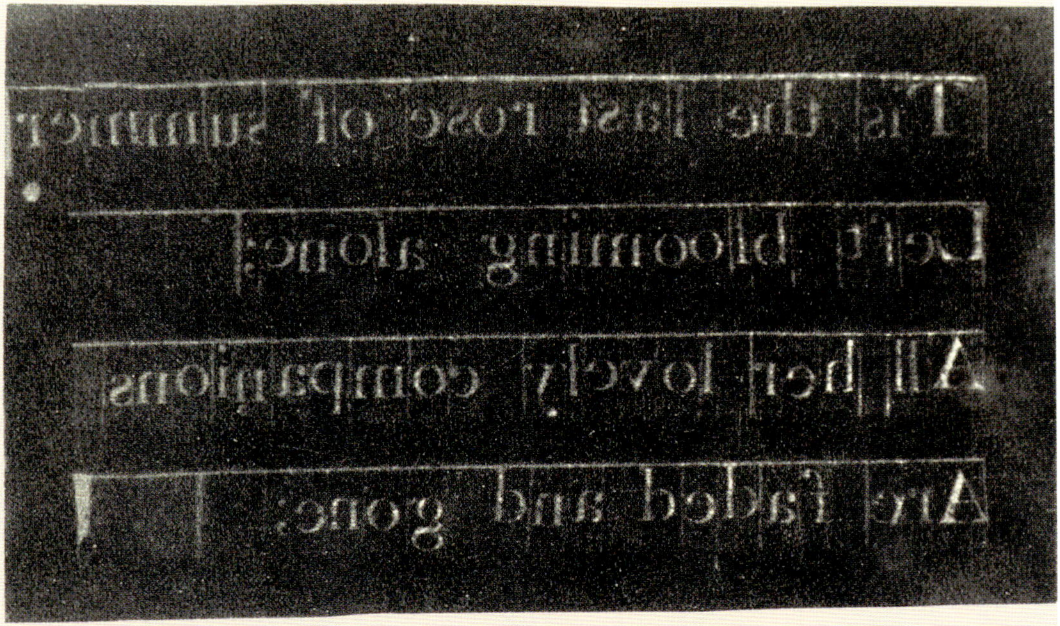

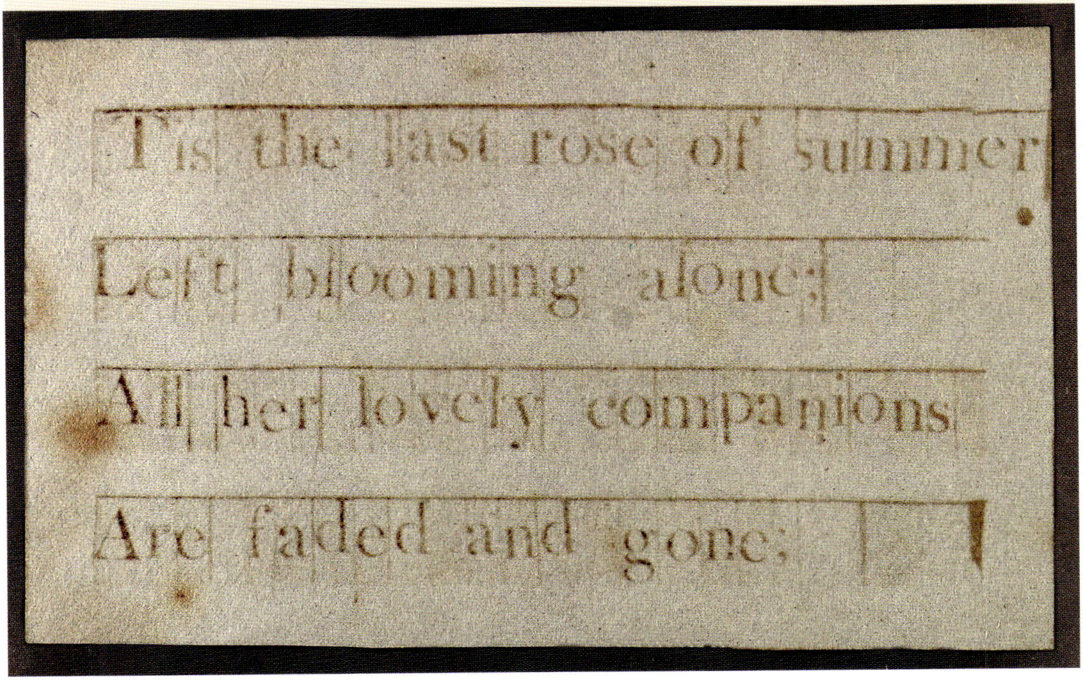
'Tis the last rose of summer
Left blooming alone;
All her lovely companions
Are faded and gone;

LIST OF WORKS

14 Robert Cumming (American, b. 1943)
1826; Niepce's Pewter Picture, 1980

16 Frederick S. Church (American, 1842–1924)
George Eastman aboard the SS *Gallia*,
en route to England from America, 1890

18 Lee Friedlander (American, b. 1934)
Peter Exline, Spokane, Washington, 1970

20 Eugène Atget (French, 1857–1927)
Fête du Trône, 1925

22 Manuel Álvarez Bravo (Mexican, 1902–2002)
Parábola óptica, 1931

24 William Klein (American/French, b. 1928)
New York Fashion, 1959

26 Guy Bourdin (French, 1928–1991)
Charles Jourdan, Spring 1978, 1978

28 Photographer unknown
Preparations for the British Exhibition of War Pictures, Grafton Galleries, London, *c.* 1917

30 Susan Meiselas (American, b. 1948)
Monimbo, Nicaragua, July 2004, 2004
From the series 'Re-framing History', 2005

32 John Stezaker (British, b. 1949)
Pair I, 2007

34 Helena Almeida (Portuguese, 1934–2018)
Inhabited Painting, 1975

36 William Eggleston (American, b. 1939)
Untitled From the *Los Alamos* portfolio, 1965–74

38 Ruth Orkin (American, 1921–1985)
American Girl in Italy, 1951

40 Gérard Castello-Lopes (Portuguese, 1925–2011)
Lisboa, 1957

42 Garry Winogrand (American, 1928–1984)
Albuquerque, New Mexico, 1957

44 Photographer unknown
Franz Reichelt, the 'Flying Tailor', demonstrates his parachute suit to the French press prior to his fateful leap from the Eiffel Tower, 1912

46 Harry Shunk (German, 1924–2006) and János Kender (Hungarian, 1938–2009)
Saut dans le vide
Photomontage of a performance by Yves Klein at Rue Gentil-Bernard, Fontenay-aux-Roses, France, 23 October 1960

48 Eadweard Muybridge (British/American, 1830–1904)
Chickens Scared by a Torpedo, 1884–87

50 Frank Gilbreth (American, 1868–1924) and Lillian Gilbreth (American, 1878–1972)
Cyclegraphic image of a woman working at a gridded table, *c.* 1914

52 Étienne-Jules Marey (French, 1830–1904)
Vertical Ball Drop, 1890

54 John Baldessari (American, 1931–2020)
From the series 'Throwing Three Balls in the Air to Get a Straight Line (Best of Thirty-Six Attempts)', 1973

56 Helen Levitt (American, 1913–2009)
New York, *c.* 1942

58 Ken Russell (British, 1927–2011)
Teddy Girl, 1955

60 Weegee (Arthur (Usher) Fellig, Austrian/American, 1899–1968)
Coney Island, 1940

62 Frances Benjamin Johnston (American, 1864–1952)
Self-Portrait (as New Woman), 1896

64 Kwame Brathwaite (American, b. 1938)
Untitled, *c.* 1966
Photo shoot at a school for one of the many modelling groups who had begun to embrace natural hairstyles in the 1960s

66 Marianne Wex (German, b. 1937)
Page from the book *Let's Take Back Our Space* (Frauenliteratur Verlag, 1984)

68 Vivian Maier (American, 1926–2009)
Contact sheet, New York, 1954

70 Chris Steele-Perkins (British, b. 1947)
Courtyard of the mental hospital run by the Edhi Foundation, Pakistan, 1997

72 Hannah Starkey (British, b. 1971)
Untitled, September 2008

74 Photographer unknown
Publicity still for Alfred Hitchcock's *Rear Window*, 1954

76 Chris Marker (French, 1921–2012)
Photograph from the film *La Jetée*, 1962

78 Gisèle Freund (German/French, 1908–2000)
Portrait of Virginia Woolf, 1939

80 Bill Brandt (German/British, 1904–1983)
Parlourmaid and Under-parlourmaid Ready to Serve Dinner, 1933

82 Henri Cartier-Bresson (French, 1908–2004)
Barge Family, Bougival, 1956

84 August Sander (German, 1876–1964)
The Notary, 1924

86 Evelyn Hofer (German/American, 1922–2009)
Queensboro Bridge, New York, 1964

88 Rineke Dijkstra (Dutch, b. 1959)
Kolobrzeg, Poland, July 26, 1992, 1992
From the series 'Bathers', 1992–98

90 Alessandra Sanguinetti (American, b. 1968)
Gauchito, 2003
From the series 'The Adventures of Guille and Belinda and the Enigmatic Meaning of their Dreams'

92 Germaine Krull (German/Dutch, 1897–1985)
Walter Benjamin, *c.* 1925

94 Florence Henri (American/Swiss, 1893–1982)
Composition, Nature Morte, 1929

96 Laure Albin Guillot (French, 1879–1962)
Narcisse, 1941

98 Saul Leiter (American, 1923–2013)
Café, Paris, 1959

100 Photographer unknown
Diego Rivera in his San Angel studio, Mexico City, 1940
From the collection of Frida Kahlo

102 Photographer unknown
Tina Modotti at an exhibition of her work at the National Library in Mexico City, 1929

104 Hannah Höch (German, 1889–1978)
Entartet (Degenerate), 1969

106 Robert Rauschenberg (American, 1925–2008)
Scanning, 1963

108 Louise Lawler (American, b. 1947)
Life After 1945 (Hats), 2006–07

110 Jason Evans (British, b. 1968)
Artwork for the Four Tet album *There Is Love in You*, 2010

112 Paul Rand (American, 1914–1996)
El Producto cigar box, 1952

114 Irving Penn (American, 1917–2009)
Frozen Foods, New York, 1977

116 Myoung Ho Lee (South Korean, b. 1975)
Tree #3, 2006
From the series 'Tree', 2006–11

170 Photographer unknown
The Federal Bureau of Investigation Fingerprint Database, 1943

172 Maurice Jarnoux (French, 1907–1969)
André Malraux at Home, 1954

174 Anastasia Samoylova (Russian/American, b. 1984)
Six Real Matterhorns, 2019
From the series 'Landscape Sublime', 2013–present

176 Dayanita Singh (Indian, b. 1961)
Conversation Chambers: Museum Bhavan, 2013 Installation View, Hayward Gallery, London, 2013

178 Claudia Angelmaier (German, b. 1972)
Hase
From the series 'Plants and Animals', 2004

180 Scheltens & Abbenes (Maurice Scheltens, Dutch, b. 1972; Liesbeth Abbenes, Dutch, b. 1970)
COS, Collections: Light Bulbs, 2012

182 Andreas Gursky (German, b. 1955)
Salerno, 1990

184 Stephen Shore (American, b. 1947)
Beverly Boulevard and La Brea Avenue, Los Angeles, California, June 21, 1975, 1975

186 Harry Gruyaert (Belgian, b. 1941)
Belgium, Waterloo, 1980

188 Lucas Blalock (American, b. 1978)
Emile, Man of the Future, 2016–17

190 Broomberg & Chanarin (Adam Broomberg, South African, b. 1970; Oliver Chanarin, British, b. 1971)
The Press Conference, June 9, 2008
From the series 'The Day Nobody Died', 2008

192 Photographer unknown
Military personnel shielded from nuclear test, 1957

194 Chris McCaw (American, b. 1971)
Sunburned GSP164 (Mojave), 2007

196 Anna Atkins (British, 1799–1871)
Cystoseira granulata
Page from the book *Photographs of British Algae: Cyanotype Impressions* (1843)

198 William Henry Fox Talbot (British, 1800–1877)
Lace, 1845

200 Helen Sear (British, b. 1955)
Untitled
From the series 'Inside the View', 2006–08

202 Thomas Mailaender (French, b. 1979)
Untitled
From the series 'Illustrated People', 2014

204 Flip Schulke (American, 1930–2008)
Cassius Clay training in a pool at the Sir John Hotel, Miami, 1961

206 Richard Avedon (American, 1923–2004)
Marilyn Monroe, Actress, New York, May 6, 1957, 1957

208 Marcello Geppetti (Italian, 1933–1998)
Anita Ekberg confronting the paparazzi, 1960

210 Eve Arnold (American, 1912–2012)
Army Manoeuvres, Fort Bragg, North Carolina, USA, 1967

212 Don McCullin (British, b. 1935)
Turkish defender leaving the side entrance of a cinema, Limassol, Cyprus, 1964

214 Luc Delahaye (French, b. 1962)
Les Pillards (The Looters), 2010

216 Alex Majoli (Italian, b. 1971)
Scene #3781, 2017

218 Pete Souza (American, b. 1954)
President Barack Obama sits in the famous Rosa Parks bus at the Henry Ford Museum after an event in Dearborn, Mich., April 18, 2012, 2012

220 Walker Evans (American, 1903–1975)
Opening pages of 'Along the Right-of-Way', *Fortune*, July 1955

222 Jürgen Schadeberg (South African, b. 1931)
Drum Magazine Office, Johannesburg, 1954

224 William Henry Fox Talbot (British, 1800–1877)
The Reading Establishment, *c.* 1845

226 Naoya Hatakeyama (Japanese, b. 1958)
River Series #4, 1993–94

228 Lorraine O'Grady (American, b. 1934)
Art Is (Girlfriends Times Two), 1983

230 Barbara Probst (German, b. 1964)
Exposure #137.5: N.Y.C., Broome & Crosby Streets, 05.01.18, 3:21p.m., 2018
For *Wallpaper** magazine, June 2018

232 Mark Neville (British, b. 1966)
Donna pregnant (Ancient Order of the Hibernian Social Club), 2005
From the Port Glasgow book project, 2004–06

234 Humphrey Spender (British, 1910–2005)
Planning Observations at 85 Davenport Street, 1937–38

236 Doug Rickard (American, b. 1968)
#96.766076, Dallas, TX (2009), 2010
From the series 'A New American Picture', 2006–10

238 Tim Davis (American, b. 1969)
Colosseum Pictures
From the series 'The New Antiquity', 2009

240 Mishka Henner (Belgian, b. 1976)
Coronado Feeders, Dalhart, Texas, 2012

242 Jules Spinatsch (Swiss, b. 1964)
Vienna MMIX – Panorama portrait of a society: 7000 Participants, 10008 Images, one every 3 seconds, 2009
Installation view, Resselpark, Karlsplatz, Vienna, 2011

244 John Divola (American, b. 1949)
Untitled
From the series 'As Far as I Could Get (10 seconds)', 1996

246 François Aubert (French, 1829–1906)
The Shirt of Emperor Maximilian of Mexico, 1867

248 Robert Frank (American, 1924–2019)
Mabou, 1977

250 Constance Talbot (British, 1811–1880)
The First Four Lines of Thomas Moore's 'The Last Rose of Summer', 1843

FURTHER READING

Claudia Angelmaier, *Color and Gray* (Leipzig: E. A. Seeman, 2007)

Richard Avedon, *Photographs 1946–2004* (Ostfildern: Hatje Cantz, 2007)

Joerg Bader (ed.) *Jules Spinatsch: Semiautomatic Photography* (Leipzig: Spector Books, 2018)

Quentin Bajac, *Luc Delahaye: 2006–2010* (Göttingen: Steidl, 2011)

Quentin Bajac *et al.*, *Stephen Shore: Solving Pictures* (London: Thames & Hudson, 2017)

Geoffrey Batchen *et al.* (eds), *Picturing Atrocity: Photography in Crisis* (London: Reaktion, 2012)

Walter Benjamin *On Photography*, ed. and trans. Esther Leslie (London: Reaktion, 2015)

Bettina Berch, *The Woman Behind the Lens: The Life and Work of Frances Benjamin Johnston, 1864–1952* (Charlottesville: University Press of Virginia, 2000)

Bill Brandt, *The English at Home* (London: B. T Batsford, 1936)

Kwame Brathwaite *et al.*, *Black Is Beautiful* (New York: Aperture, 2019)

Marta Braun, *Picturing Time: The Work of Etienne-Jules Marey (1830–1904)* (Chicago: University of Chicago Press, 1994)

Philip Brookman *et al.*, *Helios: Eadweard Muybridge in a Time of Change* (Göttingen: Steidl, 2010)

Cheryl A. Brutvan, *The Paintings of Sylvia Plimack Mangold* (New York: Hudson Hills Press in association with the Albright-Knox Gallery, 1994)

Victor Burgin, *The Remembered Film* (London: Reaktion, 2004)

Victor Burgin, *Parallel Texts: Interviews and Interventions about Art* (London: Reaktion, 2011)

Jorge Calado, *The Photography of Gérard Castello-Lopes, 1956–2006: Apparitions* (Lisbon: Banco Espírito Santo – BESart, 2011)

David Campany, *Art and Photography* (London: Phaidon, 2003)

David Campany, *Photography and Cinema* (London: Reaktion, 2008)

David Campany, *Walker Evans: The Magazine Work* (Göttingen: Steidl, 2014)

David Campany, *A Handful of Dust* (London: Mack, 2015)

Henri Cartier-Bresson, *The Mind's Eye: Writings on Photography and Photographers*, ed. Michael L. Sand, trans. Diana C. Stoll (New York: Aperture, 2004)

Charlotte Cotton and Shelly Verthime (eds), *Guy Bourdin* (London: Victoria and Albert Museum, 2003)

Jack Cowart *et al.*, *Shunk-Kender: Art Through the Eye of the Camera (1957–1983)* (Paris: Éditions Xavier Barral, 2019)

Patrizia Di Bello *et al.* (eds), *The Photobook: From Talbot to Ruscha and Beyond* (London: I. B. Tauris, 2011)

Leah Dickerman and Achim Borchardt-Hume, *Robert Rauschenberg* (New York: Museum of Modern Art; London: Tate Publishing, 2016)

Rineke Dijkstra, *Portraits* (Munich: Schirmer/Mosel; London: Art Data, 2004)

Thierry de Duve (ed.), *The Definitively Unfinished Marcel Duchamp* (Cambridge, MA: MIT Press, 1993)

Sarah Bay Gachot (ed.), *Robert Cumming: The Difficulties of Nonsense* (New York: Aperture, 2016)

Thierry Gervais (ed.), *The 'Public' Life of Photographs* (Cambridge, MA: MIT Press, 2016)

Luigi Ghirri, *The Complete Essays, 1973–1991*, trans. Ben Bazalgette and Marguerite Shore (London: Mack, 2016)

Walter Grasskamp, *The Book on the Floor: André Malraux and the Imaginary Museum*, trans. Fiona Elliott (Los Angeles: Getty Research Institute, 2016)

Maria Morris Hambourg *et al.*, *Irving Penn: Centennial* (New York: Metropolitan Museum of Art, 2017)

Janet Harbord, *Chris Marker: La Jetée* (London: Afterall Books, 2009)

Margaret Hooks, *Tina Modotti: Photographer and Revolutionary* (Madrid: La Fábrica; New York: DAP, 2017)

Margaret Iversen, *Photography, Trace, and Trauma* (Chicago: University of Chicago Press, 2017)

Daniel-Henry Kahnweiler, photographs by Brassaï, *The Sculptures of Picasso* (London: Rodney Phillips & Co., 1949)

William Klein, *William Klein ABC* (London: Tate Publishing, 2012)

Rosalind Krauss *et al.*, *L'Amour Fou: Photography and Surrealism* (Washington DC: Corcoran Gallery of Art, 1985)

Maud Lavin, *Cut with the Kitchen Knife: The Weimar Photomontages of Hannah Höch* (New Haven, CT: Yale University Press, 1993)

Kristen Lubben (ed.), *Susan Meiselas: In History* (Göttingen: Steidl, 2008)

Alex Majoli, *Scene* (London: Mack, 2019)

John Maloof *et al.*, *Vivian Maier: A Photographer Found* (New York: Harper Design, 2014)

Roxana Marcoci, *Louise Lawler: Receptions* (New York: Museum of Modern Art: 2017)

Carol Mavor, *Reading Boyishly: Roland Barthes, J. M. Barrie, Jacques Henri Lartigue, Marcel Proust, and D. W. Winnicott* (Durham, NC: Duke University Press, 2007)

Jessica Morgan and Leslie Jones (eds), *John Baldessari: Pure Beauty* (London: Tate Publishing, 2009)

Bruce Nauman, *Please Pay Attention Please: Bruce Nauman's Words – Writings and Interviews*, ed. Janet Kraynak (Cambridge, MA: MIT Press, 2005)

Murat Nemet-Nejat, *The Peripheral Space of Photography* (Copenhagen: Green Integer, 2004)

Mark Neville, *Fancy Pictures* (Göttingen: Steidl, 2016)

Filipa Oliveira *et al.*, *Helena Almeida: Inside Me* (Cambridge: Kettle's Yard, 2009)

Fréderic Paul, *Barbara Probst: The Moment in Space* (Stuttgart: Hartmann Books, 2019)

Sandra S. Phillips and Maria Morris Hambourg, *Helen Levitt* (San Francisco: San Francisco Museum of Modern Art, 1991)

V. S. Pritchett, photographs by Evelyn Hofer, *New York Proclaimed* (London: Chatto & Windus, 1965)

Leo Rubinfien (ed.), *Garry Winogrand* (San Francisco: San Francisco Museum of Modern Art, 2013)

Anastasia Samoylova, *Landscape Sublime* (In the In-Between Editions, 2016)

Gerd Sander, *August Sander: People of the 20th Century*, rev. edn (Munich: Schirmer/Mosel, 2013)

Alessandra Sanguinetti, *The Adventures of Guille and Belinda and the Enigmatic Meaning of Their Dreams* (Portland: Nazraeli, 2010)

Larry J. Schaaf, *Sun Gardens: Cyanotypes by Anna Atkins* (New York: New York Public Library, 2018)

Louise Schouwenberg, *Zeen – Scheltens & Abbenes* (Tokyo: Case Publishing, 2019)

Kim Sichel, *Germaine Krull: Photographer of Modernity* (Cambridge, MA: MIT Press, 1999)

Kaja Silverman, *The Miracle of Analogy; or, The History of Photography, Part 1* (Stanford: Stanford University Press, 2015)

Dayanita Singh, *Museum Bhavan* (Göttingen: Steidl, 2017)

Rebecca Solnit, *River of Shadows: Eadweard Muybridge and the Technological Wild West* (New York: Penguin, 2004)

Hannah Starkey, *Photographs 1997–2017* (London: Mack, 2018)

Sara Stevenson, *Magna Brava: Magnum's Women Photographers – Eve Arnold, Martine Franck, Susan Meiselas, Inge Morath, Marilyn Silverstone, Lise Sarfati* (Munich and London: Prestel, 1999)

Kathleen Stewart Howe *et al.*, *John Divola: As Far as I Could Get* (Munich and London: Prestel, 2013)

John Stezaker, *Film Still* (London: Ridinghouse, 2011)

Marie Luise Syring (ed.), *Andreas Gursky: Photographs from 1984 to the Present* (London: teNeues, 2001)

John Szarkowski, *Atget* (New York: Museum of Modern Art, 2004)

William Henry Fox Talbot, *The Pencil of Nature* (London: Longman, Brown, Green & Longmans, 1844–46)

Jeff Wall, *Selected Essay and Interviews* (New York: Museum of Modern Art, 2007)

Brian Wallis, *Weegee: Murder Is My Business* (Munich: Prestel, 2013)

Thomas Weski (ed.), *William Eggleston: Los Alamos* (Zurich: Scalo, 2003)

Marianne Wex, *Let's Take Back Our Space: 'Female' and 'Male' Body Language as a Result of Patriarchal Structures* (West Berlin: Frauenliteraturverlag Hermine Fees, 1979)

PICTURE CREDITS

Front cover: © The Guy Bourdin Estate, 2020. All rights reserved; endpapers: © A. Rodchenko, Rodchenko & Stepanova Archive, DACS, UPRAVIS, 2020; 3: The Metropolitan Museum of Art/Art Resource/ Scala, Florence; 15: © 2019 Robert Cumming/Licensed by VAGA at Artists Rights Society (ARS), NY; 17: Photo by Frederick Church/George Eastman Museum/Getty Images; 19: © Lee Friedlander, courtesy Fraenkel Gallery, San Francisco; 21: Digital image courtesy of the Getty's Open Content Program; 23: Bridgeman/Bravo © ADAGP, Paris and DACS, London 2020; 25: © William Klein; 27: © The Guy Bourdin Estate, 2020. All rights reserved; 29: Library and Archives, Ottawa, Canada; 31: © Susan Meiselas/Magnum Photos; 33: © The Artist. Courtesy the Artist and the Approach, London; 35: Courtesy Helena Almeida studio; 37: © Eggleston Artistic Trust. Courtesy Eggleston Artistic Trust and David Zwirner; 39: © 1952, 1980 Ruth Orkin. Used with special permission of the Ruth Orkin Photo Archive; 41: © Gérard Castello-Lopes, Museu Nacional de Arte Contemporânea – Museu do Chiado, Direção-Geral do Património Cultural/Arquivo de Documentação Fotográfica (DGPC/ADF); 43: © The Estate of Garry Winogrand, courtesy Fraenkel Gallery, San Francisco; 45: David Campany's personal collection; 47: © The Estate of Yves Klein c/o ADAGP, Paris and DACS, London 2020. Photograph: Shunk–Kender © J. Paul Getty Trust, Getty Research Institute, Los Angeles (2014.R.20); 49: Eadweard Muybridge; 51: The Frank and Lillian Gilbreth Collection, Archives Center, National Museum of American History, Smithsonian Institution; 53: Étienne-Jules Marey; 55: Courtesy of John Baldessari; 57: © Helen Levitt Film Documents LLC. All rights reserved. Courtesy of Thomas Zander Gallery; 59: Ken Russell/Topfoto; 61: Photo by Weegee (Arthur Fellig)/International Center of Photography/ Hulton Archive/Getty Images; 63: MPI/Getty Images; 65: Photo Courtesy of the Kwame Braithwaite Archive; 67: Courtesy of the artist and Tanya Leighton, Berlin. © Marianne Wex; 69: © Estate of Vivian Maier. Courtesy Maloof Collection and Howard Greenberg Gallery, New York; 71: © Chris Steele-Perkins/Magnum Photos; 73: © Hannah Starkey, courtesy Maureen Paley, London; 75: David Campany's personal collection; 77: Photo by Argos/Kobal/Shutterstock; 79: Photo © IMEC, Fonds MCC, Dist. RMN-Grand Palais/Gisèle Freund; 81: Bill Brandt © Bill Brandt Archive; 83: © Henri Cartier-Bresson/Magnum Photos; 85: © Die Photographische Sammlung/SK Stiftung Kultur – August Sander Archiv, Cologne/DACS 2020; 87: © Estate Evelyn Hofer, *Queensboro Bridge, New York*, 1964. Courtesy Galerie m Bochum, Germany; 89: Courtesy of the artist and Marian Goodman Gallery; 91: © Alessandra Sanguinetti/ Magnum Photos; 93: Estate Germaine Krull, Museum Folkwang, Essen. Photo akg-images/Imagno; 95: Florence Henri © Galleria Martini & Ronchetti, Genoa, courtesy Archives Florence Henri; 97: Collection of the Akron Art Museum, purchased with funds from Mrs Beatrice K. McDowell; 99: © Saul Leiter Foundation, courtesy Howard Greenberg Gallery; 101: ART Collection/Alamy Stock Photo; 103: Galerie Bilderwelt/ Getty Images; 105: Collection Landesbank Berlin, Höch © DACS 2020; 107: Collection SFMOMA, fractional and promised gift of Helen and Charles Schwag. © Robert Rauschenberg Foundation/Licensed by VAGA at Artists Rights Society (ARS), NY; 109: Courtesy of the artist and Metro Pictures, New York; 111: © Jason Evans; 113: David Campany's personal collection; 115: © The Irving Penn Foundation; 117: © Myoung Ho Lee, Courtesy Yossi Milo Gallery, New York; 119: © Noémie Goudal; 121: Courtesy the artist; 123: David Campany's personal collection; 125: © Lalla Essaydi, New York/ Courtesy Edwynn Houk Gallery, New York; 127: © Gregory Crewdson. Courtesy Gagosian; 129: Jacques-

André Boiffard; 131: The J. Paul Getty Museum, Los Angeles. Paul Nougé, © DACS 2020; 133: © Black River Productions, Ltd/Mitch Epstein. Courtesy of Sikkema Jenkins & Co., New York. Used with permission. All rights reserved; 135: Terri Weifenbach; 137: Gregory Halpern; 139: Toshio Shibata/Gallery Luisotti; 141: Jeff Wall. Courtesy of the artist; 143: © Eredi Luigi Ghirri; 145: Artokoloro Quint Lox Limited/Alamy Stock Photo; 147: © Bruce Nauman/Artists Rights Society (ARS), New York and DACS, London 2020. Digital image Whitney Museum of American Art/ Licensed by Scala; 149: David Campany's personal collection; 151: Photograph by Jacques Henri Lartigue. © Ministère de la Culture (France), MAP-AAJHL; 153: Photos © Estate Brassaï – RMN – Grand Palais. © Succession Picasso/DACS, London 2020; 155: © Succession Marcel Duchamp/ADAGP, Paris and DACS, London 2020/© Man Ray Trust/ADAGP, Paris and DACS, London 2020; 157: © Frederick & Frances Sommer Foundation; 158 and 159: Victor Burgin; 161: Image courtesy of David Zwirner Gallery; 163: Courtesy Alexander and Bonin, New York. Collection of James Mangold. Photo by Joerg Lohse; 165: Courtesy of the artist and Marian Goodman Gallery; 167: Time Inc./The LIFE Picture Collection via Getty Images; 169: David Campany's personal collection; 171: David Campany's personal collection; 173: Photo Maurice Jarnoux/Paris Match via Getty Images; 175: Anastasia Samoylova; 177: Courtesy the artist and Frith Street Gallery, London. Photograph © Stephen White; 179: © Claudia Angelmaier/DACS 2020; 181: Scheltens & Abbenes; 183: © Andreas Gursky/Courtesy Sprüth Magers Berlin London/DACS 2020; 185: © Stephen Shore. Courtesy 303 Gallery, New York; 187: © Harry Gruyaert/Magnum Photos; 189: Courtesy of the artist and Galerie Eva Presenhuber, Zurich/New York; 191: © Broomberg & Chanarin; 193: Courtesy National Archives, photo no. 111-SC-420969; 195: © Chris McCaw; 197: Anna Atkins; 199: William Henry Fox Talbot; 201: Courtesy Klompching Gallery. © Helen Sear; 203: Courtesy the artist and Michael Hoppen Gallery; 205: © Flip Schulke; 207: Photograph by Richard Avedon. © The Richard Avedon Foundation; 209: Photo by Marcello Geppetti. © MGMC/dolceVita GALLERY; 211: © Eve Arnold/Magnum Photos; 213: © Don McCullin/ Contact Press Images; 215: Courtesy Luc Delahaye and Galerie Nathalie Obadia; 217: Alex Majoli. Courtesy the Howard Greenberg Gallery; 219: Photo by Pete Souza/ White House Photo via Getty Images; 221: © Walker Evans Archive, The Metropolitan Museum of Art, New York; 223: Photo by Jurgen Schadeberg/Getty Images; 225: Gilman Collection, gift of the Howard Gilman Foundation, 2005. Accession number 2005.100.171.1, .2. Metropolitan Museum of Art, New York; 227: © Naoya Hatakeyama; 229: Image courtesy of Alexander Gray Associates, New York. © Lorraine O'Grady/ARS, NY and DACS, London 2020; 231: VG Bild Kunst, Barbara Probst; 233: Courtesy the artist; 235: © Bolton Council, from the Collection of Bolton Library and Museum Services. Courtesy of the Humphrey Spender Archive; 237: © Doug Rickard; 239: Courtesy the artist; 241: © Mishka Henner; 243: © Jules Spinatsch, Switzerland. Courtesy of Christophe Guye Gallery, Zurich, and Galerie Luciano Fasciati, Chur; 245: © John Divola; 247: The Metropolitan Museum of Art, New York, Gilman Collection, gift of the Howard Gilman Foundation, 2005; 249: © Robert Frank, courtesy Pace/MacGill Gallery, New York; 251: Constance Talbot.

INDEX

Page numbers in **bold** indicate main entries; those in *italic* refer to the illustrations.

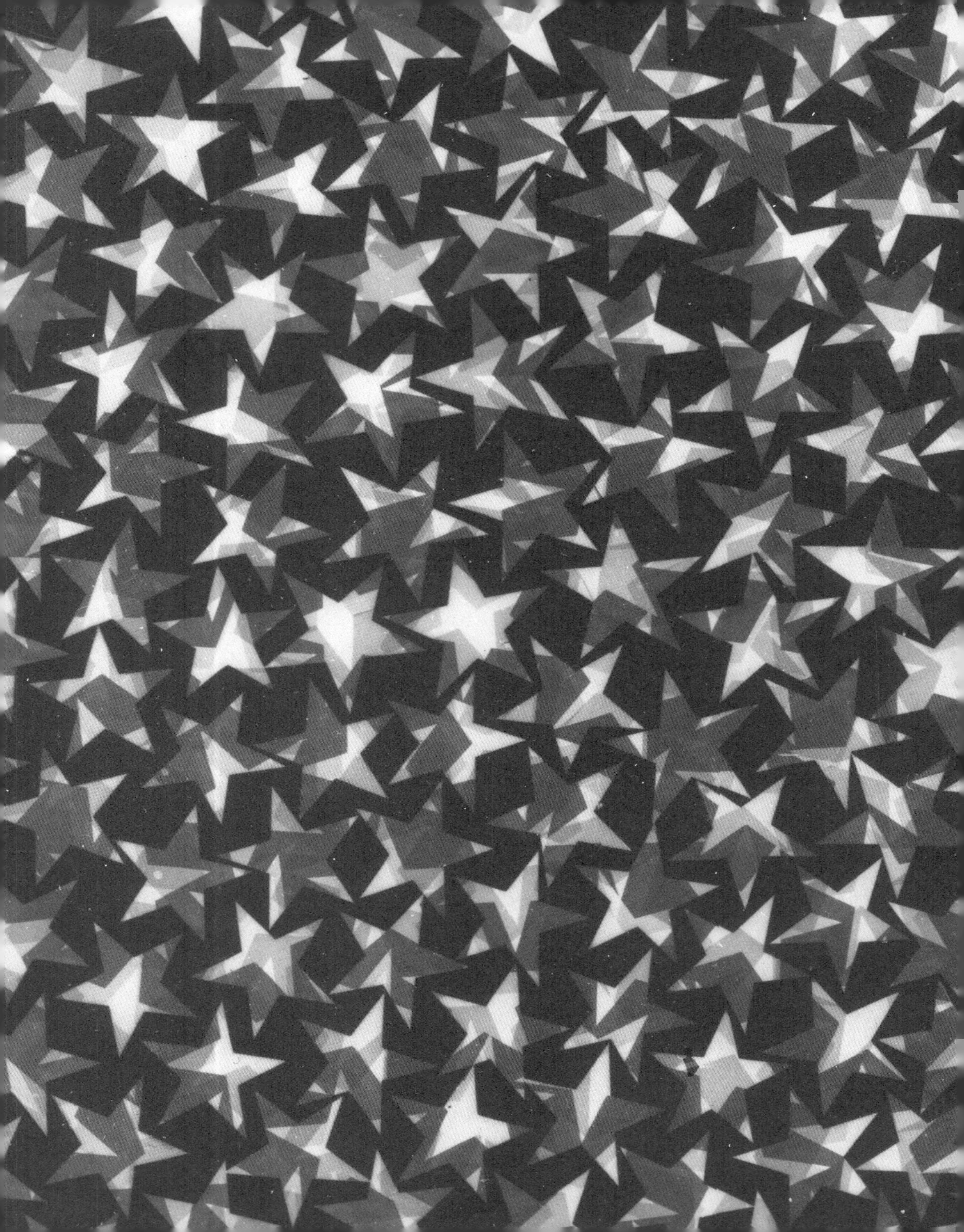